Living with Nature's Extremes

Living with Nature's Extremes

The Life of Gilbert Fowler White

Robert E. Hinshaw

JOHNSON BOOKS • *Boulder*

Published by Johnson Books, a division of Big Earth Publishing
    3005 Center Green Drive, Suite 220
    Boulder, Colorado 80301
    E-mail: books@bigearthpublishing.com
    www.johnsonbooks.com

Cover and text design by Polly Christensen
Cover: Front cover photo courtesy of CU-Boulder Publications & Creative Services, Department
    of Photography. Back cover photos courtesy of the National Geographic Society

9   8   7   6   5   4   3   2   1

Library of Congress Cataloging-in-Publication Data
Hinshaw, Robert E., 1933–
  Living with nature's extremes: the life of Gilbert Fowler White / Robert E. Hinshaw
    p. cm.
  Includes bibliographical references and index.
  ISBN 1-55566-388-5
1. White, Gilbert F. 2. Hydraulic engineers—United States—Biography. 3. Geographers—
United States—Biography. I. Title.
  TC140.W48H56 2006
  910.92—DC22
  [B]

                                            2006013540

Printed in the United States of America

Contents

Whoever wishes to take over the world
  will not succeed.
The world is a sacred vessel
  and nothing should be done to it.
Whoever tries to tamper with it
  will mar it.
Whoever tries to grab it
  will lose it.
  —Lao Tzu

Dedicated to my five children,
  twelve grandchildren,
    and six great-grandchildren
And to all the children,
  grandchildren and
    great-grandchildren everywhere
Who will need to make a difference.

Preface

Gilbert White saw more clearly than most that the earth as a natural system relies on extreme events to do its business and that catastrophe is less a natural event than a consequence of social decisions. Thanks to him, the public needs now less to be convinced of these ideas than simply reminded and kept on track.

> —**William H. Hooke, Climatologist**
> **American Meteorological Society**

Every person who buys flood insurance, or is asked to relocate out of a floodplain (and doesn't fully understand why they must do so), has been touched by Gilbert White's life in a very real way.

> —**JoAnn Howard, Administrator**
> **National Flood Insurance Program**

THIS BOOK IS BOTH BIOGRAPHY AND MEMOIR. Some of its readers will need no introduction to Gilbert Fowler White, and this Preface is primarily for those who have yet to make his acquaintance. The tributes above demonstrate that Gilbert White is an eminent, public-minded geographer whose scientific contributions in theory and practice matter to each of us. These contributions, in and of themselves, might warrant a biography. But White's ideas alone would not have persuaded me to devote five years of my life to this book. I was compelled to write it and encourage you to read it because of how Gilbert *lived* his life. He believed, with a passion, that any person can make a significant difference in this very messy world. It takes only the determination to live a life that *matters* in cultivation of a talent or an idea that is useful, and in presentation and advocacy of that idea to ensure its appreciation or adoption. Gilbert is no guru; he is neither preacher nor prophet. In fact, in many ways he has been just the opposite. His avocation throughout his life, in contrast to his vocation as a scientist, was theater, or more precisely, stagecraft. He enjoyed the production of plays and their effective orchestration. As early as high school, Gilbert was an accomplished manager, a behind-the-scenes enabler, usually reluctant to take center stage. (In grade school he avoided fisticuffs himself yet managed fist fights among his schoolmates!) And so he continued to live his remarkably effective life: backstage, imaginatively managing conflict.

Just as Gilbert's scientific ideas were controversial and required the advocacy of many colleagues and students before they were widely recognized, so his life warrants a biography and memoir to extend his legacy. May this effort to illuminate Gilbert's life persuade the reader to join the widening circle of people—in all walks of life—whose lives have been enriched, indeed, whose lives are making a bit more of a difference, because they knew this unassuming man.

Although I have known Gilbert for over half a century, I came to know him well only late in life. Undertaking this biography has been, I suppose, my baptism into that widening circle mentioned above. Gilbert (or Gil, to many) was president of Haverford College when I was a student there in the early 1950s. I was never his student, colleague, or professional associate until we teamed up in 2000 to write this book. We both moved on from Haverford in 1955, by coincidence both to the University of Chicago, where he became chairman of the Geography Department and I earned a doctorate in anthropology. In part because I became interested in natural hazards (from a career of fieldwork in hurricane- and earthquake-prone Central America), we stayed in touch until eventually we found ourselves neighbors in semiretirement in the mountains above Boulder, Colorado. The idea of producing this biography crystallized slowly, and only after several years did I broach the idea with Gilbert. He resisted initially, having already discouraged such a project by other professional geographers. As he had advised them, he also counseled me that writing his biography probably would not be the best use of my time and energy. But, perhaps because I was not part of his professional circle—more the anthropological observer than participant—he finally agreed that his life's story might serve a useful purpose in encouraging people to remain usefully "involved," to resist retirement. I think he also agreed because of our shared involvement over many years in Quaker Meetings (congregations) at Haverford College and in Chicago and Boulder. Moreover, I knew Haverford College and the University of Chicago from my own student days, and each of us had—at a very young age—served as president of a Quaker college. Once committed to this biography, Gilbert was extremely generous with his time and very forthcoming in the interviews over the subsequent five years.

&

IN THE AFTERMATH OF HURRICANE KATRINA, as this Preface is being written, world attention is focused on two ironies: (1) the discrepancy between U.S. government claims of improved readiness since September 11, 2001 to cope with disasters and the disappointing response at all levels once levees failed in New Orleans; and (2) the continued heavy reliance on structural measures (such as levees) to protect that region, despite previous massive levee failure (e.g., in New Orleans in 1927 and on the Missouri and Red Rivers of the upper Midwest in 1993 and 1997, respectively). Although saddened, Gilbert White hardly was surprised by this state of affairs. Indeed, in the late 1990s officials of the Federal Emergency Management Agency (FEMA) identified major disasters for which the nation should prepare. They concluded that the three most devastating threats were a terrorist attack on New York City, a severe hurricane in the lower Mississippi region, especially New Orleans, and a major earthquake in the Los Angeles area.

During his seventy-year career, Gilbert studied nature's extremes; the hazards they posed for humanity; and the political, scientific, and philosophical issues regarding their mitigation and effective societal response. The political issues included the role of federal, state, and local governments in disaster programs and the division of responsibility between the public and private sectors. Prior to the lower Mississippi's catastrophic floods of 1927, there was less federal than state government financing and less government than private financing of flood mitigation measures—in particular, levees and dams. Subsequently, the federal role gradually increased, with Congress initially exercising more authority than the executive branch. (One wonders why it took so long for presidents to realize how much political capital lay in their personal authorization of disaster assistance immediately after catastrophes.) Following Katrina, President George W. Bush was able to commit the federal government to leading the reconstruction of the entire Gulf Coast, including New Orleans, without much apparent congressional consultation and without offering any detailed plan, either for the funding or for the actual work involved in the largest reconstruction effort in U.S. history.[1]

The scientific issues inherent in hazards mitigation are comparably complex, beginning with the question of the comparative advantages of nonstructural and structural adjustments to reduce damage. For example, before Katrina, marshlands between New Orleans and the coast had been neglected and destroyed, as had wetlands adjacent to the Mississippi River, in unwise disregard for the protection these landforms provided against storm surge and river flooding.

Philosophical issues in hazards management include such concerns as the "wise use" of floodplains. Such areas can contain farmlands, wetlands, and woodlands and invariably are complex ecosystems of flora and fauna that must be wisely managed to ensure benefits for all inhabitants, including humans. How do we balance a river valley's long-term ecological health with shorter-term human commercial, recreational, and residential desires?

ॐ

IN ADDITION TO BEING the story of a life, this book is also the history of an idea that challenged the conventional political and engineering wisdom promulgated by the U.S. Army Corps of Engineers and its congressional supporters, virtually since the formation of these United States, about river and coastal flooding. Succinctly summarized, those assumptions (rooted in our nation's Judeo-Christian heritage, according to some) argued for controlling and bending nature to our human will: man over nature. Gilbert proposed, instead, that we work with the forces of nature. In a sense, he proposed that we accommodate flooding rather than limit our response to containing or confronting it with structural solutions (dams, levees, and seawalls). As Katrina well demonstrated, any given structure is designed for an extreme event of a given magnitude that, when exceeded, will overwhelm this presumed "protection." Gilbert's conception of natural order placed man in nature.[2]

Although not solely responsible for the shift in perspective away from control-ling nature that occurred gradually in American culture during his lifetime, Gilbert (and his students) contributed in major ways to educating government re-garding the full range of nonstructural adjustments available to manage flood-plains and mitigate losses due to flooding. Examples of these alternative approaches (most of which we now take for granted) include land-use planning to give floodwaters temporary safe places to flow; floodplain zoning and relocation of flood-prone buildings to higher ground; flood-proofing buildings to enable them to withstand flooding; forecasting, early warning, and evacuation planning; and disaster relief and flood insurance. Gilbert lobbied for several decades to reduce unwise reliance on dams and levees, prevailing eventually even to the extent of convincing the nation to implement a federally subsidized flood insurance program (the world's first such experiment on a national scale).

Gilbert's ideas and persistent advocacy engendered and inspired a remarkably multidisciplinary, integrated, and increasingly international community of natu-ral hazards researchers, government officials, and public and private practitioners involved with hazards. In a sense, this community is a collaborative circle of per-sons thinking nationally, even internationally, while acting locally. William Ander-son, a long-time public administrator and hazards scholar, is one of roughly 100 members of this fraternity who helped with this biography. Through his work with the National Science Foundation, the World Bank, and currently the National Re-search Council of the National Academy of Sciences, Anderson observed Gilbert's leadership in building this community over the past quarter-century. "Floodplain management probably would not have become an occupational field for practi-tioners and academicians without Gilbert's leadership," Anderson said.

> He brought scientists together with the key organizations and agencies such as the National Science Foundation, the Federal Emergency Management Agency, the Red Cross, the Corps of Engineers, the National Geological and American Meteorological Societies through the advisory board and annual workshops of his Natural Hazards Research and Applications Information Center he estab-lished at the University of Colorado. Friendships and perspectives were joined. Gilbert may not appreciate the magnitude of his influence on this cooperation (Anderson 2001).

☙

THE INTRODUCTION THAT FOLLOWS outlines the progression of Gilbert's scientific and public service contributions presented in the book. Because floodplain management and the nation's struggle with flood insurance are a major thread of the biography, this Preface provides an overview of a major controversy surrounding management of rivers in the United States that was ongoing from the mid-1800s until the 1930s, when White spent the first eight years of his career in Franklin D. Roosevelt's (FDR's) New Deal administration. Thereafter, Gilbert was never again directly employed by government. However, he played committee and advisory roles in each of the subsequent twelve federal administrations.

White might have retired in the traditional sense in his seventies, but he persevered in both academic and public service commitments as long as his health permitted, at least in part because of the seemingly inexorable escalation of the costs of natural disasters and his refusal to accept that trend. Just as his ideas about wise management of floodplains in particular and sustainability in use of natural resources generally have a historical context (introduced below), so likewise does Gilbert's unyielding faith in committed scientific effort and enlightened political leadership's ability to reverse ominous global trends. Accordingly, this Preface ends with a brief interpretation of how the University of Chicago first nurtured and then at midlife challenged Gilbert's idealism as he found himself at the vortex of a wrenching institutional crisis. These two pivotal scenes in his life set the stage for Gilbert White's career-long integration of faith and practice as citizen-scientist.

The Flooding of the Lower Mississippi

The Mississippi River system drains over 40 percent of the continental United States. After the Ohio, Tennessee, and Arkansas tributaries join the Mississippi below St. Louis, the river typically carries three times more water by the time it reaches New Orleans and the Gulf of Mexico than when it passed St. Louis and the mouth of its largest tributary, the Missouri. Accordingly, much of the nation's most disastrous river flooding has occurred in the lower Mississippi Valley. Indeed, the floods of 1927 generated a national response to natural disaster perhaps surpassed only by Katrina. Unfortunately for New Orleans and the Gulf Coast region generally, river flooding there is compounded by storm surges from hurricanes. Gilbert White's first career assignment upon completing his studies at the University of Chicago in 1934 involved reconnaissance for planning flood mitigation in the Missouri and lower Mississippi Valleys. There he first encountered the U.S. Army Corps of Engineers and the issues that he and the Corps debated for several decades. Gilbert's positions on virtually all those issues would in time prevail, but it is instructive to examine how Chief of Engineers Andrew B. Humphreys dominated Corps positions on the issues for sixty years (Reuss 1985).

Since the mid-nineteenth century, an inflexible consensus had evolved among most politicians, engineers, and scientists that the Mississippi was most efficiently and safely "controlled" by deepening the river's channel through the use of levees, thereby concentrating the volume of the river and accelerating the water's flow to the Gulf of Mexico. That assumption had gone largely uncontested, despite authorization by President Millard Fillmore's administration in the mid-nineteenth century of $50,000 for two independent studies, one by an eminent civil engineer, Charles Ellet, Jr., and the other by a U.S. Army Corps of Engineers expert, Andrew B. Humphreys, that in its preliminary form provided evidence to support an opposing view (similar to what Gilbert White would elaborate ninety years thereafter). Although their reports did not agree on the ancillary issues of perhaps reducing flooding by straightening the river's bed and by building dams and reservoirs to reduce channel volume, the preliminary data from the Humphreys study did not contest Ellet's principal recommendation that use of levees be judicious, given the unknowns surrounding their actual effects on the flow of rivers as large as the Mississippi and the obvious risk of their eventual failure (Barry 1997).

Ellet's study was the first to be released, in 1851, only a year after authorization of the two reports. The preliminary findings from Humphreys' team of engineers circulated the following year. Not only was Ellet more adamant in opposing levees, but also he strongly advocated for constructing manmade reservoirs and protecting outlets to wetlands bordering the river to impound and reduce the river's flow at intervals in its rampage toward the Gulf of Mexico. He also favored leaving the meandering riverbed largely unchanged. Humphreys' final report was delayed in its publication for a decade after Ellet's due to Humphreys' meticulous methodology and delays occasioned by ill health. When it finally was issued in 1861, it took issue with Ellet's recommendations on all points, even with the key issue of reliance on levees. As a West Point–trained member of the Corps who was extremely loyal to the Corps in the growing competition between army and civilian engineers, Humphreys had been chagrined by the release of Ellet's report ahead of his own and incensed by its enthusiastic reception by anti-Corps officialdom in Washington (Barry 1997). Unfortunately for the nation, the personal jealousies of these two highly competent engineers (especially on the part of Humphreys), fanned by the jealousies of their supporters, overshadowed the critical issue of the "levees-only solution," which the Corps of Engineers had generally favored and which both Ellet and Humphreys' initial findings brought into question.

Subsequently the Civil War intervened, taking the life of Ellet and diminishing the visibility of his study. By contrast, Humphreys' reputation flourished, and his final report sided with the biases holding sway within the Corps of Engineers. There was much fame and fortune to be had in levees (Barry 1997).

A Mississippi River Commission was established by Congress in 1879 to reconcile the studies and make case-by-case engineering decisions. Although the congressional bill called for three engineers from the Corps, two civilian engineers, and one member with unspecified training and loyalty, the commission president was to be a Corpsman. Gradually, over time, the preponderance of commission decisions were in keeping with the recommendations in Humphreys' final report. "In 1885 the commission stated flatly, and repeated thereafter, 'Levees designed to limit the high water width of the river, by concentration of the flood discharge of the channel . . . secure the energy of the flood volume in scouring and enlarging the channel'" (Barry 1997). Sadly, for reasons more monetary and political than scientific, the United States suffered through regular and increasingly costly floods on the Mississippi for the next forty years, even as levees lengthened and rose higher along virtually the full 1,100 miles of the lower river's channel and its tributaries.

Even with Ellet's vindication by the levees' disastrous failures during the 1927 flood, there was no effective challenge to continued dependency on structural engineering solutions until the ideas contained in Gilbert's doctoral dissertation, "Human Adjustment to Floods," found guarded reception at midcentury. In 1934, when Gilbert and his University of Chicago mentor, Harlan Barrows, were involved in the Missouri and lower Mississippi reconnaissance, their shared convictions regarding the Corps' over-reliance on structural solutions to the threat of flooding were still nascent. Even Ellet had argued for dams and their reservoirs, and the ongoing Corps and Mississippi River Commission opposition to such impoundments weakened only when the Great Depression made popular the employment provided by their construction. "It is noteworthy that so many army engineers maintained their skepticism of the value of flood control reservoirs despite the windfall of work Congress gave the Corps in the 1930s," Martin Reuss said in 1985. Indeed, White's questioning of all structural solutions, including even dams and reservoirs, in his advocacy for the broader range of nonstructural adjustments to achieve wise use of hazardous areas, might have gone the way of Ellet's cautionary counsel in 1851, were it not for White's political sagacity and the networking he accomplished during and following those eight years in Washington.

While Gilbert's challenge to the traditional, "levees-only" approach received some visibility even by the time he left White House employment in 1942, in 1939 it also resulted in his investigation by a House of Representatives committee that perceived his ideas as potentially "un-American." And, in fact, U.S. Corps of Engineers structural adjustments continued to dominate federal policies even into the 1970s, before yielding gradually to the nonstructural philosophy Gilbert espoused. By century's end, thanks in part to Gilbert White and in part to the paucity of suitable locations for dams and reservoirs, public and private interests were not building many dams and levees anymore. Predictably, as with the levees in New Orleans, those built long ago were failing at an alarming rate.

The Influence of the University of Chicago on White's Life

Chicago geographer Harlan Barrows, who early on became a member of FDR's planning team, probably contributed to Gilbert's enthusiasm regarding that group, which Gilbert joined at age twenty-two. But the optimism of a beleaguered nation during the New Deal only reinforced in Gilbert a deeply rooted idealism already inculcated by, especially, his mother and her Quaker side of his family. As described in more detail in Chapter 1, Gilbert's Baptist mother and Quaker/Baptist grandmother became acquainted with the University of Chicago's founding president when the campus was still under construction in the late 1800s. Mary White's dream, prior even to marriage, was to see her children educated at that new Baptist university.

In 1899, twelve years before Gilbert was born, as Mary and Gilbert's father, Arthur Edward, were establishing a home and family in Hyde Park, Chicago, the community was caught up in the great Baptist educational experiment that was the University of Chicago. On January 1 of that year, Mary probably was in the audience as her then good friend, President William Rainey Harper, delivered one of his signature clarion addresses to the students, faculty, and administrators of the university, ushering in the last year of the nineteenth century and anticipating the century to come. Morris Philipson, the director of the University of Chicago Press, described the event:

> In 1899 it could appropriately be assumed that [the listeners] were, on the whole, Christian believers, idealistically oriented, intellectually ambitious, and optimistic. All good things were possible, and responsible people who worked hard enough would achieve them. President Harper was able to move his audience because he and they spoke the same language. . . . Harper was a man of moral passion who believed intensely in the ideals he described and who communicated a grasp of the practical means by which an ideal—an idea of something conceived of at its best—could come to be realized. As he spoke in the 123rd year of the republic of the United States, all his energy and persuasiveness were supported by the American experience of achieving new purposes—of setting goals, of implementing plans, of pragmatically improving, of shaping and compromising, of learning by doing, and of ameliorating by hoping for yet a better world (Philipson 1970).

The attributes that Philipson ascribes to Harper and his audience were equally those embraced by Gilbert's family. Gilbert's education from age thirteen to twenty-two was at the hands of Chicago faculty steeped in Harper's pragmatic idealism, and from age forty-four to fifty-nine, Gilbert was chair of the university's renowned Department of Geography.

The world and the University of Chicago changed, however. On the seventieth anniversary of Harper's address, within a few weeks of Gilbert's difficult departure from the university, the University of Chicago Press reissued that 1899 address, "University and Democracy," and Philipson supplied the foreword entitled, "The Difference Between a Ruin and a Relic" (Philipson 1970)—an assessment of the seven intervening decades since Harper presented his optimistic, righteously Christian vision for the university. The publication followed traumatic unrest at the university in 1969, and it would be difficult to find a more sober and eloquent portrayal of the chasm that had opened between the dreams of the university's founding fathers and the reality of a bitter campus divided by the war in Southeast Asia. In a sense, the dreams were exemplified by the expectations of Gilbert's mother and grandmother and the reality by Gilbert's encouragement of dissenting faculty and his daughter Frances at a student protest and sit-in. (These events are described in greater detail in Chapter 6.)

Gilbert White identified with both eras, retaining the idealism of President Harper while protesting, by moving to the University of Colorado, the expelling of students from the University of Chicago. Indeed, Philipson might have been thinking of Gilbert's sobering resignation when he wrote in 1970:

> There is one profoundly important similarity between Harper's audience of seventy years ago and the comparable one of today. They both wish for a vastly better world, and individuals among them tend to work hard to bring that world into being. . . . What a man believes but does not understand is what makes it possible for him to do what he believes he does understand. . . . President Harper's speech is a relic of tightly reasoned American inspirationalism at the end of the nineteenth century. The hard core of his thought contains the essence of sensible, pragmatic optimism, the well-tempered idealism of a rational man. And we need all the sensible help we can get.

Chapter 1 describes Gilbert White's schooling—all of which was provided or strongly influenced by the University of Chicago—and the nurturing of such "well-tempered idealism" in one remarkably rational man. The remainder of this book describes his legacy of "sensible help."

Notes

1. In sharp contrast, in the late 1880s President Grover Cleveland vetoed a congressional emergency appropriation of $10,000 for drought victims in Texas, declaring that there was no warrant in the Constitution for the government "to indulge a benevolent and charitable sentiment through the appropriation of public funds ... [for] relief of individual suffering which is in no manner properly related to the public service" (Barry 1997).

    Even in the aftermath of the massive 1927 Mississippi flooding, "not a single federal dollar went to feed, clothe, or shelter any of the 667,000 being fed by the Red Cross. Indeed, the Army even demanded reimbursement from the Red Cross for use of its field kitchens and tents" (Barry 1997). Yet the federal government's disaster response was lauded throughout the nation as exemplary in terms of what President Calvin

Coolidge did accept as his federal mandate: to assist the Red Cross and state and local governments in rescue and evacuation—and then to plan for economic recovery and more effective flood control in the future. Coolidge had designated his secretary of commerce, Herbert Hoover, to oversee the disaster response. But Hoover's role was, in part, to organize the private sector to finance and implement these goals (Barry 1997).

2. To be sure, social scientists, theologians, and philosophers have viewed nature both as object (nonhuman and external to humans, but God-given) and as subject (more abstractly universal, subsuming human as well as all other forms of life). But in practice, "scientists tend to adopt one or the other concept of nature, sometimes adopting both consecutively, but rarely simultaneously" (Smith and O'Keefe 1980, quoted in Marston 1983a). Gilbert White was one of the latter, who adopted both simultaneously enough of the time to maintain credibility on both sides of the issue.

Acknowledgments

GIVEN THE COLLABORATIVE NATURE of this biography endeavor, there are a host of persons for whose assistance I am indebted. The list begins with Gilbert himself and his family. I became acquainted with the White children, Will, Mary, and Frances, from reading to them two afternoons each week during my sophomore year at Haverford College. Gilbert and his wife, Anne, hoped thereby to encourage Will, in particular, to read on his own. In 2000 the children were helpful in encouraging Gilbert's consent to this biography and in sharing their memories of Anne and Gilbert. Mary White shares her mother's artistic bent and was particularly helpful in selecting the book's eighty photos, most of them from the family's extensive collection. Following the photos of Gilbert's ancestors in Chapter 1, only one other photo is included before the introduction of Anne Underwood in Chapter 3. It is of philosopher Rufus Jones. We chose in this way to acknowledge Jones's unequalled influence in Gilbert's formative years, as well as his ongoing friendship with the White family, from Gilbert's involvement with Jones in the American Friends Service Committee through Gilbert's Haverford College presidency, and by virtue of the Whites living next door to Rufus and Elizabeth at Haverford the last two years of Rufus's life.

Next in importance to the White family members, among the many contributing in some way to the book's creation, are staff of the Natural Hazards Center in Boulder and of the umbrella Institute of Behavioral Science (IBS) at the University of Colorado. In particular, I am indebted to Mary Fran Myers, who, sadly, did not live to see the book's publication after acting as a liaison with funding sources and with the members of the natural hazards community nationwide with whom Gilbert has had the most involvement. Along with Mary Fran, former center director Dennis Mileti and staff member Jacquelyn Monday had themselves considered coauthoring a biography of Gilbert White. But they approached Gilbert at a point when his many other priorities did not make such an undertaking propitious. They graciously shared with me their ideas about the endeavor, assisted in outlining the book, and read and commented on drafts along the way. Natural Hazards Center office staff Diane Smith and Janet Kroeckel gave generously of their time, and past secretaries of Gilbert's at the IBS and the Natural Hazards Center, Mei Mei Pan and Fay Tracy, consented to useful interviews. At the IBS, Sugandha Brooks had for several years provided secretarial assistance to Gilbert and did so to me before lending her considerable copyediting skills as well. I am grateful to Steve

Graham of IBS for finding monies within the IBS budget to employ former Natural Hazards Center publications editor David Butler, who virtually rewrote the book in Gilbert's parsimonious style. The combined good fortune of undertaking this endeavor when Gilbert finally had the time and inclination (and yet still the requisite energy and memory) to assist and when David was available to apply his professional skills so imitative of Gilbert's writing qualifies the resultant collaboration as a memoir as much as a biography.

Beyond the University of Colorado, former University of Chicago colleague Chauncey Harris and several former colleagues at Haverford College were available for interviews. The latter included Philip Bell, Edwin Bronner, Marcel Gutwirth, Holland and Helen Hunter, Mel Santer, and board member Jonathan Rhoads. Library and archives staff at Haverford, Chicago, and Colorado were helpful, and in Philadelphia, Jack Sutters and Terry Foss kindly provided access to the American Friends Service Committee (AFSC) archives and photos.

To JoAnn Howard, former director of the National Flood Insurance Program, and Neil Furst at FEMA, I express gratitude for facilitating FEMA's assistance in funding the research and writing. To Eugene Stakhiv and the Institute for Water Resources of the U.S. Army Corps of Engineers and to Martin Reuss and the Corps' Department of History in Alexandria, Virginia, I am similarly grateful for funding and hospitality permitting my use on two occasions of the Maass-White collection of Gilbert's books and personal papers bequeathed to the Corps. Reuss also commented usefully on drafts of the manuscript. Additional funding from the Compton Foundation for the book's writing is also gratefully acknowledged, as is the asssistance of the Ecumenical Project for International Coöperation.

Other reviewers of chapters or the entire manuscript who provided helpful editing include Jacqueline Beyer, Martha Church, Stephen Collett, Susan Cutter, Douglas Heath, Nicholas Helburn, Joy King, Andrew Kirby, Larry Larson, Sallie Marston, Jan Monk, Claudia Murphy, Ann Patton, Rutherford Platt, Janet Roberts, Michael Robinson, Jack Sheaffer, Alan Taylor, Reds Wolman, Jim Wright, and Ken and Ruth Wright. Finally, I am indebted to Beth Partin for her final copyediting on behalf of Johnson Books. I thank Ken and Ruth Wright for introducing me to Mira Perrizo, publisher of Johnson Books, whose enthusiasm for this book and willingness to expedite its publication persuaded us to publish in Boulder, rather than with an academic press.

Throughout the book are references to or quotations from at least half of the over 100 professional associates, colleagues, and students of Gilbert interviewed for the book. Through these references I express my appreciation for such invaluable assistance. Since the others who were interviewed (including several lengthy communiqués in writing in lieu of interviews) also contributed to my understanding of Gilbert's legacy and in many instances directly influenced the text, I list below these names of additional interviewees: Maurice Albertson, Jay Baker, John Baskin,

Patricia Bolton, Baruch Boxer, James Callaghan, Emery Castle, Louise Comfort, John Cross, Sheila David, Tom Downing, Genady Golubev, Craig Hafner, John Harkins, Walter Hays, Jeffrey Jacobs, Jeanne Jasperson, Roger Jasperson, Jim Johnson, Andrew Kirby, Jon Kusler, Tom Malone, John Miller, Burrell Montz, David Policansky, Roy Popkin, Bill Robertson, Claire Rubin, Elena Shevchenko, Vasily Smirnyagin, John Sorenson, Philip Stern, Kathleen Tierney, Sidney Waldman, French Wetmore, Joe Whitney, and Helen and Kale Williams.

Endeavoring to name the many members of the Boulder Friends and other Friends Meetings who shared anecdotal memories of Gilbert and Anne would, I fear, leave some Friends unacknowledged. Similarly, I am indebted to many friends of the Whites who shared in writing their memories of Gilbert on the occasion of his ninetieth birthday in 2001. Excerpts from some of these, not all acknowledged, have found their way into the book as well. To one and all who have contributed to this collective labor of love, I am deeply grateful.

Finally, to my wife, Linda, I am indebted for her patience and willingness to release me for the countless sojourns in Colorado and across North America for interviewing and research and in Guatemala for writing over the past five years. The book owes much to her own reading and editing skills.

Introduction

We can be confident that action which is in accord with a few basic beliefs cannot be wrong and can at least testify to the values we will need to cultivate. These are the beliefs that the human race is a family that has inherited a place on earth in common, that its members have an obligation to work toward sharing it so that none is deprived of the elementary needs for life, and that all have a responsibility to leave it undegraded for those who follow.

—GFW

THE PRESIDENT'S BESTOWAL of the National Medal of Science on distinguished citizen-scientists is perhaps the closest the United States comes to the queen of England's bestowal of knighthood. The U.S. National Academy of Sciences also recognizes outstanding citizen-scientists with its Public Welfare Medal. Similarly, in 2000 the International Water Resources Association instituted its Millennium Award for outstanding contributions by individuals, institutions, and programs to water resources planning and management around the world. In 2000 Gilbert White received all three of these awards. The following descriptions of Gilbert White are taken from the citations accompanying his many awards.

Gilbert White is the Gustavson Distinguished Professor Emeritus of Geography at the University of Colorado at Boulder. He has been called "the most renowned geographer internationally of the twentieth century," one who "personifies the ideal of a natural resources scientist committed to stewardship of our planet." "He has educated the nation and the world on how to change the ways we manage water resources, mitigate natural hazards, and assess the environment."

The varied scientific activities in which he participated and the applications of scholarship to public policy he fostered were major contributions to the history and evolution of the twentieth century. The emergence of a global consciousness among scientific communities, public awareness of human accountability for the earth's environment, and international cooperation among policymakers to address environmental problems may well be among the most crucial developments of that century. Gilbert White was instrumental in all three.

In all this he has been "a quiet leader by example," inspiring innumerable students, colleagues, and associates to pursue a more humane coexistence with the natural world. An impressive number of the above, when interviewed for this biography, described Gilbert as the most unforgettable person they have known.

They recalled as many memories of his admirable conduct as of his accomplishments. Serious, yet full of zest for life, and as committed to enjoying nature's out-of-doors as he was to its scientific exploration, he recalled persistent reminders from his own elders as early as age ten that they expected him not only to enjoy life to the full but to "make a difference," to be someone whose life would *matter*. He succeeded beyond his own humble expectations and expected his students and friends to do the same.

How does any one person come to matter that much to his profession, to a nation, to our planet? And as accomplished as he became, why is he not more popularly "famous"? Because he worked unobtrusively at the margins, bridging several academic disciplines, and networking quietly behind the scenes in his public advocacy roles, Gilbert White is hardly a household name. His biography addresses this paradox. By surveying his committed career, disciplined mind, and humanitarian spirit, these questions and two more are addressed: Thinking globally, in today's complex world, what constitutes effective leadership in decision making that will leave our planet a better place for our presence? And thinking locally, how important for humanity's and the earth's future is it that *our* lives matter—that we each make a difference, if only in our immediate environs?

෴

IN 1973 GILBERT WHITE succinctly summarized one central focus in his career:

> How does man adjust to risk and uncertainty in natural systems, and what
> does understanding of that process imply for public policy? This problem,
> raised initially with respect to one uncertain and hazardous parameter of a
> geophysical system—floods—in one country—the United States—provides a
> central theme for investigating on a global scale the whole range of uncertain
> and risky events in nature.

Seven years before President Bill Clinton conferred on Gilbert White the National Medal of Science, the upper Mississippi River and several of its northern tributaries flooded more disastrously (in terms of property loss) than the United States previously had experienced. That flood of 1993 resulted in a presidential commission to study the mitigation needed to avoid another such catastrophe. When invited by President Clinton to chair that endeavor, Gilbert declined after much deliberation because of the weight of other commitments. He was sorely tempted to acquiesce because it was exactly sixty years since his assignment to another Mississippi Valley Committee on flood prevention fortuitously had set the course of his career.

From 1933 through 1939, he served as staff secretary on a succession of water and land committees under National Resources Planning Board auspices, becoming convinced that it was folly to occupy floodplains assumed safe from normal flooding because they were protected by dams and levees. Increased occupancy, he foresaw, would only result in increased losses when extreme flooding overcame these structural barriers. Challenging the national philosophy and the U.S. Army Corps of Engineers policy of controlling rivers in his 1942 doctoral dissertation, Gilbert advocated nonstructural adaptations to flood hazards (such as not permitting construction in flood-prone areas) and called for the management of river floodplains as complex, essential ecosystems that provide benefits beyond human occupancy, economic development, and recreation.

Although the argument regarding the best approach to floodplain management was sometimes contentious, the even-handed, constructive way in which White approached the discussion is perhaps reflected in the fact that the Corps of Engineers Department of History is the repository for White's personal papers and library of water-related publications (among the largest private holdings on the topic in the world).

From the New Deal era of optimism regarding our ability to cope politically and socially with our collective problems despite the setback of the Great Depression, Gilbert White's career spanned seven decades of diminishing national confidence in the political will, if not the ability, to manage the natural resources of the United States wisely. In 1966 he chaired a Bureau of the Budget Task Force on Federal Flood Policy that recommended experimenting with a national flood insurance program. Congress acted on that recommendation, but too rapidly and ambitiously—without due experimentation and the depth of planning Gilbert's task force had advised—resulting in a conundrum of never-ending challenges with which White stayed the course through government consulting and committee work for the remainder of his career. The flood insurance program was subsumed in 1979 under the Federal Emergency Management Agency (FEMA). By century's end FEMA was helping communities adopt ordinances that restricted floodplain occupancy and was purchasing and removing structures suffering repetitive losses. But despite progress on many fronts, property losses from flooding continued to escalate.

Toward the end of his career, Gilbert and two of his former students looked back and pondered why increased knowledge had not done more to stem the losses from flooding. They asked: Is the knowledge still insufficient? Sufficient but not used? Used ineffectively? Used but with an unanticipated lag in taking effect? Or used with positive results that have simply been overwhelmed by increased vulnerability due to population growth, economic expansion, and in some instances greater poverty and lack of empowerment? (See White, Kates, and Burton 2001.) Population growth in the United States and especially its increased concentration in hazardous locales certainly are important explanatory factors. Nationally, the U.S. population increased from 123 million in 1930 to 300 million in 2005, concurrent with only a twentyfold increase in the gross national product. The picture is therefore more encouraging when recent annual losses from disasters (averaging $6 billion annually at century's end, prior to the catastrophic 2005) are viewed as a percentage of gross national product.

That translates to losses averaging approximately $20 per capita per year prior to hurricanes Katrina and Rita (see Chapter 9).

∝

While White was chairing the University of Chicago's Department of Geography (1955–1969), the program became recognized as a national leader in environmental research. The initial study to formulate the plan for the National Flood Insurance Program was carried out at the University of Chicago. White's career thereafter at Colorado expanded his research from studies of water use and the extremes of flooding and drought to include other extreme events of nature (i.e., earthquakes and tsunamis, volcanoes, landslides, high winds and tornadoes, hurricanes and coastal storms, wildfires, snowstorms, and avalanches). As with flooding, he argued that people should reduce their risks by wisely managing natural resources and considering the full range of adjustments to nature's extremes available for mitigating their negative effects. White maintained that many natural hazards become disasters only when humans get in their way—an apparently simple idea with profound implications.

White's vehicle for pursuing this agenda of mitigating an expanded range of disaster losses became the Natural Hazards Research and Applications Information Center under Colorado's Institute of Behavioral Science (which he chaired). Established in 1974, the center is perhaps best known among persons involved with hazards and disasters for its annual workshop that hosts scholars of many disciplines, policy makers, and practitioners from throughout the world who convene to share their collective wisdom, frustrations, questions, and answers. There were many frustrations at the outset. Hazards study as a profession was inherently risky: multidisciplinary in the extreme and marginal to all the academic disciplines involved. No wonder that its community members—always looking for "trouble" from nature—initially were looked at askance by not only academe but also the usual academic funding sources.

Herein lies another irony, all too well illustrated by Hurricane Katrina. For the twentieth-century pioneers in hazards study as an academic discipline (of which fraternity Gilbert White is the oldest living member), funding for hazards research and a legislative agenda to more effectively mitigate disaster losses unfortunately advanced on the backs of disaster victims. Government has a history of reaction in coping with calamity, and the hazards community was constantly planning, anticipating the next disaster for the funding opportunity it might provide to advance their (and our common) cause.

Against considerable odds, hazards study as an academic discipline and the Boulder Natural Hazards Center gained momentum, in part on the coattails of White's lengthening reputation. By 2005 there were a host of such academic centers in the United States and a dozen abroad. In 1942, the year that the University of Chicago conferred on White his Ph.D., his was one of but seven dissertations accepted by U.S. universities with topics even remotely dealing with natural hazards and disasters (Mitchell 2001). By century's end, hazards-related dissertations numbered many dozens annually.

ಞ

TO THIS POINT THE INTRODUCTION has reviewed White's involvements with natural hazards. Concurrently his career commitments expanded considerably. Following four years of World War II humanitarian relief and reconstruction service in France and Germany under the auspices of the American Friends Service Committee (1942–1946), and a decade as president of Haverford College (1946–1955), Gilbert expanded his applied research and service to include more international scientific, humanitarian, and political action work. He became involved, often in a leadership role, with the National Research Council of the National Academy of Sciences (and through the NAS with its counterparts in other nations), the International Geographical Union, the International Council of Scientific Unions and its Scientific Committee on Problems of the Environment (SCOPE), Resources for the Future, and related foundation-financed consultation and research abroad. Theodore Munn, editor of SCOPE publications for three decades, credits White with bringing to international consciousness the real and potential environmental impacts caused by alterations in biological/geological/chemical cycles (global warming, for example, and the threat of nuclear winter accompanying nuclear war). Gilbert's citation accompanying the Sustained Achievement Award, given him by the Renewable Natural Resources Foundation (RNRF) in 1992, applauded White's role in ensuring that a SCOPE report on the environmental effects of nuclear war appeared in the halls of Congress and the United Nations in time to influence the International Nuclear Freeze Treaty negotiations between the United States and the Soviet Union. White's efforts in this regard were acknowledged with his induction into the Russian Academy of Sciences.

White also directed U.N. committees investigating arid zones, human-made lakes, and integrated river development, as well as several high-profile missions assessing environmentally appropriate economic and political arrangements among nations sharing the Nile, Mekong, and Jordan Rivers and the Aral Sea. Most visible of these was his task force's 1962 report on the economic and social aspects of Lower Mekong River development, prepared for the Committee for Coordination of Investigations of the Lower Mekong basin. The report set forth a program of economic development to help stabilize the region in hopes of reducing the escalating tensions that led to the Vietnam War.

Although Gilbert's primary concerns may have been with water and drought, his work and interests were far broader. During the 1960s, he was a member of the committee that recommended that the Peace Corps be established, president of the Association of American Geographers, and chair of the American Friends Service

Committee. During the 1970s, he chaired the steering committee of the Ford Foundation's Energy Policy Project (the first national assessment of energy resources and policy options), the International Geographical Union's Commission on Man and the Environment, and three major units of the National Research Council of the National Academy of Sciences. In the 1980s and 1990s he served on two committees (chairing one) that examined problems related to nuclear waste storage under Nevada's Yucca Mountain. By then he was also focusing increasingly on the global environmental trends that were placing the planet more at risk due in part to human population increase and potentially unsustainable exploitation of natural resources. In 1984 he served on the steering committee of a World Resources Institute study, *The Global Possible: Resources, Development, and the New Century,* among the first global assessments of resources and environmental trends.

Prior to the four recent honors mentioned above, Gilbert White received (among the many other honors listed in Appendix 2) the Volvo Environment Prize, the U.N. Sasakawa International Environment Prize, the National Geographic Society's Hubbard Medal, the Tyler Prize for Environmental Achievement, the International Geographical Union's Laureat d'Honneur, and the Vautrin Lud International Prize in Geography.

Despite these accolades, Gilbert eschewed the spotlight. Although his name appears on over 400 publications, the majority involve shared authorship with students and colleagues, often across disciplines. Moreover, these publications consistently focused on policy and the real-world implications of research, rather than on either geographic theory or the promotion of a career within academia. He wrote almost exclusively for academic, professional readers, explaining in large part why his is not a popularly recognized name. White believed that scientific knowledge is sought primarily to inform public policies serving the common good, and a persistent question to his graduate students regarding their own research was, "What are the policy implications?"

Gilbert White remains the consummate citizen-scientist who works equally in his community, nation, and world to better the human condition. At age ninety-four, his efforts on behalf of flooding and wildfire hazard mitigation in Boulder County have abated but little. His greatest legacy may lie in the example he offers those despairing of our society's ability to cope with the environmental challenges we face. Despite society's ever-deepening dilemmas, Gilbert's faith in humankind's potential for improvement has never dimmed. He has helped not only individuals, but groups as well, nurture that potential and achieve beyond their expectations.

One of Gilbert's deepest beliefs has been in the dignity and worth of each individual (the divine spark within everyone) and hence in the importance of group discernment in setting direction and staying on course. He was attracted to the Society of Friends in his early adulthood in large part because Quakers share these convictions. Active membership ever since in the Society of Friends has strengthened his related beliefs in pacifism (nonviolent resolution of differences) and

Cartoon sent as a gift to Gilbert by the artist, Rob Pudim. Image courtesy of the artist.

social justice (conserving natural resources so that they might be more equitably shared among and within societies and across generations). Gilbert White recognizes no foes, either in human form or in nature's extreme events; we are all part of one Planet Earth (or Planet Water), and sustainable cohabitation here can succeed ultimately only through understanding and cooperation in balancing the contending needs of all its life forms.

White worked best at resolving differences behind the scenes, where listening, candor, wise counsel, honesty, and a deep desire to reach consensus served disputants well. If encouragement of comprehensive scientific and political management of floodplain ecosystems was a major thread of Gilbert White's career, a parallel thread was nurturing and modeling his skills (as he said, more an art than science) to move from disagreement to agreement in effective problem solving. The contexts for these labors were many over the course of his career, but most important to Gilbert were the dozens of conferences for diplomats sponsored by the American Friends Service Committee, spanning half a century, that brought together midlevel career diplomats to address informally the most contentious international political, economic, and environmental issues. These conferences, held almost yearly around the world from 1952 until 1997 and often chaired by Gilbert, allowed him to marry his scientific and spiritual commitments.

Gilbert's major career commitments mentioned above, and a number of others, are discussed in more detail in this biography than would be possible had the decision been made to cover all of his wide-ranging memberships and activities. Many of his less significant career endeavors are not discussed, even in passing. Therefore, a chronology of almost all of Gilbert's commitments is appended (Appendix 1), with dates, to round out the picture of his life and to give readers an appreciation of his myriad involvements during any given year of his adulthood.

The body of the book integrates Gilbert's scientific research and public policy advocacy with his service to the Society of Friends more intentionally than it integrates his public and personal/family life. That was a difficult decision necessitated by considerations of the book's length. After the opening chapter's attention to ancestral roots and Gilbert's "growing up" years, family life receives only passing attention (except for his collegial as well as his matrimonial partnership with Anne Underwood White). The richness of his and the family's foreign travel and their summer vacations in the Rocky Mountains surrounded by a multitude of friends receive short shrift. The biography focuses decidedly on Gilbert's work, not his play. To be sure, there was much more of the former than the latter, as his and Anne's three children were quick to attest when interviewed. His longevity was a saving grace in this respect; in the children's adulthood the family made up for past sacrifices endured in the interest of enabling Gilbert to be true to his calling.

In my discussions with Gilbert about the book's organization, we agreed to integrate his scientific, public service, and religious commitments throughout as much as feasible. Nonetheless, because his involvements with Quaker institutions were concentrated largely in the first half of his career, Chapters 3–6 (following his University of Chicago schooling and FDR New Deal employment in Chapters 1 and 2) focus primarily on those Quaker endeavors from the 1940s through the 1960s. Readers who may be less interested, at least initially, in that dimension of Gilbert's life will find more concentrated discussion of his scientific roles and contributions in Chapters 7 to 12.

Specifically, Chapters 7–9 constitute a chronological review of the nation's quest for unified floodplain management at the national level, including the contentious history of the National Flood Insurance Program, into the twenty-first century. Chapter 10 then brings that story alive through the local experiences of two cities with which Gilbert was specifically involved, Boulder, Colorado, and (to lesser degree) Tulsa, Oklahoma, perhaps the nation's exemplar in accomplishing by century's end what would have been deemed impossible several decades previously. Chapter 11 might advisably have come earlier in the book insofar as it reviews chronologically from the 1960s through the 1990s Gilbert's legacy in advancing the discipline of geography and specifically the efficacy of its instruction at all levels. Chapter 12 similarly reviews chronologically the story of growing consciousness of a planet at risk and of the consensus among scientists of the deleterious impact of humans on the planet's ecosystems and cycles of elements basic to maintenance of life in its myriad forms.

The two closing chapters attempt an interpretation of Gilbert's life, first in terms of his character, convictions, and behavior and second in terms of his legacy and impact on associates. I hope that readers initially interested in the book because of Gilbert's involvements with nature's extremes (and who may move directly from Chapter 2's commencement of that career focus to Chapter 7's resumption of such involvements) will return upon completion of the book to three decades (Chapters 3–6) when Gilbert's genius in leadership evolved in such exemplary manner. The Epilogue assesses the critical need for that style of leadership and invites our collective efforts to build such personal and institutional capabilities before "the candle between a descending darkness and any bright future" (Gilbert's motto late in life) is extinguished.

❧

FOR READERS WISHING to go beyond this book in deepening their familiarity with Gilbert's legacy, an excellent website is available at **www.colorado.edu/hazards/ gfw/bio/html**. It lists all his publications. Former students Ian Burton and Robert Kates coedited a two-volume festschrift of Gilbert's excerpted writings (volume 1), and thirteen invited essays (volume 2) (Kates and Burton 1986). U.S. Army Corps of Engineers historian Martin Reuss interviewed Gilbert at length about his life and career through the 1980s for a series, *Water Resources, People, and Issues* (Reuss 1993a). Gilbert wrote a chapter assessing his principal career contributions (from his perspective) in an anthology of such autobiographical essays by sixteen geographers (White 2002). A similar book introducing youth to twenty inspirational Quakers of the twentieth century has a chapter on Gilbert (Baker 2004).

❧

IN MANY WAYS, this biography is a typical account of doing and achieving—of a career—but equally it is an example of being—of relating to and loving the people and world in which one finds oneself. Commitment to science and application of its findings for the common good constituted the career of Gilbert White. Commitment throughout that career to the testimonies and practices shared by Quakers, as a Society of Friends, constituted his living witness as a responsible human being. Revealing the extent to which each informed the other in Gilbert's life is the biographer's challenge. In a larger sense, that is the challenge we all face: to do as we believe, to share our convictions, experience, and wisdom, and in the process to make the world a more peaceful and sustainable home. We all need as much help in this pursuit as we can find. The example of Gilbert White both stimulates and challenges us to emulate.

1 Roots, Childhood, and the University of Chicago

Living in the neighborhood of the University of Chicago and working summers on a Wyoming ranch, my mental images were a mix of Gothic campus, raw city streets, lakeshore, semi-arid mesa, mountain forest, and tumbling river. Geographic field work in the early 1930s exposed me to Wisconsin fisheries, Ontario forests degraded by smelter-fumes, decaying British estuarysides . . . [and] well-tended alpine meadows.
—GFW

Family Roots

Gilbert Fowler White was born and raised in Hyde Park, a half-dozen miles south of downtown Chicago and a quarter of a mile from Lake Michigan. The University of Chicago, also in Hyde Park, was just a few blocks from his home. Indeed, in retrospect, the university was part of Gilbert's destiny almost from its founding in 1892. His family's devotion to the university began with a grandmother's wish to attend the Chicago World's Fair. In 1893 Julia Fowler Guthrie and her daughter Mary Guthrie traveled by train from Atchison, Kansas, to Chicago, where Julia's Baptist minister had arranged for the two to stay in one of two adjoining Baptist guesthouses in Hyde Park. Temporarily residing in the neighboring house were Dr. and Mrs. William Rainey Harper, the newly arrived president of the University of Chicago and his wife. The university, whose principal founders were Baptists, was under construction a few blocks away. Both Guthries were very much impressed by the Harpers and William's liberal philosophy of learning, and Mary determined then and there that her children would someday attend the school.

In 1896 Mary married Arthur Edward (A.E.) White, an employee of the Chicago, Burlington, and Quincy Railroad. A year later A.E. was transferred from Cameron Junction, Missouri, to Chicago. Although it entailed a cross-city commute to work, A.E. honored Mary's ardent wish to live near the university. The couple had a daughter, Julia, born in 1899, and two sons, Arthur, Jr., born in 1902, and Warren, born in 1904. That was to constitute the White family, but seven years later Mary was pregnant again. On November 26, 1911, a neighbor in the Whites' apartment complex on Dorchester Avenue stopped in to share tea with Mary. Mrs. Angell asked when the baby was due, and Mary calmly replied, "If you wait about ten more minutes, you will be present!" Startled, Mrs. Angell left, and, indeed, minutes later Gilbert Fowler White was born. As his mother wished, he was born

1

Gilbert's parents, Mary Guthrie and Arthur Edward White, 1917

Gilbert at three years of age, at Ingleside in Atchison, Kansas, 1915

figuratively, and almost literally, in the shadow of an institution—the University of Chicago—that would shape his life for the next sixty years. At the end of those years, in protest, Gilbert left the university, but he remained indebted to the school the rest of his life. In Gilbert, the university produced one of its most productive, distinguished, and loyal graduates.

Neither of Gilbert's parents attended college. A.E. might well have done so (his father and grandfather attended Dartmouth), but he dropped out of school at age twelve when his father, William Wallace White (W.W.W.) died prematurely at the age of fifty-four and left a wife and eight children financially strapped. (The family story was that W.W.W. became distraught about financial affairs following the Black Friday crash of 1869 and committed suicide a few months later. Banks were going under, and W.W.W. was a banker. He also was the mayor of Burlington, Iowa, and his position in the community may have been one reason that the cause of his death was not reported in the local newspaper.)

W.W.W. was the son of Phineas White, a member of the U.S. Congress from Putney, Vermont, who had inculcated in his children a love of good literature and an appreciation of responsible citizenship. W.W.W. moved west at a young age and married Frances Atherton before establishing a career as a lawyer in Burlington. During the Civil War he served as quartermaster for a fleet of Union riverboats on the Mississippi.

Frances and W.W.W. had seven other children in addition to A.E., none of whom produced cousins for the children of A.E. and Mary. Gilbert's memories and the stories from A.E. about his siblings and parents were tinged with melancholy, and to that side of the family Gilbert attributed much less influence in his life than to his mother's family.[1] This assessment applied to his father as well, in part because A.E.'s employment required long absences from home. Yet, A.E. indirectly was responsible for his son Gilbert's interest and career in geography. After dropping out of school following W.W.W.'s death, A.E. was hired by a Mr. Perkins, a neighbor and vice president of the newly established Burlington Railroad. A.E. worked as a water boy during the construction of the railroad across western Iowa, the start of a career that led to his becoming supervisor of the railroad's food services. Gilbert recalled A.E. designing china for his dining cars. As a railroad employee, A.E. came to love the open spaces of Wyoming traversed by the Burlington tracks, and within a few years of moving to Hyde Park with Mary, he and an associate purchased a ranch in northern Wyoming to produce food that could be served in the Burlington dining cars. They named it the Quarter-Circle-Bell.

∝

IN CONTRAST TO THE MEMORIES of his paternal ancestors, Gilbert's childhood memories of and the stories passed down about his mother's ancestors, the Fowlers (the "F." in Gilbert F. White), were more numerous, cheerful, and vivid. Born into a Quaker family in Virginia, Gilbert's great-grandfather William Fowler was a member

Gilbert's maternal grandparents, Julia Guthrie and Warren William Guthrie, en route to Europe in 1900

of the Indiana state legislature before moving to St. Joseph, Missouri, where he served as postmaster and mayor during the Civil War. A daughter, Gilbert's great-aunt Emiline, married Benjamin Loan, representing western Missouri as a part of the "radical Republican" group in Congress and prior to that a brigadier general in the Union Army. Emiline passed down to Gilbert's family the gloves, fan, and necklace from the 1865 inaugural ball at the White House, where she danced with President Abraham Lincoln. Gilbert's first clear memory, from age three, was of Emiline in her deathbed the last weeks of her life. "She held court every day right up until a day or two before she died. One of her amusements was to have me come in and take orders for the groceries for that day.... I had been greatly interested in going with Louisa to shop at the grocery store" (White 1994a). Louisa, Emiline's sister, was the most accomplished and popular of the three Fowler sisters. She became a writer, socialite, and political activist in a city identified with Lincoln and the North during the Civil War. As daughter of the city's mayor, she and her sisters were once threatened by a Confederate commander intent on invading St. Joseph. The raid never happened, but because it had been rumored that the commander intended to rape the Fowler girls, they were hidden in caves along the Missouri River for a number of weeks (White 1994a). Louisa never married; rather, she cared for Emiline and the Fowler family property after Emiline's husband died.

Nor did any of the Fowler sons marry, and none of them particularly distinguished themselves. Hence, all the subsequent Fowler descendents were offspring of the youngest daughter, Julia, and her husband, Warren William (W.W.) Guthrie, Gilbert's maternal grandparents. Ironically, it was not Julia that the young lawyer Guthrie first courted. Initially, it was Louisa he visited and for whom he crossed the Missouri River from Brown County, Kansas. (That was probably not a particularly safe trip at the time. The courtship occurred at the time of "bloody Kansas"—the period, prior to the Civil War, of brutal fighting in Kansas over the permission or prohibition of slavery in that territory. At the time, pro-slavery advocates from Missouri would enter Kansas to vote—and fight—for their side.) During those visits, Julia would simply sit quietly in the parlor during the conversations. Finally W.W. (not to be confused with Gilbert's paternal grandfather, W.W.W.) went to William Fowler and asked for the hand of his daughter in marriage. When Fowler said yes, it was all right for the young lawyer to marry Louisa, W.W. replied, "No, I want to marry young Julia."

And he did. The wedding was a notable occasion because W.W. and his best man, both Kansas legislators, had to reach St. Joseph by jumping from one block of ice to another on the almost completely frozen Missouri River (White 1994a).

The couple subsequently moved to Atchison, Kansas, where they resided for many years at "Ingleside," a 12-acre tract of land with orchards and a vineyard; tennis and croquet courts; and a stately home with six bedrooms, a library, and a drawing room with piano among its sixteen rooms. W.W. and Julia built the house while living initially near the station for the Pony Express. They named their first son Warren, Jr., and their second son Gilbert, after Julia's brother, a disappointed gold miner who had died on the slopes of Mt. Shasta. This second Gilbert in the family was the namesake and favorite uncle of Gilbert White. From him, Gilbert learned many of the stories of his maternal ancestors and eventually inherited his most prized piece of furniture, the desk of his grandfather, W.W. Guthrie, the first attorney general of Kansas.

W.W. died shortly before Gilbert's birth, and thereafter Julia focused much of her attention on her four grandchildren by her daughter, Mary—in particular on Gilbert, the youngest. So did her son, Gilbert's namesake and uncle. As a mining engineer, the elder Gilbert traveled to exotic destinations, such as Japan, Siberia, South Africa, and northern India, that intrigued his nephew. His service on the European front during World War I also impressed Gilbert White. Gilbert White had few memories of his uncle Warren, due to Warren's untimely death after having escorted his mother, Julia, around the world soon after her husband's death.[2]

With no Quaker congregation in St. Joseph, the Fowlers had joined the Baptist church, but (in Gilbert's memory) Julia remained steadfastly Quaker, even though she promoted the Baptist faith among her children. How strongly this Quaker heritage influenced his other ancestors, Gilbert cannot say, but he vividly recalls one morning when he was about ten years old, helping his uncle Gilbert weed a garden. "We were talking about my studies, sports, and friends. Then he asked, 'Do you think you will ever amount to anything?' I wasn't sure what he meant at first. But then I understood he wasn't asking about doing well in school, or making money after college. He was asking whether I would be honest, tell the truth, and help people. It wouldn't be a matter of how I would be regarded by others. It would be for me to decide for myself whether at the end of my life I had really mattered" (White 1994a).

Gilbert's maternal uncle and namesake, Gilbert Guthrie

Gilbert determined then and there "to matter." Each year, when he visited his grandmother, Julia would sit Gilbert down and interrogate him about his progress. From Julia, Gilbert received, pondered, and retained bits of Quaker history and Quaker beliefs: the spark of divinity in and respect due all humans, the spiritual equality of women and men, the value of nature and the need for stewardship of natural resources, and the importance of nonviolence in resolving differences. Most notably, through her letters from nine months of circumnavigating the globe, Julia inspired in her children and grandchildren a sense of global citizenship and responsibility. Perhaps Gilbert's warmest memory of Julia was her sending him $50 before he left for London prior to his senior year in college; with the money he was instructed to visit Germany and France. His grandmother worried that Gilbert would be overly impressed with London and become an Anglophile. She felt that he should be more cosmopolitan and that he needed to visit Berlin and Paris, in part to practice his German and French. Indeed, Gilbert credited his grandmother for his determination to learn all the major European languages, including Russian, which he did.

Early Education

The Whites resided in two Hyde Park apartments, the second on Dorchester Avenue, before purchasing the house at 5607 Dorchester the year following Gilbert's birth. It was conveniently located just one block from the Ray Elementary School. Because his mother passionately supported her children's education and was actively involved with the Ray School and its faculty, Gilbert completed the usual eight years in seven. "Mother was a delightful hostess and was so known throughout the neighborhood. She entertained not only the neighbors but the teachers at the Ray School" (White 1994a). Both his parents were dedicated readers; Mary was involved in book clubs organized by others. She took great pride in her home and flower garden, letting others take the lead in community affairs beyond Ray School and the local Baptist Church.

Hyde Park was a diverse community, and the White children had friends and schoolmates from a stimulating mix of racial, ethnic, and economic backgrounds. The Ray School was a short distance south of east-west-running 55th Street, which divided the mixed university community from a heavily black neighborhood. Gilbert's closest friends included the son of a Chicago mafia boss with whom Gilbert never ventured anywhere except by limousine with a bodyguard—whether to theaters or to the book stores the two loved to frequent. Another of Gilbert's Ray School friends was killed in a gang fight, and several others served jail terms. Gilbert's brother Art was held up one night by one of Gilbert's schoolmates, who promptly apologized and sent Art on his way when he realized whom he had accosted.

Gilbert White was as independent as he was precocious—benefiting as he put it, "from parents' weariness with disciplining my older siblings"—and he got into his own share of mischief. The White home at 5607 Dorchester included an old barn from the days when that part of Chicago was still rural. By the time Gilbert's family occupied the house, the barn's upper loft was largely empty, and Gilbert once used it to stage a prizefight between two boys from Ray School (where fighting was prohibited). The Chicago police noticed the gathering crowd and halted the match before it began.[3]

There was no distinction between the university children and the 55th Street children at Ray School, but when they left the elementary school and went to high school, that changed; they went many different ways (White 1994a). Gilbert's university schooling actually began in 1924 at the University High School, commonly known as the Lab School because of its experimental approach to secondary instruction. Its founder was John Dewey, a philosopher and psychologist who became a strong proponent of the philosophical school of pragmatism associated with Harvard philosopher William James. Dewey joined the university as professor of philosophy, psychology, and education in 1894 and moved on in 1904. Gilbert did not meet him until midcentury in Dewey's New York City apartment shortly before his death.

Gilbert White acknowledged the influence of William James's philosophy of pragmatism on his own thinking but felt less intellectual indebtedness to Dewey. Nevertheless, there were certainly indirect influences from Dewey through some of Gilbert's teachers at the Lab School and at the university itself, including some of the geography faculty. Dewey defined geography as "all those aspects of social life which are concerned with the interaction between the life of man and nature; or . . . with the world considered as the scene of social action . . . or with changes introduced in this environment through the life of man" (Dewey 1895–1898, quoted in Wescoat 1992). In an article comparing the work of Dewey and White,

James Wescoat points out that Dewey's definition anticipated by thirty years the representation of geography as human ecology by Gilbert's mentor at Chicago, Harlan Barrows. In the article, Wescoat asks, "What is the philosophy that eschews theoretical discourse, prefers an inductive approach, insists on practical application, and prizes collaborative inquiry? I argue that White's approach was influenced by the pragmatic tradition of American social thought, and most notably by the work of philosopher John Dewey" (Wescoat 1992).

Dewey believed that strong identification with place (one's home and neighborhood) and appreciation for regional relationships were important in development of character and, therefore, that schools should offer early, thorough grounding in geography. Such training was apparent in Gilbert's lifelong commitment to recording the details of his neighborhood at the time (be it a German prison camp or a Colorado ranch).

The influence of his Lab School secondary education is apparent in Gilbert's own later pedagogical commitments. Throughout his teaching career, Gilbert participated in and espoused integrated curricula taught by faculty teams representing related disciplines, and he promoted experiential learning. Teaching was both more integrated and more individualized in the Lab School than the instruction Gilbert had experienced in the Ray School, and achievement was monitored more through informal consultation and written evaluation than through grades and the accumulation of credits. Projects emphasized cooperation rather than competition and individual effort.

At the time that Gilbert enrolled, the Lab School introduced a reorganized curriculum, integrating history, geography, sociology, economics, political science, and the reflections of cultural heritage found in art and music. The social and economic environment became the basis for mastery of oral and written language, thereby strengthening knowledge and skill in both English and the social sciences and reinforcing the relationship between the two. As the proposal for reorganization stated, "High school students need to learn to weigh evidence, to cultivate habits of intellectual sympathy and tolerance, and to develop a sincere desire to promote human welfare. All these factors demand that the school devote more time to history and the social sciences" ("A Report of the Proposed Program of Studies for the New Three-Year High School and the First Two Years of the New College of the University of Chicago—President's Papers 1925–45").

Gilbert's classmates at the Lab School were mostly the children of university faculty and staff and other professionals in the Hyde Park neighborhood. Many of these students accompanied Gilbert through undergraduate and graduate study at the university, and he developed several very close friendships, especially with the students who shared his interest in reading and theater. Initially, he experimented with acting but early on concluded that he much preferred the production side of stagecraft. As president of the drama club as well, Gilbert was very much in charge. This, despite being on average a year younger than his Lab School classmates by virtue of having skipped a grade while at the Ray School.

Further, since the Lab School encouraged its students, after three years of high school, to proceed to two years of integrated general studies in the university's undergraduate college, Gilbert was only sixteen when he graduated from the Lab School and enrolled in the University of Chicago. He was one of the first students to do that, anticipating university president Robert Maynard Hutchins's later policy of offering early admission based less on years of schooling than on student preparedness and his or her potential to benefit from the university's innovative philosophy of education.[4]

Graduation from the Lab School "recognized achievement of defined goals: emotional balance, capacity for self-direction and self government, a sense of social responsibility, and an ability and disposition to cooperate in socially desirable activities" ("A Report of the Proposed Program of Studies for the New Three-Year High School and the First Two Years of the New College of the University of Chicago—President's Papers 1925–45"). Gilbert fully satisfied these expectations. Despite his young age and even younger appearance, Gilbert at sixteen was acknowledged by many of his colleagues and teachers to be mature beyond his years. As Philadelphia family friend Betty Emlen said, "He was grown up when he was born! He was forty by the time he was twenty and stayed that way the rest of his life" (Emlen 2001).

Wyoming

Gilbert White matured early in part because of the summers he spent in Wyoming from age ten to eighteen, sometimes in the company of a brother and always with his responsible older sister, Julia. The two became ranch hands on the Quarter-Circle-Bell Ranch near Dayton, Wyoming. As mentioned earlier, their father and a railroad associate had purchased 6,000 acres along the Tongue River, hoping to produce meat to sell to the Burlington Railroad, which passed nearby. The ranch shifted from cattle to sheep, chicken, and honey production, each summer raising 3,000 lambs in the Bighorn Mountains for slaughter in the fall.[5]

Gilbert attributed much of his early interest in environmental and natural resource problems to his summers in Wyoming:

> Helping clean the irrigation ditches, stack the hay crop, and tend sheep camp in the national forest sensitized me to some of the environmental problems there. When and how was the forest land overgrazed? When was there inadequate drainage, leading to soil degradation? What systems of land use made for prosperity or poverty in the local community? . . . I was continually alerted to issues of use and deterioration of natural resources. One of my chores while tending sheep was to count black sheep periodically as a means of telling whether the band was intact. Since on average there were 20 white sheep for every black one, I was regularly exposed to the problems of inference from statistical samples (White 2002).

In retrospect, Gilbert also attributed his sociological and anthropological interest in people of different cultural backgrounds in part to the eight summers he spent

Gilbert in Wyoming in 1992, on the Eaton Guest Ranch near the family's Quarter-Circle-Bell Ranch, where he spent summers in his youth and came to love horses

dealing with Scottish wranglers, Spanish and Basque sheepherders, and Crow Indian friends.

Gilbert was frequently the object of the hired hands' mirth. He was given a pony, which wranglers helped him train. He entered it in a Fourth of July race in Dayton, but he had neglected to train the pony for the pistol shot at the start. When the gun went off, the pony bolted in the opposite direction. Despite that humiliation, which the ranch hands would not let him forget, Gilbert developed an enduring love of horses, mules, and donkeys.

While Gilbert and Julia were in Wyoming, their mother or a classmate would sometimes join them on the ranch. A.E. spent little time there and eventually sold his interest to his associate after the Depression, drought, and the loss of 700 sheep in a late winter freeze nearly bankrupted the operation. A.E. had also become concerned about his daughter Julia's extended trips to Wyoming, staying year-round after she finished college. Indeed, Julia joined one of the ranch's horse trainers in his mountain cabin for an extended visit one winter, and on learning of it, A.E. ordered her to return home. Stubbornly, she explained that the gentleman had been castrated by a bullet during the war and was no threat to her virginity. Besides, he was a delightful companion who enjoyed literature as much as she. A.E. said that could well be, but that it was the appearance to the community that counted. She returned home (White 1994a).

Gilbert's close friendship with Julia, who never married, became even stronger because of those many summers together and the adventures they shared. For example, they were introduced to Yellowstone National Park by their Hyde Park neighbor, Stephen Mather, founding director of the National Park Service. (Mather asked them to join him in showing the park to the beautiful wife of a French diplomat; he was afraid that traveling with her alone would raise eyebrows.)

The University of Chicago and Gilbert White

Gilbert White entered the College of the University of Chicago in the autumn of 1928. His siblings Julia and Arthur had already graduated from the college (their brother Warren showed little interest in higher education). Arthur had been an active fraternity member, and Gilbert joined Alpha Delta Phi. He was elected class president his freshman year, the only position of leadership in his life for which he could recall campaigning.

Gilbert White was blessed from an early age with a remarkable memory—an ability that helped him throughout his career. One of the first tangible benefits came during his employment in the university's Faculty Exchange, where daily he delivered campus mail to all employees. In Gilbert's sophomore year, Robert Maynard Hutchins (like President Harper, a young and innovative educator from Yale) became president of the university. When he learned of Gilbert's familiarity with everyone on campus, Hutchins invited Gilbert to accompany him (discreetly) to alumni functions and similar public assemblies to help him attach names to the many faces.[6]

In addition to working at the Faculty Exchange, Gilbert was employed by the campus chapel, where he supervised ushers and the collection of contributions. The chapel dean, Charles Gilkey, was a Baptist and friend of Mary White (Gilbert's father was an avowed agnostic and attended church only once a year to donate the family's annual contribution). Although he was not otherwise active in the chapel, toward the end of his freshman year Gilbert did—on his mother's advice—seek out Reverend Gilkey for counsel regarding ROTC. Gilbert had joined the campus ROTC field artillery chapter because it provided an opportunity to work with horses, but after a year of ROTC drills, when he thought about the implications of the military service that would follow, Gilbert had reservations.

His talk with Gilkey led to two fortuitous evening fireside conversations, several weeks apart, with two visiting chapel speakers: Haverford College's Quaker philosopher, Rufus Jones, and New York City's Riverside Baptist Church minister, Harry Emerson Fosdick. By coincidence Fosdick at the time was editing the personal papers of Rufus Jones for a biography. Both were outspoken opponents of warfare as a means to political ends, and Gilbert was sufficiently impressed by their counsel to begin reading Quaker literature as part of his research regarding the integrity of his continuing with ROTC. While discussing tenets of Quakerism beyond the pacifism that had prompted their fireside talk, Fosdick suggested that Gilbert also read William James's *The Varieties of Religious Experience,* and Gilbert did.

William James was a psychologist turned philosopher who, at the outset of the twentieth century, attempted an even-handed description of the full range of reli-

Rufus Jones, Haverford College philosopher and Quaker leader, in his office at home, 102 College Circle, next door to the Whites. Photograph by Tyler Fogg.

gious experiences, focusing on their functional benefits to believers (his philosophy's pragmatic approach). The lectures that constitute his widely read book describe the results of a variety of religious paths, the necessary prior step to judging their merits. "The best fruits of religious experience are the best things that history has to show," he said.

He drew an initial distinction between "two birth" and "one birth" religions. The former assume humans to be by nature selfishly sinful and in need of divine intervention, salvation, and rebirth. The latter assume humans to be intrinsically blessed with an adequate moral compass without such intervention. Early on, Gilbert White inclined decidedly toward "one birth." In James's words, "Such is the Emersonian religion. The universe has a divine soul of order, which soul is moral, being also the soul within the soul of man." The "religion of healthy-mindedness," as James labeled it, was little concerned with the origin and manifestations of evil in God's creation. As for the mysticism of sects such as the Quakers, James respected, even lauded, the products of such convictions, although he admitted never having a personal experience of the divine with the immediacy that Quaker and other mystics typically described.

Regarding such mysticism, Gilbert was impressed with the personal testimony of Rufus Jones in a 1930 leaflet, *An Interpretation of Quakerism.* "The Light Within which is the central Quaker idea, is no abstract phrase," Jones wrote.

> It is an experience. It is a type of religion that turns away from arid theological notions and that insists instead upon a real and vital experience of God revealed to persons in their own souls, in their own personal lives. . . . We no more need to go somewhere to find God than the fish needs to soar to find the ocean or the eagle needs to plunge to find the air. . . . Quakerism proposes to drop overboard the whole heavy load of theological "notions," including the innate depravity of people; it proposes also to jettison every shred and relic of . . . religious mediation for one person by another. . . . All people *must be religious for themselves* or they will never have the fruits of religion.

In essence, the message from Jones, Fosdick, and James was the biblical injunction, "By their fruits shall ye know them." The way that Rufus Jones had put it to Gilbert during their fireside chat made the most impression: when taking a man's measure, watching his walk tells you more than listening to his talk. Jones had helped establish and been named director of the American Friends Service Committee immediately following World War I, and during their fireside conversation Rufus related that history to Gilbert. Jones's fervor and dedication were contagious and instilled in Gilbert a desire to become similarly involved with the humanitarian service arm of the Society of Friends—a hope that would be fulfilled with the onset of World War II. Following that evening with Rufus Jones, until Jones's death two decades thereafter, Gilbert "watched the walk" of no one with more admiration.

Gilbert decided not to resume his ROTC involvement his sophomore year. His return to the Quakerism of his grandmother Julia had begun, but he chose not to make an issue of his church membership, remaining, while at Chicago, nominally Baptist out of respect for his mother's firm Baptist commitment. He did not seek out the fellowship of Chicago Quakers (who held their worship services in the basement of a Unitarian church only blocks from Gilbert's home); he only began practicing Quaker worship in Washington, D.C., a half-dozen years later.

In the meantime, Gilbert's Lab School interest in drama continued into college, and he became president of the college's Dramatic Association. He began to work closely with a young Chicago professor and playwright, Thornton Wilder, and was stage manager for two of his plays that premiered at the university. However, some tension developed between Gilbert and Wilder because Gilbert preferred challenging productions, whereas Wilder preferred a minimum of props. Nonetheless, Wilder remained Gilbert's favorite playwright for the rest of his life.

Gilbert also served on the staff of the literary publication, *Owl and Serpent,* was editor of the *Student Handbook,* and served as president of the Undergraduate Student Council. He graduated Phi Beta Kappa and was appointed Head Marshall of his graduating class by President Hutchins in recognition of "high intellectual attainment coupled with leadership in non-academic activities." His active membership in the Alpha Delta Phi fraternity continued beyond his Chicago years; in Washington, D.C., he was an officer in the regional chapter.

In his second year of college, Gilbert had decided to become a geographer after taking one course and realizing that in this field he could explore his interest in natural resources, especially water and land, that he first experienced during his summers in

Gilbert on completing his undergraduate studies at the University of Chicago, age twenty

Wyoming. The timing of Gilbert's decision was fortuitous—for Gilbert, for the discipline, and for Chicago's Department of Geography. Chicago's was the first full-fledged geography department in the United States, founded by a tall and stately Scot, Rollin Salisbury, assisted by an even larger giant of a man, Harlan Barrows, who was chair when Gilbert enrolled in the graduate program in 1932. These first two department chairs had been greatly influenced by Charles Van Hise, author of one of the first books on conservation of natural resources published in the United States. Gilbert was particularly attracted to Barrows's focus on the intersection of geography, ecology, and culture, a subfield Barrows labeled "human ecology" in his 1922 presidential address to the Association of American Geographers. As an undergraduate, Gilbert also took courses in the department from John Morrison, Charles Colby, Wellington Jones, and Griffith Taylor.

Gilbert's sterling undergraduate performance was rewarded by an invitation to spend the summer preceding his senior year in England studying with Henry Leppard, who had written a thesis under Barrows on the ecology of a Canadian river valley. Eventually, for his own master's thesis, Gilbert used information on delta land use in the Humberside estuary in England, which he examined with Leppard in 1931. As Gilbert recalled, "Geographic field work in the early 1930s exposed me to Wisconsin fisheries, Ontario forests degraded by smelter-fumes, decaying British estuarysides, a celebration of colonialism in Paris, well-tended alpine meadows, and Berlin students debating the merits of Hitler versus Hindenburg." By the end of 1933, as the coursework for his doctorate neared completion, Gilbert White—just turned twenty-two—was identified by chairman Barrows as a most promising geographer.

᪣

EARLIER THAT YEAR, Barrows and a colleague in political science at Chicago, Charles Merriam, had been appointed by Secretary of the Interior Harold Ickes to positions with President Franklin Delano Roosevelt's newly established National Planning Board under the Public Works Administration. Merriam was appointed directly to the Planning Board. Barrows was appointed to the Planning Board's subsidiary Mississippi Valley Committee. More specifically, he was assigned to the Missouri basin, and, while on assignment in Washington in January 1934, he offered Gilbert White his first job. Barrows needed help for several months with Missouri basin reconnaissance, and he implied that he might need Gilbert's services even beyond the initial assignment. Gilbert promptly accepted. He wrote to Barrows:

> It was with the greatest pleasure that I read your letter, not only because it offered me a position which I am eager to fill, but because it also indicated the acceptance of your plan for the study of the Missouri basin. The launching of such a project will, I am certain, mark a new and scientific approach to the problem of large-scale planning. I feel complimented that you should consider me eligible to take part in the work. . . . I am looking forward to hearing more about the study from you on your return to Chicago. Until then I shall apply myself to the completion of my master's thesis, and to preparation for the examination (White 1934).

Had Barrows not made this offer, Gilbert might well have remained allied with the University of Chicago even more closely than he did. Several years after taking the job in Washington, he was again approached by Barrows, this time regarding a possible teaching position in geography at Chicago. Gilbert was readily willing then and there to resume his career as a scholar and teacher at the University of Chicago. His family expected no less, and Gilbert would have been extremely happy with the position. But the assistant professorship never materialized, and Gilbert resumed his work in the heady world of Franklin Delano Roosevelt's New Deal, where several highly regarded public servants had identified Gilbert White as an uncommon man. For the rest of his career, Gilbert never sought a job or position. Invariably, others pursued him, often for assignments for which he would have assumed himself inadequately prepared.

"Unassuming" is one of the most frequent adjectives offered to describe Gilbert White. It is particularly complimentary for a Quaker. Yet close friends and colleagues have wondered about this quality of Gilbert's and have posed a recurring question: with such remarkable leadership abilities, with such a keen mind and gift for profound insight, would Gilbert White's legacy have been even more far-reaching had he more aggressively competed for influence in high places?

Notes

1. In 1993, when Gilbert and his children cleaned out the attic of Gilbert's boyhood home and looked through the scores of boxes and trunks there, they found a number of boxes that had been brought from Burlington in 1920 after the last of A.E.'s siblings had died. In one was a set of nine fine women's dresses from about 1870. Several of them had never been used; others had been used only slightly; all were bright, colorful and beautifully sewn. Gilbert's hypothesis is that when W.W.W. died, the ladies in the family put away their finery, went into mourning, and never wore these colorful clothes again. In any event, the dresses were still in excellent condition, and they are now distributed among the family (White 1994a). Gilbert's most treasured keepsake from his paternal grandparents is a set of *Harper's Weekly* saved by his grandmother Frances throughout her life. Gilbert's second daughter is named Frances in her honor.

2. Gilbert's other maternal uncle, Warren, died of typhoid fever after accompanying his mother, Julia, on a nine-month voyage around the world following the death of W.W. Gilbert White inherited his grandmother's extensive correspondence from that tour, carefully edited into a two-volume book by Louisa. Warren went to Yale Law School, was the first owner of an automobile in Atchison, and watched the Wright brothers' first flight on the beach at Kitty Hawk.

3. In 1978, the house at 5607 Dorchester was reputedly one of the two oldest homes still standing in Hyde Park, as described in Jean F. Block's booklet, *Hyde Park Houses: An Informal History* (1978). It remained in the Whites' possession until the mid-1990s.

4. By Gilbert's third undergraduate year, President Hutchins had instituted a policy of encouraging the enrollment of sixteen-year-olds, resulting in 40 percent of entering college students being that age by the time Gilbert returned to the university as a faculty member in the mid-1950s. Opposition from Chicago public schools to losing many of their best students halfway through high school led the university to abandon the policy soon thereafter (Stein 1971).

5. The ranch also leased 20,000 acres of grazing land on the adjacent Crow Indian Reservation north of the Montana line. In later years a major dam on the Bighorn River was named for a Crow neighbor, Robert Yellowtail, who each summer visited the Quarter-Circle-Bell with his family to renegotiate the lease.

6. Twenty years later, when he was president of Haverford College, Gilbert would impress the campus by mastering the names of all new students within two weeks of the opening of school. When a board member asked in jest at an annual dinner how many of the several hundred faculty, administrators, and Board of Managers present he could name, Gilbert rose and amiably introduced them all. The dazzled board member made a notable contribution to the college that same day.

2 *Washington and the New Deal Era*

It was important that I not offer personal opinions . . . just be honest in presenting the points of view expressed by others.

—GFW

Gilbert F. White in the New Deal Administration

Gilbert White's career spanned the last two-thirds of the twentieth century and addressed numerous problems, particularly the management of natural resources and the mitigation of natural hazards. At twenty-two, he found himself in the right place at the right time—in the executive office of the White House one year into Franklin Delano Roosevelt's (FDR's) New Deal response to the Great Depression. Because of his outstanding record at the University of Chicago and the consequent support and recommendations he received from the Geography Department chair, Harlan Barrows, Gilbert became part of the nation's first (and last) concerted effort to centralize national planning in the White House. His introduction to Washington politics and governmental maneuverings was necessarily quick and sometimes harsh. He became thoroughly involved in both executive and legislative efforts to determine law and policy regarding water and land. In addition to the pioneering but controversial Tennessee Valley Authority (TVA), FDR's New Deal initiatives included greatly expanded employment programs, primarily under the Works Projects Administration (WPA) headed by Roosevelt's friend, Harry Hopkins. By 1936 over 3.5 million people were employed in various WPA programs, which included the Civilian Conservation Corps, the National Youth Administration, and the Public Works Administration. Among other things, these programs were mandated by law to involve the Depression's unemployed in conservation of natural resources such as national forests, parks, and other public lands, as well as rivers and river drainage basins.

Gilbert White joined Harlan Barrows in Washington in March 1934, to assist with river planning. They were assigned to review plans for big dams on lower Mississippi tributaries, construction of which would be funded under the Public Works Administration administered by Harold Ickes, secretary of the interior (and another University of Chicago graduate). As Gilbert recalled, "The reviews went on very rapidly so they could get the dirt moving, get the money moving, and generate employment." And as he listened he began wondering what effect those dams were going to have and what the alternatives might be (White 1991a).

The following year Harold Ickes dedicated Hoover Dam, the largest of them all, with the words, "Pridefully, man acclaims his conquest of nature." Hoover Dam, employing over 10,000 of the Depression's unemployed, eventually spawned a half-dozen other dams on the Colorado River, reaching even into Mexico. From his vantage point seven decades thereafter, Jacques Leslie (2005) reviewed the good, the bad, and the ugly of the Hoover Dam's legacy. Suffice it to note that its hydroelectricity built the planes and ships in southern California that contributed to an Allied victory in World War II, that its water impounded in Lake Mead permitted the population of the Southwest to swell by 25 million people, and that the millions of tons of salt in that water (which otherwise would have emptied into the Pacific) "have instead been strewn across the irrigated landscape, slowly poisoning the soil." Without Hoover and companion dams on the Colorado, there would be no Las Vegas, Phoenix, modern Los Angeles, or San Diego, but "the Cocopa Indians, whose ancestors fished and farmed the delta for more than a millennium, might have a chance of avoiding cultural extinction" (Leslie 2005).

In July 1934, after completing their reconnaissance of conservation options in the Missouri basin, White and Barrows stayed on to work with the Water Resources Committee (WRC), which replaced the Mississippi Valley Committee. The WRC reported to the National Resources Board (NRB), created in 1934 and chaired by FDR's uncle, Frederic A. Delano. The NRB was supplanted within a year by the National Resources Committee, which in turn became the National Resources Planning Board (NRPB) in 1939. A number of subcommittees were established in 1935, and Gilbert became staff secretary to the subcommittee on water, chaired by Johns Hopkins University professor Abel Wolman, a highly regarded pioneer in water resource management. Gilbert subsequently also became secretary to the subcommittee on land, chaired during most of his tenure by Charles Colby (another Chicago geographer).

A centralized planning commission reporting directly to the White House was neither Roosevelt's nor Harold Ickes's idea. It was the dream of Charles Eliot II, an architect/planner and son of a Harvard president, who became the executive officer of the resultant string of umbrella planning committees (and hence Gilbert's supervisor). Ickes, Delano, and Eliot, together with political scientist Charles Merriam (yet another Chicagoan) and economist Wesley Mitchell, all served throughout the several reincarnations of centralized planning.[1] These five oversaw three operational divisions and eventually a staff of more than 200. That two of these five were Chicagoans, coupled with White's, Barrows's, and Colby's association with geography at Chicago, was a remarkable testimony not only to the university's reputation but to the perceived importance of the social sciences and in particular of a geographical perspective in this New Deal national planning. It is difficult to imagine a more exhilarating commencement of a career. Gilbert's optimism and high expectations of federal government during his Chicago schooling, buoyed by Quaker Herbert Hoover's leadership in spite of the Depression, quickened with his introduction to the Washington of Franklin D. Roosevelt.

Harlan Barrows and Abel Wolman, as chairs of subsidiary water committees, outlasted Gilbert White with the NRPB because Gilbert moved to a parallel planning role with the Bureau of the Budget during his last eighteen months in Washington. There he monitored all legislative initiatives concerned with water and land resources until his departure in the summer of 1942 to work with war refugees in France.

Becoming a Washingtonian

During his eight years in Washington, from age twenty-two to thirty, Gilbert shared an apartment with his Chicago classmate George Vanderhoef, his closest friend, with whom he had visited Berlin and Paris following his master's thesis research in England. Vanderhoef was a scholar of Victorian literature, student of martial arts, and fencer (he had been captain of the University of Chicago fencing team) who later joined the U.S. Marine Corps. An ambitious and able cadre of other Chicago alumni shared the apartment building, and they, along with Gilbert, were active in Washington's alumni chapter.[2]

Gilbert's world was almost exclusively a man's world his first two years in Washington. Neither Gilbert nor George Vanderhoef had time for dating. They joined a racquet club and played tennis, hiked near Washington and along the Appalachian Trail, rowed on the Potomac, bowled, played billiards and poker, smoked cigars, drank beer and brandy, and enjoyed Gilbert's lifelong addiction—fine chocolates. Gilbert also accommodated Harlan Barrows's fondness for professional baseball and joined him to watch games at stadiums from Washington to New York.

But in 1936 Gilbert began dating a young sociology student named Helen Wheeler, and for the next four years his social life and preferences for entertainment became more refined. He attended concerts and, especially, theater. Indeed, attending a play became an almost weekly pastime for the remainder of his years in Washington.

As Gilbert took on various roles in government, his circle of professional companions rapidly expanded. (In 1939 he sent Christmas cards to sixty good friends, forty of whom visited him in the hospital following an emergency appendectomy a few months later.) He also became increasingly involved with the Society of Friends and regularly attended worship and business meetings of the Florida Avenue Friends Meeting. His knowledge of the inner workings of and access to the FDR administration attracted the interest of Washington's socially concerned and politically active Quakers.

In addition to his professional acumen, Gilbert commanded attention because of his distinct appearance. He was over 6 feet tall beneath an additional 2 inches of crew-cut brown hair. Yet he was small-boned and thin to the point of gauntness, weighing only 137 pounds at the time. His decidedly boyish face framed disarmingly penetrating blue eyes—a serious mien accompanied by a keen, sometimes sharp wit.

Throughout his life, Gilbert was a man of few, well-chosen words, preferring to listen and synthesize other's ideas and desires and, often, to ask a few considered questions rather than offer opinion. However, when Gilbert did speak, his employers, colleagues, and friends listened. He cultivated a sober public appearance (perhaps to counterbalance his youth), and he had a closet full of uniformly dark suits, white shirts, and red and maroon ties—a time-saving approach that also announced his serious purpose.

Gilbert was remarkably disciplined in focusing his personal resources on the goal of pursuing science and scholarship in the public interest, and his discipline led to regimens. Within a year of his arrival in Washington, he began to record assiduously, but with little commentary, his daily activities and appointments. The record of his daily activities for the remainder of his life is now documented on index cards that fill several cabinet drawers. At the same time, Gilbert never kept a diary and seldom engaged in introspective letter writing. His professional correspondence was voluminous but characteristically brief, even terse.

At about the same time that he began keeping daily records, Gilbert also began daily meditation modeled after Quaker worship. The unprogrammed worship of Friends is not based on creed and does not involve prepared sermons or ritualized activities other than group meditation and the voicing of shared convictions. This approach appealed to Gilbert's basically agnostic view. Two years after he began attending the Florida Avenue Friends Meeting, he observed in his journal, "There is need for a new type of Meeting, not religious but ethical, not partisan but political, not class but economic, no salaried leaders other than teachers, perhaps music, certainly quiet and simplicity on a Sunday morning." Gilbert began to devote a half hour daily to "centering"—focusing his attention in quiet contemplation. Sometimes he did that at the end of the day, but more frequently at the beginning, as he weighed objectives and planned appropriate action. Quaker practice encourages such daily meditation, but more for spiritual, rather than intellectual, reasons. Gilbert was reluctant to describe this regimen as a spiritual exercise like Zen meditation (in which he showed little interest). Nor did he use meditation to try to determine the subconscious significance of his dreams. In fact, he would have preferred to be spared dreaming in his life: "it just gets in my way," he once said.

In his second year in Washington, Gilbert learned through a White House associate of a physical exercise regimen being taught within a block of the White House by a physical therapist. Two days after noting an almost miraculous change in his colleague's appearance due to the exercise, Gilbert tagged along to observe and subsequently adopted this regimen of calisthenics. For the remainder of his life, whenever time and place would permit, he faithfully devoted 20 to 30 minutes each morning to the series of standing and prone exercises. For him, this discipline was independent of the centering of his mind, although he came to recognize the power of the two in combination to relax and energize his body and focus his thought. Toward the end of his life, Gilbert calculated that he had allocated almost one full year to the calisthenics and another to centering.

In part because of his daily regimen of physical and mental exercise, for seven decades Gilbert White retained a much admired capacity to remain alert and focused. He could put in long days and short nights working away from home and maintain his intellectual edge through long meetings. Often at such meetings he appeared to slip into a trance or sleep when the moment required attentive listening. But to the relief of many moderators and anxious masters of ceremony, at the moment he was expected to speak, Gilbert would open his eyes and, more often than not, provide insight or a new perspective regarding the issue at hand. His ability to almost hibernate, while mentally reviewing detailed notes sometimes assembled days earlier, enabled Gilbert to address audiences at length without notes. Stewardship of natural resources was an early career passion of Gilbert's. Stewardship of the mind and body was a comparable commitment. This approach to caring for himself, in combination with (and probably contributing to) the uncommon longevity of Gilbert White's career, explains in part his remarkable productivity. At ninety-two he completed his final book, *Water for Life*, after fifteen years of research and writing (Wescoat and White 2003).

Gilbert occasionally noted New Year's resolutions in his daily record. On the eve of 1938 he mentioned the continuing need to learn to concentrate and listen to others. The latter discipline became particularly important in the ensuing months as his father struggled with jaundice. A. E. White died in May. Shortly before his death, father and son traveled together on one of their few shared vacations. When he returned to Chicago to help the family assemble a photo album in A.E.'s memory, Gilbert rededicated his efforts to the "3 Cs: concentration, consideration, cultivation." On the eve of 1941 his resolutions were to "perfect the technique of progressive relaxation; no drinking and less smoking; minimum 'front,' exaggeration, biting words, and jealousy; one constructive Friends charity; Mother and Julia (sister); save $1,000; simplicity; first aid; study philosophy; and finish the Ph.D." To study philosophy, he promptly enrolled in a St. John's College "Great Books" seminar (made famous by Robert Maynard Hutchins at Chicago). He also enrolled in a first aid class, graduating to an advanced class before the year ended. His concern about alcohol resulted from an especially disturbing hangover following a party. His parents had no objection to alcohol, and almost all his close relatives drank in moderation. However, his brother Warren had become an alcoholic. Once he resolved to abstain, Gilbert rarely drank the remainder of his life. On rare occasions he joined his wife in a glass of sherry. Although the writing of his dissertation was behind schedule, the central ideas were forming rapidly. In large part they reflected what Gilbert had learned in Washington.

FDR's New Deal White House

The New Deal programs with which Gilbert was involved reflected the agendas of not only Franklin Delano Roosevelt but also of his predecessor, Herbert Hoover. Although Hoover looked first to public-private partnerships rather than to the federal government to address the problems caused by the Depression, he recognized that the construction of flood control works could help ease unemployment. This idea was adopted by Harold Ickes, FDR's public works administrator and secretary of the interior, and it led to the creation of the Mississippi Valley Committee—the institution that had brought Gilbert White to Washington.

In the opinion of Gilbert White, FDR's greatness lay more in his charisma—his ability to attract and manage human resources—than in his own conceptual and planning skills. Although he was passionate about the American wilderness, the farm belt, the nation's forests, and soil conservation, FDR showed, at least initially in his administration, little interest in Gilbert's central concerns for water and flooding (Arnold 1988). Rather, it had been Herbert Hoover who, as commerce secretary during the 1927 Mississippi floods, initiated Tennessee River basin studies by the Corps of Engineers that subsequently led to the creation of the Tennessee Valley Authority during FDR's administration.

The Wilson Dam was constructed on the Tennessee River by the Corps during World War I for the primary purpose of facilitating production of nitrates for the manufacture of explosives. Completed too late for this war purpose, its electricity-generating potential for domestic use became the center of intense controversy between private energy interests and those favoring federal operation of the dam's hydroelectric generating capacity. Presidents Calvin Coolidge and Hoover had succeeded in blocking the latter, but in 1933 FDR "paid an emotional visit" to view the dam at Muscle Shoals, Alabama:

> Roosevelt now saw the great dam, symbol of progressive frustrations and progressive hopes, for the first time. He was struck by the sight and sound of the foaming water roaring unused over its massive spillways. In the vast surrounding valley of the Tennessee, families nightly lit their cabins with kerosene lamps and cooked on wood stoves. To Roosevelt, the contrast was intolerable (Kennedy 1999).

On April 10, Roosevelt requested that Congress create the Tennessee Valley Authority to build additional dams in conjunction with the Wilson Dam for controlling floods, generating electricity, combating soil erosion and deforestation, producing fertilizers, upgrading health and educational services in the depressed valley, and attracting new industries to the region (Kennedy 1999). It was a major advance from single to multiuse planning for river valley/floodplain management.

Although he admired FDR's optimism and leadership, Gilbert equally appreciated Hoover's political wisdom and foresight.[3] Hoover, when president, had redrawn the boundaries of all Corps of Engineers districts so that they would better correspond to the major river drainage basins of the nation. The initial recommendation to recognize river basins as natural management units had come three decades earlier from John Wesley Powell, an engineer and the chief surveyor of the arid American West. (Hoover, also an engineer, stopped short of implementing Powell's related recommendation to create river basin "commonwealths" to replace arbitrarily drawn state boundaries.)[4]

∞

THE CONSUMMATE DEMOCRAT HIMSELF, FDR was blessed with Democratic-controlled legislatures from his first term through the first half of his third term in 1942 (when the Republicans briefly regained control of the House of Representatives), the entire decade between the onset of the Depression and U.S. entry into World War II. Perhaps the principal benefit of this power was the uncommon opportunity FDR enjoyed to experiment with increased executive prerogative, expanding federal agencies as well as creating new ones, such as the Bureau of the Budget (BOB) and the National Resources Planning Board. The planning board had no precedent, nor has there been a successor agency since FDR that comprised such concentrated expertise responsible directly to the president. Prior to the 1939 Reorganization Act, in which Congress approved and funded the NRPB, predecessor planning committees depended on ephemeral funding from within the White House budget. This uncertainty and intermittent funding account for the confusing name changes of both the umbrella board and the subsidiary water committee from 1935 to 1939 (Meyer and Foster 2000). While this succession of planning bodies enjoyed congressional approval (or at least toleration) for many years, suspicion of expanding executive power steadily grew until the Republican-controlled Congress cut off NRPB funding in 1942.

The comparably innovative BOB survived, however. From its initial advisory role, when Gilbert White was a young employee, it evolved into a regulatory authority—an evolution that Gilbert critically observed as he consulted for BOB over the course of his career. His involvement with these agencies, particularly his employment by BOB during FDR's third term in office, deepened Gilbert's understanding of the inherent tension between the legislative and executive branches of government. But prior to his stint at BOB, while involved with the NRPB, Gilbert observed even more closely tensions within just the executive branch over the allocation of funds and the direction of New Deal programs.

National Resources Planning

With respect specifically to rivers and flooding—the topic of Gilbert's Ph.D. dissertation—there were basically four contentious issues that plagued executive branch planning. First, with regard to providing useful work for the unemployed, the White House had to decide whether to rely chiefly on the Army Corps of Engineers or on an expanded Public Works Administration under Harold Ickes. Much was at stake for the Corps of Engineers in this debate, for Ickes was set on removing the Corps from water management. From his position with the Water Resources Committee, Gilbert watched the struggle to defend the innovative Public Works Administration and the power and authority of Harold Ickes against mounting opposition from other federal agencies as well as Congress.

The Corps had begun construction of Hoover Dam while Hoover was still president, and Roosevelt followed Hoover's lead, authorizing construction of the Port Peak Dam in 1933 and the Grand Coulee Dam in 1934, in large part as emergency job measures. But by 1937, when FDR requested the National Resources Committee (the predecessor to the NRPB) to prepare his public works recommendations, there were several other New Deal agencies also involved in such unemployment relief efforts. Roosevelt approved a six-year effort that would require congressional approval for implementation of specific programs, but he stopped short of including the always contentious water projects. Nonetheless, within a month, under pressure from the subcommittee on water for which Gilbert worked, he agreed to endorse water-related programs. FDR's efforts to create a permanent federal public works department were thwarted, however, because of agencies' fears that Harold Ickes, if named the department's secretary, would have too much power (White 2000–2005).

A second, jurisdictional, problem existed. The Corps of Engineers and the Department of Agriculture/Soil Conservation Service (and to a lesser degree the Department of Interior and Bureau of Reclamation, which were responsible for developing the Colorado River and California's interior valleys) shared responsibility for river basin management and development. The Corps had preeminent and undisputed authority regarding issues of navigation and harbor management along major waterways ("big waters, big dams"), but when it came to controlling rivers for irrigation and flood control, the Department of Agriculture exercised considerable authority over "little waters, little dams and reservoirs" in upper drainage basins (Leopold and Maddock 1954). In Gilbert's words,

> The basic difference between the Department of Agriculture and the Corps of Engineers in early flood control investigations was the difference between engineering and ecology. The engineers saw themselves as being the valiant and competent technicians who set out to curb a stream on rampage, to keep the father of waters from invading the homes of the sons of man along his shores, in short, to harness a recalcitrant nature. The Department of Agriculture people saw themselves essentially as trying to harmonize man's actions with what they regarded as ecological principles so long as the measures were those which the Department customarily proposed to land owners (White 1969, quoted in Platt 1986).

Water and soil are equally important resources, and Gilbert found himself in the middle of competing interests when he became staff secretary for both the land and water committees. The upstream issues, primarily of concern to farmers, were land management issues; the downstream issues, primarily of concern to flood-plain residents (and thus to engineers), were control of rivers and flooding. Of course, the agricultural concerns could also involve structural alterations of rivers, often done by the Corps of Engineers, but in the regions of "little waters" the locally constructed and maintained dams and levees were often privately financed. Early on, Gilbert realized that Morris Cooke, the first chairman of the WRC under whom he served as secretary, was principally interested in the upper watersheds and "little dams." Cooke steered the committee's research toward the mapping and land management of such regions, in part because of his primary interest in rural electrification of the United States (Reuss 1993a). He had comparatively little interest in the control of rivers to mitigate flooding, which put him (and accordingly his committee) at odds with the Corps. Gilbert was intrigued with Cooke's slyness but shared Harlan Barrows's concern over the antagonism Cooke generated. Over lunch in January 1937, they debated, "Is or is not Morris Cooke an s.o.b.?" For Gilbert's part, his friendship with Morris Cooke steadily grew and endured after Cooke resigned as WRC chair to establish, with FDR's blessing, the Rural Electrification Administration.[5]

From Gilbert's perspective, the tensions manifested in the discussions of appropriate water policies and programs that constructively focused attention on the multiple uses and benefits provided by the structural modification of rivers. Dams and reservoirs served not only to control floods up to certain magnitudes but also to generate power and provide other benefits such as recreation. He went even further; he described and advocated the full range of adjustments to floods (both structural and nonstructural) in the interest of protecting not only people but also the ecological integrity of floodplains. The central tenets of his eventual doctoral dissertation gradually were forming. The passion Gilbert brought to his subject flowed from his deepening familiarity with the limitations of existing policies, resulting from his three years' involvement with the National Resources Committee's fledgling effort at what later would be labeled environmental impact assessment.[6]

The third problem with executive branch planning for rivers and flooding was the FDR administration's inability to establish autonomous administrative bodies, other than the Tennessee Valley Authority, to manage river basins. Supporters of the TVA lobbied in vain for congressional authorization of comparable integrated management of other major river basins. Ironically, the success of the TVA threatened existing federal agencies that shared jurisdiction over water and land resources. The closest the WRC came to realizing FDR's dream for regional authorities in other river basins was the establishment of eight regional committees to analyze the major river basins of the United States. However, all subsequent efforts to establish in these basins the degree of authority enjoyed by the TVA were defeated by concerted agency and congressional opposition.[7]

Even though comprehensive river basin management was never realized, Gilbert's committees had some major successes. Toward the end of Gilbert's first year in Washington, the National Resources Committee issued a report, Regional Factors in National Planning and Development (Renner et al. 1935), containing what two leading planners in 1979 retrospectively judged "the most sophisticated treatment of the regional concept available in an official government planning document, even today" (Friedmann and Weaver 1979). The report led to the establishment of two regional planning agencies in which Harlan Barrows had keen interest: the Pacific Northwest Regional Commission and the Northeast Regional Planning Commission. Unable to gain support for similar commissions in other regions, the National Resources Planning Board subsequently advanced a modified concept of "area analysis" and issued analyses of fifteen smaller geographically determined areas. Gilbert White and Barrows were involved with these analyses, including those for the Delaware and Potomac River basins, South Florida, the Lower Rio Grande, the Lower Mississippi, and the Northern Great Plains. Gilbert toured these regions to promote cooperation among their regional authorities, the national planning committees, and federal agencies. However, in his daily notes he reported that these efforts at facilitation were usually discouraging:

> Fort Tuthill Agriculture conference with experts from all relevant sciences endeavoring to understand basic environmental problems of Great Plains and Great Basin. Most missing the boat with details or with unapplied principles. Following day with North and South Great Plains Commissions, with no mention of the NRPB . . . impression of educating but not advancing thought. All concerned with slowness in initiating Northern Great Plains projects, due largely to Bureau of Reclamation's field organization being highly ossified and not suited to new problems. No longer taking leadership (September 1939).[8]

Concerning the Potomac, Gilbert wrote:

> Sad lack of direction as to what the new Potomac Interstate Commission should do once organized. All talk and no thinking for past three years (October 1939).

Concerning the Lower Mississippi:

> Colonel Parker reports that Army hasn't bothered to consult TVA in preparing its revision of Lower Mississippi flood control plans (October 1939).

Concerning the Northwest:

> Agriculture has failed to treat the interdependence of rural relief and urban activities. Internal migration can balance economic opportunities. Staff meeting reveals highly superficial approach to national planning problems (November 1939).

But when meeting with the Chicago Land Committee, Gilbert experienced the "first real attempt to discuss national land policy ... proposing acquisition of lands as a major tool of readjustment in land use."[9] Barrows and White, joined by President Roosevelt, were also encouraged by the possibilities in the Columbia Basin of selling Grand Coulee Dam power for entrepreneurial industry and irrigation to support migrant workers and the "Grapes of Wrath unemployed." However, the daunting challenge of balancing Department of Agriculture and Interior bureaucracies discouraged Gilbert from directing the Grand Coulee study, even though Barrows urged him to do so.

The fourth issue that Gilbert identified concerned contradictions inherent in the structure of the National Resources Planning Board and its committees. Gilbert detailed these internal struggles in his correspondence with Harlan Barrows. There was a paradox, he said, in the WRC reviewing the work of the very agencies represented on the committee while depending on the cooperation of those agency's representatives to accomplish the WRC's mandate. Tension also arose from this mandate failing to clarify the WRC's role in the initiation of and lobbying for legislation that might forward the committee's objectives. Harlan Barrows was particularly eager to pursue legislative implementation of the water committees' recommendations. Gilbert was inclined to do so as well but recognized that Brigadier General Thomas Robbins, representing the Corps of Engineers, was adamantly opposed to any drafting of legislation by the NRPB or its subsidiary committees. Disinclined to compromise, Robbins maintained the position that each member of the committee should have the right to protect the specific interests that he represented and for which he was responsible.[10]

The other people centrally involved in this issue were Abel Wolman, who chaired the WRC; Charles Eliot, executive staff for the NRPB; Vice Chairman Charles Merriam; and Chairman Frederic Delano. Although Eliot was prepared to work actively with Congress, as a staff member he needed authorization. For his part, Merriam was strongly opposed to any NRPB lobbying of Congress by committee or staff. Merriam felt the NRPB's planning mandate ended with recommendations to the president and his agencies. In contrast, Frederic Delano, a planner by training who was accustomed to seeing his plans implemented, was not averse to lobbying Congress; still, being uncle to the president, he had to be cautious. Meanwhile, Wolman inclined with Merriam toward the advisory role, and because he worked under Wolman, Gilbert White's hands were tied. He could not actively lobby for any of the approaches he espoused.

The lack of a clear mandate regarding the promotion of legislative initiatives in support of its planning objectives hobbled the water committees under first Morris Cooke and then Abel Wolman. It was particularly frustrating as the committees dealt with back-to-back flooding disasters in New England (1936) and the Ohio Valley (1936 and 1937). The initial reports from the Mississippi Valley Committee had stopped short of providing a legislative plan the president could take to Congress. From Gilbert's perspective, the WRC did not learn from that experience and thus was doubly remiss when, in 1936, it again failed to provide congressional committees with the recommendations needed to ensure sound flood control legislation.

Only after Congress submitted to FDR its single-purpose Flood Control Act (the major flood control legislation of the decade) did FDR receive from the WRC a proposal for an integrated, multifaceted program for basinwide natural resource conservation and utilization. The Water Resources Committee was critical of the heavy reliance on structural adjustments in the pro-Corps bill that originated in Congress, and the committee recommended a presidential veto. However, FDR signed the bill, and the 1936 Flood Control Act became law (Arnold 1988). Gilbert White then drafted a 1937 memorandum that did persuade Roosevelt to veto a joint resolution of Congress that assigned authority for planning flood control projects to the secretary of war, bypassing broader review by regional, state, and local planning bodies. When amending legislation in 1938 removed cost-sharing provisions of the 1936 Flood Control Act, allowing federal assumption of the entire cost of both dam and channel modification projects, the WRC again recommended a presidential veto. But FDR again signed the legislation.

It was to the credit of Harold Ickes, and ultimately FDR, that the talented men on both sides of this legislative mandate issue were first assembled and, perhaps more remarkably, kept together. The inherent tensions in the NRPB were held largely in check by the staff—Eliot and under him Gilbert—until early 1941, when Harlan Barrows finally took such personal offense at his treatment by Wolman that Barrows had to leave. In December 1940, after months of hard work and dedicated leadership in chairing the National Water Policy working group under the WRC, Barrows submitted a report to Wolman and headed home to Chicago for the holidays. His report advocated a strong, proactive role with Congress, a stand that most of his colleagues endorsed. Barrows felt that forthright legislative recommendations were needed, particularly in light of the way forces had allied to defeat earlier attempts in 1908 and 1917 to formulate a unified national water policy. But Abel Wolman, on behalf of the WRC, softened Barrows's recommendations before forwarding the report to Frederic Delano for transmission to the president. Unfortunately, Wolman took this action without consulting Barrows.

Upon learning of the changes, Barrows fired off a sharp letter of protest with a copy to Gilbert White. After reading the letter, Gilbert replied to Barrows (whom he, affectionately, had taken to addressing as Simon Legree, the truculent ogre of *Uncle Tom's Cabin*), "Mr. Wolman has neither telephoned nor called during the past two weeks, and I have not sought him out. . . . Perhaps your letter of January 15 helps explain his absence. Before reading it, I sat down as you had suggested. Unfortunately, the letter slipped from a then-steaming hand and burned a hole in my pants on its way to the floor. For the time being it has been filed in the icebox. Sometimes I agree that the name 'Legree' is inappropriate—it is too gentle!" (White 1941).

The rift between Barrows and Wolman did not affect Gilbert's working relationship with either man. When they died, Gilbert coauthored fitting tributes to both friends (White and Colby 1961; White and Okun 1992).[11]

Reduced funding and erosion of confidence within the National Resources Planning Board resulted in rapidly decreased board effectiveness by the end of the 1930s. As scholarly as he was, even Gilbert lamented the excessively academic tone of many NRPB reports. Moreover, federal agencies, many represented on the board and its subsidiary committees, used the NRPB reports (finally numbering 370 with 43,000 mimeographed pages) more than congressional committees did (Clawson 1981). The NRPB's work did not seem to be making a difference in national policy.

As early as November 1939, following a reorganization of the Bureau of the Budget in 1938, Gilbert was aware of BOB's proposed involvement in some of the planning functions of the NRPB, including review of all departmental reports going to Congress. FDR and Harold Ickes were issuing memoranda suggesting that BOB should intervene in interagency controversies that were not being resolved within or by the NRPB (GFW daily notes in late 1939 and early 1940). Through his housemate E. Johnston Coil's involvement in the State Department, Gilbert was also aware of discussions about the implications for defense and postwar planning in the event of U.S. entry into World War II. Early on, Coil, soon to become the founding executive of the new National Planning Association, kept Gilbert informed of the extent to which planning for war and reconstruction had begun to dominate the agendas of the president's cabinet and federal agencies. With the approach of war, these discussions often had a common underlying theme of how to use the pending crisis to shake up government and reclaim some of FDR's diminished executive advantage. It would not be the first time that a war or disaster shifted the balance of power from the legislative to executive domain.[12]

The Bureau of the Budget

Gilbert White had little experience with congressional politics until his appointment to the Bureau of the Budget. At BOB, he regularly dealt with the flow of legislative proposals to the White House regarding land and water. By chance, his office with the NRPB was adjacent to BOB offices, and he developed friendships with several people in the bureau. Proximity, friendship, and recognition of his abilities led BOB occasionally to enlist Gilbert's help. After preparing an executive order requiring all federal agencies to submit construction proposal plans to the bureau for review prior to submission to Congress, Gilbert was invited to come aboard to help implement that order relative to land and water projects. His salary would be $5,600, an increase of $1,000 over his NRPB employment.

At the time, he was considering another offer to move to the Bureau of Reclamation. Gilbert had heard that cuts in the NRPB would result in reduced budgets for the Water and Land Resources Committees, and Gilbert's job would be in jeopardy. The careful, studied approach to decision making that Gilbert already had developed by age twenty-nine is reflected in his correspondence to Barrows regarding his options:

> Since talking to you yesterday I have given much thought to the questions having a bearing on my decision to leave the NRPB. . . . Work involving problems of conservation of natural resources and requiring research rather than administration seems to offer the most certain prospect for satisfying returns. I believe that I could perform more effectively in study rather than in administration. I also believe that I would prefer and would be least inept in handling problems of national scope rather than local scope, many-sided problems rather than narrow problems, problems of integration of data rather than collection of data, problems the solution of which involved deciding with many people rather than a few people. . . . The burden of administrative work and the method of operating prevent careful study of any problem. Much of the activity is fruitless. Those conditions coupled with the disagreeable personnel situation and the lack of any immediate prospect for a sound organization of the Board lead me to the decision to make a break (White 1940b).

With the Bureau of the Budget, he would be at the center of policy issues, some involving water. The Bureau of Reclamation, in contrast, would provide useful field experience. In the end, the attractions of the Bureau of the Budget were stronger, and in January 1941 he was sworn in by Fred Bailey, head of BOB's Legislative Division. After his first day, Gilbert observed in his daily journal:

> Impression of much staff rivalry. Bailey's invaluable "black book" of statements on budget procedure is the first order of business, giving illuminating lessons from British budget procedure and organization. Black book details history of Budget's subtle transition away from destructive, critical attitude toward all agency requests. Army and Navy budgets each cut a billion each . . . they don't know what they want. Advised to avoid Budget appearances before Congressional Committees because other witnesses know too much. FDR has put his finger on any additional appropriations for J. Edgar Hoover or Thurman Arnold; he seems to be down on them both.

Gilbert's first assignments included drafting a memo on three major legislative issues regarding water resources: improvements in evaluation, survey authorizations, and construction authorizations. Gilbert felt very much at home. His was a very small desk in a very large White House office—the largest office he would have in his career. "My job," he said,

> was to prepare for FDR the materials necessary for deciding what he wanted to do with legislative recommendations coming from legislative committees and Cabinet members. One cabinet member might favor one bill, and he would give his recommendation, while another would be in support of a competing bill. It was important that I not offer personal opinions . . . just be honest in presenting

the points of view expressed by others. We were wanting from FDR his opinions on what legislation was in accord with his program, what wasn't, and any suggestions he might have. Harold Smith, as Director of the Budget, or occasionally one of us in the office would then take the work we had prepared to FDR each morning and pick up the decisions FDR had made on the previous day's delivery. Often FDR would still be in bed. Just once we offered our opinions. There was a piece of legislation recommending authorization of money for a Harvard University celebration. We assumed he was probably going to approve it, so I wrote a little poem to FDR. And he wrote back in the same fashion—a bit of doggerel. I wish I had saved copies of the exchange. Some years back I tried to locate it at the archives in Washington . . . but I guess they didn't think it important to keep the President's poetry (White 2002).

Gilbert's history with the NRPB—of planning for regional authorities and floodplain management—would seem to imply that he would be given similar responsibilities with BOB. Unfortunately for Gilbert, FDR remained firm that Harold Ickes should retain oversight of regional authorities, despite warnings from congressmen stopping by BOB offices that Ickes's involvement would kill the new regional authorities bill. Gilbert and Fred Bailey dragged their feet to buy time, until Ickes's irritation over the delay forced them to proceed with the bill's recommendation to FDR. And as they predicted, the legislation failed (GFW daily notes, September 1940).

Gilbert's other assignments ranged from drafting bills establishing the Inter-American Highway and Inter-American Statistical Institute to legislation for a census of business and industry. In addition, because a replacement for him with the Land Resources Committee of the NRPB had not been found, he continued to assist there until, in April 1940, he moved into a new area of planning in association with his housemate, E. Johnston Coil.[13]

Coil's dream of establishing a new National Planning Association (NPA) had become a reality, with a forward-looking postwar reconstruction agenda that addressed production and labor, social services, U.S. foreign policy, and global political trends. Drawing on his prior involvement with Morris Cooke when Cooke ran both the Mississippi Valley Committee and the Rural Electrification Administration, Coil turned to Cooke to chair the NPA.

White, Haushofer, and the Onset of World War II

At the close of the initial planning meeting of the NPA, Gilbert suggested to Morris Cooke that the theories of German political geographer Karl Haushofer were heavily influencing Adolf Hitler's plans for world domination and therefore should be included in the NPA's study of global political trends. Cooke agreed and, at the same time, urged Gilbert to lead a study of the economics of large-scale social movements. This latter invitation resulted in Gilbert joining with S. W. Boggs in the State Department and Charles Colby on the NRPB to plan an atlas for world reconstruction. The Carnegie Foundation agreed to contribute $3,500 to the NPA for the project, and the National Research Council (NRC) of the National Academy of Sciences agreed to supervise the study (GFW daily notes, May 1941). Gilbert accepted the NRC appointment to outline Haushofer's theoretical contributions, but because he wanted to complete his dissertation, he turned down an accompanying salaried position to direct the geographical mapping for the atlas. In hindsight it was fortuitous that he declined; shortly thereafter the Japanese attacked Pearl Harbor. U.S. entry into World War II led Gilbert to hurriedly complete his dissertation, since he anticipated working as a conscientious objector with the American Friends Service Committee.

Pearl Harbor also led to Gilbert's involvement with Milton Eisenhower's War Relocation Authority (WRA). Eisenhower was asked in 1942 by FDR to oversee the relocation of Japanese American citizens to camps in the western United States. In March Gilbert turned down an invitation from the WRA to work on the program. Unwilling to take no for an answer, Milton Eisenhower took Gilbert to lunch to press his case, arguing that Gilbert could help recruit sensitive people to manage the relocation projects. Eisenhower was convinced, sad though the prospect was, that isolating Japanese Americans in internment camps was the most feasible way to protect them from the animosity generated by Pearl Harbor, and Eisenhower needed an assistant director of the WRA. Gilbert agreed only to give as many days to recruitment of personnel as his progress on the dissertation and work on the Haushofer project would permit.

The National Planning Association issued a booklet, *The Strategy of World Conquest: Territorial Foundations of the German Aspiration,* the following month. As the following excerpt attests, the booklet would have benefited if Gilbert, the master of clarity, had had a hand in the writing:

> The existence since before the First World War of detailed German General Staff plans for conquest overseas as well as in Europe, the establishment since the end of that war of agencies for gathering and collating information about all parts of the earth, and the success of military operations in many theaters of war since 1939 stand as proof that no part of the world has been omitted from the comprehensive and painstakingly worked out plan of conquest. The incompleteness of published items about plans for regions far from Germany may be explained by the fact that all, or nearly all, the articles and books written since 1920 on the subject of territorial aggrandizement have been prepared mainly to apprize the German public of plans afoot with the object of eliciting the country's support for them. Haushofer, the leader of this educational propaganda, has openly adopted the rule of moving one step at a time in conditioning public opinion to the grandiose idea of conquering the world. To enlist popular backing for aggression is easiest if moves are to be made against nearby states. Their opposition to German objectives is common knowledge, and needs only skillfully phrased reiteration to inflame the public mind. As the war has shown, public opinion readily keeps up with advancing conquests.

This proves the shrewdness of the [German] geopoliticians in letting open discussion of remote regions wait.

FDR also received the booklet. He was already well aware of Karl Haushofer's ideas because of his friendship with American political geographer Isaiah Bowman. FDR and leaders of allied governments in the war were not blind to Hitler's imperial aspirations, but, at least initially, they may have been overly confident of their ability to meet the Hitler/Haushofer challenge. Believing that any European confrontation could be confined to a short-lived air war, FDR's focus in 1938 was on the postwar U.S. response following a quick victory. In contrast to Hitler's use of Karl Haushofer to plot a global empire, FDR employed Isaiah Bowman in 1938 to plot with equal confidence the global resettlement of the 10 to 20 million refugees the Allies anticipated following their victory.

Gilbert White left his White House position satisfied that he had at least shared his premonitions about the gravity of the Nazi threat and the eventual commitment of U.S. forces to the ground war in Europe. Part of White wished very much to share FDR's optimism about avoiding such troop commitment, but Haushofer's writings and Hitler's ambitions were clear. Gilbert had an uncommon understanding of the events in Europe, from his reading of German political geographers and especially from his visit to Berlin with George Vanderhoef just prior to Hitler's victory at the polls in 1932. The two Chicagoans had listened to heated debates among German geography students at the University of Berlin over the pros and cons of Paul von Hindenburg's and Hitler's campaign platforms. Hitler's charisma and the appeal to those youth of Hitler's idealistic designs, however grandiose, were clearly apparent.

Virtually everyone, including Quakers, had underestimated the Nazis. Gilbert gradually came to understand how Hitler and his Gestapo had managed, even manipulated, the periodic visits of European and North American Quaker emissaries (including Rufus Jones) on behalf of Jews. The Gestapo always opened such meetings with expressions of gratitude for Quaker-distributed food and seed, which had saved many German lives following World War I. Perhaps because of such tact, Quakers on both sides of the Atlantic failed to recognize, perhaps more than many other people, the inhuman objectives of the Nazis. As John Greenwood said, "He who sups with the devil needs a much longer spoon than Quakers, or even Popes, possessed" (1975).[14]

Germany's surprising success in September 1939, overwhelming Poland in less than one month, was followed by a comparably unexpected pause in Nazi aggression at the outset of World War II. FDR hoped that Hitler was having second thoughts, and he sent euphoric greetings of hope at year's end to Catholic, Protestant, and Jewish leadership in the United States. But then, in early 1940, Germany quickly overtook Denmark and Norway, invaded the Low Countries, and attacked France. France's military capitulated within a few weeks, overwhelmed by the German blitzkrieg, and the German army occupied Paris on June 14, taking 2 million French militia prisoners. Under an armistice signed a week later, Germany occupied northern France as well as a strip along the Atlantic coast. Southern France remained in control of the now nominally neutral French government, with the capital in the city of Vichy. In return for the resignations of pro-Western French government leaders and the expressed loyalty to Germany of their replacements (General Philippe Petain and Prime Minister Pierre Laval), the Nazis agreed not to occupy this region, and Vichy France became a buffer state. Under the watchful eye of the Nazis, the Vichy government maintained diplomatic relations with the United States and welcomed refugee relief, reha-

Gilbert on leaving Washington, D.C., to perform AFSC relief work in France, 1942

bilitation, and emigration programs from American church groups, including the American Friends Service Committee, endorsed by the U.S. State Department.

What Gilbert Learned

Before examining Gilbert White's service in France and Germany during the war, I want to summarize the principal lessons in leadership that he learned in FDR's New Deal White House. First, Gilbert learned that being a true servant in public service is a key to effective leadership, regardless of the level of one's official authority, and that the servant role begins and ends with listening. From FDR, among others, Gilbert learned to listen and to be patient before disclosing his own views. FDR not only had the ability to listen; in some situations he would disguise his own position and give those with competing points of view the impression that they enjoyed the president's support. He could thus solicit thorough and honest statements regarding disparate approaches to an issue. However, Gilbert also learned the downside of this tactic, which at times resulted in feelings of having been misled or even betrayed.[15] Thus, he also deepened his commitment to honesty and integrity. These qualities, coupled with humility, underlay his sincere listening—to associates and, in particular, to subordinates or those with whom he differed.

From Harlan Barrows, Gilbert acquired many of the ideas concerning river basin and floodplain management that appeared in his dissertation and for which he would receive major credit. Gilbert is the first to acknowledge his intellectual debt to Barrows. At the same time, not all the lessons Barrows demonstrated were positive. For example, making friends, establishing allies, and exercising influence are as important in accomplishing political goals as is dissemination of useful scientific knowledge. Frequently, scholars focus on the latter and fare poorly with the former. Fortunately, on the water committees for which White and Barrows worked were other people whose public relations skills Gilbert could study and emulate, even as he sadly observed Barrows's comparative ineffectiveness in exercising influence. Both Morris Cooke and Abel Wolman were highly effective chairpersons, but with very different objectives and styles of leadership. Cooke was idealistic yet shrewdly opportunistic, using his chairmanship to promote his agenda of rural electrification. Although intrigued by Cooke's political savvy, Gilbert understood from his own reactions to Cooke's opportunism how confidence in such leadership, however able, gradually dissipates.

Wolman, in contrast, was a patient, persistent, and persuasive negotiator whose only goal as chair was to produce consensus from diverse interests. With a somewhat less impassioned personal agenda or a willingness to suppress that agenda, Wolman enjoyed a distinguished career of chairing committees that addressed many diverse problems.[16] From Abel Wolman's example, therefore, Gilbert learned prudence in accepting only service assignments that helped him further his goals. From Harlan Barrows he learned parsimony, to accept opportunities for which his qualifications and interests were most appropriate. From his grandmother Julia, Gilbert had learned that things worth doing are worth doing well.

At a deeper level, Gilbert grew accustomed to working with highly talented people whom he respected and who in turn learned to respect him. After his eight years in Washington, he was not easily impressed or overawed. Gilbert concluded that at the heart of politics lies power and its exercise by strong egos. He would have none of it, himself, for the remainder of his career, but he did not thereafter disparage it in others. He learned to disarm it to considerable degree among his associates, but in the interest of getting things done rather than in casting judgment. Accordingly, it did not get in the way of friendships or learning what such associates could teach him. Unfortunately, however, the Washington world of government was almost exclusively a man's world. Gilbert had few female exemplars, and he risked slipping into the chauvinism typical of government circles at that time. It would be a blessing, therefore, that within a year of leaving Washington, during his work with refugees in France, Gilbert would work with several strong, middle-aged women from assorted European backgrounds with remarkable courage and resilience. They would prove to be every bit as capable as his male teachers. If Gilbert left Chicago feeling that he had become a successful fish in a small campus pond and left Washington realizing that he could swim successfully in much larger pools, he would leave France and Germany chastened by the examples of fortitude and wisdom provided by these women.

To summarize, in the third decade of his life Gilbert observed a great deal of conflict and learned much about its management. In his role as staff secretary to the National Resources Planning Board committees, he witnessed behind-the-scenes infighting that seldom surfaced in the official meetings of the NRPB and its several committees. The most contentious quarrels were between civilians and Corps of Engineers personnel. As already suggested, a growing concern of Corps' critics was its bias toward controlling rivers with structures such as dams and levees, rather than adjusting human uses and occupancy near them. Gilbert's views on this subject, even before the 1945 publication of his dissertation, *Human Adjustment to Floods: A Geographical Approach to the Flood Problem in the United States,* were well known to Corps personnel on the water and land committees. But from his first Washington assignment, during which he worked with Corps employees in the Lower Mississippi basin, Gilbert developed—through conscientious listening—a rapport that would enable him to work with and influence his friends in the Corps. He demonstrated genuine respect for Corps personnel, and that respect was reciprocated throughout his career. With tact and patience Gilbert White successfully challenged the Corps' approach to river management and flood control, substituting for their exclusively structural solutions, wherever feasible, the full range of nonstructural adjustments for which Gilbert became the nation's leading proponent (Arnold 1988).

These nonstructural approaches were available and used, albeit in embryonic form, during the 1930s. For example, in flood control legislation passed in 1938, the Corps was instructed to consider evacuating an area at risk instead of building levees, if the cost of the former was less than the cost of construction. However, that instruction largely fell on deaf ears. That same year Gilbert attended a national planning conference in California where he boldly suggested that federal funds for constructing flood control dams in California should not be spent unless legislation was enacted to control any further encroachment into floodplains. When word of these radical views reached California's congressional delegation, it promptly called for an investigation of the youthful staff member of the National Resources Planning Board who was promoting un-American ideas. Gilbert survived the congressional hearing (White 2000–2005).

Much, perhaps most, of what the NRPB's subsidiary water committee tried to introduce into the nation's water policies was never implemented during the life of the NRPB (1939–1942). Yet, Marion Clawson, in his review of the influence of the NRPB (1981), judges the Water Resources Committee's work to be the basis for everything that happened in U.S. water planning in the intervening four decades. Moreover, insofar as its work spawned Gilbert's dissertation, the WRC can take credit for inspiring what many regard as "perhaps the most influential piece of public policy research ever published by an American geographer" (Cutter 2001).[17]

Notes

1. Mitchell and Merriam were involved in executive office planning dating back to 1929 when, as chair and vice chair, they served on President Herbert Hoover's Research Committee on Social Trends (Meyer and Foster 2000).

2. In their apartment building they were joined by fellow Chicagoans Huntington Harris, Charles Dearing of the Brookings Institution, and E. Johnston Coil, who, after sharing assignments with Gilbert on the Mississippi Valley Committee, became an officer of the Rural Electrification Administration. Shorter-term housemates included Charles Thompson, also with the Brookings Institution, and William Aydelotte, whose father, as president of Swarthmore College, became Gilbert's mentor during Gilbert's overlapping tenure as president of Haverford College, Swarthmore's sister college.

3. Gilbert also gained respect for Hoover's leadership from serving on a committee on natural resources, chaired by Hoover within the Commission on Organization of Government under Harry Truman in 1948.

4. Paradoxically, waterways that seemingly "naturally" produce state boundaries, in many instances warrant management as river basin wholes. That is the case despite (and because of) the simple fact that flooding may affect bordering states differently. States on both sides of the Mississippi, for example, affect or are affected by river use and channel alterations of all states up and down and on either side of the river. Individual states have their rights, of course, but river management along state lines makes coordinated action (with respect to water quality and flooding, for example) difficult. Hoover understood that well.

5. Although the Corps of Engineers and Department of Agriculture frequently clashed because of their conflicting interests, their shared concern over FDR's possibly empowering Harold Ickes at their expense sometimes made them bedfellows. In May 1937, when the National Resources Committee was considering recommending the establishment of an Ohio–Lower Mississippi flood control committee under Ickes's leadership (building on Barrows's and White's work with the Mississippi Valley Committee), the Corps opposed the move. Not surprisingly, the Corps preferred regional valley authorities under Corps direction. Agriculture was generally supportive of the National Resources Committee proposal but sufficiently wary of Ickes's power to threaten siding with the Corps to block Ickes. As chair of the Water Resources Committee, Abel Wolman counseled Gilbert to stay out of this fray (information taken from Gilbert's daily notes).

6. "It soon became apparent that the files were full of horror stories of reservoirs that leaked, dams that failed, dams that didn't serve their purpose, drainage projects that destroyed large areas of wildlife habitat without proportionate gains in economic production. . . . The group recommended to the President that he issue an executive memorandum telling all agencies that before they started a new water-storage project or a

new land-drainage project they should let the others know. That was done. A system of regular reporting was established. Subsequent experience showed that the agencies could wait until they were about to launch a project and then inform the others. It then became very difficult for the others to have much influence on the proposed development" (Reuss 1993a).

7. Several years after he worked for the National Resources Committee, while employed by the Bureau of the Budget and at FDR's request, Gilbert drafted legislation mandating regional authorities, but it failed to gain congressional approval. After leaving Washington, Gilbert continued to pursue and promote this idea, first during the Truman administration when he was asked to serve on the Commission on Organization of Government chaired by President Hoover, and subsequently during the long tenure of the Water Resources Council from 1965 through its dismantlement by President Ronald Reagan two decades later. During the twentieth century, although a succession of administrations recognized the logic of river basin authorities modeled on the TVA, no president could overcome the opposition of well-entrenched agencies. Gilbert even lived to see the effectual end of the TVA's river basin management authority when Congress terminated TVA funding in the mid-1990s.

8. En route to Fort Tuthill, while visiting Mesa Verde, Gilbert learned of Neville Chamberlin's declaration of war against Germany, followed by FDR's radio assurance of neutrality.

9. Gilbert maintained keen interest in Chicago regional resources planning, eventually working with the city and contributing to that city's reputation for pioneering adjustments to floods when he joined the University of Chicago's Geography Department in 1955.

10. From this experience, Gilbert learned an important lesson in facilitation. Effectiveness as a committee chair or staff secretary requires strict neutrality. Trust is gained only through such rigorous impartiality (even though all concerned may know the chair's personal bias). At the outset, the chair should try to gain agreement that blocking progress because of partisan loyalties is unacceptable, given the committee's charge. The relation of this lesson to Gilbert's beliefs as a Quaker is manifest.

11. True to his truculent nature, Barrows, when he retired from the University of Chicago soon after his falling out with Wolman, dismayed his Geography Department colleagues and the University Archives by burning his personal and professional papers after learning that he had been denied his anticipated postretirement office space.

12. Lincoln became a strong president because of his management of the Civil War. Afterward, for four decades there were no major natural disasters in the United States or a major war involving the nation until the 1898 Spanish-American conflict. Throughout this time, under its legislative mandate to protect waterways for transportation, the Corps of Engineers was the single federal agency addressing the threat of floods. The levees and dams the Corps deemed necessary were seldom contested, and during the last half of the nineteenth and early years of the twentieth centuries, such works virtually never failed. Only in 1916, when structures failed to control Mississippi flooding, did the House of Representatives establish a Committee on Flood Control to determine the programs and funding needed to aid all areas of the nation facing the threat

of severe flooding. Support for the Committee on Flood Control arose in part because of growing opposition to the pork-barrel relationship between the Congressional Rivers and Harbors Committee and the associated Corps of Engineers Board for Rivers and Harbors. Legislators and private citizens alike were concerned over flood-prone congressional districts dominating Corps' priorities in the appropriation process. However, this growing tension over Corps authority played out not within the executive branch but within Congress. Corps supporters argued that flood crises benefited from the Army's rapid-response capabilities. Opponents pointed out the inequities and escalating federal expenditures if a single agency with congressional support were to monopolize both funding and planning.

13. Twice following his transfer to the Bureau of the Budget, Gilbert turned down entreaties from NRPB leaders to return to his staff position there, each time despite the offer of a higher salary. Even though Gilbert was unwilling to return, the obvious needs of the struggling NRPB made it difficult for BOB not to loan Gilbert to the board intermittently.

14. "The Nazis knew how to maintain the Quaker silence, as they knew how to manipulate so many things. . . . At one period insistent questions about concentration camps were stilled by allowing a few carefully controlled visits in which the visitors were never permitted to speak to any prisoners freely or alone. . . . Goering, Heydrich and Hanfstangle answered the Quakers' letters with bland reassurances and made concessions in particular cases, mingling genuine if oily acknowledgements of Quaker help to Germany with a veiled and ominous atmosphere of threat. Hitler even received the pacifist leaders George Lansbury and Percy Barlett. Such concessions were enough to prevent the Quakers from telling all they knew" (Greenwood 1975).

15. Harlan Barrows shared with Gilbert an apt example of this approach by FDR. In North Dakota the Corps had proposed damming a river, thus creating Devil's Lake. The local community was in favor of the dam, but communities downstream were generally opposed because of recent shortages of water. During the drive from the airport with FDR to the town meeting where Roosevelt had agreed to speak, the Chief of the Corps and Barrows offered their respective opinions. Barrows pointed out the risk that any dam poses, should it fail, for people living downstream. The Chief of Engineers pointed out the economic advantages of the dam. The two went into the meeting not knowing what FDR was going to say. After acknowledging in his remarks the economic advantages that would accrue to the local community in the short run, he expressed his deep concern about the risks involved in the long run for all the people and property downstream should the dam fail. Reluctantly, he concluded that the river should not be dammed. Barrows, in relating the story, pointed out that there was an election coming up, and FDR had made the decision to court support from the residents downstream. It was the right decision, as far as Barrows was concerned, but not necessarily for the right reason (White 2000–2005).

16. Gilbert presented the 1999 Abel Wolman Distinguished Lecture, under National Research Council auspices, reviewing the principal changes in U.S. water management and environmental policy of the twentieth century. In 1962, for the Committee on

Natural Resources of the National Academy of Sciences, Wolman had assessed the more significant technological problems in the water resources field and related areas of research needing attention: ground-water processes, techniques for evaluating systems of water management, evaporation suppression and transpiration control, and improved water-purification methods and techniques for forecasting pollution damage. His voice joined White's at that time in pleading for broader interdisciplinary training of students in the water resource arena (White 1999b).

17. At century's end, two eminent geographers were invited to assess, in retrospect, the influence of Gilbert's dissertation, *Human Adjustment to Floods* (1945). Timothy O'Riordan's assessment is mentioned in Chapter 8. Rutherford Platt's placement of White's ideas within the context of nascent ideas of others at the time, including even the Corps of Engineers, bears inclusion here:

> Like Ebenezer Howard, the father of the garden cities movement at the turn of the century, Gilbert White drew together diverse strands of policy and action, synthesized them into a grand design and thereafter worked persistently to realize his vision. . . . It is of course very difficult to evaluate the actual contribution of Human Adjustment and its progeny to the reduction of flood losses, although many researchers have examined the effects of individual strands with some success (e.g., the recent work of Raymond J. Burby, Stephen P. French, Peter J. May, Eve Grundfest, Burrell Montz, Earl J. Baker and this writer among many others. . . . Whatever its exact statistical contribution, the USA and the world are safer because it was written, and because the author continues tirelessly to advocate, personally and through his warm encouragement of others, the perfectability of human settlements on the earth (Platt 1997).

3 *Love and the Onset of War*

The only obligation which I have a right to assume is to do at any time what I think right.

—Henry David Thoreau
On Civil Disobedience

Anne Underwood

"Deep friendships." On November 26, 1941, Gilbert chided himself for making so little progress in developing deeper friendships. On his thirtieth birthday he was reviewing the New Year's resolutions he made eleven months earlier. How to proceed? The previous week he had gone out to dinner with Anne Underwood, a tall, attractive, somewhat reserved young woman whom he had met at a holiday party a year earlier and who was home from Vassar College for Thanksgiving. That dinner was their first time alone together in six months. Their few encounters that fall occurred following Sunday Quaker worship when she was in town or when Gilbert had been invited to join her with other friends—who usually included Alfred Dennis, a Princeton friend whom Anne dated intermittently. Anne had spent her summer among the poor in Appalachia at a Tennessee work camp sponsored by the American Friends Service Committee (AFSC).

The holiday party where Anne and Gilbert first met was at the Dennis home. Gilbert had accompanied George Vanderhoef, a friend of Alfred's as well as of Alfred's mother, with whom George worked at the Federal Housing Authority. Anne had come by taxi, so George and Gilbert suggested dropping her off en route to their apartment. Only on that drive home did Gilbert and Anne begin to talk in depth and discover their shared interest in Quakerism. Anne had heard Gilbert's exemplar, Rufus Jones, give a talk following his return from a December 1938 meeting in Berlin with Gestapo agents to offer assistance to Jews wishing to emigrate to the United States. Jones's presentation and ideas prompted Anne, as they had Gilbert, to explore Quakerism, and while attending Friends meetings, she discovered the AFSC's summer work camp service program. Anne joined the Florida Avenue Friends Meeting in Washington but had not attended often because she was attending Vassar. Hence, somewhat serendipitously, Anne and Gilbert first met at a party.

Gilbert was intrigued and not a little surprised that this quiet, serious, mature young woman was eight years younger than he. Moreover, Anne was beautiful—a stately, brown-eyed brunette. Her stylish yet unadorned dress and understated

Anne Underwood in 1942

makeup and jewelry bespoke a welcomed independence and self-assurance. For Gilbert, it was particularly refreshing to encounter such an attractive woman who was as thin and almost as tall as he. But he was reluctant to get back in touch with Anne because of George's friendships with both her apparent boyfriend and his mother. George, however, badgered Gilbert to give Anne a call. Gilbert did, finally, and her response was encouraging: "I have been awaiting your call!" Anne and Gilbert spent the next evening dining at fashionable Normandy Farm, and in his notations before retiring Gilbert observed, "easily the nicest gal yet, or perhaps ever."

Anne and Gilbert got together two more times before Anne returned to Vassar for the spring semester. On one of those occasions Gilbert met her mother, whom he perceived to be none too friendly; he surmised that Anne's family was none too happy about her Quaker involvements. In March 1941, at a Sunday Friends meeting in Washington, Anne accepted Gilbert's invitation to lunch (only at this time did Gilbert learn that her name was spelled with an "e"). However, because Anne was away all summer and was still accompanying Alfred Dennis when they next met in the autumn, Gilbert began dating another woman. The understanding that he and Anne shared in subsequent meetings was that they were friends because of their shared Quakerism, but probably nothing more.

Moreover, Gilbert was wary of any serious relationship for reasons he was not ready to share with Anne. For many months prior to their first date he had not been dating at all, following his many years of courting Helen Wheeler. He and Helen had come to the brink of announcing their engagement before Gilbert's intuition told him to back off. Within three weeks Helen announced her engagement to another man, and at her wedding Gilbert (with no regrets) kissed the bride goodbye. Subsequently he had begun to feel that his high expectations—or hopes—of beauty, intellect, and shared values could not be found in one woman. But, despite her relative youth, Anne Underwood did have all three, and during their recent Thanksgiving vacation dinner, Gilbert felt renewed warmth from and for her. With his resolve "to get on with deep friendships," he invited Anne on several long walks over the following Christmas holiday, where he found it "down right worrisome" that they shared so much in common. On the eve of Anne's January 1941 return to college for her final semester, he recorded before retiring, "for the first time I could tell Anne how much I think of her."

Because of the war in Europe, the couple faced the prospect of Gilbert's departure for AFSC work abroad that summer and the even grimmer prospect that he might not return, at least not for a long time. With all that he had to do in his few remaining months in Washington, opportunities to share time together were rapidly evaporating. In fact, the two spent more time that spring working together frantically on his dissertation than in pursuing romance. When they did take a break and go out, their conversation inevitably returned to the implications of being a Quaker and the problems they had explaining to their friends and relatives their pacifism and the importance of conscientious objection to a military draft.

By this time, Anne and Gilbert presupposed marriage eventually, and together they viewed the world and conversed as a couple cast adrift from familiar ties and beliefs, with only each other and their shared values to rely upon as their convictions were tested by World War II. They were reassured by the fact that they had chosen the Society of Friends for the same reason: Quakerism confirmed basic convictions they had derived quite on their own. Apart from pacifism, those convictions included belief in the spiritual worth and brotherhood of all persons, the value of humanitarian service to those less fortunate, and the need for simplicity in lifestyle to reduce social inequities.[1]

Despite their growing intimacy, it seemed unwise to Anne and Gilbert to announce an engagement in view of the uncertainty of Gilbert's future—indeed, the uncertainty of the world in general. They resolved to wait—and hope that Gilbert would come home from his AFSC service in Europe.

Being a Conscientious Objector

The 1940 Selective Service Act, mandating registration for military service but allowing exemption from bearing arms for reasons of conscience, permitted substitution of civilian humanitarian service at the discretion of local draft boards.[2] This provision resulted in part from lobbying by the three Protestant churches that shared the strongest beliefs in pacifism or the refusal to take human life: the Church of the Brethren, the Mennonites, and the Society of Friends. Anyone could apply for a conscientious objector (CO) exemption, but it was assumed (incorrectly), both by the general public and by some draft boards, that the provision was intended to accommodate only members of these denominations. This understanding, unfortunately, made it much more difficult for men who had no religious affiliation or were members of other religious groups to receive such an exemption.[3]

Prior to the passage of the Selective Service Act, Gilbert purposely had not joined the Society of Friends, despite his active participation in the Florida Avenue Friends Meeting. He had decided that if military service became mandatory, he would pursue alternative service as a CO. However, if he were forced to take that stand, he wanted his application for CO status judged on its merits, not prejudiced either way by his having joined one of the peace churches. Hence, Gilbert decided to postpone membership in the Society of Friends until his dealings with his draft board and his status under the Selective Service Act were decided.

Prior to World War II, Quakerism to the average American (particularly in the eastern United States) was associated primarily with the founding fathers of Pennsylvania and with the many prominent Quaker schools up and down the East Coast. Americans also probably associated Quakerism more with humanitarian service (for example, nineteenth-century assistance to escaping slaves via the Underground Railroad) than with pacifism and opposition to war.[4] The association of pacifism with not only political pragmatism (i.e., a foreign policy of isolationism), but also the moral imperative of refusing to take human life, gained global consciousness as the world witnessed Mohandas Gandhi's nonviolent opposition to British rule during and immediately following World War I. His satyagraha (civil disobedience) movement married pragmatic and moral pacifism within the broader context of Hinduism. At the onset of World War II, the introduction of compulsory selective service in the United States, providing a nonmilitary alternative to fighting for those morally opposed to killing, further strengthened public awareness of the moral imperative in pacifism. (Identifying such pacifism primarily with "peace churches" ended in the

1960s with the civil rights movement and the prominence of America's "Christian Gandhi," Martin Luther King, Jr.)

These nuances of pacifism in 1940 explain, in part, the incredulity with which Gilbert's conscientious objection was received within his Washington circle of professional acquaintances. It was particularly difficult for his colleagues to understand how he could leave his enviable government position in protest of the United States going to war. A Washington group of COs and the Florida Avenue Friends Meeting supported Gilbert's stand, but among his larger circle of government associates and University of Chicago friends, he stood alone in this affirmation of his pacifism. His closest friend, George Vanderhoef, and his Chicago mentor, Harlan Barrows, were among those most incensed with Gilbert's willingness to give up, or at least to interrupt, his promising career and risk alienating those people who would support or promote that career. Neither friend had any patience with Gilbert's pacifism. Even Abel Wolman, a true gentleman, seemed to cool toward Gilbert for the same reasons. It was a heavy burden, and at one point the pressure seemed to get the best of Gilbert. After several days of indecision he abruptly announced to Wolman that he had decided not to seek CO status (from Gilbert's daily notes, 10/15/1940).

What changed Gilbert's mind back again? Perhaps it was his reading Thoreau's *On Civil Disobedience* and Plato's *Crito* (a treatise on the moral questions of conscientious objection and civil disobedience, posed as a dialogue between Socrates and his acolyte, Crito, in the final days before Socrates' death). Perhaps it was the unflagging encouragement of his CO support group. Perhaps it was the calm resolve and influence of Anne Underwood, who independently had arrived at the same pacifist convictions. At the Bureau of the Budget, Director Harold Smith was initially nonplussed by the prospect of losing Gilbert because of his unexpected avowal of pacifism. Gilbert's decision seemed even stranger and more unnecessary since he had already received a Selective Service exemption from military service: it was considered to be of national importance that he continue his government employment in time of war. Smith implored Gilbert to reconsider, and that pressure may have been the reason for Gilbert's temporary vacillation. But once Smith became convinced of Gilbert's resolve, he readily agreed not to oppose Gilbert's draft board petition unless his opinion was invited.

Smith's opinion was not sought, and at Gilbert's one hearing before his draft board, his request to undertake nonmilitary alternative service abroad as a conscientious objector was partially granted. His request for conscientious objector status was tabled on the grounds that he already was doing work of national importance. Moreover, the law required that alternative service by conscientious objectors be done within the United States. Nonetheless, apparently impressed by his turning down an automatic deferment, the draft board unanimously recommended Gilbert for nonmilitary foreign service in the national interest.

The Onset of War

En route home after attending the Florida Avenue Friends Meeting the first Sunday in December 1941, Gilbert decided to stop at his office in the Executive Office of the President, adjacent to the White House. Government limousines crowding the parking areas and the sight of Secretary of War Henry Stimson and Secretary of the Navy Frank Knox rushing from the State Department were Gilbert's first clue that something of major importance had happened. Inside, he passed by the cabinet conference room, where he encountered a mix of shock and, oddly, apparent relief over the word—just in—that the Japanese had attacked Pearl Harbor. Cabinet staff were issuing emergency orders for response and preparing the president's "Day of Infamy" speech to be presented to Congress the next day. Gilbert left for home concerned but also somewhat relieved that he did not have to be involved in the preparations for war. He had overheard relieved—even pleased—talk of possible U.S. reprisals but had heard no one discuss actions of the United States that might have provoked the Japanese. He reflected back on policies and programs that might have antagonized the Japanese—foreign trade policy or embargoes, for example. This questioning of motives, this desire to understand how others perceive their place or predicament in the world and thus why they undertake the actions they do became a hallmark of Gilbert's approach, both to scholarship and human understanding. After December 7, Gilbert resolved that in his career and service work he would always try to assess the possible reasons for others' actions, as well as the indirect effects of his own actions upon all people involved, even though such assessments would be difficult.

An interesting but sad resolution to Gilbert's concerns on December 7 appeared over forty years later. Under persistent pressure from journalist Robert B. Stinnett, the government's files on Pearl Harbor finally were made public in the 1980s. They showed that FDR and his closest circle of advisers had anticipated an attack by Japan against the United States. Indeed, U.S. military intelligence had recommended a series of U.S. actions in the Pacific that would provoke Japan into a war that President Roosevelt had concluded was inevitable. For FDR, it was sufficiently important politically for Japan to be the aggressor in the eyes of Americans and the Allied world that a surprise attack was deliberately invited. In his book, *Day of Deceit: FDR and the Truth About Pearl Harbor* (2001), Stinnett reconstructs the increasing U.S. provocations in the Pacific. Pearl Harbor was a surprise to the Allied world, but to FDR and a small coterie in his administration, the surprise lay only in the details of timing and location. Reading Stinnett's book in 2003, Gilbert found the answer to the question he pondered on December 7, 1941: "Why are some of these people so pleased with this terrible news?" The answer dealt a major blow to Gilbert's respectful memory of FDR.

Four days after Pearl Harbor, Germany declared war on the United States. Gilbert then telephoned the Philadelphia office of the American Friends Service

Committee to ask about alternative service, preferably abroad. Within two weeks, he received and accepted an offer to serve with the AFSC delegation in unoccupied France.[5] Gilbert wrote to Harlan Barrows:

> Since writing last I have received word from the AFSC that it believes I could be of real help to them in connection with its European relief program. At present, there is a small group of Friends headquartered at Marseilles which is handling the feeding of 80–100,000 French children, the distribution of Red Cross clothing, the inspection and assistance of concentration camps, the rehabilitation of several war-torn villages, and the delivery of foreign funds to refugees stranded in France. At least two-thirds of the children in France have either lost or have not gained weight during the past six months, and the rest have gained less than the normal minimum. Inasmuch as I still feel deeply opposed to the war effort, this would seem to afford a chance to help in the kind of constructive effort which I think will aid in bringing about a lasting peace; to give more concrete expression to a position which so far has been largely passive; and to do so under somewhat difficult circumstances. (White 1942a)

Quaker Relief Assistance in Europe

Quakers in England had communicated with North American Quakers regarding humanitarian issues worldwide throughout the nineteenth century. But the former remained in the forefront of humanitarian service to victims of war and persecution until the second half of the twentieth century. Prior to the establishment of the American Friends Service Committee, American initiatives abroad lacked the centralized organization of British efforts.

Rufus Jones was the principal organizer of the assembly of American Quakers that founded the AFSC one week after the United States entered World War I in 1917. Jones agreed to serve as chair. At the same time, he chaired the philosophy department at Haverford College, outside Philadelphia. Fortuitously, the director of the Red Cross in France had been a student of his at Haverford. Together they arranged for Haverford and the AFSC to gather material, organize personnel, and provide Red Cross training on the Haverford campus. One hundred Americans subsequently joined European and British Quakers in the effort to aid France, until one year after the 1919 armistice, when Herbert Hoover, as U.S. food administrator, asked the AFSC to assume leadership of relief efforts in Germany.

Herbert Hoover, a Quaker himself, had been involved in U.S. government relief in Belgium and France since 1914. He also coordinated aid from England and France to starving Europeans until the United States entered the war. By 1918 Hoover had become chairman of the Inter-Allied Food Council, and at war's end he was elevated to director-general of the Commission for the Relief and Reconstruction of Europe, handling over $3 billion in relief funds and 23 million tons of food, medical supplies, and clothing distributed among thirty countries. U.S. law debarred Hoover's council from providing this relief to Germany and Austria until a signed peace agreement formally ended the war. To circumvent this prohibition, Hoover offered to sell to the AFSC all the food it could buy, and by the end of June 1920, 1,200,000 German children were receiving a hot meal daily through a program organized by a Quaker team supervising 40,000 German assistants (Greenwood 1975). When the Treaty of Versailles (June 28, 1919) officially terminated Allied relief to Germany, Hoover further circumvented the treaty to ensure continued aid under AFSC auspices. He insisted that the feeding be done under the American flag but had no objection to the program's identification with Quakers. "My own impression is that the pacifism of the Quakers, which is of centuries standing, would certainly not be amiss if applied to the German population" (Greenwood 1975).

British and American Quaker relief continued in a variety of forms in various areas of Europe throughout the 1930s. The last major effort prior to the outbreak of World War II was in Spain during the 1936–1939 Spanish Civil War. As Franco's Nationalist forces moved toward victory over the Republican Loyalists in 1938–1939, British and American Quakers worked on both sides of the conflict, with refugees pushed north and south out of Spain into France and North Africa. (Gilbert's first assignment with the AFSC in 1942 was to assist some of the 300,000 Spanish refugees living in France.)

In a parallel development, in 1938 Howard Kershner, a Quaker, founded the International Commission for the Assistance of Child Refugees with funding from twenty-four nations and a number of private groups, including Quakers in Geneva. During the Spanish Civil War, the commission tried to provide every refugee child at least one hot meal a day. As refugees were forced out of Spain into southern France, Kershner moved with them and there oversaw the establishment of sixteen Spanish children's colonies; fifteen schools; a maternity hospital; and the provision to these institutions of food, clothing, and school supplies. However, in 1940 these efforts were superseded by a much larger problem, when the Germans invaded France and took control of the northern two-thirds of the country, sending hundreds of thousands of refugees to southern France to reside under the nominally neutral French government in Vichy established by the peace agreement with Germany. To assist in this relief effort, Helga Holbek, a Danish Quaker who had been working in the children's colonies with the Kershners, moved south to Toulouse, a city of 200,000 that had swollen to 1 million in a matter of days. In June, several Quakers (Margaret Frawley and Rosanna Thorndike, representing the AFSC, and Toot Bleuland van Oordt from the Netherlands) moved their center of operations in France from Paris to Marseilles, on the south coast. Kershner accepted the AFSC's invitation to continue his earlier work in this smaller, more manageable, program, assisted by the above-named foreign Quakers and several French Quakers. The French involvement was both direct, through Secours Quakers supplying official cover for foreign Quaker involvements, such as the AFSC, and indirect, through parallel efforts such as those of Pastor André Trocme and his congregation in Le Chambon, who hid more than 5,000 Jews (Hallie 1979).

The AFSC in Lisbon, Portugal

Almost a year later, in the spring of 1941, the AFSC opened an office in Lisbon, Portugal—like Vichy, neutral in the conflict—to support Kershner's program in Marseilles. A small staff, consisting of Philip Conard, Russell Richie, Dorothy Thumwood, and a Portuguese errand boy, took on the monumental task of helping refugees from Nazi persecution in Europe and northern Africa find asylum in the United States, Great Britain, and Latin America. Portugal's population had mushroomed by almost a quarter million the previous year, following the defeat of the French armies that were overwhelmed by the six-week German blitzkrieg. From December 1942, until December 1943, AFSC staff on both sides of the Atlantic were able to resettle only 7,000 of the tens of thousands of refugees stranded in Portugal (Wriggins 2004). The obstacles to obtaining exit visas for entry into the United States were several: Portugal's government, under President Antonio de Oliveira Salazar, was a repressive police state walking a tight rope between friendship with Great Britain (which maintained a naval blockade of Lisbon to limit German access to war matériel) and friendship with the nearby Germans, who were suspicious of overzealous assistance to those fleeing Nazism. Salazar's financially pressed government wanted to get rid of the refugees and yet adhered strictly to the receiving countries' regulations regarding immigration. Moreover, because they came through Spain, most of the refugees entering Portugal also had to have proper Spanish entry and exit visas. In short, acceptable Spanish and Portuguese paperwork was a prerequisite for obtaining entry visas to the Americas or Great Britain, and obtaining such paperwork often required months of waiting in France, Spain, Portugal, or Casablanca, Morocco, during which the Quakers and Allied relief agencies provided financial assistance for those considered most likely to gain asylum.

Meanwhile, to support the European efforts, in the United States the Philadelphia AFSC staff worked to find American sponsors for refugees—the critical prerequisite to obtaining entry visas from the U.S. Immigration Service. They also lobbied for liberalization of immigration quotas, since the U.S. quotas during the early 1940s heavily favored northern European over southern European immigration. However, the Immigration Service clearly did not support their efforts, and the United States simply did not want a large number of poorly documented aliens entering the country.[6] A member of the Lisbon AFSC team, Howard Wriggins, when meeting with the U.S. ambassador in Lisbon, George Kennan, was surprised to hear Kennan tell him, "Of course you realize, Mr. Wriggins, that the activities of your committee and the others are tearing a hole in the security of the United States. . . . You have no way of really knowing about the identity of the people you are helping. You have their stories but you have no way of confirming their veracity" (Wriggins 2004).

⁂

OVER THE COURSE of that year in Lisbon, as hope for finding asylum abroad for many refugees faded, the AFSC shifted its efforts to assisting refugees within southern France who had no hope of leaving Europe. Hence, the Philadelphia office of the AFSC decided to increase the number of personnel in Marseilles, and on June 13, 1942, Anne Underwood watched Gilbert White depart for Marseilles via Lisbon on the steamship *Nyassi*. In addition to the clothes he was wearing, Gilbert carried one box of chocolates, one-fourth pound of tea, three pairs of socks, an extra pair of shoes, a flannel shirt, and snapshots of Anne and his mother.

Sailing with Gilbert and the 100 other Americans headed for Lisbon were German Americans being deported because of their suspected Nazi affiliation. It took a full day on the dock in New York City to examine these latter individuals' possessions, including birth certificates and personal correspondence, which were confiscated. En route to Lisbon, a German submarine surfaced and monitored the steamship's passage. It was then six months since the United States had entered the war against Germany and five months before the successful Allied attack on German and Italian forces in North Africa. After several days of briefing in Lisbon, Gilbert left for Marseilles via train through Spain. As he traveled through the night, Gilbert pondered why the Nazis allowed France's southern border to remain open and why the U.S. State Department continued to condone and facilitate the AFSC presence in occupied France.

At least part of the answer to the second question might have been that, although U.S. civilian officials in Portugal and France may have been skeptical of the worth of Quaker relief efforts, the presence of such efforts served U.S. military objectives by reducing Axis concern over any imminent U.S. attacks that would place U.S. personnel at risk. Indeed, as detailed in the following chapter, the AFSC presence in France—insignificant as it may have seemed in the total scheme of things—may have been one reason that General Dwight D. Eisenhower's invasion surprised the Axis armies in North Africa. And in part because of the AFSC group's eventual imprisonment with the U.S. French embassy personnel in Germany, the Nazis would succeed in negotiating the exchange of two German prisoners of war for each U.S. detainee—a trade that returned to the front 1,000 Axis troops captured during the Allied invasion of North Africa. In short, the AFSC volunteers were unwitting pawns used by both sides of a conflict. The entire scenario was another lesson for Gilbert regarding the unintended consequences of one's actions.

Gilbert did not have to go to Europe and become involved in the conflict, but he chose to do so. He went to help reduce suffering and to demonstrate ("bear witness to" in Quaker terminology) the Quaker tenets of pacifism and humanitarian service. But in the face of such overwhelming physical need, numbing cruelty, and ironic manipulation by larger forces, Gilbert and his Quaker companions would struggle to justify their presence in Europe in 1942. Gilbert could only conclude that his work mattered simply because he was there, bearing aid and goodwill and demonstrating a more humanitarian approach to human suffering.

Notes

1. For Gilbert, however, simplicity was necessary not just to reduce inequities: his idea of simplicity was much broader. As he was often to reiterate, he endeavored to focus on just the things that really "matter." He chose clothes not for adornment but because they were appropriate and necessary for his work and career. Indeed, he had several sets of basically the same clothing, always the same colors, to eliminate decisions about what to wear. At the same time, his simplicity did not equate with shoddiness; he bought quality clothing that would last a long time. Many people, including Gilbert, see a quiet elegance in the plain dress of traditional Quakers—a dress that permits only the essentials: solid and somber colors with a minimum of frills for women and typically an absence of collars for men. Gilbert didn't go that far in his modesty: he didn't cut the collars off his shirts and coats, but they struck him as superfluous. Sarah Nathe, employed in the Natural Hazards Center in the mid-1970s, recalled when Gilbert "showed up in the office one day in a new light blue shirt with a slightly big collar, as was the style in those days. It was a dramatic change from his usual white shirt with utilitarian collar. Being then a graduate student and very much of the time, I thought the shirt was great and told him so. He thanked me and allowed as how it had been a gift. I then said I especially liked the dashing collar, and he responded, 'Doesn't it seem like a waste of cloth?'" (Nathe 2002). He endured a fair amount of teasing over his unQuakerly red (or maroon) ties. But he had his rejoinders to those criticisms— for example, Ralph Waldo Emerson's reminder that a foolish consistency is the hobgoblin of simple minds and the example of the red rose: Roses come in about every color except "Quaker gray" and everything one needs to know about simplicity can be learned from a rose. "There is nothing extraneous about a rose. Everything that should be there, is. Everything unnecessary is gone" (Wright 2003).

2. There also had been provision, under the Furlough Law of 1918, for noncombatant service (usually as medics or work with Friends Reconstruction Units) during World War I. The visibility of this provision was low, however, outside the "peace churches" (the Society of Friends, Mennonites, and Church of the Brethren), and no more than fifty men were assigned to relief work in France under Quaker auspices. A larger number of conscientious objectors opted for noncombatant roles within the armed forces during World War I. Only thirteen Quakers went to prison for refusal to accept the option of noncombatant service (Schmitt 1997).

3. Some COs refused even to register for the draft, thus engaging in civil disobedience in objection both to the draft itself and to the inequity of some draft boards. If identified, these young men were usually imprisoned. When he became president of Haverford College, Gilbert White testified before draft boards on behalf of several student COs and visited in prison at least one Haverfordian who refused to register during the Korean conflict. He vividly recalled his own loneliness in seeking exemption from combat only a decade earlier.

4. The word "pacifism" in popular usage during the early twentieth century referred less to moral opposition to taking human life than to staying out of war in Europe—that is, isolationism, as advocated by Presidents Woodrow Wilson and Franklin Delano Roosevelt prior to U.S. entry into World Wars I and II. Roosevelt's position in this re-

gard was supported by most congressional Democrats and by many Republicans as well. Harry Woodring, FDR's first secretary of war, was a staunch isolationist who opposed U.S. rearmament. Even after Germany invaded Poland, Denmark, and Norway, General George Marshall, secretary of war in 1939, testified before a Senate subcommittee, "I am more of a pacifist than you think. I went through one war and I do not want to see another" (Fromkin 1995). Despite the apparently unavoidable impending commitment of American soldiers to the war in Europe following Nazi occupation of France in 1940, FDR won reelection to a third term with the avowed Midwestern pacifist, Henry Wallace, as his running mate. Also in the Midwest, the University of Chicago's highly visible president, Robert Maynard Hutchins, publicly espoused pacifism until war was actually declared.

5. Abel Wolman's high regard for Gilbert is reflected in the letter of recommendation Wolman sent to the AFSC personnel secretary:

    I have known Mr. White for eight years and have worked with him in various capacities during a great part of that period. I can speak of him only with the greatest enthusiasm. He is one of the most unusual young men with whom I have ever worked. He has all of the qualities of maturity of judgment and of stability which one ordinarily associates with people twice his age. His intelligence is of a superior level and his capacity for work surpassed that of most people whom I know. He has a most attractive personality and has managed to negotiate understandings under all types of circumstances in the most skillful and satisfactory manner. I know of no individual of his age who has comparable characteristics. I suspect that you might consider that these encomiums may be largely sheer flattery, but I assure you that they rest upon a long experience with him and a strictly objective review of his characteristics. I have no doubt whatever that they would be confirmed by all of his older associates. I cannot conceive of any individual who could be more useful to your enterprise, if you are searching for someone who has intelligence, energy, tact and attractive personality. The combination is rare in one person but he has it. I am glad to register the fact (Wolman 1942).

6. Quakers subsequently learned that Breckenridge Long, director of the Office of Refugee Affairs, was politically allied with those in the U.S. government determined to slow the influx of refugees from throughout the world wherever possible. In this regard the office may have been responding both to American anti-Semitism and to the paranoia many in the United States were feeling toward the Japanese Americans who were interned following Pearl Harbor (Wriggins 2004).

4 *World War II: Humanitarian Service, Internment, and the Return Home*

More than the clothes or the food or the messages, the feeling that someone genuinely cared seems to have given greatest comfort.

—GFW

B Y THE MIDDLE OF 1942, the agenda of the American Friends Service Committee in Marseilles and its three branch offices in France was greatly overextended and no longer manageable, given the small AFSC budget. In addition to administering the remnants of the Spanish and Alsace-Lorraine refugee programs instituted by Howard Kershner and his predecessor of the International Commission for the Assistance of Child Refugees (notably the sixteen children's colonies under Helga Holbek's coordination), the Quakers had to deal with rapidly increasing numbers of Jewish refugees from Germany and the other Nazi-occupied countries of Europe. These refugees fled to the port city of Marseilles, hoping to find their way to safety abroad if they were unwelcome in France.

Unoccupied France was required to send material assistance to occupied France under the terms of the armistice with Germany. Further aggravating the problem, the amount of food per person in France steadily declined from 1940 through 1942, as supplies from abroad dwindled due to an unfavorable currency exchange and transportation problems brought on by the war. Because resources were strained, the Vichy government introduced food rationing, even for the native French. Due to these problems, many French residents felt enmity and resentment toward refugees, especially newly arrived Jews, who sapped the already scarce food supply. Consequently, the AFSC included supplemental feeding of non-refugee French children in its program.

At the same time, with other relief agencies and relatives wanting to assist and stay in touch with refugees, the AFSC found itself coordinating the work of Jewish aid groups, Mennonites, and Unitarians. It also aided the British Friends Service Council, which was transmitting even more money and communiqués to individual refugees in Europe than was the AFSC.

No one in the Marseilles or Philadelphia offices of the AFSC had the heart to say no to this crush of ever-expanding work. When he arrived in Marseilles, Gilbert found fifty employees trying to deal with these problems; the three branch offices in Toulouse, Montauban, and Perpignan employed about the same number. Virtually all the employees were native French with no Quaker affiliation. Many of the branch employees were refugees themselves, since, by employing them, the offices hoped to protect them from deportation to concentration camps in Germany. Only seven employees were American Quaker delegates, and ten others were European Quakers or "friends of Friends" selected by the Marseilles director of Secours Quaker, the French committee established to assist the AFSC and provide legitimacy for its operation on French soil. Of these ten, almost all of whom were women, Helga Holbek (Danish), Alice Resch (Norwegian), and Mary Elmes (Irish) in particular impressed Gilbert. A memoir of Alice Resch's sojourn in France was published posthumously (Resch Synnestvedt 2005).

With the Quaker imprint so faint on the programs financed by the AFSC, most aid recipients perceived the AFSC to be simply a good-hearted but partisan U.S. aid program designed to encourage popular support for the United States in the impending war. The image of the Americans was not helped by all but two of the AFSC workers being such young men on only one-year assignments with no prior experience assisting refugees. Moreover, most of the Americans spoke only limited French, German, or Spanish. Gilbert White alone was fluent in French, with a fair knowledge of German and Spanish as well. In contrast, most of the European employees were older women with considerable refugee relief experience and open-ended assignments. Because of these different employee backgrounds, the branch offices, under the leadership of the strong, experienced European women (notably Helga Holbek), were understandably skeptical of the Marseilles office and of Kershner's attempted leadership there.[1]

Exacerbating this problem, Howard Kershner, who had been on leave in the United States for several months, tendered his resignation as program director on the eve of Gilbert's sailing for Europe. Consequently, Gilbert carried with him instructions regarding periodic reporting and other information that the AFSC in Philadelphia needed—much of which was overdue. Lindsley Noble, who had been filling in, agreed to serve as acting director until a successor could be found. However, Lindsley was also working with Swiss Quakers, hoping to expand the AFSC refugee program to Switzerland, and shortly after Gilbert's arrival he left for Geneva for three weeks. Gilbert already had made an immediate, strong impression on the group, reflected in Lindsley's request of Gilbert to oversee operations in his absence, including the preparation of the reports requested by the Philadelphia office. For the duration of the team's service in unoccupied France, Gilbert continued to provide informal leadership—with both enthusiasm and apparent success.

During the remainder of July 1942, Russell Richie, another young volunteer who had just joined the American team from the Lisbon office, accompanied Gilbert on a tour of the myriad AFSC projects in southern France. On their return, Gilbert prepared for Lindsley and mailed to the Philadelphia office his assessment of program strengths and weaknesses. Reflecting a concern that continued in virtually every aspect of his later career, Gilbert stressed the need for systematic monitoring of the results of policies in the interest of effective stewardship of limited resources. Although basically critical of the lack of consensus among the branch offices regarding priorities and the need for central leadership that problem reflected, he did not shy away from assessing, as well, the enthusiastic and capable leadership in those offices under the strong-willed Helga Holbek. "They are doing a difficult job with great energy and sympathy. Perhaps they are working a little too intensively for the best interest of the entire program. They lack the time to keep in touch with other relief and rehabilitation programs and needs and, indeed, with other phases of the Quaker program."[2]

Two weeks after reviewing the branch offices' activities, Gilbert mailed the overdue report on all programs for June. The statistics for that one month were impressive, given the AFSC's limited resources: 7,200 adults and 800 children fed in concentration camps and hospitals daily; 500 children fully supported in Quaker colonies and 2,000 supplemental feedings given daily in other children's colonies used for temporary care of orphans and badly malnourished concentration camp children; 230 children fed in private homes; 3,100 French children given supplemental food in school canteens; 1,700 persons provided related relief (largely clothing); 1,500 persons interviewed for and some assisted with emigration procedures; at least 100 workers supported in Spanish and Lorraine refugee cottage industries and concentration camp workshops; and 1,200,000 francs, transmitted by the British Friends Service Council, distributed to 550 refugees.

Expanding on his earlier concerns regarding program effectiveness and flexibility, Gilbert added that the Marseilles office was working on a complementary and much more difficult report relating to relief needs in France through the coming winter. Various sources of official information, including interested social, relief, and medical agencies, were being canvassed to determine the probable needs of different segments of the population in the principal regions of distress (White 1942c).

When Lindsley returned (the AFSC program was never extended to Switzerland, although the number of Jewish refugees fleeing illegally into Switzerland reached 2,000 per month by October), Gilbert joined the small delegation in Montauban. Gilbert was pleased with the assignment, given the long history of that region's involvement with Spanish refugees and hence with refugee rehabilitation beyond emergency relief. Experiments with cottage industries and housing rehabilitation in villages largely abandoned because of the industrial-age exodus from farm to city, as well as experiments with diversified forest and agriculture production, interested not only the humanitarian but also the scholar in Gilbert—so much so that months later, during his internment by the Nazis, Gilbert somehow found the library resources to draft a detailed history and analysis (unpublished) of the abandonment of those villages. The oldest, Puycelci (Heaven's Mountain), was a walled city high in the mountains that served as a hiding place for Catholics who had left the church during the Albigensian Inquisition. Alice Resch described neighboring Penne du Tarn, with its castle ruin at its highest point, as "an arm with a fist reaching toward the heavens" (Resch Synnestvedt 2005).

In Montauban as many as 1,000 Spaniards were fed in the canteen every day. There was a school, run by a former Spanish minister of education for Spanish children who could not speak French, and a small factory that manufactured artificial limbs for Spaniards who could only be released from concentration camps to perform labor if they had an artificial arm or leg. (All the employees of that factory were themselves amputees with artificial limbs manufactured by Spanish colleagues.) The deserted villages of Puycelci and Penne had been taken over for the care of the refugees early in 1941, an endeavor spearheaded by Helga Holbek over the initial objections of Kershner in Marseilles. At Puycelci, refugees from Lorraine concentrated on making furniture from wood harvested from the nearby forest. At Penne du Tarn, Spanish refugees made toys out of available wood. However, because the cost per person to the AFSC of such long-term rehabilitation greatly exceeded the cost per person of feeding and clothing destitute children, Gilbert sided with Kershner's earlier judgment that it should not be the AFSC and American Quakers directing such long-term rehabilitation. Unitarians, who had been involved with the project from its beginning, fortunately increased their leadership. For the duration of his six-months sojourn in southern France, Gilbert kept an eye on the Branting Farm near Gaillac, which had been purchased for the project with funds raised throughout Europe by Helga Holbek and Joseph Weill of the American Unitarian Service Committee. The Branting Farm long had provided villages in the region with wheat, vegetables, milk, and meat.

Burritt Hiatt, a Quaker businessman from Ohio, assumed leadership of the Marseilles AFSC office toward the end of Gilbert's three months in Montauban. During his orientation tour of the branch programs, Hiatt noted that Gilbert White was single-handedly dealing successfully with some unpleasant personnel issues requiring great diplomacy. Hiatt mused that, if given Helga Holbek's leadership authority, Gilbert could, in spite of his youth, resolve a number of unfortunate situations. "He has the superiority in intelligence and feels what the Quaker objectives in these projects should be: simplicity, friendliness, and a demonstration of a way of life that would make the world so much happier if it were extended further to whole regions" (Hiatt 1942–1944a). In fact, it had been Helga Holbek who, after purchasing the Branting Farm, assigned Gilbert to its oversight.

When Hiatt arrived in early October 1942, the deportation of Jews to Nazi concentration camps had been under way for several months. To his horror, he realized that they were being deported to be exterminated. It had been many weeks after the deportations began before the Quaker team became convinced of this. Suspicious, they began giving postcards to deportees to send back. Not one was returned. The deportation, particularly of children, accelerated suddenly in August and September, possibly so that more of the diminishing food supply in southern France could go to the non-Jewish French. By the time of Hiatt's arrival in October, 10,000 Jews had been deported since August, loaded into boxcars and shipped away in guarded convoys.

In his notes, Gilbert indicated that during the wholesale deportation of foreign Jews from France in the late summer, the French officials prepared lists of those scheduled to be exiled, if found. The lists were based on selection policies established at Vichy. Usually, the selected persons were not certain that they were "on the list" until the gendarmes caught them. Some persons hid for weeks in fear of being caught, when, in fact, they were not being hunted. Others were included on the lists by mistake, but once caught—often without papers and cut off from friends—they were unable to help themselves. In some regions the Quakers were the only group that could and would go openly to the police to request information about the lists, since their integrity was respected by police and Jews alike. Through these efforts many mistakes were corrected.

But sometimes the Quakers weren't successful. On one occasion Gilbert thought that he had obtained all the paperwork that would enable a string quartet of musicians to escape into Spain. They were in the holding pen with others who had been rounded up for deportation back to concentration camps, and when they were next in line to board the boxcar, Gilbert intervened with the paperwork. But when the guard checked the papers, he found visas for only three. The young men conferred quickly before embracing, and one climbed the ramp into the car. "His companions and I just stood there. . . . There was nothing more I could do" (White 1942e).

Gilbert also recounted the story, from the same period, of a Jewish refugee, his wife, and their sixteen-year-old son who slept in their clothes every night and never answered the door after sunset. In August 1942 they were on a list of Jews slated for deportation, but because of Quaker intervention they were exempted. Still, they never knew how long their amnesty would last, and as they saw other German Jews being rounded up and shipped off, they grew more and more nervous. They spoke often of fleeing but had no place to go. The man's work suffered, and his wife became ill. The constant tension and the relentless, methodical departure of their fellow refugees almost became too much for them. They would never, they said, be delivered to the train alive. They would commit suicide. In this resolution they were not alone; some of their neighbors did end their lives when they finally heard the knock at their door (White 1942e).

Despite these difficult and often painful circumstances, in the fall of 1942 Gilbert reflected:

> In the middle of this it is refreshing to look occasionally to the basic ideas behind the work, and I have been tremendously encouraged and stimulated to find those ideas keenly appreciated both by the refugees and by the officials involved. In camps where the physical conditions of living have been abominable, the phase of our work most gratefully and happily received has been our expression of sincere, friendly concern. More than the clothes or the food

or the messages, the feeling that someone genuinely cared seems to have given greatest comfort. In the recent hectic days of departures there has been no need to explain why we were there to help as best we could. Understanding could be read in the eyes of those who departed, or, happily, remained. At the same time, the effect of our position upon the attitudes and action of the French themselves has been, in some areas at least, profound. I believe it is fair to say that the firm Quaker insistence upon the sanctity of the individual and upon friendly treatment regardless of race or creed, has done more than anything else to keep alive a desire to act humanely. In some places, we have been the only group which stood out openly and clearly for those principles, and our stand has encouraged others to follow in part. . . . The leavening effect is extraordinary, and it reaches deep into local institutions that are largely lacking in any other sort of encouragement from outside (White 1942f).

Working with Refugee Children

In June 1942, as Gilbert was en route from New York to Lisbon, sixty-four Spanish refugee children had crossed his path en route to Staten Island. Quakers had successfully orchestrated this first effort to settle refugee children in the United States. Earlier, Alice Resch, one of the European women in the AFSC program, had managed to smuggle six Jewish boys across the French and Spanish borders to Portugal and on to the United States (Resch Synnestvedt 2005). (This act was made public only in the late 1990s, when the boys invited Alice to the United States for a celebration of the fifty-year anniversary of their escape.) It will never be known how many other refugees were smuggled out of France by Europeans involved with the AFSC program, but for their part, the American Quakers were wary of such initiatives and agreed that they could jeopardize the integrity of the entire AFSC program. Nazi spies, posing as refugees, could easily have uncovered such activities, and indeed, following their exile to Germany (recounted below), the Americans learned that an Irish Quaker in their group, Mary Elmes, had been imprisoned in France for about one month, presumably for overstepping.

When the deportations of children suddenly escalated in the late summer of 1942, the Philadelphia AFSC office asked the U.S. State Department for 1,000 visas to resettle a second shipment of children—this time German Jews. Secretary of State Cordell Hull agreed to the request, suggesting that if this effort was successful, the State Department would consider allowing 5,000 more émigrés. When approached by the Quakers, the Vichy government initially was skeptical of this plan, fearing that Jewish émigrés would disseminate negative propaganda in the United States. But when the U.S. Embassy urged acceptance, the Vichy government relented and agreed to issue a maximum of 500 exit visas, subject to one condition—that all youth receiving visas would be bona fide orphans. Any children whose parents had been deported to "work camps" in Germany were not to be included; French authorities continued to insist that deported adult Jews were simply being

Refugee children in Vichy, France, eating a meal provided by the AFSC, 1942. Photo courtesy of the AFSC.

sent temporarily to the camps for the common good. This condition was unacceptable to the AFSC, and when the Quakers made their case that no more than 100 confirmed orphans lived in all the camps and children's colonies under their care, the Vichy government relented.

On November 7, the first group of children from the camps and colonies arrived in Marseilles. As fate (or the U.S. State Department, which had set the Lisbon arrival date for the children's ship from the United States) would have it, the next day General Dwight D. Eisenhower launched the Allied invasion of North Africa. Within two days the French border with Spain was closed. Although Vichy officials maintained that exit permission might yet be negotiated for the émigrés, it was never granted. Indeed, the French staff of Secours Quakers, who assumed responsibility for the distribution of Quaker aid after the Americans were forced to leave, learned that German officials behind the scenes had prevented the children's departure, possibly in retaliation for the U.S. ruse of timing the evacuation ship's arrival on the eve of the invasion—a subterfuge that may have contributed to German and Italian complacency.

The U.S. ship docked at the Lisbon harbor on schedule, with twenty-one American escorts for the orphans on board, but after waiting a few days it returned to the United States with no children. The sixty-three orphans who had assembled in Marseilles were under French police surveillance when the border was closed, and those authorities released no information as to the children's fate.[3]

With this sorry end to the AFSC efforts on behalf of the orphans, Burritt Hiatt became despondent: "When I came over here my greatest hope was that the children of the Jewish couples could be sent to America. I now believe that behind all of these negotiations with the French government stands the Germany military which looks with detachment upon the death of Jews and the malnourishment of their orphans. I go to bed wishing that I were not convinced of this" (Hiatt 1942–1944b).

Relocation

Responding to the Allied invasion of North Africa, the Germans invaded unoccupied southern France and in the first week of December ordered all Americans (including journalists, diplomatic personnel, and relief workers) out of Marseilles into neighboring departments until they could be repatriated. The seven Americans in the AFSC Marseilles office left for the village of Petuis in an old ambulance bearing an American flag. They had arranged with Secours Quaker for the relocation of the other program personnel and substantial remaining stocks of food and clothing. Thirty-eight tons of clothing had been received from the Philadelphia office in August and September, and in the interim only one-fifth of the bales had been sorted and inventoried (as required by the International Red Cross). Those 400 bales were transported to the Branting Farm warehouses outside Gaillac, while the remaining 1,600 bales remained in Marseilles under the control of Secours Quakers. Because Gaillac was centrally located in the region, orphanages could continue receiving clothing if and when Secours Quaker assumed supervision of operations from the Americans. White and Richie relocated to Gaillac to oversee the continuing sorting of clothing by a half-dozen local employees.

By mid-December, the Germans were in full control of all France and had decided that Americans who could be exchanged for Axis prisoners of war should be ordered to assemble at the city of Lourdes. This directive was cabled to the Quakers, but because of confusion regarding whether it was a German or AFSC directive (and if from the AFSC, whether it was a command or a recommendation), only Hiatt and two others (the oldest and the youngest members of the delegation) complied. White and Richie chose to remain in Gaillac as long as possible, and the remaining two members of the delegation decided to take their chances outside Marseilles and work with the Secours Quaker staff.[4]

Besides its central location, another reason White and Richie chose to move to Gaillac was its low visibility and comparative isolation; it was small and rural yet located at a rail and highway crossroads. Nonetheless, as the deadline came and

Gaillac, France, where Gilbert and Russell Richie supervised aid distribution from the Branting Farm warehouses before internment in Baden-Baden, Germany

went for all Americans to report to Lourdes, White and Richie kept knapsacks containing essentials at hand, should they be arrested. In his notes Gilbert recorded:

> The worker at the creaking gates of the warehouse where we stored the food, clothes, and medical supplies called to warn me, "Gilbert, the hour has arrived. You're wanted!" I put on my knapsack and went to the door to see a German Sergeant and two armed soldiers approaching. The Sergeant politely explained that the German Army General Staff had just moved into town and the Commander had requisitioned a fine house in which the toilet did not work. They had been told that the best plumber in town was working for the Quakers. "Would I release Jean to go at once to the General's house?" I consulted with

Jean who agreed, providing they would return him that same day. When he returned, the repair done, Jean reported that the General was surprisingly friendly. In due time we learned that the General as a boy in war-torn Germany following the First World War had been fed and clothed by Quaker workers. He ordered that we were not to be touched, while all around us the military occupation took charge of the town. What was this? Happy chance? A miracle? As I look back over the truly crucial events in my life I realize that they were not planned long in advance. Albert Einstein said, "There are only two ways to live your life. One is as though nothing is a miracle. The other is as though everything is" (White 1942g).

White and Richie's good fortune was not to last. With their work readying supplies for distribution by Secours Quaker completed, they pondered the possibility of escaping the country on their own, perhaps by finding their way over the Pyrenees into Spain. They even talked to the local French Loyalist underground about escaping, until one day they learned from those same Loyalists that all the Americans in Lourdes were leaving by train for Lisbon at 7:30 A.M. the following Thursday. They hurried to Lourdes, arriving Wednesday, and found the hotel where the Americans were staying. The guards at the door wouldn't let them in.

> We said, "but we are Americans." They said, "That's impossible. The Americans are *inside*." So we asked to see someone in charge and were taken to see the head of the Embassy staff, Pinkey Tuck. He wasn't particularly cordial and asked where on earth we had been . . . hadn't we been told a month ago to come to Lourdes? We acknowledged we had but said "We had work to do." "So why'd you come today?" he asked. "Well, we got good information that you are going to Portugal and we'd like to join you." Tuck was amused, and said, "You fellows really know how to handle things! You're off on just one small point . . . we're leaving tomorrow morning, all right, but we're going to prison in *Germany!*" (White n.d.)

After the war, Gilbert was surprised to learn that, possibly, his French Loyalist contact had set them up, knowing full well that White and Richie would be interned in Germany if they went to Lourdes. While representing the AFSC after the war on the first mission of the American Council of Voluntary Agencies to Europe to explore options for providing relief to Germans in occupied Germany, Gilbert shared a compartment on a train from Frankfurt to Paris with a man who looked at him for a long time before asking if he was Gilbert White. Gilbert acknowledged that he was and asked how the man knew him. The fellow explained that he had been a colonel with the underground French intelligence (the Maqui) stationed in Gaillac and had been assigned to work in the garage where Gilbert had kept his car. He was to report on Gilbert's activities, which he had done faithfully, except for the weekend of November 17, 1942, when he couldn't account for Gilbert's whereabouts. Gilbert thought back and recalled that although he routinely traveled to the same supply distribution points, that day he had gone to a different orphanage to check on their needs. With that puzzle solved, the Maqui colonel explained that the French Loyalists couldn't understand why, after the deadline had passed for all Americans to report to Lourdes, the Germans in Gaillac were so unconcerned about Gilbert and his partner. The Maqui had suspected that the two amiable Americans were in fact German agents.

Internment in Germany

One hundred thirty-seven Americans were taken to the Bremmer Kur Hotel in Baden-Baden, Germany, on January 15, 1943, where they were interned until February 20, 1944. The facilities were surprisingly luxurious, the food adequate, and treatment humane—even cordial—by most of the Gestapo guards and resident staff. Although confined, the group had opportunities to attend local church services, explore the environs on supervised day-long hikes, and receive correspondence and Red Cross supplemental food (including luxury items such as coffee, cigarettes, and chocolate).

Why internment in Baden-Baden rather than in Lourdes? In his journal, Burritt Hiatt speculated that the Germans were not comfortable with the camaraderie the Americans enjoyed with the Swiss consulate in France. Switzerland had agreed to represent both American and German prisoners of war during the negotiations for repatriation, which stretched out interminably. The Swiss authorities in Germany appeared to be more compliant with German directives and more deferential to German authorities.[5]

Two letters from Gilbert to his mother suggest the good humor with which he faced his confinement. The first is included here, and the second is in the endnote:

> One side of our hotel faces out across that garden on a small mountain stream. On the other side is the main park promenade, and on sunny afternoons and warm evenings there always is a parade to be seen there: elderly couples here to take the cure, young mothers with children, convalescent soldiers. On the whole they are very polite and only stop for a few seconds to get a glimpse of us creatures on the other side of the rocky stream bed. The net effect is in some respects like Brookfield Zoo at its best: contented animals, a sense of being in their native habitat, no unseemly bars of iron, and a nicely landscaped moat in between. On the bookshelf in the living room you will find, I believe, a copy of David Garnett's A Man in the Zoo. He, however, elected to be on display. Some of the animals sun themselves like boa constrictors oblivious to the public gaze, others pace singly or in pairs around the prescribed paths making nimble turns at each barrier, others are tucked away inconspicuously on over-hanging balconies, and others rarely leave their interior quarters. Their demeanor is faultless and usually dignified except, for example, on such special occasions as when a case of lemons came calmly floating down the stream in open formation and soon attracted a barefoot salvage expedition (White 1943a).[6]

The group of interned Americans consisted of nine male newspaper reporters and six of their wives, sixteen Red Cross personnel, the Quakers and three Mennonite relief volunteers, a few unaffiliated Americans—including a young, Russian-born man with no winter clothing to whom Gilbert gave one of his two suits and a pair of shoes—and a large contingent of embassy personnel, including many wives and over a dozen children. Other than Gilbert White, none of the Quakers and few of the other adults were still living when I began this biography.

Not surprisingly, Gilbert was one of the more energetic and disciplined internees, determined (despite losing over 20 pounds on an already slim frame) to keep his spirits up and his mind active and productive. By contrast, Burritt Hiatt's morale continued to flag throughout his imprisonment. His diary reveals his increasing reliance on Gilbert's quiet strength:

> Gilbert joined me in the garden. He is determined that this internment shall not be an operation in deep-freeze where we remain static until liberation. He has seen the crack-up of individuals in internment camps and knows that close detention has its social and mental hardships even though we are confined in comfortable quarters. We're very much in contact with other people, and the relationship to each other is extraordinarily close. Every month, every week and every hour is of importance. Our daily actions are demonstrating our beliefs.... Gilbert said that whether our internment became a deep-freeze or not depended a good deal upon the leadership available (Hiatt 1942–1944c).

In Gilbert's memory, the only leadership provided by Pinkey Tuck, head of the embassy contingent, was morale maintenance through throwing parties. Fortunately, a newspaper journalist and Rhodes scholar, Philip Whitcomb, assumed a more creative and disciplined approach to maintaining morale. Whitcomb had directed an educational program in another internment camp, Bad Nauheim. Early on, he discussed with Gilbert his detailed plans for educational activities, including the creation of a "university," with a list of possible courses for adults and children that included geography. That was the birth of Badheim U., to which Gilbert probably devoted as much energy as did any of the other 69 instructors of 168 courses in 3,053 class sessions over the three terms of the university's existence. Indeed, one of the internees received a year's credit in an American school on the strength of his certificate from Badheim U.

Whitcomb was named president of the university,

> founded at Bad Nauheim in execution of the last will and testament of Ichabod Badheim IV, under pedagogical principles laid down by the great Professor Wurlitzer (whom God preserve), temporarily closed at 9:30 P.M. on May 12th, 1942, by the enthusiastic withdrawal of its entire teaching and student body, but reopened amid scenes of unprecedented gloom on Monday, January 27, 1943, in its present gilded setting in Baden-Baden. The fundamental principles of the university are: (1) A university should be a fog with a student at one end and the professor at the other; and (2) Badheim is forever dedicated to the proposition that education of the ignorant, for the ignorant, and by the ignorant, must not perish from the earth. General Note: Parents are assured that

students are fully protected during the tender formative years from contact with the rough, outer world (White n.d.).

Gilbert's contributions included a geography class for twelve embassy children, a seminar on Karl Haushofer's geographic theories (mentioned in Chapter 2), and a cooperative seminar on the wartime German economy led by one of the internees. (Ironically, after repatriation, Gilbert received a letter of commendation from the U.S. Office of the Secret Service for his participation in intelligence gathering while interned at Baden-Baden. It turned out that the leader of the cooperative seminar, to which even the camp's German supervisor's was invited to contribute, was an OSS agent who had devised this means of gathering information, which he somehow secreted out of Baden-Baden to Allied intelligence. The experience was yet another lesson for Gilbert White regarding unanticipated consequences, despite the best of one's intentions.)

Gilbert took courses in four languages, including Russian from Olga MacGowan, an American citizen but a native Russian who sometimes gave her class while reclining in bed. He practiced his German conversation with the Gestapo guards, one of whom had been fed by Quakers following World War I. From Lindsley Noble he took accounting—"the only instruction in accounting I've ever felt I needed!"

Gilbert joined Hiatt, Richie, and Noble in another university endeavor: a sort of colloquium exploring the pros and cons of establishing an internationally sponsored war relief agency to which private agencies such as the AFSC could contribute funding and personnel. While the fact that their delegation in France had been organized and funded under the auspices of an American agency had worked to their advantage at times, Gilbert early-on became convinced that, on balance, international sponsorship would have enabled the AFSC to promote more effectively the Christian tenets underlying its humanitarian service. The extent to which they had been used and compromised, with counterproductive consequences, resulted in large part from the AFSC clearly being an American agency.

That was one of the principal conclusions/recommendations contained in a forty-three-page report to the Philadelphia office that the full Quaker group conscientiously drafted as their self-imposed university assignment. A related issue with which they struggled was the scale of programs: the more refugees whose needs the France program had endeavored to address, the more impersonal and less meaningful the effort became in terms of their witness to (affirmation of) Quaker tenets of faith. As the scope of the work increased, hiring became less discriminating, and the lack of adequately trained personnel proved counterproductive to achievement of many goals, in terms of both quantity and quality of service.

As Gilbert questioned, "Since the role of individual relationship and friendly understanding is so important, should AFSC ever undertake large scale programs, or should the extent of its activities always be restricted in order to give the best results to the Quaker testimony?" (White et al. 1943).

Gilbert's bias was evident in his and Rosanna Thorndike's (the one American woman in the Quaker group) editing of the final report. From his first involvement with the AFSC, Gilbert developed a strong conviction that Quaker service to alleviate physical needs and social injustice—to improve the quality of life for others—ought never to supersede the personal witness—the personal fulfillment and understanding—that they gained through this act of volunteering. Quaker service is as important an experience for those giving as for those receiving. In fact, the AFSC, and Gilbert in his myriad involvements with the organization, would struggle with this issue for decades to come.

University class attendance tapered off as time wore on and boredom, if not depression, set in. At the same time, it became clear that the Baden-Baden American contingent did not include enough diplomatic brass to hurry Washington into a prisoner exchange with the Nazis. Rosanna Thorndike wrote:

> If Badheim U. had not declared a holiday at Easter it would have had to shut its doors for lack of students, for classes were dwindling away to nothing. It's the mental "torpitude" that gets one (if only there were such a word—"torpor" is too superficial) and you learn you can't rest if you are without your liberty, though it is ridiculous that that should be so. . . . Gilbert named seven members of the Foreign Service who attended no classes. . . . And while Gilbert knows much about the geographical distribution of sources of water over the earth, his subject could be completely vanquished by a report that we would have a sardine on Friday, or an apple tomorrow (Thorndike n.d.).

Food was an overriding preoccupation, even for Gilbert, who maintained his own garden. Gloom set in when he realized that the white powder he had mixed with water for whitewashing the walls of his room was in fact powdered milk! In another letter to his mother and sister, he wrote:

> There was a proud display of local window-box gardening and washstand jam making. Most of the people lavish care on a window-sill plant or two, and they struggle with common geraniums and nasturtiums and mint and egg-plant and tomatoes and parsley—anything that might possibly grow. The jam making dates from berries which we have had a chance to pick on walks in the forest, but the sugar supply doesn't encourage it to last long. I am nursing a collection of mint, ivy, geranium, and a primrose, and hardly a day goes by that, spotting with anxiety a foreign insect, I do not think of you and Guthrie in the garden. . . . The march of the seasons—the weather, the plants—has meant more to me this year than ever before. It is said that frustrated adults tend to revert to their attitudes and interests of some earlier age, and it would seem in my case that I am making a much greater leap backwards to the spirit of that other Gilbert White, the gentle old English clergyman who wrote *The Natural History of Selbourne,* and charted the arrival of the wrens, the budding of the linden trees, and like events of his little parish of Selbourne. So that if my notes seem to be on the bucolic side, you may understand (White 1943c).

When at last the Americans' impending repatriation and departure via the steamship *Gripsholm* was announced at the end of January 1944, Badheim U. held a commencement, with Quakers in the limelight, as they had been throughout the year in university activities and extracurricular drama productions. Following the reading of the class will and prophecy, Lindsley Noble recited someone's speech about the Haitian freedom fighter Toussaint Louverture. And after Gilbert was voted one of the two most popular instructors, Roderick Davison's alma mater composition was sung by his male quartet:

> *Badheim U., we hail thee,*
> *Founded on the sand;*
> *Earnestly we're hoping*
> *Thou wilt not ever stand.*
> *Proudly on the Oosbach*
> *Waves thy black and blue*
> *Badheim, now we raise our caps*
> *Loyal—to you!*
> *Now we part forever*
> *From these hallowed halls,*
> *Scenes of great endeavor,*
> *Ivy-covered walls.*
> *Sterner life awaits us*
> *On the briny foam;*
> *Graduate courses will be held*
> *On the—Gripsholm.*

The printed certificates awarded by President Whitcomb bore the university's magnificent seal—a keyhole with a key that obviously didn't fit, two squirming fish, and the inscription *Sine die* (adjournment indefinitely)—its colors black and blue. Finally, always looking for a reason to hold a party, Pinkey Tuck officially closed the university and invited everyone to the prom.

On February 24, 1944, the group boarded the train for Lisbon. They were joined by wounded American servicemen, a contingent of South Americans, and an odd assortment of other Americans rapidly assembled to make up the 500 Allied repatriates needed for the two-for-one exchange with the Nazis. Indeed, before boarding the *Gripsholm*, the group watched 1,000 Axis repatriates from the United States and Brazil disembark.

During a Christmas eve meeting for worship just two months earlier, the Quakers and several others at Baden-Baden had pondered the paradox of their being ransomed for German soldiers—two soldiers returning to the battlefield in exchange for each relief worker repatriated. The irony was not lost on their nonpacifist companions, one of whom suggested that they might consider the propriety of their accepting American Red Cross food rations in view of their enabling twice as many enemy soldiers to return to the war. One of the Quakers further expressed growing doubts about pacifism in wartime, questioning whether, on balance, the benefits of their relief work were not outweighed by their relative impotence, especially during the internment. Perhaps the role of pacifists should be limited, this person suggested, to peacetime education in techniques of nonviolent resistance and coping with oppression in the event of occupation by an invading army. Burritt recorded the discussion:

> Gilbert replied by saying that there is no direct evidence that the long history of relief work has had any appreciable influence on the foreign policy of any nation. Quaker peace-makers have often advocated policies which they had little hope of seeing adopted in their generation. They took their stand on these proposals regardless of their expectation of immediate implementation. They have had insights into the methods and objectives of foreign policy and have acted on these insights at an early stage of history. Ultimately the validity of the approach must rest on the validity of conclusions concerning the fundamental nature of the universe; of man and the relationship of God to man. To the extent pacifists are unsound at these points so will their approach to relief work be unsound (Hiatt 1942–1944d).

During his nineteen months in France and Germany, Gilbert White (who was only thirty-two when he returned to the United States) found his own answer to Einstein's options for living one's life. Every day given to us, no matter how miserable its context, "matters," he concluded. Each is a gift to marvel at, to learn from, but never fully to comprehend.

Repatriation, Anne Underwood, and Marriage

Following his release by the Germans, Gilbert injured his back when rough seas threw him against a deck support en route to New York from Lisbon. He did not receive medical attention on board, and consequently he endured subchronic pain throughout his life. However, Gilbert found that he could alleviate the discomfort with firm back support when seated and good posture when standing—habits that contributed to the ramrod figure Gilbert presented for the rest of his life.

The accident, together with a respiratory infection, prohibited the happy, carefree reunion Gilbert had anticipated when the *Gripsholm* docked in New York in mid-March. A Vassar friend had loaned Anne her apartment in New York City, and Anne in turn had reserved a nearby hotel room for Gilbert. When the ship finally docked, it was rumored that the passengers would not disembark until the next day, and, with rooms at a premium, Anne cancelled the reservation. Late that evening she received a disgruntled phone call from Gilbert, who was waiting in the hotel lobby where he had expected to rendezvous. The couple finally spent the few remaining hours of the night talking in Anne's borrowed apartment before Gilbert left the next morning for a medical examination and reunion with his mother and sister in Chicago. Gilbert, who had always been trim, had lost 30 pounds because of intestinal worms. He was gaunt and feeble and remained frail for several years after his return.

Anne returned to her Labor Relations Board job in Atlanta. She heard from Gilbert so infrequently in the ensuing days that she began to doubt his intention to proceed with their wedding plans. Her boardinghouse companions, sensing her despondency, were therefore skeptical when she announced that she was getting married in April. (They had had a collective wager that the first to marry would claim a fancy nightgown. Anne had already lost that bet, so they took her out to dinner and presented her with a cookbook, which was more to her liking anyway.)

In fact, there was little advance notice of Gilbert's repatriation and hence little time for Anne and her family to plan a Washington wedding. But under the care of the Florida Avenue Friends Meeting, they were married on April 28, 1944, in the Quaker tradition, with no presiding minister, no music, and few flowers. Perhaps more than anything, this espousal of Quaker "plainness" demonstrated to her family and friends that Anne had left her Episcopalian High Church traditions. (Not to be completely denied, someone in the family defied her instructions and spiked the punch, and for the rest of his life Gilbert enjoyed relating how memorable the occasion was for his very merry, but none the wiser, teetotaling Quaker friends.) Some time thereafter, Anne's mother fretted on learning that some Quaker weddings had considerably more floral accompaniment—even music—than Anne had permitted.

Unlike Gilbert's paternal ancestors in New England and his maternal Quaker ancestors in Delaware who had moved to the Midwest, the Underwoods on Anne's father's side and the Bayards on her mother's side had roots in the Washington area (except for her paternal grandfather, who was from York, Pennsylvania). Her paternal grandmother (like Gilbert's maternal grandmother) had a Quaker background. Gilbert remembers Anne's father, Norman, as more accepting than her mother of Anne's and Gilbert's interest in Quakerism. Norman was not bothered by his brother's openly gay sexual orientation. When Gilbert knew him, he was chief chemist in the Bureau of Printing and Engraving, in charge of the inks for stamps and currency. Although opposed to desegregation, he trained his black employees as diligently as the others. (During the presidency of Warren Harding, he was fired for being a Democrat but was reinstated after Harding's death by President Calvin Coolidge.) Gilbert credits Anne's simplicity, even frugality, to her father.

Anne's mother, Anne (Nan) Bayard Underwood, had enjoyed a privileged upbringing, frequently in the company of her maternal grandmother and aunts, who were members of one of Washington's more distinguished and politically visible families, the Deakins. Nan's father, James, briefly had served as lieutenant governor of the Arizona Territory but was handicapped by alcoholism. Gilbert and Anne's children described their maternal grandmother as always having a girlish charm, even in her eighties. Nan had an artistic appreciation for fine things, was a scholar of lace (giving lectures at local clubs on the subject), and could recreate a couture

Wedding of Anne and Gilbert in Washington, D.C., April 28, 1944

evening gown in a matter of days, having only examined the original once. Some of Anne's most beautiful evening gowns, in her youth, were created that way since money was never plentiful and Nan spent what they had wisely. Nan supported women having careers; shortly after her husband Norman died in his nineties, she told her granddaughter Frances how prudent it was to get a Ph.D. and have a career. After all, what did she (Nan) have in life now that her husband was gone, since she had never taken up a career.

Anne's maternal great-grandfather, like his father and grandfather before him, had been a U.S. senator from Delaware. In that role in 1877, when the popular vote threw the outcome of the presidential election into the Electoral College, he unfortunately voted for Samuel Tilden who, despite having won the popular vote, lost the election. He resigned from the Senate in 1885 to serve as secretary of state during

Grover Cleveland's first term and as ambassador to the Court of Saint James (England) during Cleveland's second term. Consequently, Nan's mother and aunts led a very formal social life in the diplomatic world of London and returned to Washington with a social status that Nan's husband's Underwood ancestors could not match. The three generations before Anne Bayard Underwood on her mother's side had been a matriarchal dynasty, which Anne was relieved to put behind her when she married Gilbert, a self-assured yet unassuming man eight years her senior. The social skills that come with such privilege had been passed down, however, and in her life with Gilbert, Anne would have many occasions to put them to good use.

Although capable of dressing well—even formally—when the occasion required, Anne was a free spirit when it came to appearance. She had begun smoking at Vassar but gave it up while working with the Labor Relations Board, when her predominantly male colleagues insisted on her smoking their cigars. She disliked wearing hose, regardless of the occasion, and especially when she became pregnant, she raised her mother's ire with her dress. Anne was always quite conservative in her dress, and although she did not share her mother's interest in fashion, she bought very good quality clothes (she referred to them as "good goods") and wore them well. Her style was simple but elegant and practical.

Anne's three maternal great-aunts doted on her and her brother, Bayard; none of the three had children of their own. Of them, Florence in particular was Anne's champion, intrigued with her independent thinking. In Anne's teenage years, Florence had showered her with attention, rewarding her for her graduation in 1938 from the Madeira preparatory high school in Washington with a summer sojourn to France and Italy. They shopped in Paris for Anne's "coming out" wardrobe for her debutante ball during her first year at Vassar, and Anne recalled (late in life, when recording her early memories for her children) being "very ambivalent about it because by then I had some exposure to a different sort of socialist leaning, and here was this upper class stuff going on and I thought it was terrible." Florence had married a geologist, George Becker, a member of the National Academy of Sciences who died before Anne was born.

Although from very different Protestant backgrounds, Anne and Gilbert had moved toward remarkably similar beliefs, values, and lifestyles before their marriage. During their courtship and in the early years of their marriage, they explored the writings of their Quaker contemporaries, William Wistar Comfort and Thomas Kelly (both affiliated with Haverford College), and their predecessors, Quaker founder George Fox, early theologian Thomas Barclay, political pioneer William Penn, and social activist John Woolman. Anne was no more inclined than Gilbert to delve very deeply into the theological underpinnings of either Christianity or Quakerism, but she was as sympathetic as Gilbert to Thomas Barclay's disavowal of the orthodox Judeo-Christian belief in an essentially sinful human nature. Despite their coming to Quakerism by "convincement" rather than by birth into Quaker families, Gilbert and Anne decided early in their marriage to use the "thee, thou, and thy" familiar forms of address with each other, which Quakerism had retained well after other English speakers shifted to the informal "you." As do a growing number of contemporary Friends, they found the "plain language" endearing in their marriage.

Their children described both parents as unusually self-disciplined. Anne, as was typical of mothers of her generation, did not have the time to focus on scholarship or a career as intently as did Gilbert. Perhaps that was fortunate, given the role Anne played helping Gilbert, collaborating with him, and keeping him mindful of his myriad commitments. The children did not recall Anne's ever complaining about Gilbert's single-mindedness, his focus on work, or his leaving so much of the parenting to her. To some degree she protected Gilbert from the children's demands on his time. With him she presented a united front with respect to discipline. In fact, the children witnessed little bickering between their parents. Just as Anne and Gilbert inclined toward decorating their homes with often austere, formal, and sometimes uncomfortable antique furnishings, their demeanor struck the children as formal and controlled. Gilbert could be stern, but more often was just too busy to be "present." Anne was described by the children as respectful, dignified, and calm.

Given the difference in their ages and Gilbert's determination to be true to the high expectations he and others had for his career, it would have been understandable had Anne used parenting as an excuse to release herself from comparably high expectations for a career beyond her family, especially involving academic pursuits that would force comparison with Gilbert's accomplishments. Instead, she chose to identify fully, or perhaps even more, with her husband's than her children's needs, which may explain their children feeling about as distant from their mother as from their father. Anne chose the greater challenge of casting her lot fully with her husband, with the consequent risks of feeling inadequate to the needs of all who depended upon her. That choice was testimonial to her self-assurance and conviction that she was intellectually fully Gilbert's equal, an essential partner in their "making a difference."

Life and Work in the United States, 1944–1946

Gilbert continued to work with the American Friends Service Committee after returning to the United States, and the newlyweds rented their first residence in Philadelphia at the corner of Mole and Cherry Streets, one block from the AFSC offices and the adjacent Race Street Friends Meeting House. A stray cat, their first of innumerable family animal companions, promptly wandered into their lives. In good geographical form, they named it "Racmolcha" for the neighborhood streets of Race, Mole, and Cherry.

A cobbler's bench from General George Washington's Valley Forge era was one of the newlyweds' house purchases, for just an additional ten dollars—the first piece of Gilbert and Anne's collection of antique furniture. To this day, much of the furniture still in use in Gilbert's and his children's homes was handed down from ancestors on both sides of the family. In fact, so much of their furniture qualified as antiques that the children (and guests) joked about lacking comfortable places to sit in their succession of homes, and the children had to remind friends not to romp on the chairs for fear they would collapse. "Anne used to color in the thread-bare parts of their oriental rug in the living room with ink so it didn't look so worn . . . but it was a very comfortable and old-fashioned-feeling home—well worn" (communiqué from Frances).

After they moved into their new home, the Whites began collecting and cherishing friends as well, and the collection grew rapidly, with attrition only brought about by deaths. Once a friend of the Whites, always a friend, and Anne and Gilbert worked hard to nurture these friendships through personalized gifts, aid, or comfort offered in times of need. Some of the friendships were carried into the marriage from their prior single lives. For example, the Whites' next-door Philadelphia neighbor, Betty Emlen, had been a classmate of Anne's at Vassar, and like Gilbert and Anne, Betty and her husband, Woody, lived in the neighborhood because of their involvement with the AFSC. Indeed, eighteen months after the Whites moved to the neighborhood, the Emlens embarked upon one of the first overseas assignments for couples allowed by the AFSC. Still, those eighteen months were sufficient time for Gilbert and Woody to build a lifelong friendship as close as Betty and Anne's. Both friendships were important and helpful when the Whites moved on to Haverford College and later to Gilbert's leadership of the AFSC.

Betty described Anne during their Vassar years as brilliant and highly respected, due in part to Anne's courage in majoring and excelling in economics. During the two years that Gilbert was in France and Germany, she had begun a career based on her college work in labor relations, but with her marriage to Gilbert she was eager to begin training that would be helpful in the AFSC overseas assignment that she and Gilbert assumed would follow his two years of administrative service in the national AFSC office. In fact, she began training in medical lab technology, only to realize six months into the marriage that she was pregnant.

During Gilbert's initial months in the Philadelphia office, he was assigned to assist James Vail, secretary for AFSC foreign programs. Gilbert directed fund-raising for the AFSC's China-Bangladesh program, raising $2 million through a Community Chest Drive he orchestrated.[7] The drive was particularly noteworthy because of the enthusiastic joint leadership that Gilbert coaxed out of rival AFL and CIO labor union organizers in Philadelphia. Sixty years later, Gilbert and the children still maintained a close familial friendship with Trudy Jeramias, whose husband, Jerry, had been a collaborator in that philanthropy.

Impressed with Gilbert's administrative abilities and ambitious fund-raising, Executive Director Clarence Pickett invited him to become his first assistant director. Anticipating the end of the war, Pickett had compiled a list of goals, and the second was an objective equally dear to Gilbert's heart: to shift the AFSC personnel recruitment priority and policy from finding people for jobs to finding jobs that matched the talents and experience of concerned Friends. During the war, the situation in France had understandably justified rapidly hiring whoever was available with the requisite skills. But Gilbert had witnessed the consequences of this emergency approach, including, among many of those new employees, a lack of understanding—sometimes a lack of interest—in the precepts underlying AFSC service. Pickett and Gilbert were in agreement regarding the need to create volunteer service opportunities within the Society of Friends. Deeply motivated persons were eager to serve—often felt divinely led to serve—and deserved AFSC assistance in finding worthy assignments that matched their qualifications.

An especially appropriate opportunity for Gilbert to aid potential service volunteers came at the end of the war, when General Lucius Clay of the U.S. Army Corps of Engineers became the director of U.S. postwar relief in Europe, including Germany. A decade earlier, Gilbert had worked with the National Resources Planning Board committees on land and water on which Clay had represented the Corps—often reluctantly and with little enthusiasm for the committees' goals. When he accepted his postwar role, Clay felt that the U.S. military would need little, if any, assistance from private agencies. Nevertheless, in 1946 the AFSC joined with seven other U.S. voluntary agencies to survey food, housing, clothing, and medical needs in Europe and meet with General Clay to report their findings. Gilbert was appointed to the mission in part because of his recent experience with relief efforts in the region. After many weeks in the field, the team obtained an audience with General Clay in Frankfurt, and Clay finally agreed to selected relief assignments. However, Clay denied the agencies' request for assistance with air transportation back to the United States, except to transport one member of the team who had become ill. For that, Clay granted two seats on a transport plane. The team drew lots to determine who would escort the invalid, and (to Gilbert's amusement) the priest who offered to lead the group in requesting divine blessing on their endeavor drew the assignment. Then, to his chagrin, Gilbert was the last to be granted passage home on a troop ship after several days' delay; he suspected that Clay was responsible for the delay.

Notes

1. Alice Resch described the relationship between Helga and Howard Kershner: "He was a wise and friendly man, who unfortunately lacked Helga Holbek's flexibility and ability to do the right thing at the right time. We had worked independently all summer, so it took some adjusting suddenly to have to ask permission for everything. When and if permission was granted, it was often too late" (Resch Synnestvedt 2005).

2. Many specific suggestions and questions followed:

   > A review of the work in progress at each delegation frequently raises these questions: Are food distributions being made to the classes of people most in need or most deserving? Are the areas selected for the various types of distributions (including distributions through children's colonies) the more needy? Is the aid given the most effective per dollar expended? . . . A more nearly complete appraisal of relief needs in France might suggest the drastic curtailment of certain phases of the program, and the expansion or innovation of other phases. . . . Another part of the difficulty is the lack of information as to food and its uses. For example, extra feedings are being given in several camps without any careful analysis of its physical effects, and as to the relative values of the different foods singly or in combination. Medical examinations are haphazard and uncoordinated for the most part. Records of diet are generally poor. This knowledge becomes highly important as the stores of food dwindle, and it is more than ever essential to avoid unnecessary uses (White 1942b).

3. Some of the escorts who had made the crossing elected to remain in Portugal, eventually helping over 300 children gain asylum in Spain and Morocco and eventually reach foster homes in the United States (Wriggins 2004).

4. Gilbert's mother and Anne Underwood were understandably distraught upon learning through the Philadelphia AFSC office of Gilbert's decision to disobey the directive. Once again, Anne endeavored to communicate with Gilbert via the AFSC and once again was informed by Margaret Frawley that "regulations do not permit our communicating with the American group in France. Both the Lisbon and Geneva offices are sending us news that they have from the workers in France, but we are not allowed to reciprocate. Our only communication with them has been an official recommendation made through the State Department and at the State Department's request. We have sent a cable recommending that they either go to Lourdes for repatriation, or, if possible, to Switzerland" (Frawley 1942).

5. None of the other Americans kept journals, fearing they would be confiscated. Even though Gilbert and Burritt talked almost daily while circumnavigating the grounds seventeen times (1 mile), Burritt never mentioned his journal. In 1993 Roderick Davison, the youngest member of the Quaker team, did document his recollections of Baden-Baden, and, for a book that he was writing on the war, John Baskin tried to interview as many of the French AFSC group still living in the 1990s as he could track down. It was through Baskin that, over half a century after the Baden-Baden imprisonment, Gilbert first learned of Hiatt's journal, then in the possession of Hiatt's daughter-in-law, Muriel Hiatt.

   There is, therefore, considerable information available on the Baden-Baden experience from a range of internees' perspectives. As with the account of Quakers in Vichy, France, the story presented here of the Americans' internment in Germany relies primarily on Burritt Hiatt's journal and Gilbert's memory and correspondence with the AFSC and his family. Unfortunately for Anne, his fiancée, Gilbert had no direct contact with her his entire time in Europe.

6. The second letter:

> The food here is not exactly the kind we used to have for Thanksgiving dinner, but it is adequate, and stands in pleasant contrast to that which those of us who did not use diplomatic or Black Market connections had in France last year. There the sense of a mild hunger was almost constant, and could not be dodged simply by eating quantities of tomatoes or carrots. Here, we have meat in small portions on the average of once or twice a day; all the potatoes and black bread that we care to eat; a good many beans and fresh salads; and dessert of fruit or custard. People who like it and wish to pay for it can have a little wine each week. We enjoy rations larger than those of the ordinary people, and in addition, of course, have the Red Cross packages every two weeks. These carry a good assortment of items that have given me a new and deeper appreciation for the largesse of the American countryside. Never again will Columbia River salmon, or Florida orange juice, or Mr. Hershey's chocolate, or Cudahy's corned beef, or California prunes, or Kansas City oleo have a prosaic meaning for me. They are magic, romantic things, incomparably better than any lobster from Harvey's or roast duckling from Normandy Farm. They almost, as I started by saying, remind me of a pre-war Thanksgiving on Dorchester Avenue (White 1943b).

7. In Bangladesh over 2 million people had perished in the 1944 Bengal famine, due not only to hunger aggravated by the war's interruption of agriculture and shipping but also to flooding. Survivors received food, medicine, and medical equipment before the AFSC shifted its priority to supporting local cooperatives. In China, the AFSC objective was to procure drugs from American, British, and Canadian Red Cross Societies for distribution by the Friends Ambulance Unit to Chinese citizens caught behind Japanese lines.

5 Haverford College

Inevitably, those of us who have come after Gilbert White are largely custodians of what White wrought. . . . I should like to think that our commitment to excellence, coupled with [our] sense of community, has meant that we have maintained the academic integrity which . . . White gave us.

—Robert Stevens
    President, Haverford College

A New Job and a New Home

In the spring of 1946 Gilbert was asked by his first AFSC supervisor, James Vail, to make presentations on AFSC priorities and programs to regional gatherings of friends, supporters, and associates of the AFSC. Gilbert obliged but later learned that Vail had hidden motives for asking Gilbert to take on this task. Vail was wearing two hats, the second as a member of the Board of Managers of Haverford College. Haverford is a small, liberal arts school, founded in 1833 in a suburb of Philadelphia by the Society of Friends. At the time, it was an all-male institution, although now it is coed. Gilbert's name had come up in the board's search for someone to replace the retiring president, Felix Morley. Because of Gilbert's youth and recent arrival to the Philadelphia area, Vail was using the regional presentations to expose Gilbert to the Friends in the area and vice versa. Gilbert passed these initial tests, and when finally informed of Haverford's interest, he agreed to a dinner meeting with board members.

The Whites' hopes for a joint AFSC foreign assignment had ended when their son, William Deakins White, was born on July 13, 1945. At the same time, however, Gilbert was again exploring a possible assistant professorship in the Department of Geography at the University of Chicago. Undecided between the two positions but inclining toward Haverford, he sought the advice of President Robert Maynard Hutchins at Chicago. Gilbert wryly recalled, "When I went to discuss this decision with Hutchins he leaned back, flicked a cigarette ash, and remarked that Haverford did not have a really good undergraduate program but it was probably the best there was among small colleges" (White 2002).

Gilbert described it as the most difficult job decision he ever made. He was just thirty-four years old and looked no older than Anne, who was twenty-six. They both could have been (and would be) mistaken for college students. Anne, especially, had

Gilbert's inauguration at Haverford College, autumn 1946. Anne and Gilbert are facing Frank Aydelotte, former president of Haverford's companion Quaker institution, Swarthmore College.

had her heart set on service abroad, and she knew that, as a college president's wife, she would be saddled with the entertaining and social life she had gladly left behind in Washington, D.C. Moreover, Gilbert was eager to return to research in geography and to experience teaching at the graduate level. In fact, the couple had decided to turn down the Haverford offer when Gilbert left for the board meeting that was called for his decision. Anne was asleep when he returned, and he waited until morning to tell her what had happened.

After listening to the board's plans for Haverford, he realized that such an opportunity might never come his way again. Although an undergraduate institution, Haverford had begun experimenting at the graduate level with programs focusing on postwar relief and reconstruction. The job and the school presented a unique opportunity for Gilbert to pursue his ideas regarding both inculcating community values at the undergraduate level and training for efficacious service at the graduate level. Gilbert would become the youngest college president in the country, but the board had convinced him that his employment with the AFSC had provided the requisite administrative and fund-raising experience. Moreover, although his return to geography research would have to wait, he could teach. The board agreed that Gilbert could teach one geography course annually. He accepted the job.

Both the Whites and the Haverford Board of Managers might have had some trepidation about the decision; certainly neither realized how fine the match would be. Hutchins, from his vantage point as a student of innovative education and long acquaintance with Gilbert, may have understood the benefits that Gilbert would provide Haverford. (Although Hutchins's tenure at Chicago would overlap Gilbert's at Haverford by five years, Gilbert had little contact with him, apart from brief meetings at reunions of their shared fraternity, Alpha Delta Phi. He accepted one speaking engagement at Haverford during Gilbert's tenure.) Gilbert acknowledged the influence that his education at Chicago during Hutchins's presidency had on the ideas promulgated at Haverford. Chief among them were the institution of tripartite freshman core courses in social sciences, physical sciences, and the humanities (labeled metaphysics by Hutchins at Chicago) and an insistence on postponing any applied programs until completion of four years of pure liberal arts and sciences. Gilbert, however, despite (or perhaps because of) having entered the College of the University of Chicago at sixteen and commenced graduate study at twenty, did not share Hutchins's belief that capable high school students should be allowed admission to college two years sooner than the American norm.

Their move to Number One College Circle on the Haverford campus made the Whites and Rufus Jones next-door neighbors. Although Jones had retired from teaching at the college, his friendship with Gilbert had deepened because of their association with the AFSC. Rufus had served as chair or honorary chair of the AFSC since its founding. Sadly, a year after they moved to Haverford, not only Gilbert and Anne, but also their young son, Will, lost a very close friend when Rufus Jones died. The Whites' friend, Betty Emlen, recalls Will watering his friend's grave, "hoping that with the flowers' appearance perhaps Rufus would come up, too." Gilbert had the small consolation of inaugurating the Rufus Jones Memorial Study in the college library. Gilbert also became well acquainted with David Hinshaw, biographer of Rufus Jones, during David's sojourn at Haverford researching the biography (Hinshaw 1951).

Will had two sisters: Mary Bayard, born July 25, 1947, and Frances Anne, born July 10, 1950. The three (Frances in particular) were cared for by Helen Cadbury-Bush, the widowed daughter of biblical scholar Henry Cadbury, who had taught at Haverford before joining the Harvard faculty. "Bushy" lived in the Whites' third-floor apartment throughout Gilbert's tenure at Haverford, not only taking care of the children but also assisting with the Whites' entertaining. Other faculty wives also helped Anne, and the Emlens regularly helped host dinners at Number One College Circle (entertaining dinner guests with Gilbert while Anne managed the kitchen).

As mentioned earlier, both Anne and Gilbert repeatedly were mistaken for students. At campus social events Anne grew accustomed to being asked out by unsuspecting freshmen. Gilbert's greatest national notoriety (in his lifetime, Gilbert claimed) came when newspapers across the nation reported on the "boy-president" sidelined with mumps! (Thereafter, when he learned that a Haverfordian was in the infirmary with mumps, Gilbert would pay a condolence call.)

Gilbert's Legacy

The college may never have had a president and spouse more popular with students than were Gilbert and Anne. Today, this enduring popularity of the Whites is matched by a comparable respect for Gilbert's leadership. He is now considered one of Haverford's most influential presidents, perhaps second only to Isaac Sharpless, the college's president from 1887 to 1917 (Cary 2001). Gilbert's legacy was that he returned Haverford to the national prominence it had enjoyed a half-century earlier under Sharpless, who had succeeded in emancipating the college from its founding mandate to provide Quakers with a narrow, religiously guarded, liberal arts education.[1] As Rufus Jones once observed, a college education that is both guarded and liberal is a contradiction in terms. At the end of Sharpless's tenure in 1917, all Quaker institutions were struggling as their pacifism placed them at odds with many other citizens and institutions of a country at war.[2]

The three Philadelphia colleges founded by Quakers were Haverford, Bryn Mawr, and Swarthmore. Haverford was by far the smallest of the three. With its many fewer faculty and more traditional liberal arts curriculum (involving no programs in engineering, as at Swarthmore, or in teacher education, as at Bryn Mawr), Haverford's stature waned in relation to the other schools following the Sharpless years. Moreover, because of the Quaker doctrine of pacifism, during World War II, Haverford's competitive edge with schools such as Harvard, Princeton, and Yale (Haverford's three principal Ivy League rivals) also grew smaller. Still, that same Quaker conviction strengthened Haverford's reputation within the Society of Friends, which was increasingly beleaguered because of its opposition to a popular war. Resolute pacifists among the faculty, students, and alumni of the college welcomed President Felix Morley's principled denunciations of the war, but he paid a price for his stand: it became more and more difficult to raise money for the college. Even within Philadelphia's sizable Quaker population, 75 percent of the men eligible under the draft chose military over alternative service. With the end of the war in 1945 and enactment of the GI bill, private colleges faced the prospect of rapidly increasing competition from public institutions of higher learning. By midcentury, public postsecondary enrollment surpassed that in private colleges and universities nationwide. Haverford was much in need of and ready for new, strong leadership.

Gilbert White had served honorably in Vichy France. As a former prisoner of war, he would be well received by returning veterans. Furthermore, his vision of academic excellence was essentially a return to the vision of Isaac Sharpless. Gilbert rejected as fully as did Rufus Jones any anti-intellectual bias remaining from orthodox Quakerism's mysticism and especially its quietism. In 1983, in talking about Rufus Jones, Haverford president Robert Stevens said to Philadelphia's Newcomen Society, "Rather than emphasize the Bible, he emphasized the universal approach of mankind to God. This de-emphasis on the more Orthodox biblical tradition has been important, especially for the Haverford of today, in which only twenty percent of our students are practicing Protestants." Stevens could as well have been referring to Gilbert White.

At Haverford, Gilbert was equally committed to acquisition and dissemination of knowledge and to its use for human betterment. As a scientist, he maintained a corollary commitment to the advancement of understanding of human nature and the ways human behavior could be modified to minimize negative impacts on the environment. Proceeding from these commitments were the pedagogical goals of honing the intellect, cultivating veracity, and distinguishing between cognitive and evaluative judgments. Central to Gilbert's Quaker faith was his belief in the necessity and efficacy of collective discernment and consensus regarding correct ends and means to meet such commitments and goals. Discernment involved imagination (and illumination), and the communal seeking of truth underlay all other values. An unusually small college, Haverford provided an ideal laboratory for realizing these beliefs. Perhaps Gilbert and the Haverford board saw that for postsecondary education in the United States, time was running out on opportunities to achieve excellence in such integration within colleges as small as Haverford.

In Gilbert's opinion, the size of Haverford's student body was critical. He argued aggressively, even obstinately, with faculty and the Board of Managers that an enrollment above 450 made it impossible for himself as president or for any other community member to know at some meaningful level—at minimum by name—every other member of the community.[3] The argument was not easily sold, especially to faculty, since institutional size related then, as now, to the financial resources available to support the faculty and the development of a broad, competitive curriculum. That is particularly the case the more those resources are dominated by tuition income, in contrast to endowment, annual giving, and public or private grants. As compared to other Quaker and Ivy League schools (and competition) Haverford's income was disproportionately tuition-based when Gilbert became president. The school had barely balanced its budget the year prior to his arrival (1945). During Gilbert's first year as president, with the GI Bill in place and Haverford committed to readmitting any former student who had entered the service, enrollment topped 500 for the first time in Haverford's history. Over 50 percent were returning veterans of military or alternative service. Fall enrollment reached 556 in 1948, before declining to 528 in 1949 (with veterans constituting only 15 percent of the student body by then). Gilbert saw enrollment return to 450 only in 1953.

To achieve his goal of limiting enrollment, as soon as he accepted the presidency Gilbert set out to reduce the college's dependence on tuition income. His first objective was to double the school's endowment, and he succeeded. From less than $4,500,000 when Gilbert arrived in 1946, the endowment increased to over $11,000,000 when he left in 1955. (By contrast, in the three decades prior to Gilbert's arrival, the endowment had increased by less than $2,000,000.) Gilbert and the Board of Managers were determined not to let the drop in enrollment affect the richness of the curriculum or the size and quality of the faculty. Indeed, raising faculty salaries was another of Gilbert's ongoing (and accomplished) goals throughout his tenure. The increase in endowment was one of the principal means to that end. Not content simply to raise salaries, Gilbert also set out to enlarge the faculty even as enrollment declined. Some endowment bequests were solicited specifically to add faculty, but the faculty and curriculum were also enriched through grants. Gilbert wrote many foundation applications himself, primarily to the Carnegie and Rockefeller Foundations, since he had no development staff initially. (Two years into his tenure, Gilbert hired Lester Haworth as the college's first development director.) Such "soft" money supported semester- and year-long visiting faculty, as well as a host of shorter-term lecturers and campus speakers.

Tuition increased intermittently over Gilbert's decade as president, but the increases were largely offset by increased financial aid, which not only helped the school to retain students but also broadened Haverford's student diversity. Very few black students attended Haverford at the time, and Ira Reed, in sociology, was the only black professor. Greater geographical (including international), racial, and ethnic diversity became a major objective of the college, and achieving such diversity required increased financial aid to students. Such support quadrupled during Gilbert's presidency, thanks in part to significantly increased annual giving from alumni, parents, and other friends of the college, which in turn was aided by the formation of an Alumni Council.

To strengthen the college fiscally while simultaneously lowering enrollment was an idealistic gamble—a gamble that Gilbert won admirably—but the ten years immediately after World War II probably constituted the last decade in which he, or anyone, could have achieved such success. The faculty remained divided over the wisdom of Gilbert's enrollment policy throughout his tenure, and under his successor, Hugh Borton, enrollment increased sharply. Gilbert's tenacity in pursuit of deeply held convictions and the Board of Managers' unwavering support were the keys to his remarkable success. His was a bold experiment, which by century's end had become legendary among the presidents following Gilbert and especially among the students who had graduated from Haverford during those ten years. Gilbert returned to Haverford by alumni request for most of the forty-, forty-five-, and fifty-year reunions of the classes that graduated during his tenure.

Community and Community Service at Haverford

Community service was neither more nor less valued by Gilbert than knowledge acquisition and effective dissemination. However, research by Haverford psychology professor Douglas Heath suggests that Haverford was particularly successful in nurturing community values during the Gilbert White era.[4] In the early 1960s Heath initiated longitudinal studies of student maturation from freshman to senior year and thereafter from their twenties into their midforties (Heath 1968, 1999). He was pleasantly surprised to discover that their Haverford experience ranked

Work Day at Haverford (Gilbert is center-left). Photo courtesy of Theodore Hetzel.

eighth out of fifty possible determinants (such as type of occupation or spouse's personality) in its contribution to their growth since graduation (Heath 1999). This success may have been due in part to two weekly rituals required prior to and throughout Gilbert's presidency. One was the Fifth Day (Thursday) meeting for worship. The other was the Collection (convocation) of the campus community members to hear announcements, observations from the president, and usually a visiting speaker. Both ended under the subsequent administration, when increased enrollment made it difficult to accommodate the entire campus community in either the Haverford Friends Meeting House or the Collection auditorium. Obligatory participation was always controversial, but Gilbert felt strongly that these weekly assemblies and meditation involving all sectors of the community were the linchpin of Haverford's claim to be a Quaker college, a family of seekers. Professor Douglas Heath strongly agreed. Among the students studied by Heath were many who, while at Haverford, rebelled against required attendance at Fifth Day worship (less than 10 percent were Quakers). Yet of the more than thirty indicators of maturation during their adult years that Heath monitored, appreciation for the influence of meetings for worship was the only one that showed increased salience between graduation from Haverford and the follow-up interviews fifteen years after graduation (Heath 1999).

Gilbert frequently spoke at Collection; he rarely spoke at meetings for worship, where the Quaker elders of the community regularly would "speak from the silence" of meditation. Anyone was free to thus offer their ministry, and—even if the right never was exercised—this democratic approach directly reflected basic tenets of

Quakerism: the divine spark in all persons, the essential equality of all worshippers in this gift of spirit, and the expectation of all members of a community to participate in the discernment of wise actions. Two remarks, one from Collection and the other from a faculty meeting, demonstrate Gilbert's convictions in this regard.

From Collection:

> At base the relation between student and teacher at the college level is an act of faith in the capacity of man to think for himself and to recognize the truth for himself. Without this it is a mere training process in which someone is trained to do what someone else has done before him. It serves its purpose only when teacher and student alike believe in the ability of the other as children of God to sense something of the divine purpose of the universe.

To the faculty:

> The good teacher gives this service by example and precept. We may be warranted in operating a college for a student for four years if only once there comes to him clearly the illumination of viewing his own powers in relation to a divine purpose, if only once he feels that warming fellowship of the seekers of truth that cuts across the lonely barriers of complexity and purposelessness that seem to surround each one of us. The whole history of great teaching is rich with men who helped their fellows reach across these barriers for inspiration and comradeship.

Gilbert considered the reintroduction of Quaker procedure into faculty meetings his greatest contribution to building a sense of community within the faculty. As president he was expected to chair faculty meetings, and initially he observed Robert's Rules of Order. Early on, however, when deliberations bogged down in contentious dispute, he suggested experimenting with discerning "a sense of the meeting" and offered to clerk (or chair) the process.

Some background on Quaker business procedure may be helpful to readers unfamiliar with the Society of Friends. When serving as clerk, one sets aside one's personal preferences in the interest of discerning the group's common preference or will. If he or she has such trust, the gifted clerk will lead a consensus-building process, expanding the common ground through careful listening and patient reasoning. The implicit expectation is that there is a right decision that will emerge from such reasoning and discussion. A related expectation is that the clerk will summarize that consensus for the group, often in stages as it evolves. Those who are least committed to the emerging consensus (as articulated by the clerk, written down by a second "recording clerk" and affirmed by the group) have the right, indeed the responsibility, to express their reservations and, if they prefer, to "stand aside." If unwilling to stand aside, then as few as one dissenter can delay a decision until additional "threshing" (dialogue) resolves the objection. The resultant consensus is what Quakers term "the sense of the meeting." It differs from a majority vote, insofar as once this kind of consensus has been articulated by the clerk and accepted by the group, standing in the way of the decision's implementation is out of order.

Even within these parameters, an able clerk can influence outcomes both through his or her formulation of the evolving consensus and by talking privately during recesses with anyone having difficulty with the emerging group opinion. (Once, when he was asked if he had used committee or task force chairmanships to promote outcomes he personally favored, Gilbert acknowledged that on many occasions he had exercised the latter prerogative of "laboring privately" with members, usually so that he could better understand their opposing views and determine ways to accommodate them. Otherwise, he assiduously avoided pushing his own agenda.) Abel Wolman, whom Gilbert watched chair committees under the National Resources Planning Board, demonstrated these lessons well, and Rufus Jones and Clarence Pickett reinforced Gilbert's belief in this approach during his years with the American Friends Service Committee.

The Haverford faculty guardedly voted to try this approach for one year, the last vote they took until a year later, when they voted to continue using the procedure. More than half a century later, faculty meetings continue to be conducted "after the manner of Friends."

Changes at Haverford

Faculty support of Gilbert's strong opinions and leadership understandably was divided. They were unaccustomed to a president being so assertive in rejuvenating their ranks, so interested in the total curriculum, and so eager to experiment with pedagogy. Among the few faculty of that era interviewed for this biography, opinions differed. Some agreed with Gilbert that he simply endeavored to nurture faculty creativity and to experiment along the lines of institutions such as the University of Chicago, Oxford University, and Reed College. For example, Gilbert was intrigued with the tutorial approach he experienced later as an exchange professor at Oxford. In Gilbert's words:

> My concern was not to establish a particular program, but to get the faculty to think about something new about which they could be enthusiastic, and which I then could support. So I did not go into it with a conviction that there was a particular program that should be adopted, rather that there should be a program that fit Haverford faculty inclinations and essence. And that's the way it evolved through faculty committees.

When questioned concerning Gilbert's leadership, Stephen Cary, a fellow administrator at the time, responded:

> From my advantage as a Haverford observer for over 30 years, those who know Gilbert well say that he was the last president who ran the College from the President's office. . . . Gilbert got away with it because he was profoundly respected as a scholar. There was no resentment of his strong leadership to my

Commencement at Haverford in 1955, the last during Gilbert's tenure as president

knowledge. He enjoyed great confidence of faculty because of his clarity of thought, articulation of ideas, and the good luck of being president before the era of faculty domination set in. It was a simpler administrative environment then, but one where Gilbert was preeminently the leader. And because the faculty were so supportive, I think this was an example of where Gilbert thought he was giving faculty the leadership role. But, I tell you, Gilbert White was running this place, not the faculty! (Cary 2001)

Others, recalling that era, felt that Gilbert's biases toward interdisciplinary and team teaching, and especially toward strengthening the natural and social sciences, were readily apparent. However, because funding for curriculum experimentation and faculty expansion and development was secured largely at Gilbert's initiative, most faculty were willing to follow his lead. In Gilbert's defense, if he rebuilt the natural and social sciences at some expense to the humanities (apart from English), the humanities had long been Haverford's strength. Philosophy and history, behind only English, continued to be the most popular majors throughout Gilbert's presidency. Fortunately for Gilbert, the presence on campus of Rufus Jones (albeit retired) and Douglas Steere, a renowned professor of philosophy and religion and a prominent Quaker, freed Gilbert to be a scientist-president rather than the pastoral leader that otherwise would have been expected of a Haverford president in that era. (Indeed, any more competition in preaching might well have made the Fifth Day worship services even more entertaining for the students on the back benches, who wagered on who would be the next to rise and for how long that person would minister to the captive audience.)

As keen as Gilbert was on strengthening the natural and social sciences, he was equally concerned that Haverford students obtain a holistic, interdisciplinary perspective in these sciences and the humanities. To that end, he secured faculty support for three core courses in these divisions. The courses were team-taught by representatives of all departments in each division, and participating faculty were expected to attend the classes taught by others. The longest-lived of these core course experiments was freshman English in the humanities division, modeled on the Oxford tutorial system. The course was consciously designed to complement the experiential learning supported by the Collection gatherings, meetings for worship, the honor code, and related extracurricular activities. A number of new faculty were hired for this interdisciplinary program, and as many of the newcomers were Jews as Quakers.[5]

In cooperation with other Philadelphia Quaker colleges and the AFSC, Haverford provided nonacademic credit for service courses that introduced students to weekend work camps in low-income inner Philadelphia neighborhoods, as well as summer work camps in rural Mexico and a nearby Norristown mental health facility. In part because of his wife, Anne's, transforming experience working in a similar AFSC camp while an undergraduate at Vassar, Gilbert was determined to advance college-AFSC cooperation wherever possible. Consequently, he obtained funding from the Carnegie Foundation for a comprehensive assessment of the impact of work camps on the values and attitudes of youth. Gilbert obtained the services of Harvard University's Henry Riecken to direct the 1948–1949 Work Service Evaluation Project. Riecken was assisted by several Haverford faculty, AFSC staff, and a remarkable team of renowned social scientists, including Gordon Allport, David McClelland, Harold Garfinkel, Talcott Parsons, and M. Brewster Smith. Questionnaires were administered to Haverford students prior to, during, and ten months following their participation in three summer work camps. The results resoundingly confirmed the positive impact of such voluntary service and thereby provided the Society of Friends in the person of Gilbert White possibly its strongest advocate for such service. "To summarize the results of testing our expectancies," Riecken wrote,

> we can say quite briefly that campers became enduringly less prejudiced, more democratic, and less authoritarian. They also became more service oriented in their choice of vocations, more concerned to help their fellow men, better adjusted, less anxious, more autonomous, and less frustrated. Further we concluded that campers' personal maturity had increased—they had become more self-confident, less dependent, less hostile, and had, in short, developed greater ego-strength. On the other hand, their ideological views on nonviolence were not changed, nor did they become more liberal in their political and economic views.
>
> . . . Lastly, it is not clear that they became any more capable of coping constructively with problematic or stressful situations, and they seem to have become somewhat more compliant and withdrawing in the face of stress (Riecken 1952).

The sophistication and thoroughness of the study and the utility of its findings strengthened Gilbert White's conviction that postaudits, or rigorous retrospective assessments, of institutional practices and public policies are indispensable and, in particular, are an absolutely necessary feature of any program aimed at responsible stewardship of resources (White 1988).

The Korean War accelerated Haverford's experiments with service-related technical training. In the 1950–1951 academic year, over fifty students enrolled in a not-for-credit course in mechanics, motor transport, and first aid. The war also led to the initiation of a master's level graduate program in social and technical assistance (STA), an experiment that had been one of the reasons Gilbert accepted the presidency of Haverford. However, the program continued only three years and attracted at most twenty-two students. By Gilbert's own assessment, it failed to live up to the expectations generated by Haverford's highly successful relief and reconstruction training program during and following World War II. "We didn't get financial support for it," Gilbert said, "and we didn't have the power of our convictions as to the success of the effort" (Bronner 1993).

If he was discouraged with the STA program, Gilbert was similarly unimpressed with what other Quaker colleges did during the Korean War. Heads of Quaker institutions, including the AFSC, met a number of times in this regard, with Gilbert questioning the appropriateness of midwestern Quaker colleges' willingness to dilute their traditional undergraduate liberal arts curricula with applied technical and area studies programs. While recognizing the vocational utility and service ideals motivating such innovation, Gilbert was concerned that the inclusion of technical training at the undergraduate level, for academic credit, would subvert the broader goal of providing a liberal education. Without the foundation of such an education, the vocational and service work that might follow college would likely be neither as effective nor as personally enriching as it might otherwise be.[6]

For Haverford College, at least, liberal education would continue to be the focus of the academic curriculum at the undergraduate level. Indeed, a University of Chicago consultant had judged that Haverford was not expecting enough academically of its students and advocated increased rigor (Heath 2001). In contrast, psychology professor Douglas Heath, while outspokenly supportive of Gilbert's campus community-building efforts, questioned whether, by the end of his tenure, the focus on academics had gone too far. Heath asked whether "a liberal education, at least of the Haverford type, should not balance its excessive analytic, logical, critical, and deductive bias by nurturing sympathetic, intuitive, appreciative, and inductive forms of judgment" (1976).[7]

Because Haverford had much to gain (including heightened visibility) from increased cooperation with Bryn Mawr and Swarthmore, Gilbert strongly promoted interschool linkages. In time the amount of cross-registering and cross-majoring between Haverford and Bryn Mawr led some administrators, faculty, students, and alumni to question whether one or both of these single-gender institutions should follow Swarthmore's example and become coeducational.[8]

Gilbert refused to accept as much credit as others would give him for Haverford regaining, even surpassing, the eminence enjoyed under Isaac Sharpless. He credited Lester Haworth for establishing the financial foundation that enabled the school to regain the six-to-one student-to-faculty ratio it enjoyed under Sharpless, and Gilbert was also quick to recognize the invaluable service Vice President Archibald MacIntosh provided in selecting students especially well suited for Haverford. Gilbert particularly acknowledged the avuncular counsel the older and seasoned "Archie Mac" provided regarding how to deal with entrenched administrators, several of whom tried Gilbert's patience.

Moving On

Toward the end of his tenure, Gilbert invited anthropologist Margaret Mead to speak at Haverford. Over dinner that evening, Mead talked about research in which she was interested, and Gilbert mentioned related research that he was hoping to pursue. Mead's blunt response kept Gilbert and Anne awake much of the night. She said that Gilbert never would return to significant research, now that he had been away from research so long and had been successful in administration. The offers that he could anticipate would be in administration from other academic institutions and funding sources such as foundations. Indeed, Gilbert already had been approached by a foundation, and soon thereafter Brown University invited him to become a candidate for its presidency.

In connection with Brown's interest, a Brown trustee wrote to University of Chicago president Lawrence Kimpton, inquiring about Gilbert's reputation within the Department of Geography. Kimpton turned to Chicago's geographers, one of whom, Chauncey Harris, sent a card to Gilbert asking whether he was, indeed, considering another presidency. Gilbert responded that he had been approached but that he would prefer a post in geography. Upon learning that, Harris canvassed fellow geographers and the chair of the Division of Social Sciences at the University of Chicago and, with their agreement, met with the Whites at Haverford during a trip to the East Coast. After attending his first Quaker meeting for worship with the Whites, Harris promptly offered Gilbert the chairmanship of the University of Chicago's Geography Department (Harris 2001). If the decision to go to Haverford was his most difficult employment decision, accepting the Chicago offer was Gilbert's easiest. He was ready to return home.

President Robert Stevens's closing remarks to the Newcomen Society in 1983, in commemoration of Haverford's 150th birthday, provide a fitting summary of Gilbert's term at Haverford:

> Inevitably, those of us who have come after Gilbert White are largely custodians of what White wrought. We live in a more democratic age. Since the 1960s, stu-

dents have been consulted in a way unheard of in the 1930s, even in a college which talked freely of community and consensus. . . . Indeed, I suspect the greater involvement of faculty and students has brought us closer to the Quaker ideal of community than in the period when the contact of the College with the Religious Society of Friends was much closer. I should like to think that our commitment to excellence, coupled with this sense of community, has meant that we have maintained the academic integrity which Sharpless and White gave us. It would certainly be an inspiring thought on our 150th birthday (Stevens 1983).

Twenty years following Stevens' remarks the college dedicated a new science library in Gilbert's name.

White, the Scientist and Scholar, 1932–1955

Gilbert managed to remain surprisingly productive as a scientist during his years of employment with Quaker institutions.[9] Every year he taught a geography course for Haverford students on natural resources, incorporating what he was learning from serving on a series of national and international commissions, two of which were under President Harry Truman's administration. The Truman administration bore none of the animosity toward Herbert Hoover that the Roosevelt administration had, and Truman promptly turned to Hoover to chair the Commission on the Organization of Government. Hoover in turn invited Gilbert to join the subsidiary Task Force on Natural Resources. Subsequently, he was also invited to serve as vice chairman of Truman's Water Resources Policy Commission. Hoover was critical of the Corps of Engineers. Indeed, over dinner one night he recounted for Gilbert and several colleagues his long and difficult experience with the Corps. Gilbert agreed that if Hoover had Truman's and congressional support for removing both the Corps and the Bureau of Reclamation from flood control, a new, effective, national water management agency might be instituted. But Gilbert did not share Hoover's antipathy for the Corps and therefore advised the former president to stick with the existing agencies, which had deep roots in communities and the Washington bureaucracy, if consensus on establishing a new umbrella agency could not be reached. Hoover followed Gilbert's counsel.

The birth of the United Nations in 1945 resulted in invitations to serve on various committees and boards. White chaired first the Scientific Conference on Conservation of Resources, held at Lake Success, New York, in 1949, and then the United Nations Educational, Scientific, and Cultural Organization's Advisory Committee on Arid Zone Research from 1953 to 1956.[10] These diverse, high-level appointments enabled Gilbert to monitor not only the evolution of floodplain management specifically, but the whole spectrum of natural resource supply, demand, and conservation issues generally. Although Gilbert was the only social or behavioral scientist at the Lake Success conference, representatives of two dozen academic disciplines from fifty nations served on the Arid Zone Advisory

President Harry Truman's Water Resources Policy Commission, 1950. Morris Cooke, chair of the commission, is seated in front of Gilbert, the vice chair (far right).

Committee. Gilbert established relationships with scientists worldwide, some of whom—especially researchers in Egypt, the Middle East, the Soviet Union, and Southwest and Southeast Asia—would become lifelong friends and join Gilbert in collaborative research and consultation.

The lessons Gilbert learned from the collective review of knowledge about arid lands paralleled the lessons that river basins taught him: dams and levees were to floodplains as canals and wells were to arid lands. The prevailing societal response to water scarcity in arid lands was somehow to produce ever more water; in floodplains it was to control and reduce water. But just as dams and levees promoted increased occupancy of the regions they were intended to protect, canals and wells supported populations that only increased the demand for water, ultimately resulting in physical degradation of soil and water alike. Addressing a University of Arizona audience, Gilbert presented a startling dilemma: as many acres of irrigated land worldwide were being lost to agricultural production because of salinization and waterlogging as were needed for new irrigated production, presumably to meet the needs of the expanding population.

> Without fanfare . . . salt accumulation is taking as much as 40,000 acres a year in West Pakistan. More than sixty percent of the irrigated lands of Iraq are seriously affected by salting, the product of over-application of water and unsuit-

able soils. In the fruitful delta of the Nile, as much as one-quarter of the land is threatened by a high water table resulting from inadequate farm drainage. Declining yields of cotton testify to the curtailed productivity. There now is doubt that the investment in massive new works is any more than offsetting the inconspicuous dissipation of old investment in farms that are abandoned to salt-crusted fields and soggy soils. Cities are also beginning to steal irrigated land, as in Southern California where the demands of urbanized areas are accompanied by a retreat and an intensification of agriculture on the urban fringe (White 1960).

The dilemma could be resolved, Gilbert argued, by increasing the efficiency of irrigation. Doing so would not only replace the acreage lost to salting and water-logging but also would fill the needs of the expanding population as well, without requiring an increase in the water supply. For example, according to the Agricultural Research Service in the mid-twentieth century, the doubling of irrigated acreage in the western United States would require 307 million acre-feet of new water if no improvement in efficiency were made. But if water managers implemented known and tested methods of conservation, not only a doubling but half again as much new acreage could be irrigated with 307 million acre-feet of new water. In short, the cure for impending or existing water shortages was not necessarily more water; it was better water management.

Gilbert recognized that judgments of "too little" or "too much" water reflect human concerns about human welfare and comfort. They are evaluative, not cognitive, judgments and typically do not take into account the entire needs of complex natural ecosystems (which science still struggles to comprehend). In the mid-1950s, the term "sustainable development" had not yet been introduced. Nor was the growing disparity between haves and have-nots within and among nations widely appreciated; "right (or fair) sharing" of resources was not yet a popular adage. Rachel Carson's *Silent Spring,* the book that first described an "earth at risk" due to industrialization, was not published until 1962. Moreover, Gilbert was the first to acknowledge that a commitment to sustainability, although laudable, says nothing about what sustainability actually means (see Chapter 12).

The increasing wealth of a few at the expense of the many became a popular theme in Gilbert's public speaking to all audiences, with sensitivity to the difficulty of younger audiences to process such information without being overwhelmed to the point of despair. The facts Gilbert condensed from multitudinous sources were indeed sobering: In 1950 the United States constituted 8 percent of the Earth's land area and was occupied by 9.5 percent of the "free" world's population. Yet this 9.5 percent was consuming fully half of the free world's production of materials. In the first half of the twentieth century, U.S. consumption of petroleum products increased thirty-fold, use of coal increased two and a half times, and consumption of iron ore increased three and a half times. Forest and agricultural consumption was similarly

Left: Gilbert at age forty-four, on leaving Haverford in 1955. Right: Anne White and their children, Will, Mary, and Frances, on leaving Haverford.

taxed; the nation shifted from a production-compared-with-consumption surplus of 15 percent in 1900 to a production deficit of 9 percent by 1950. Moreover, the depletion of known reserves of natural resources was proceeding at a higher rate in the United States than in any other country. The Paley Report (1952) projected that, at midcentury rates of consumption, the 9 percent production deficit would reach 20 percent at century's end. Compounding the problem, as demand increased, the cost of production (even of water) had begun to climb by midcentury, following a half-century of steady decreases in the cost of most resource production.

In hindsight from the early twenty-first century, fifty years ago Gilbert White clearly anticipated the dilemmas faced by the United States and other wealthy nations as they endeavor to maintain their increasingly privileged position with respect to the use of global resources. In 1953 Gilbert shared the political and moral implications of these trends, first in an unpublished speech to business executives in Michigan and then in an article for conservationists in the *Journal of Soil and Water Conservation* (White 1953). To the audience of business executives he presciently forecast that "so long as the United States faces an increasing dependence upon overseas areas for basic materials—and self-sufficiency seems both economically and physically impossible—it will be involved in the maintenance and stability of those areas. Much more basically, as long as the United States wishes to act in a spirit of Christian and democratic friendship toward its fellow nations it must be prepared to share in their efforts to improve their own positions." Gilbert then characteristically provided a concrete, positive example coupled with a strong warning against underestimating the challenge.

In the end, Gilbert's career was a tightrope act, balancing optimism with realism, eschewing both effusive enthusiasm and apocalyptic gloom. Addressing the global population dilemma, he expressed his own persistent bias: his optimism about our collective ability to make morally responsible political adjustments if science can inform policy makers in timely fashion. Gilbert White never yielded to despair. The closest he came, after setting forth an essential agenda, was to acknowledge that its realization, while unlikely, was not quite impossible.

> The prospect which we now face is not as discouraging as that presented in some of the recent conservation literature which ominously maintains that the United States itself already is overpopulated in terms of its available resources, and that other densely settled areas will continue to be explosively over-populated unless drastic measures are taken to curb population. At the same time the evidence does not seem to support the assertion by some business leaders that given freedom of research and enterprise, and stable investment possibilities, there is no need to fear any shortage of materials. It seems neither as hopeless nor as hopeful as these views would suggest (White 1953).

Notes

1. As Robert Stevens, president of Haverford from 1978 to 1987, said in a speech commemorating the 150th anniversary of the school, "In many senses, it was [Sharpless's] ability to adapt Orthodox Quakerism, to move it back from a concern with rules to a concern with the spirit that was vital both for the Society of Friends in general and, in particular, for the liberation of Haverford from the sheltered atmosphere that had characterized its founding" (Stevens 1983).

   In the College   (until its removal by President Stevens, to the consternation of some faculty), Sharpless was quoted as saying:

   > I suggest that you preach truth and do righteousness as you have been taught, where in-so-ever that teaching may commend itself to your consciences and your judgments. For your consciences and your judgments we have not sought to bind; and see you to it that no other institution, no political party, no social circle, no religious organization, no pet ambitions put such chains on you as would tempt you to sacrifice one iota of the moral freedom of your consciences or the intellectual freedom of your judgments.

2. Haverford was more disadvantaged by this pacifism than were the other Philadelphia Quaker institutions, both because its Quaker constituency was more committed to pacifism than were the Swarthmore and Bryn Mawr communities and because Haverford was an all-male college. Swarthmore had an ROTC program and was coeducational. Bryn Mawr was dedicated to the education of women. It was primarily Haverford's constituency, under the leadership of Rufus Jones, that established the Quaker service arm, the American Friends Service Committee.

3. Gilbert was able to determine the limit of his own memory of campus names as enrollment fluctuated over his nine years between 450 and 550. To his satisfaction, his personal experience was confirmed by David McClelland's social-psychological research findings: if a group was larger than 450, individuals would not make an effort to know the rest of the members. An institution might as well have 1,000 as 500 students if sense of community, measured by mutual acquaintance, was not a goal.

4. Thanks to Heath's longitudinal study of sixty-eight Haverford graduates of the 1950s, from their freshman year through their midthirties, the impact on graduates of their Haverford experience at midcentury is well documented. The extensive data (Heath 1968, 1976, 1999) provide one measure of Gilbert's legacy. His annual reports to the Board of Managers provide another. (College historian Edwin Bronner, who conducted a long interview with Gilbert in 1990 [Bronner 1993], described these reports as among the finest produced by Haverford presidents.) A tribute to Gilbert presented by the college library Quaker collection curator, Thomas Drake, and the aforementioned assessment of Gilbert's presidency by former president Robert Stevens (1983) are yet others. These sources, in addition to interviews, provide the details of Gilbert's years at Haverford presented here.

5. In conjunction with an initiative called the freshman English experiment, Gilbert made one of his most notable faculty appointments when he enticed Wayne Booth from the University of Chicago to move to Haverford. Booth stayed with the experiment until its end and then returned to Chicago and became dean of the College within the University of Chicago just as the college was projecting a doubled enrollment. The proposal Booth made to the board of the University of Chicago was to enlarge the faculty to ensure the requisite instruction for a number of programs, or collegiate divisions, each serving approximately 400 students "to preserve the small college flavor important to students, despite the doubled enrollment" (Boyer 1999). Gilbert, by then also a member of the University of Chicago faculty, had good reason to feel vindicated in his comparable struggle to peg Haverford's enrollment at 450.

6. The midwestern Quaker college curriculum of which White was most critical for its applied B.S. degree options belonged to Wilmington College in Wilmington, Ohio. In that era of the late 1940s and early 1950s, President Samuel Marble received national visibility equaling White's at Haverford, but for very different reasons. Marble instituted extracurricular (noncredit) work-study programs on an ambitious scale, including persuading an automobile parts factory to locate near the college and to employ primarily Wilmington students on shifts that accommodated their class schedules. The students also constructed one of the dormitories under Marble's imaginative leadership. Majors in not only elementary and secondary teacher education but in industrial education and agriculture (with Ohio State University, the only two degree-granting agriculture programs in the state) were among the most popular in the curriculum.

    I obtained permission from Haverford to enroll at Wilmington College my junior year, upon marrying a Wilmington student. The work-study program enabled me and my wife to marry and both of us to remain in college, and subsequently we returned to Haverford for my senior year and graduation. We later returned to Wilmington for the five years of my presidency (1970–1975). The college's applied programs had, if anything, strengthened in the two decades between my student and administrative roles at Wilmington. Moreover, it was primarily because of the even greater blending of traditional liberal arts and applied sciences at the undergraduate level at Bethel College, in North Newton, Kansas, that I accepted an invitation in the 1980s to serve as Bethel's academic dean. As a Mennonite college, Bethel had even fewer reservations about including applied majors than I had encountered at Wilmington. Training in industrial arts and teacher education was joined by undergraduate majors in nursing, social work, and agriculture/ rural development in foreign contexts. A center for conflict resolution and peace studies was established at Bethel in support of a major in peace studies, while in the same era Haverford College concluded that peace studies would not provide sufficient focus as a disciplinary major (Wallace Collett, personal communiqué). Haverford has since instituted a Center for Peace and Global Citizenship that "stitches a new layer of understanding on top of our strong but traditional course of study" (as described by President Tom Tritton in the "State of the College 2005").

I remain deeply indebted to Haverford for the excellent liberal arts education the college provided. And of the tenets of educational philosophy espoused by White, it was only the restriction of credit-bearing education to the liberal arts through age twenty-two with which I have taken issue in my own career decisions.

7. Three student suicides during the last two years the Whites were at Haverford were a major concern. But even greater concern arose in Heath's mind during his final interviews with the aforementioned cohort of 1950s Haverford graduates. "For many, the more important kinds of skills they needed were to make judgments with very incomplete information available, to sensitively size up an interpersonal situation and react appropriately, to incorporate their feelings into their judgments. . . . Their over-intellectualized higher education trained them to distrust their feelings. It inhibited learning that most of the important decisions they were to make in their adult lives were ones of judgment, not of analytic logic" (Heath 1976).

8. Swarthmore had been coeducational since its founding in 1864. Some felt that the issues raised by Douglas Heath's research would be ameliorated if Haverford had a coed student body and faculty. This idea had gained considerable momentum on both campuses in the late 1960s when Gilbert was invited by Bryn Mawr's president to join the Bryn Mawr board, under the assumption that Gilbert would favor both Bryn Mawr and Haverford remaining single-gender institutions. Although Anne strongly felt that women's higher education was more fairly served when women were not competing with men, Gilbert did not take a position on the issue. He declined the Bryn Mawr invitation, and Bryn Mawr remained an institution dedicated to serving women, while Haverford became coeducational in the mid-1970s.

9. Gilbert produced seventeen scientific publications from 1944 through 1955. While in Washington from 1935 to 1942, he had seven articles accepted for publication. His unpublished public addresses were much more numerous. They were about evenly divided between Quaker audiences (on topics relating to education and Quaker service) and nonchurch audiences in higher education, business, and industry on topics relating to education and management of natural resources.

10. White's interest in arid zones dated back to a report he wrote in 1935 about the effects of the dust bowl, the 1934 midwestern drought. The Natural Resources Committee asked him soon after his arrival in Washington to prepare a report based on survey data gathered with the help of the American Water Works Association. Bob Kates and Ian Burton, when editing a festschrift in White's honor (Kates and Burton 1986), selected this first publication of Gilbert's to introduce excerpts from selected publications throughout his career. In it Kates perceives:

> the elements of form, function and findings that would continue to characterize his professional work. ... First, droughts are "acts of God," but drought losses are largely acts of man. The greatest drought in history actually affected the public water supply of only 2 percent of the American people and created difficulties only in areas already vulnerable either because of prevailing physical problems of supply or the underprovision of capacity. Second, there are few truly national (and even fewer global) problems. Most environmental problems are regional problems, with considerable difference between regions. It is the geographer's duty to carefully document the regional difference and suggest ameliorative action matched specifically to the needs of a place. Finally, even "quick and dirty" data, limited by issues of definition, accuracy, and coverage, can be better than ignorance in making policy decisions (Kates and Burton 1986, vol. 1).

6 The American Friends Service Committee and Southeast Asia

We must learn something that no nation or group of nations yet has mastered: the art of helping others to improve their lot even as differences between them grow.

—GFW

The Conferences for Diplomats

When Jacquelyn Monday, Gilbert White's junior colleague and secretary briefly at the University of Colorado, was asked what words Gilbert brought to mind, she replied, "Serendipity! Gilbert appreciates serendipity" (Monday 2001). As focused as he can be, Gilbert also cultivated imagination and alertness to opportunity. Early in 1951, halfway through Gilbert's Haverford tenure, Clarence Pickett, who only the year before had retired after twenty-one years as executive secretary of the American Friends Service Committee, broached an AFSC idea with Gilbert. Leaders in academic disciplines from political science to psychiatry who shared interests in interpersonal, intergroup, and international relations had been meeting regularly the previous year to determine how pertinent research in their fields could be transferred to and implemented by the people planning and administering government programs with potential impact on relations among peoples, political systems, and cultures (Collett 2002). The New Hope Foundation had funded these preliminary discussions and upon their conclusion had invited the AFSC to consider expanding the dialogues to include potential government users of such research findings. For Gilbert, science in the public interest was an enduring cause, and the possibility of it becoming central to an AFSC program was intriguing. Gilbert agreed to help, the beginning of his forty-five-year commitment to a unique AFSC venture.

Gilbert first offered to assist the program by providing introductions to his Washington contacts. Clarence Pickett hired Harold Snyder, former director of international programs of the American Council on Education, to direct the endeavor, and the three men set about recruiting key scientists and members of government for a seminar on "The Impact of U.S. Policies, Programs, and Personnel upon Other Peoples." Those invited from government were carefully selected from middle management in federal departments and bureaus, frequently at the recommendation of their supervisors. They were invited with the understanding that they were participating as individuals rather than as representatives of their governmental domains. In six monthly meetings at the AFSC's Davis House, the group of a dozen regular participants met with an invited topic specialist and an AFSC facilitator.[1] The questions addressed were, What American cultural values are reflected in our system of government and foreign policies? and How do these values influence images and stereotypes of the United States abroad and ultimately affect global stability? The plan was for several AFSC staff to chair the seminars, but Gilbert's success in eliciting participation, keeping discussions on track, and succinctly summarizing the areas of agreement and dissension in the first seminar resulted in his chairing all but one of the six meetings that launched the Washington seminars.

The early consensus was to keep the discussions strictly off the record and to commit to regular attendance. Proxies were not permitted, and participants proved remarkably faithful. Before continuing with the program beyond the initial six-month trial period, Gilbert made certain that all participants were asked by Harold Snyder to assess the program and offer suggestions for improvement. Gilbert's own appraisal was that, useful as the dialogues may have been, the AFSC risked spreading itself too thin if it continued as sponsor. Overreaching in AFSC programs, in terms of having both requisite knowledge and human resources within the Society of Friends, was then and remained a major concern of Gilbert's. Clarence Pickett, however, wanted to push ahead; the New Hope Foundation had encouraged the AFSC to present a proposal not only for continuation but expansion of the experiment. After participants resoundingly endorsed the program, Gilbert acceded to the consensus within the AFSC to continue. The experiment not only continued, with Gilbert chairing two of the nine monthly meetings of government officials the following year, but comparable series were initiated with personnel directors of federal agencies (in cooperation with the Federal Personnel Council), foreign affairs journalists, embassy officials, members of Congress, and administrators of educational exchange programs.

Gilbert's participation might have ended then, had the experiment not been expanded to Europe in the summer of 1952. That year, at St. George's School in Clarens, Switzerland, overlooking Lake Geneva, twenty-five officials from the foreign ministries of fifteen North Atlantic nations convened for unrecorded conversations on "National Interest and International Responsibility." Gilbert invited Ralph Bunche to cochair this first Conference for Diplomats and two successor conferences the following year. Women were included from the start, and in the second conference representatives of eleven Asian countries joined those from Europe and the Americas. By the third year, the conferences had been lengthened to two weeks, and participation had grown to three dozen. Unexpectedly, the conferences began attracting older and higher-placed representatives from foreign ministries, although the

Participants in the 1954 Conference for Diplomats, in Clarens, Switzerland. Gilbert and Anne White are first row, center. Photo courtesy of the AFSC.

organizers initially had targeted diplomats in midcareer, between thirty and forty-five years of age. Gilbert White, still within this age range himself, again chaired the discussion—this time on "The Task of Diplomacy in a Disunited World."

By then, the United Nations was nine years old, with membership having expanded gradually following World War II to include nations that had been on both sides of that conflict. Similarly, the Conferences for Diplomats attracted wider representation as counterparts from governments on opposing sides of issues found it useful to meet and talk face to face. Indeed, the conferences reflected a major transformation in diplomacy, from strictly bilateral toward multilateral dialogue. Prior to the United Nations, each country's interests and its citizens' welfare eclipsed concern for the planet's and humanity's general welfare. By focusing on participants as private individuals rather than as public national representatives, the Conferences for Diplomats expedited the emergence of the idea of a universal "family of man" and the recognition by diplomats of the need to consider implications broader than just short-term national interests. Also, by inviting middle-level rather than upper-level experts within foreign ministries, the AFSC stood popular wisdom on its head; Gilbert and his colleagues understood that heads of foreign ministries were often spokespersons for policies developed and advocated by the staff reporting to them. Unfortunately, the perspectives and net of contacts of these middle-range staff members were circumscribed geographically and restricted by protocol. To help address these obstacles, AFSC staff maintained and distributed alumni directories containing, by program's end, contact information for about 2,000 diplomats and resource personnel from ninety-one countries. As these directories were updated, it became apparent that the great majority of alumni remained active in their governments' design, implementation, and interpretation of foreign policy.

Participation in the conferences was always by invitation. Initially, many of those invited declined, and others only accepted hesitantly. When first invited, one French minister exclaimed, "What an odd idea, inviting diplomats to express personal viewpoints on issues of national policy!" Gilbert recounts a Canadian ambassador's confession years later that he made alternative housing plans in the town near the conference center in the event that the conference turned out to be a failure or, at the least, unsatisfactory. Similarly, a Swiss participant recalled having arranged for his office to call him every day in order to provide an excuse to return to Bern if the Quakers were a disappointment. In the end, however, many ministry representatives of races, religions, and political ideologies at deep odds became good friends because of their two weeks of unavoidable association at the conferences (Collett 2002).

Gilbert remained the chair of choice throughout the first decade of the Conferences for Diplomats. During that decade, twenty-five conferences brought together 550 foreign ministry officers from fifty-three countries and consultants from twenty-eight. The list of consultants and public servants invited to help lead the conferences reads like a Who's Who of the world's most distinguished diplomats at midcentury. Brock Chisholm, the first director-general of the World Health Organization (WHO), regularly for fifteen years gave the closing talk on "Developing a Sense of International Responsibility." Ralph Bunche's role has been mentioned. Lord Caradon, Lester Pearson, and Philip Noel-Baker, among others, also followed the program around the world over several years. Funding from the Ford and Carnegie Foundations sustained the program for another fifteen years. By 1977 fifty conferences at Clarens and another fifty in other locations in Europe, the Middle East, Africa, and Asia had hosted 1,400 diplomats. Thereafter the program metamorphosed into new forms under the auspices of the Quaker United Nations Offices (QUNO) in New York and Geneva, and the Quaker International Affairs Representative programs in regions around the world.

Stephen Collett, director of the New York City Quaker United Nations Office from 1986 to 1998, wrote a history of these Quaker seminars and conferences in which he detailed several instances in which the Conferences for Diplomats succeeded in bringing together representatives of countries deadlocked on issues, some of which in time would yield to diplomacy: East-West Cold War struggles, including the unification of East and West Germany; Pakistani-Indian claims on

Kashmir; Arab-Israeli confrontations on a number of issues; and China's representation in the United Nations (Collett 2002). In 1970 a conference for diplomats was held at Rastenfeld, Austria, dealing exclusively with this latter issue. The following year the U.N. General Assembly voted by a two-thirds majority to replace the representatives of Taiwan with those of the People's Republic of China (PRC). Quakers generally supported the PRC taking China's seat in the Security Council, and that same year (1971) the AFSC sent a delegation to the PRC, the first such visit by an American nongovernmental agency. Gilbert was included.[2]

Looking back over his forty-five years of involvement with the Washington Seminars and Conferences for Diplomats, White attributed the success of these experiments in large part to the high visibility of the AFSC at midcentury. American Quakers had been very active in postwar efforts following World War II, rivaling the efforts of British and Irish Friends. In 1947, five years prior to the first Conference for Diplomats, the Nobel Peace Prize had been awarded jointly to both the AFSC and the joint British/Irish Friends Service Council. Gilbert accepted little of the credit accorded him by Collett for the accomplishments of the meetings. Yet his skill and reputation both as a scientist and facilitator certainly were essential in moderating the delicate conversations among diplomats that led to increased confidence in multilateral diplomacy.

When leadership of the Conferences for Diplomats passed to QUNO in the 1980s, East-West issues, including weapons reductions and the fall of the Berlin wall, dominated the agenda.[3] Gilbert returned to chairing conferences in preparation for the Third Special Session on Disarmament in 1988, when his connections from the Washington years helped secure John Kenneth Galbraith as keynote speaker. But his more pivotal role was as liaison between these diplomatic initiatives of Quakers and the efforts of scientists internationally to focus research on the environmental effects of nuclear war. Three colloquia in 1991 and 1992 drew mostly ambassador-level negotiators from the leading nations in preparation for the Rio de Janeiro U.N. Earth Summit agreements. Then, after Rio, Gilbert also chaired colloquia in New York for negotiators of the Convention to Combat Desertification in Nairobi. White's final involvement, in the late 1990s, was to chair some of the first QUNO conferences on reform and revitalization of the United Nations (Collett 2002).

Science in the Service of Humankind

In 1969 the International Council of Scientific Unions (ICSU) established a Scientific Committee on Problems of the Environment (SCOPE), governed by representatives of thirty-four national academies of science and fifteen international scientific unions. Gilbert was invited to join SCOPE the following year and went on to serve as its president from 1976 to 1982. In 1983 SCOPE in turn established a U.S. Committee on the Environmental Effects of Nuclear War (ENUWAR). Gilbert moved from the presidency of SCOPE to ENUWAR's nine-person steering committee. Simultaneously (from 1983 to 1992) he became an executive editor of *Environment* magazine during the height of concern over the effects of a nuclear winter, and in 1988 he was able to orchestrate with QUNO the wide distribution to United Nations personnel of an issue of *Environment* (volume 30, no. 5) containing the ENUWAR research findings.

Gilbert joined thirty other scientists from ten countries for ENUWAR's first conference in Stockholm in 1983, after the steering committee, in its initial planning session earlier that year, had heard committee member S. K. Bergstrom present World Health Organization findings on the anticipated medical effects of nuclear war. ENUWAR decided to confine its studies to the longer-term effects of such a holocaust (e.g., food and water availability globally) as opposed to the more immediate problems of disruption of communities by the blasts, electromagnetic pulse, and consequent loss of infrastructure. Gilbert was involved in two of the dozen subsequent ENUWAR workshops convened in eight countries in 1984 and 1985. He also wrote the Foreword (White 1985) of the final report and was instrumental in securing funding for ENUWAR's activities from the Carnegie Corporation, Rockefeller Brothers, General Services Foundation, and the Andrew Mellon Foundation.[4]

In 1985, in recognition of his SCOPE and related United Nations efforts, Gilbert was awarded both the United Nations Global 500 and the United Nations Sasakawa International Environment Prize. The following year, in Switzerland at the twenty-first General Assembly of the ICSU (now the International Council for Science), he provided the closing remarks on the consequences of nuclear war.

Thereafter, from 1986 to 1998, the Quaker United Nations Office in New York arranged seventeen Conferences for Diplomats. A few focused on the reform and revitalization of the United Nations; the others, on almost a yearly basis, laid the groundwork for major U.N. conferences on human rights, population, women, social development, and, especially, the environment. Gilbert participated in one of four conferences in preparation for the 1992 Earth Summit in Rio. His final involvement in the Conferences for Diplomats occurred in 1997 at a conference on protection of forests. He was then eighty-six years old.

Returning to Chicago

This chapter in the lives of the White family began with Gilbert's relocation from Haverford College to the University of Chicago. His academic career during this tenure as chair of the Department of Geography is the topic of Chapter 7. The remainder of this chapter is a continuation of his involvements with the Society of Friends, specifically the American Friends Service Committee. As mentioned in the Preface, the war in Southeast Asia influenced Gilbert's regard for the University of Chicago and to some extend led to his and Anne's decision to relocate one last time to another academic home (the University of Colorado) in 1970. And not only that relocation decision, but also Gilbert's decision to become active in SCOPE in 1970 coincided with the end of

Gilbert's involvements with the American Friends Service Committee. Indeed, it was in part his growing discouragement with the AFSC that freed him to became so rapidly and heavily involved with SCOPE and related international endeavors. In retrospect at century's end, he considered it fortuitous that his simultaneous discouragement with both the University of Chicago and the AFSC (theretofore his two deepest loyalties) led to the opportunities for international as well as national service to science and public policy that set his agenda for the balance of his career.

⁂

THE WHITES MOVED to Hyde Park, Illinois, at the end of 1955, renting an apartment at the corner of 56th Street and Dorchester Avenue, across the street from Gilbert's ancestral home at 5607 Dorchester, where his sister, Julia, still resided. Their apartment, conveniently close to the university, was also close to the Friends Meeting that had purchased a house on 57th Street during Gilbert's absence from Hyde Park. The Whites promptly transferred their Quaker membership from Haverford Friends Meeting.[5] The ancestral house at 5607 Dorchester remained in the family until 1998, becoming in 1984 the home of Gilbert and Anne's son Will and his wife, Olivia, while Will was employed in Chicago. Thus, even after the Whites moved from Chicago to Colorado in 1970, for another quarter-century their Hyde Park home (where his sister, Julia, resided until her death in 1984) remained open to Gilbert in his comings and goings across the United States and around the world. It was the same neighborhood he had known from earliest memories, quite remarkable given the geographical longitude and latitude of Gilbert's career involvements.

But during the 1960s, the Hyde Park community was crippled by racial and economic tensions that resulted in a major administrative initiative under university president Lawrence Kimpton to heal the problems. Both Anne and Gilbert promptly joined the Hyde Park–Kenwood Community Conference, founded to promote a more viable interracial, interclass neighborhood, and Anne joined a group of faculty wives working on these goals within the public schools. Several months after their arrival, Gilbert accepted an invitation to chair the executive committee of Chicago's regional office of the American Friends Service Committee, where racial justice and integration also headed the agenda. Organizing weekend work camps that brought blacks and whites together in neighborhood betterment projects was a major priority of the regional office. Indeed, even while he was at Haverford College, Gilbert's own first work camp experience was in Chicago, planning a weekend project for college educators.

The Whites' children were also affected by the racial integration struggle in Hyde Park. Instead of the Ray School of Gilbert's youth, all three children attended the university's elementary school, the Lab School of Gilbert's high school experience. Ray School, in a predominantly white neighborhood during Gilbert's youth,

School of Geography, Oxford University, where Gilbert was a visiting professor in 1962–1963

had integrated markedly over the following decades. Enrollment during the 1960s was about equally divided between blacks and whites, and racial tensions frequently interrupted classes and occasionally shut down the school. After graduating from the Lab School's elementary program, all three children opted to attend a small Quaker secondary boarding school in West Branch, the birthplace of President Herbert Hoover, near the University of Iowa in southeastern Iowa. Scattergood School offered a community experience in the John Dewey tradition, similar to the Lab School, but in a rural setting.[6]

Chairing the American Friends Service Committee

Gilbert White was invited to become the national leader of the American Friends Service Committee a few days after he received another invitation to spend the 1962–1963 academic year as a visiting professor at Oxford University. On July 17, 1962, Anna Brinton sent Gilbert a note on behalf of the Philadelphia office of the AFSC. It read in part:

> This is an important communication. I hope it may receive your earnest consideration. The AFSC is faced with the need of discovering a chairman. You are the first choice of Board and staff. I remember that when we were seeking

From left to right: (back) Gilbert, Anne's parents, Anne and Norman Underwood, (front)
Frances, Anne, and Mary White, at Oxford University in 1962 [son, Will, took the photograph]

Colin Bell and before Harold Evans was appointed you gave the Service Committee some hope that at a future time you might be willing to consider becoming its chairman. Has that time come?

Gilbert accepted on condition that he could do justice to the role while remaining in Chicago and could delay the start until the family returned from England.
The Philadelphia AFSC office promptly agreed. The year at Oxford provided a
much-deserved respite from Chicago pressures at the midpoint of Gilbert's and
Anne's fifteen years in Chicago. Moreover, Mary and Frances were able to accom-

pany them. Will opted to remain at Scattergood School in Iowa and to join them following his graduation. Gilbert wrote a letter to a student, Jackie Beyer, similarly abroad, doing fieldwork, describing their surroundings:

> Our house here has a garden that slopes down toward another garden and another street and thus on to the floodplain of the Charwell River, a pleasant green area that over long reaches has managed for 900 years to evade any permanent occupance other than the lock-keeper's house, a pub or two, a decorative display of houseboats, and the college playing fields. This was due, according to the persistent remarks in the local topographies, to the 11th century monks of Abingdon not wanting to get their feet wet at time of high water. It is a suitable spot from which to send greetings to water addicts.

Anne, especially, reveled in the leisure, writing creatively and sharing with Gilbert dutiful correspondence with students, colleagues, and friends abandoned in Hyde Park.

> Life whirls on apace here, with glorious tulips and forget-me-nots swirling in the cold, wet wind of spring. I ushered in this month of May from the top of Maudlin Tower, where at dawn the choir boys sing an ancient song, and the stone roof pitches like a channel steamer when the bells ring, as it has done for the last more than three centuries.
>   The rest of the family was below, where they could watch, in the streaming rain, the boys and girls of the University scrambling from sinking punt to sinking punt on the Charwell.

The Oxford area's many theaters provided rich fare, their favorite pastime. In April they sojourned in southern France, visiting the towns where Gilbert had been involved with AFSC relief efforts and then traveling to Germany to visit his internment hotel in Baden-Baden. Gilbert was persuaded to take up skiing, at fifty-two, during a side trip to the Austrian Alps. Anne's parents crossed the ocean (her father's first time east of the Atlantic) to share the Whites' outings and comparative leisure.

Gilbert used the year to assemble and share on campus a series of lectures regarding what his consultation and participation in the U.N. Educational, Scientific, and Cultural Organization's Advisory Committee on Arid Zones (see Chapter 5) had taught him about human occupancy of arid zones. These lectures formed the bases for a series of publications on arid lands (White 1966b–d) and reinforced his determination to continue in the upcoming years his heavy involvement in Africa, examining human-made lakes, river basin development, domestic water supplies, and sanitation.

Gilbert began his six years of national AFSC leadership at the November 1963 meetings of the Executive Committee and corporation.[7] His introductory remarks focused on managing land and water for humanity's welfare. He balanced enthusiasm with caution regarding the profound scientific revolution that was expanding humankind's

Gilbert (left) and Colin Bell, executive secretary (far right), honoring Hugh Moore (with Mrs. Moore) on the occasion of Hugh's retirement from fund-raising with the AFSC. Photo courtesy of the AFSC.

ability to use and abuse the earth. Despite increased sophistication in scientific tools, such as improved evaluation procedures for measuring the consequences of public policies, many interrelated environmental and social problems were deepening because of imprecision in setting goals and lack of political will to monitor the effects of policies. Gilbert was suggesting an action agenda new to the AFSC.

Gilbert's patience was about to be tested. He came to the chairmanship with immense respect for an institution he cared about deeply. Many of those welcoming him were convinced that the AFSC needed to reassess its priorities in a world in revolution, and Gilbert shared that conviction. Some were open to an agenda more focused on environmental issues. Yet Gilbert clearly understood that it was not his task to set AFSC priorities. As chair his duty was to fashion a consensus among increasingly disparate communities of North American Quakers and an even more diverse staff. To this end his "brilliance in moving complex agendas forward in Friends' ways" (Clark 1997) served well and left a lasting mark on the AFSC. However, his commitment to science in the public interest would be largely ignored within the AFSC and its programs (apart from the central role he concurrently played in the Conferences for Diplomats program).

Procedural issues within the AFSC proved particularly divisive and frustrating, since the broadening war in Southeast Asia deserved increasingly concerted action. Some staff and Friends had developed significant differences regarding the degree of autonomy permissible to regional offices when those offices were determining their program priorities and seeking funding. Another issue was the appropriate division of responsibility between the national corporation and its Executive Committee and between these governing entities and the paid staff, which numbered in the hundreds in Philadelphia and around the world. Having served as a regional executive committee chair in Chicago, Gilbert favored as much decentralization of operations as the size of the organization could accommodate while believing that the Society of Friends, through its representation in the corporation, should lead in establishing priorities and policies. The AFSC was (and is), after all, a service instrument for the "witness" of Quakers, even though employees increasingly were hired because of their expertise rather than because of their affiliation or experience with the Society of Friends.[8]

Gilbert believed strongly that the AFSC was neglecting a role it had played with remarkable success in earlier decades: finding meaningful service opportunities to fit the skills, experience, and commitment of Friends young and old. An alternative approach dominated: identifying social needs and hiring personnel from or experienced in those (mostly minority) social contexts. Programs dealing with black-white relations in the cities and border issues in the Southwest were bringing many African Americans and Hispanics into AFSC programs. These staff clearly sympathized with AFSC goals, but by the mid-1960s, fully half had no prior involvement with the Society of Friends. This distinction was also true of donors to the AFSC; most funding came from non-Quaker sources by midcentury (Tjossem 2001). In the opinion of the Whites and many other alumni of earlier voluntary service programs of the AFSC who subsequently joined the Society of Friends, Quakerism was suffering from these hiring and funding trends.

Initially, while Colin Bell and then Stephen Cary were executive secretaries of the AFSC, Gilbert's working relationship with the Philadelphia office was excellent, hampered little by his heavy academic commitments at Chicago. But the leadership styles of Cary's successor, Bronson Clark, and Gilbert White were quite different and contributed to Gilbert's growing disenchantment with the organization.[9]

The long-standing focus on race relations in the Chicago regional office, applauded by Gilbert, increasingly became a priority at the national level. As tensions escalated in the South during the civil rights movement of the early 1960s, the AFSC used Ford Foundation funding to preserve and promote community-level leadership. The committee deepened its cooperation with the Southern Christian Leadership Conference and also supported southern rural groups interested in finding land and sources of income. Martin Luther King, Jr.'s personal opposition to the war in Vietnam further strengthened civil rights movement ties with the AFSC. Indeed, he had the support of AFSC national and regional offices in April 1967, when he launched a nationwide "Vietnam Summer" initiative to recruit 10,000 volunteers to lobby against the war. A year later, when Dr. King was assassinated in Memphis, the AFSC continued to support the strike by sanitation workers that originally brought Dr. King to Memphis and helped host the enormous influx of people who arrived for memorial services.

Gilbert White represented the AFSC at King's funeral in Atlanta. He marched with the funeral procession, led by the mule-drawn cart carrying the body of Dr. King, from Wheat Street Church to the services at Ebenezer Baptist Church and afterward to Morehouse College. To Gilbert these events demonstrated—particularly for the many participants who had never before identified with pacifism—the importance of nonviolence in achieving social change. He asked the AFSC Board of Directors to consider what increased role the AFSC might play, beyond simply helping to preserve order in the South, in redressing grievances and promoting social justice. This precipitated lengthy debate regarding endorsement of the Poor People's Campaign and March on Washington. In this and similar debates a primary concern of Gilbert's was to discern carefully the relationship of any specific policy or action to long-term goals. The range of choice among means to any given end dictated careful assessment of which measures were most appropriate, which actions or programs would be most efficacious, and, among these choices, which ones the AFSC was most qualified to do well.

Southeast Asia

In his personal life and academic career, Gilbert practiced careful selection of goals and the proper means to their achievement. In the early 1960s he fervently hoped that war in Southeast Asia could be avoided, and his distinguished role as a geographer advising a United Nations committee on cooperative economic management of the Mekong River complemented and added credence to his AFSC leadership during the Vietnam era. Beginning in 1961 he chaired a four-person Ford Foundation mission, representing the Netherlands, United Kingdom, and United States, that advised a U.N. Mekong River Committee comprising representatives of Cambodia, Laos, Thailand, and Vietnam—the countries that shared the lower Mekong drainage basin. (The Ford Foundation's mission's mandate and recommendations are discussed in more detail in Chapter 7.) Gilbert learned much from the Mekong assignment, including one particularly critical lesson: that planning for the use and development of any major international river basin involves shared interests so fundamental to human welfare that they demand cooperative effort even among political adversaries. Gilbert used the Mekong to illustrate to his AFSC audience the magnitude of the global challenge:

> We must learn something that no nation or group of nations yet has mastered: the art of helping others to improve their lot even as differences between them grow. In a world increasingly organized on principles of individual and national equality, this will be a staggering test of sensitive understanding, cooperation, and communication.

Gilbert propounded this lesson eloquently in an article titled "Vietnam: The Fourth Course" (1964a), in which he advocated ambitious pursuit of Mekong cooperation as a fourth alternative to attempting to contain the Vietcong and Pathet Lao guerrillas, carrying the war to North Vietnam to try to cut off support of those guerrillas, or endeavoring to neutralize the region with a U.N. peacekeeping force. The Mekong collaboration involved nations on both sides of the unfolding war, yet succeeded despite those political differences.

Copies of "Vietnam: The Fourth Course" were circulated with a cover letter on AFSC stationery to 1,150 carefully selected recipients. The committee received 165 replies, 92 from government, almost all of which were encouraging. Through contacts with the White House, the "Fourth Course" proposal reached President Lyndon Johnson, who incorporated the thesis into an address at Johns Hopkins University on April 7, 1965.[10] At that point several foundations and private businesses had pledged almost one billion dollars to the implementation of the plan adopted by the U.N. Mekong River Committee, and yet the total U.S. contribution to this endeavor was less than the cost of four days' military aid to South Vietnam. When President Johnson's personal papers were released three decades later, the world learned how deeply anguished he had become prior to entering the conflict against the Vietcong and carrying the war to North Vietnam. He was convinced that U.S. involvement was ill-conceived, that this was a war South Vietnam and its allies could not win. In view of this disclosure, Gilbert White never ceased wondering whether the initiative proposed by President Johnson might have reversed the march toward war, had Johnson received the proposal and the Ford Foundation report sooner. Such regret was somewhat assuaged, perhaps, and superceded by his ensuing heavy involvement with the Vietnam movement as a faculty member opposed to the University of Chicago administration's support of the war and as chair of the AFSC. Gilbert's involvements on both fronts peaked in 1968.

Opposition to the Vietnam War

If 1968 was the most turbulent and painful year in the United States between World War II and September 2001, it was also probably the most traumatic in the life of Gilbert White. In Vietnam the year began with the Tet Offensive by the Vietcong in January, which raised major questions about the U.S. ability to pursue this war in Southeast Asia. In the United States, Martin Luther King, Jr., and Robert F. Kennedy were assassinated in April and June, respectively. Over 200 campus demonstrations sparked by Vietnam and racial tensions occurred between the particularly violent demonstration organized by Students for a Democratic Society (SDS) in April at Columbia University and the riots surrounding the August Democratic National Convention in Chicago (Boyer 1999).

Even prior to 1968, the University of Chicago had experienced a large number of student sit-ins concerning issues of student prerogative and authority. The university, under President George Beadle, was one of the schools most in support of U.S. military involvement in Southeast Asia. Despite his love for his alma mater, Gilbert became one of the university's most outspoken critics. Since his first year at Chicago, Gilbert had served as faculty adviser to the campus Peace Club, and in April 1967 he had participated in a Vietnam teach-in, one-month prior to receiving the Quantrell Award for excellence in undergraduate instruction. One week following this honor, Edward Levi, at that time dean of the Law School, telephoned Gilbert and asked his assessment of the campus mood regarding Vietnam: Should the administration take seriously the rumors of an impending Vietnam "study-in" with the potential to disrupt the campus at semester's end? Gilbert excused himself from comment, since he had to catch a plane to Philadelphia to attend his son Will's commencement at Haverford. Despite Levi and White having been classmates and close friends throughout their secondary, college, and graduate schooling at Chicago, the war strained their friendship.

The campus was surprisingly quiet during the tumultuous Democratic National Convention in Chicago, and it remained calm throughout most of the fall semester. However, student involvement in campus governance continued to be a significant political issue. At the November meeting of the university's Committee on Academic Affairs, Gilbert voted with the majority, first, to invite the faculty and student body to appoint two representatives each to attend meetings of the University trustees and, second, to invite student representation at committee meetings. Later that month Edward Levi was promoted to provost. Members of SDS attempted to disrupt Levi's inaugural dinner, and one month later there was strong student reaction to a university decision not to renew the contract of a sociology professor, Marlene Dixon, popular with students active in the SDS. When students failed to persuade the administration to involve students in a review of this decision, hundreds of students occupied the Administration Building on January 29, 1969. Under pressure from vocal senior faculty to call in the police, Levi responded, instead, by threatening severe administrative sanctions, including expulsion, against protestors. By the end of the first day of the sit-in, 116 summonses to disciplinary hearings had been issued. The stalemate continued for over two weeks, at which point the 175 students still in the Administration Building withdrew.

The ensuing two months of debate over the fairness of the disciplinary measures gradually involved more of the faculty, including Gilbert, who organized a silent vigil in front of the administration building. Sixty-five faculty participated in the hour-long vigil, and over 100 signed the circulated petition explaining that "we stand in silence to express our concern with the effects which recent disciplinary actions are having upon our students and upon the life of the University. We oppose the irregular procedures of the disciplinary committee and the harshness and inconsistency of the sentences imposed" (quoted in Boyer 1999).

The Whites' youngest daughter, Frances, had joined the sit-in, and now her father was the principal spokesman for senior faculty opposed to the administration's actions. In a personal letter to Levi, Gilbert protested the administration's position on the matter and expressed his deep disappointment with the university's open endorsement of the war. Levi was incensed and unforgiving. Despite efforts by both the Whites and Mrs. Levi to heal the breach, Levi remained aloof and unapproachable to Gilbert from then on, even at a chance encounter at an alumni social gathering many years later.[11]

∝

ALTHOUGH RECOGNIZED on campus for his stand against the war, Gilbert was even more prominent nationally for this opposition as chair of the AFSC. On May 5, 1968, he headed a White House vigil with 1,400 sympathizers, including most board members and East Coast staff of the AFSC. Following a meeting for worship at the Florida Avenue Friends Meeting House, at 11:30 in the morning the group marched silently two by two to the White House, standing silently until 4:00 that afternoon. President Richard Nixon had been apprised of the group's plans and had been invited to discuss the conduct of the war with Gilbert and four other vigil participants. Nixon arranged for Henry Kissinger, his national security adviser, to stand in for him. The delegation used the opportunity to tell Kissinger about efforts being made to alleviate civilian suffering on both sides of the conflict.

The most visible effort was a prosthetic center in Quang Ngai, which manufactured and distributed prostheses to 3,000 civilians who had lost limbs in the war.[12] But the AFSC, the Canadian Friends Service Committee, and the Friends Service Council in England also had been trying to determine a means for providing critical medical supplies, especially penicillin, to civilian health care providers in North Vietnam. At issue for the Americans was whether to await a license from the Commerce and State Departments to join legally in this collaborative endeavor. Seven months earlier, when they had met with State Department officials, Gilbert and two colleagues had been told that a decision would be forthcoming in forty to fifty days. Because that time had elapsed, Gilbert hoped that he could use the meeting with Kissinger to gain help. But Kissinger likewise asked for more time, three to six months, and added that if the United States had not commenced pulling out of Vietnam by then, the protestors could "kick down the gates" of the White House. He was tight-lipped about policies, agreeing only to a subsequent July meeting with the group. Unwilling to delay further the shipment of medical supplies already assembled, the AFSC decided to continue shipping through the Canadian Friends Service Committee to the International Committee of the Red Cross for delivery to health officials in Hanoi. (By the time the State Department's decision was received in January 1969, rejecting the request, the AFSC had shipped in this

Gilbert talking with reporters at the May vigil after meeting with Henry Kissinger. Photo courtesy of Theodore Hetzel.

circuitous manner $100,000 in supplies to civilian health care providers in regions controlled by the National Liberation Front as well as to Hanoi.)[13]

The May audience with Henry Kissinger led to subsequent meetings between him and AFSC representatives over the ensuing seventeen months. Kissinger appeared intrigued with the rapport Quakers had achieved with leadership on both sides of the conflict and tried to use these informal, off-the-record dialogues to listen—even obliquely respond—to North Vietnam's concerns. The AFSC delegation returned from the last of these meetings very pessimistic. Kissinger had stressed the administration's fear that any U.S. withdrawal from the region would produce a domino spread of communism to neighboring countries.[14]

AFSC opposition to the war only increased with the threatened erosion of civil liberties as both the war and opposition to U.S. military involvement escalated. Gilbert represented the AFSC in testifying before a Senate committee that was hearing congressional proposals to restrict or remove tax exemptions for contributions to not-for-profit organizations opposing the war. Governor Wallace of Alabama had been particularly outspoken in calling for withdrawal of AFSC's tax-exempt status. However, the AFSC efforts to gain support and meet the threat to freedom of speech were successful, with organizations such as the Rockefeller Foundation joining Gilbert's defense of the AFSC.[15]

At the March 1969 AFSC board meeting, Gilbert announced his desire to step down as chair by autumn. Even those closest to the Whites had not anticipated the announcement. "The ensuing silence was so deep you could have heard a pin drop" (Tjossem 2001). Gilbert's decision resulted in part from the same concerns over procedures and program priorities that he had brought with him initially. He had periodically reminded his colleagues of these concerns in committee deliberations, but he had resisted using his chairmanship to lobby for resolution of these issues behind the scenes. He remained faithful to his charge as clerk and to the process of discerning the group's collective judgments. After he had offered his counsel for the last time in the January and February meetings, he chose to step aside.[16] The AFSC was a beleaguered organization in the late 1960s, losing funding in some quarters while gaining new support in others because of the divisive issues in which it was involved. The effectiveness of its work, of its "witness," might be compromised if the criticisms of the head of the organization became public. Accordingly, not even Philadelphians in staff and board leadership positions were privy to Gilbert's reasons for resigning.[17]

During his tenure as chair, and again briefly from 1972 to 1975 when he acceded to Stephen Cary's urging to serve a three-year stint on the board, Gilbert felt that the agenda of the AFSC was unwisely determined more by staff than by the board.[18] He also felt that the gradual decline in numbers of American Quakers was in part the consequence of reduced opportunities for voluntary service and career development available to Quakers through the AFSC. Many, perhaps a majority, of those associated with the AFSC at midcentury (like Anne White) had learned of Quakerism and in many instances had become members of the Society of Friends as a result of voluntary service during high school or college in AFSC-sponsored work camps. The AFSC largely abandoned the work camp program during the 1960s for reasons that Stephen Cary considered valid, albeit unfortunate. They included working primarily in minority communities whose residents became resentful of help volunteered by wealthy outsiders when the communities' own youth did not have jobs and could not participate, and dealing with issues concerning drugs and sex, with which Quaker youth sometimes were ill-prepared to cope when thrust into different subcultures and societies (Cary 2001).

Simultaneously, in the 1960s, the AFSC strongly embraced affirmative action, recruiting staff and volunteers in numbers proportional to national averages of not only racial and ethnic minorities but also gays. In much of middle America where persons openly homosexual were frequently discriminated against in hiring, the AFSC seemed almost a sanctuary to many gays and lesbians. Some regional offices responded to the inequities and discrimination by altering their hiring practices, ironically alienating other Quakers, who objected to this apparent favoritism in staffing (Tjossem 2001).

Gilbert's concerns about the staffing composition of the AFSC and service opportunities for Friends did not abate. In 2003, when the chairmanship transferred to Paul Lacey, retired from the faculty of Earlham College, former chairs were queried for any counsel they might wish to share with Lacey in his role. Gilbert took the opportunity to inquire into the percentage of AFSC staff who were members of the Society of Friends and the number of young people who had served for a week or more in service projects the previous year. Lacey's research revealed that 57 of the roughly 400 staff, worldwide, or slightly more than 15 percent were members. The additional number who attended Friends meetings and might thereby consider themselves to be Quakers was undetermined.

As for the numbers of youth under eighteen years of age annually involved in AFSC projects, ranging from weekly and monthly gatherings to pursue peace and social justice work to weekend workshops and conferences (including young children involved in service activities, such as gathering funds or assembling school kits for Afghanistan, etc.), the total number was estimated at 2,000. As for work camps specifically, most AFSC involvement involved cosponsorship with assorted Friends congregations and was a "very small aspect of AFSC work."

> I am sorry the AFSC has not found an adequate replacement for the work camps, interns in industry and interns in mental hospitals which were so powerful a learning opportunity in the past. I have not given up the hope that we will find the right form of service projects for the AFSC in the near future. At a Board meeting last year, I asked for a show of hands of those who had first encountered AFSC while in high school. . . . A substantial majority of Board members had first encountered AFSC between grade school and college (Lacey 2003).

Moving from the AFSC to Voluntary Service Opportunities

Gilbert and Anne persisted in their search for meaningful service opportunities for the young as actively after Gilbert's employment with the AFSC as they had before. For Quaker youth in the western states, the network of Friends meetings succeeded in establishing work camps among Native Americans. On a much larger stage, in late 1960 and early 1961, as John F. Kennedy campaigned for president and then assumed that office, Gilbert served on an advisory "Point Four Youth Corps" study committee. In early 1960, Wisconsin representative Henry S. Reuss had sponsored legislation that eventually became an amendment to the Mutual Security Act passed later that year; it proposed a study of the "advisability and practicability" of a Point Four Youth Corps of young Americans willing to serve their country in public and private technical assistance missions outside the United States at a soldier's pay. Oregon senator Richard Neuberger sponsored an equivalent bill. Gilbert went to Washington to offer Reuss his support in lobbying for the legislation. It became law in August 1961, and the International Cooperation Administration (ICA) was mandated to oversee the exploratory study.

Under the umbrella of the ICA, the study committee examined a number of private initiatives, including the AFSC's Voluntary International Service Assignments (VISA), which consisted of two years' work abroad in Third World community development and empowerment (Collett 2002). Such work was not unique to the AFSC; VISA volunteers in some countries worked with papal volunteers from the Catholic Church who were serving in very similar roles. In the ICA deliberations Gilbert shared his concerns stemming from the AFSC's experience with the VISA program: (1) whether selection of volunteer applicants would benefit from sufficient information about applicants' abilities to perform useful work in a manner that would improve international relations and (2) whether interest in potential host countries would be sufficiently broad that a Youth Corps program would not be perceived as an extension of American foreign policy.[19]

Before the ICA committee could present its findings and recommendations, Kennedy's campaign organization took the idea and incorporated it into the young senator's presidential campaign. Polls indicated a very close race, and following Hubert Humphrey's suggestion, on October 14, 1960, Kennedy included the youth corps proposal in a speech at the University of Michigan. Although his plane arrived after midnight in Ann Arbor, a patient audience of several thousand received the idea so enthusiastically that Kennedy promised to unveil its details when speaking next in San Francisco. For one thing, Kennedy wanted a title for the program more inspiring than "Youth Corps." Earlier, Hubert Humphrey had suggested "Peace Corps," in legislation he had introduced in the Senate, despite Soviet "peace" mongering having discredited the term somewhat in the West. Kennedy accepted that name, seeing this as an opportunity for the United States to reclaim the term. In San Francisco one week prior to the election, Kennedy unveiled his Peace Corps proposal. It essentially nationalized the American Friends Service Committee's VISA program and offered two years of community service abroad (usually in rural areas), at the invitation of host countries (usually in the developing world), at subsistence wage for persons of college age or above.

On November 8, Kennedy was elected president, in part on the strength of his Peace Corps proposal. Indeed, the corps became the first legislation enacted by his administration, and Kennedy named Sergeant Shriver, his brother-in-law, as director. Shriver in turn invited Gilbert to join him as his assistant. The invitation was tempting, but Gilbert had only relatively recently returned to the University of Chicago, and the move did not seem wise.

Gilbert's selection for the Youth Corps ICA study committee resulted in part, he assumed, from his familiarity with AFSC voluntary service programs dating back to the Philadelphia inner-city work camps cosponsored, at his suggestion, by the three Quaker colleges in Philadelphia. But even at that time he had considerably more ambitious ideas concerning international voluntary service. In 1952 at the Twenty-First *New York Herald Tribune* Forum, Gilbert proposed what was essentially the Peace Corps, but internationalized under the United Nations (White 1952). In retrospect at century's end, given the success of the Peace Corps in

The White family enjoying their ranch vacation home in Sunshine Canyon, Boulder County, Colorado, in the late 1950s

Gilbert readying burros Peter and Jack for a family pack trip in Sunshine Canyon

providing both service opportunities to youth and useful assistance abroad, Gilbert chided himself for not urging its internationalization more actively when conditions might have been more favorable for U.N. sponsorship than in 1952, during the Korean War and the height of the Cold War.

Home and Family in the 1960s

Chapter 7 examines Gilbert's years at Chicago as a scientist and scholar concerned with natural hazards and, specifically, floodplain management in the United States. In the 1960s these interests and commitments, along with his Quaker public service, resulted in Gilbert being away from Chicago as much as he was at home. Even when he was at home, the long hours he devoted to university duties essentially meant that Anne parented single-handedly. Had any of the children elected to remain in Hyde Park during their high school years (instead of attending Scattergood School in Iowa), the demands upon Anne would have been considerable. As it was, she managed the household without domestic help, entertaining geography students and faculty when Gilbert was in town. Her strength of spirit was reflected in and nourished by the poetry she read and increasingly wrote. In 1961, when Gilbert was on his U.N. Mekong River Committee assignment in Southeast Asia, Anne wrote:

The Weather Here

I would the weather
Were yours as well as mine.
Snow in Denver
Can mean a mass of air
Soon cold in Chicago.
But half the world away
Has not this weather here.
However long I wait
Only the moon will circle
And turn a face from you to me.

Gilbert tried to combine multiple commitments when he traveled and consequently could be gone from Chicago for as many as ten weeks at a time. As the children's time in Chicago steadily lessened, Anne began to join Gilbert for at least some part of these trips. Together they toured North and East Africa, Japan, southern and central Europe, the Soviet Union, England, and the Yucatan peninsula in Mexico. In March 1968 they toured Germany in a Mercedes Benz they had ordered from Chicago and that they subsequently shipped home. The car was Gilbert's idea, and his children kidded him relentlessly about it, given all his parental admonitions about "living simply, that others may simply live."

Beginning in the summer of 1956, the family, with or without Gilbert, began spending summers in the mountains of Colorado. At the time, Frances was experiencing severe attacks of asthma, and a high, dry retreat during the summer provided relief. Gilbert had become familiar with the Front Range of Colorado's Rocky Mountains through speaking engagements in Denver and Boulder, and the family hoped to locate a rural property with housing in the foothills above Boulder that could be rented during the summers. Gilbert coveted for his children ranch experiences similar to what he had enjoyed in his youth. Upon inquiry among the several graduate students from Colorado, he happily learned through Jackie Beyer (his first Ph.D. student) that friends of hers had spent the previous summer living in the home of Leonard and Bea Wittemyer in Sunshine Canyon while the Wittemyer family herded their cattle to higher pastures. Gilbert learned that indeed the Wittemyers were interested in renting their place for the summer in return for care of a stallion and any sick animals not up to the trek to summer grazing lands. Gilbert and Leonard quickly struck a deal, and over the course of the summer the White children helped round up cattle and brand calves before herding them to summer pasture. Soon thereafter, the family purchased a neighboring property, hoping to build there eventually.

The impetus to build came sooner than expected; a couple of winters thereafter a fire damaged the Wittemyer home. The following summer the Whites rented another house near their property, while they constructed a modest cabin. (That home eventually was replaced by a year-round home in Sunshine Canyon above Boulder when the family moved to Colorado in 1970.)

Throughout Gilbert and Anne's marriage, the home in Sunshine Canyon helped to maintain and strengthen family ties, even as the children moved to the East and West Coasts. It was not only the house that provided the family a sense of place and belonging but also a succession of much-loved horses that carried family members along familiar trails to their favorite places in the hills, occasional donkeys, and invariably a dog. In fact, Gilbert owes the last four decades of his life to one of those family pets, a Rhodesian Ridgeback dog named Shona that Mary brought from Oakland in 1969.

One very cold autumn evening, returning home from his Boulder office in a blizzard, Gilbert's Jeep stalled in snowdrifts a quarter-mile from home. Thinking he could make it home on foot, he set off up the steep driveway, only to pass out due to hypothermia still a considerable distance from the house. Because telephone service had broken down and Gilbert kept irregular office hours, Anne was not concerned about his being late until Shona became agitated, prompting Anne to open the door to let the dog out. The dog took off across the field, and Anne followed with a flashlight. She found Shona licking her husband's face. Gilbert regained consciousness, returned home, and fully recovered. No one knew what to make of Shona's intuition, but the dog's anxiety and Anne's decision to follow him were certainly serendipitous.

Drawers of Water

Both Gilbert and Anne treasured the summers they spent in their first cabin up Sunshine Canyon, but they may have cherished even more the time they spent together conducting research for their landmark study of domestic water use in East Africa. The couple first discussed conducting scholarly research together in 1964, when they celebrated their twentieth wedding anniversary at the Indiana dunes on Lake Michigan's southern shore. "We spent the 28th of April in the rain with hepatica, trillium, claytonia, marsh marigold, and kink cabbage," Gilbert recalled. He also recalled his grandmother Julia's advice to seek interesting and useful things to do with his wife. "Good marriages depend on doing more together than rubbing tummies," she counseled. With Frances, the youngest child, entering Scattergood School that fall, the time seemed propitious for an ambitious, collaborative undertaking.

The following January Anne joined Gilbert for five weeks in Uganda before he continued on to Southeast Asia. While in Egypt and East Africa conferring on the Aswan Dam and the challenges posed by human occupancy of arid zones, Gilbert began to consider an approach to understanding these problems: Why not study in detail the decision-making process of obtaining water for domestic use? Obtaining and using water represented perhaps the oldest and most widespread human decisions about the environment. They were traditionally the domain of women, and East Africa was ideal for such a study. The region offered cultural variations in social organization, a range of economic differences in rural and urban standards of living, and remarkable environmental diversity—from dry grasslands to tropical rain forest. The Whites had finally found the opportunity they had long sought to work together. In November 1964 Gilbert returned to East Africa to help plan a proposed merger of several small, struggling, East African universities that had been established when their nations gained independence. Specifically, he had been hired by the Carnegie Foundation to assist business managers of the universities in developing a budget for the proposed merger. Gilbert was chosen for this unusual assignment because of his successful leadership in earlier cooperative ventures among Haverford, Swarthmore, and Bryn Mawr Colleges that were funded by Carnegie. Gilbert had agreed to serve on the board of Makerere College in Kampala, and at a banquet for college personnel and visiting dignitaries, he found himself seated beside David Bradley, a visiting medical researcher from London studying schistosomiasis. The two soon realized that they had converging interests in the Whites' proposed study of domestic water procurement and usage. Bradley suggested that the survey consider water purity as a variable in the selection of sources of drinking water and that it include an analysis of the effects of those choices on subsequent contamination and

Left: Two of Tanzania's "drawers of water" interviewed during fieldwork

Below: Anne with children in Kenya during fieldwork for the Drawers of Water *volume, late 1960s*

household health. Since Bradley was on long-term assignment to Makerere, funded by the Rockefeller Foundation, his participation would not only be valuable but also affordable. By happy coincidence Gilbert also had $50,000 available in unsolicited Rockefeller funding for research of his choosing.

Much of that money was spent hiring and training personnel. Anne's experience conducting surveys while working for the Department of Agriculture and the National Labor Relations Board led to her managing the study survey—both questionnaire design and administration. The study involved a cultural challenge, since those doing the interviewing would be male and those being interviewed (the "drawers of water") would be women in most of the households examined. Anne was able to enhance the accuracy of data gathered by anticipating and investigating the barriers to easy communication that this dilemma presented. She also assisted with data compilation and analysis back in Chicago.

In the spring of 1965 Anne and Gilbert returned to Kampala for ten weeks, joining Bradley in refining the research methodology and selecting and training thirteen student assistants from universities in Dar es Salaam, Nairobi, and Kampala. As part of the instruction, Anne directed two weeks of training in gathering reliable data. To verify that students were digesting the instruction, Anne and Gilbert set up an experiment in which Gilbert broke into the room during Anne's lecture to request her help with a car accident. He gave a host of details rapidly, including instructions to her, which he had noted on paper in advance. As she dismissed the class some time later, she pretended to have forgotten the details of the accident and Gilbert's instructions and asked students to remind her what he had said. They initially claimed to know nothing. Polite custom dictated that the students demonstrate oblivion to everything going on in their presence if it involved higher-status Caucasians. But then Anne informed the students that they were being tested and that she really needed to know exactly what they recalled. On paper each student wrote down what he remembered, and to the Whites' pleasant surprise, all remembered virtually verbatim everything that Gilbert had said. Once trained to the Whites' satisfaction, these students traveled terraces, forest trails, and city streets visiting 700 households in 34 rural and urban sites in Tanzania, Kenya, and Uganda.

The three researchers analyzed the resulting extensive data over the next three and a half years, heavily involving the University of Chicago's fledgling statistical lab in processing the study's many boxes of punch cards. The major challenge of measuring the health costs of water procurement and use decisions fell largely to Bradley. In the end, *Drawers of Water: Domestic Water Use in East Africa* (White, Bradley, and White 1972) provided more precise information than had ever been gathered previously in the developing world on household decisions in selecting sources and quantities of water; the costs incurred in time, calories, and money; and the health implications of the choices made. The findings were shared both with the households surveyed and international agencies concerned with domestic water projects.[20]

A decade later, in 1982, a Peace Corps water technician working in Kenya read *Drawers of Water* and found it directly relevant to his work. John Thompson wondered what had changed in those thirty-four field sites since the Whites and David Bradley did their study. Several years later, Thompson was studying at the Graduate School of Clark University in Massachusetts and fortuitously met Anne and Gilbert when they were campus visitors. Thompson asked if they had ever considered revisiting East Africa for a longitudinal restudy. In Thompson's recollection, Gilbert responded, "You know, we have thought about it, but we think it might be something more fitting for a younger person to pursue."

> With their and David Bradley's endorsement, that is precisely what I did. I mounted two attempts to repeat the study in its entirety. The first effort, in the late 1980s, ended in disaster thanks to the lack of vision of one particular international agency that will remain unnamed here. It would be another ten years before I managed to launch a second attempt. This time we were successful. . . . Why stick with a project that has taken nearly twenty years to complete? Not only because I think the issue—how people use water and the determinants of that use—is worth investigating in its own right. And not simply because Gilbert and Anne maintained meticulous records that have given us a unique baseline from which we are able to measure change in use over time. But also because, through all the many highs and lows, the periods of financial and institutional uncertainty, Gilbert, Anne, and David stuck with us. Gilbert, in particular, provided not only intellectual guidance and moral support, but also financial assistance as well. In fact, he gave us our first seed grant to help get the project off the ground. Without his vision, commitment, and patience, *Drawers of Water II* would never have gotten off the ground (Thompson 2001).

Development agencies in England, Denmark, Sweden, and the Netherlands funded the replication study in 1997 at precisely the same sites. The behavioral adjustments generated by the initial study constituted exactly the kind of postaudit Gilbert always championed. A team from London, Dar es Salaam, Kampala, and Nairobi reported their findings at the Rockefeller Bellagio Center in Italy in 2001. Gilbert and David Bradley attended, and they provided the preface to *Drawers of Water II* (Thompson et al. 2002).

The Children and Their Father

With both parents involved for so many years with the East African research, the White children began to take greater notice of and appreciate their parents' careers. Indeed, it may have been only after they left home and began building their own careers that Will, Mary, and Frances understood the remarkable accomplishments of their parents, in particular those of the father who was so often away during their childhood and adolescence. How do children come to regard a parent's accomplishments as any more significant than those of their friends' parents in academia? Certainly not from perusing esoteric academic journals. For Will and Mary the revelation of Gilbert's standing among his peers came when they read a September 1968 article in the *New Yorker* by Gerald Jones. It was based on an interview with their father in which Gilbert reported what the American Friends Service Committee had been doing in Vietnam as well as within the United States to address social problems. The children's appreciation also increased as they watched their father decline a series of invitations while at Chicago to take on new positions and tasks. In addition to the Peace Corp job under Sergeant Shriver, John D. Rockefeller invited Gilbert to join the Population Council as executive vice president, while the Rockefeller Foundation suggested a visiting professorship at the Rockefeller Institute. Resources for the Future, which Gilbert chaired for many years, also proposed that he assume its vice presidency for science and coordination, and Stewart Udall, secretary of the interior under Kennedy and Johnson, offered Gilbert the directorship of the Water Resources Council. As Gilbert's children became young adults, their growing appreciation of their father's civic and scholarly work helped heal any sorrow, pain, or feelings of neglect they might have had. In retrospect they concurred that although Gilbert might not have been available as regularly as they needed, when he could, he gave them his undivided attention. For example, in an effort to utilize to better advantage the limited time at home he did enjoy, Gilbert (who rarely cooked) whenever possible on Sunday evenings prepared grilled cheese sandwiches and parfaits for the family.

Notes

1. Earlier, following his release by the Nazis and subsequent return to the states, Gilbert had been asked by Clarence Pickett to evaluate a large downtown residence in Washington that had been offered to the AFSC. The committee felt that an AFSC conference center at a convenient location in the capital could serve multiple uses. Gilbert conducted an extensive assessment, concluding that the high cost of utilities would prove prohibitive. Shortly before Gilbert was inducted into Washington's Cosmos Club after he had become president of Haverford, the club purchased and relocated to this property at 2121 Massachusetts Avenue, N.W. It immediately became Gilbert's favorite home away from home when in Washington. In the meantime, the AFSC acquired the less grandiose Davis House at 1822 R Street, N.W., and it became his second-most-frequented Washington location in the ensuing decades.

2. When he returned home to the University of Colorado, Gilbert's public reenactment of the AFSC delegation's reception in China was memorable. Dressed in the formal attire of the delegation's government guide, Gilbert mimicked their host's inscrutable effusion and polite, although totally uninformative, responses to the delegation's carefully crafted questions. It was one of the few times when Gilbert, the passionate admirer of theater, stepped out of character and publicly revealed his acting skills.

3. The first of several Conferences for Diplomats in nonaligned Sweden focusing on Cold War tensions followed on the heels of the initial ENUWAR conference (discussed in the next section), also held in Sweden. At the QUNO-sponsored Conference for Diplomats, the American ambassador heading the U.S. delegation was at first reserved, even defensive. He quickly reassured the Quaker hosts that they should not think "that we don't talk to the Soviets." But he warmed and soon was actively talking with his Soviet counterpart. At the end of the conference, he thanked the hosts, saying, "Thank you very much. This was different!" (Collett 2002).

4. William Roberts was a key contact in this network of funding sources for SCOPE endeavors. Loaned initially by the National Research Council of the National Academy of Sciences to assist SCOPE as Gilbert's presidential assistant, Roberts subsequently joined the Andrew Mellon Foundation, where he continued to assist Gilbert in obtaining environmental program funding. Through Roberts's efforts Gilbert secured an endowment that helped preserve Resources for the Future when the Ford Foundation withdrew most of its RFF funding during Gilbert's tenure as chair of that organization, 1974–1979.

5. The Meeting's most prominent member at the time was Senator Paul Douglas, a member of the university faculty, whom Gilbert recalls slipping into the rear of the meeting room as unobtrusively as possible on Sunday mornings, hoping that his presence would not be noticed by members who were inclined to use the hour of unprogrammed worship to lobby their legislator. (In Quaker worship, anyone is free to "speak from the silence" to share promptings of the spirit, which not infrequently might be better characterized as secular promptings of the mind. This latitude could easily degenerate into discussion and debate, were it not considered improper to respond in kind to such secular thoughts and to speak more than once in any given meeting for worship.)

6. Gilbert and Anne's son Will, in particular, blossomed at Scattergood, going on to Haverford College and Harvard. He studied for three months at Cambridge prior to alternative service as a conscientious objector at Massachusetts General Hospital from 1968 to 1970. At Scattergood, the White's oldest daughter, Mary, found her calling in the arts, subsequently studying in London and receiving her master's in fine arts at the California College of Arts and Crafts before commencing a lifelong career in glass sculpture and eventually ecoart. Frances studied cultural anthropology after Scattergood, attending the College of the University of Chicago before obtaining her doctorate in cultural anthropology at the University of Wisconsin.

   Throughout the decade that the children attended Scattergood, Anne White participated actively in governance of the school, serving as the governing committee's chair for several of those years. Kale and Helen Williams, among the Whites' closest Hyde Park friends, shared the driving between Chicago and Iowa City, since their children also attended Scattergood. Kale was executive secretary of the Chicago American Friends Service Committee throughout most of the Whites' years in Chicago and was a helpful confidant to Gilbert during Gilbert's chairmanship of the national board of the AFSC.

7. The meeting was interrupted by news of the assassination of President John F. Kennedy (JFK), producing (as Gilbert recorded in his daily notes that evening) "a

shock and pall beyond any expectation." Visiting their daughter, Mary, at Scattergood the following week, Gilbert and Anne found her shaken by JFK's death and questioning the utility of working for anything anymore. All service institutions—Scattergood School and the AFSC alike—were now faced with the challenge of channeling the despair and anger of the nation's youth.

8. Five years into Gilbert's term as leader of the AFSC, the organization took steps to strengthen the authority of the governing board. The committee revised its bylaws in November 1968, providing for (1) fewer but longer corporation meetings, (2) more authority mandated to the Executive Committee, (3) the appointment of corporation members (rather than simple nomination) by Quaker Meetings across the nation, and (4) a smaller corporation with advisory powers more clearly specified.

9. Stephen Cary was asked to serve as interim executive secretary following the early resignation of William Lotspeich (due to illness that soon took his life) and the selection of Bronson Clark as his successor. As mentioned, the leadership styles of Clark and White were quite different. When asked during an interview for this biography, "What was Gilbert's relationship with Bronson during the one year of their overlapping tenures as Chairman and Executive Secretary?" Stephen Cary replied, "I don't think it was very good. Bronson was very charismatic, very black and white. He spoke vigorously, always trying to validate his position. Gilbert has told me that the selection committee made a mistake in choosing Bronson over me. It wasn't the thing to do in Quaker culture to seek a leadership role. I wanted the position. I knew that Gilbert's and Bronson's relationship wasn't very strong. Bronson reflected the very things that Gilbert was unhappy about" (Cary 2001).

10. "Neither independence nor human dignity will ever be won by arms alone. It also requires the works of peace. The American people have helped generously in times past in these works, and now there must be a much more massive effort to improve the life of man in the conflict-torn corner of the world. The first step is for the countries of Southeast Asia to associate themselves in a greatly expanded cooperative effort for development. . . . For our part I will ask the Congress to join in a billion-dollar American investment in this effort as soon as it is under way. And I would hope that all other industrialized countries—including the Soviet Union—will join in this effort to replace despair with hope and terror with progress" (speech by Lyndon Johnson, reprinted in Raskin and Fall 1965).

11. One of Gilbert's colleagues related how divisive these events were. In March 1969 Gilbert had accepted an offer to join the University of Colorado, one month before informing Provost Levi of that decision. Learning of it from Levi, Dean of Social Sciences D. Gale Johnson expressed his deep regret over Gilbert's departure and the loss it would mean to the Department of Geography and the social sciences. However, upon learning subsequently of Gilbert's role in organizing the faculty vigil and drafting the petition, Johnson confided to a mutual friend that it was high time Gilbert left (Harris 2001).

12. The 3,000 amputees fitted with prostheses represented just 10 percent of the civilians handicapped by the fighting. The volunteer physician who initiated the program trained Vietnamese to make and fit the prostheses. In association with the prosthetic

center, a day care center was also established by David and Mary Stickney, codirectors of the AFSC presence in South Vietnam that provided preschool care and education for seventy-five children under Vietnamese supervision.

13. Then Executive Secretary of the AFSC Bronson Clark recalls this drama in his autobiography: "David Stickney (director of the Quang Ngai prostheses program) had gone to Saigon to interpret our actions to the Ministry of Health of the Saigon government and to the United States Ambassador, Ellsworth Bunker. Later Gilbert White, Charles Read, and I met with Under-Secretary of State William Bundy to inform him of our action. I recall this meeting vividly. Gilbert White had known William Bundy for years and informed him that as religious organizations, the American Friends Service Committee and the Quakers did not allow the U.S. government to decide to whom they would make humanitarian shipments. William Bundy looked absolutely thunderstruck!" (Clark 1997).

14. "The administration appeared to us to have a rigidity that made it unable to respond creatively to the growing public clamor against the war. This did not bode well for an early end of the war or for the avoidance of confrontations here in the United States. Unknown to us, there would not be another meeting. Major escalations of the war were shortly underway, not the least of which was the bombing and invasion of Cambodia" (Clark 1997).

15. Other tax issues also concerned the American Friends Service Committee. The AFSC filed suit contesting the requirement that employers withhold estimated taxes for the Internal Revenue Service, including the portion supporting the war, which some employees wished to deny the government. A 1971 decision in favor of the AFSC by the U.S. District Court, Eastern Division of Pennsylvania, was upheld by the Federal Court of Appeals in 1974 before being overturned by the Supreme Court later that year on the grounds that the government's right to withhold taxes could not be impinged. At about the same time the government imposed a telephone tax, in part to fund the war, precipitating considerable debate among the AFSC board, which finally concluded that loss of telephone service because of nonpayment of the tax would result in too heavy of an impact on other dimensions of AFSC work (Clark 1997).

16. On January 31, 1969, Gilbert addressed a memorandum to the Program Perspectives Committee at the board's request after the personnel secretary's verbal report to the board at a January 24–25 meeting apprised the board of those recommendations. The result of Gilbert's actions was some reordering of program priorities by the Program Perspectives Committee, orchestrated by Stephen Cary. These reordered priorities, elevating attention to service opportunities for Quakers, were passed along to the board. Gilbert's position—that service work should be found to fit the needs and desires of concerned individuals, not vice versa—clearly was a minority view, and even Stephen Cary remained unconvinced. When questioned about the memorandum (reproduced below), Cary replied, "As to the issue of whether the AFSC role is to be the servant of the Society of Friends, addressing Quakerism's service needs, or a representative of the Society to the wider world, I have differed fundamentally with Gilbert on this. I think we needed to address the world's needs, and the first 30 years we did this in relief work with the excel-

lent help of folks like Gilbert. I think we needed to move into the wider social changes occurring globally at mid-century" (Cary 2001). Gilbert's memorandum stated:

> The Personnel Department report at the Board's January meeting seemed to me to pose the basic question which the Board should face regularly: to what extent should AFSC seek to provide channels for service for concerned people in contrast to undertaking work which it considers to be socially significant. Obviously, no activity ever falls wholly into one class or the other: it is the emphasis that is important. I strongly feel that the emphasis should be on providing channels for service. Were this view to be accepted— and I realize it is not at present—it would leave the Committee with responsibility for looking for ways of meeting the expressed needs of the young people, the intermediate professional group, and the retired people about whom we heard at the Board meeting.
>
> At this point, two other questions are pertinent. One is whether possible solutions should be offered as a plan, or as a range of possible alternatives among which choice could be expressed? Here, I would favor a process by which the Board and other responsible groups would be presented with a range of choice in a preliminary fashion. But what of the process? Again, I would favor a process that placed emphasis on decentralized decision making so far as practicable. Such emphasis would stress devices of the types we have discussed before: e.g., spread of choice among regional offices, expressions of preference by givers, grant of bequest funds for non-renewable projects, invitation to local groups to submit their own proposals, encouragement of activities such as draft counseling which become self-supporting and are continued only as local enthusiasm permits, and various others. It seems to me that much of our machinery already is adjustable to this style of decision-making, and that a fundamental choice is between that and the style toward which we have been drifting steadily, centralized setting of social priorities.

17. Most of the AFSC leaders from that era were no longer alive when interviews were conducted for this biography, but Stephen Cary, acting executive secretary during the tumultuous year of 1968, consented to two helpful interviews before his death (Cary 1999, 2001).

18. The second interview with Stephen Cary began with a suggestion by the author that he focus on the issue of AFSC organization, specifically the division of responsibility between staff and board that increasingly concerned Gilbert during his years as board chair in the 1960s. Cary replied, "I thought he was more concerned about the trend toward decentralized decision-making, the shift of autonomy to regions. And this decentralization continues to be contentious. I don't think we can be criticized for endeavoring to centralize power in Philadelphia when we're working with $35 to $40,000,000 and upwards of 500 employees worldwide. We have to have structure. We haven't built in bureaucratic structures as the way opens, but only as they have closed in behind us. We badly need controls over who speaks for the whole. As to whether staff are too central, I think they are. The board hasn't been willing to exercise due control. And Gilbert in my opinion was correct in his belief that the right balance has not been struck. This currently is being worked on very hard."

19. In 1987 Gilbert and Anne, to replace their earlier Sunshine Canyon mountain abode, purchased a cabin retreat near Allenspark, Colorado, above Boulder, only a few miles from the summer residence of fellow scientist and humanitarian, Maurice Albertson,

professor of civil engineering at Colorado State University (CSU). Albertson had served as principal staff member on the ICA Point Four Youth Corps Committee, and CSU became the first recipient of funding to implement that committee's recommendations. Reuss's original legislation had provided only $10,000 in federal funding on the assumption that private funding would be forthcoming for such a popular initiative. Albertson and his assistant Pauline Birky obtained $25,000 in additional funding from the Rosenthal Foundation, enabling them to launch feasibility studies in pilot locations in ten countries on four continents. Albertson conducted the feasibility assessments in three Asian countries, and CSU colleagues carried them out in South America and Africa (assisted in Africa by Albert Schweitzer). Albertson subsequently launched at CSU the first and longest continuous Peace Corps training program in the nation (Albertson 2003; Birky-Kreutzer 2003).

20. Robert Kates and Ian Burton, in Volume 1 of their two-volume festschrift in White's honor, *Geography, Resources, and Environment* (1986), give useful introductions to three of White's seminal publications dealing with the range of choices regarding use of resources and formation of public attitudes. *Drawers of Water* is one of those three publications. The excerpts that Kates and Burton provide offer a useful introduction not only to this East African research but also to the wider theoretical issues of decision making and risk perception regarding natural resources and the hazards they can represent.

Norman Moline, when a graduate student under Gilbert White at the University of Chicago in the 1960s, was introduced to Gilbert's decision-making model (or framework for analyzing decisions about human uses of environments). Moline subsequently summarized it succinctly for his own teaching in the following handout for students (Moline 2001):

> A broad problem in resource management is explaining why resource use differs from place to place. We are not concerned here with the larger question of why a particular type of farming localizes in a given region or why urban use concentrates in a particular river valley. We are asking only why a particular course of action is chosen among those possible and why this choice is often different from choices made in other places with relatively similar environments. The answers can come only in a framework of decision-making which includes economic efficiency but is not restricted to it.
>
> One possible decision-making schema includes consideration of six basic elements that apparently enter into decisions involving natural resources. One element is the perception which persons have of the theoretical range of choices open to them. This theoretical choice can be defined as the choices which have been made in all similar environments plus an unanticipated innovation. Second is the perception which persons have of the physical characteristics and processes related to the resources in question. For example, the perceptions of the average citizen, the trained scientist, and the government official may be radically different. A third element is the technology perceived by the person, i.e., to what extent does he have command of the technology available for use in the particular resource situation. Fourth is the person's perception of economic efficiency, both generally and specifically, to the given resource use question. A fifth element is his recognition of the extent of spatial

linkages between his action and resource use in other areas. Finally, all of these elements are affected by a complex of social constraints including official governmental statutes as well as the less tangible but equally as real societal norms and values.

This model is descriptive rather than normative. It simply states that conditions necessary to making a decision are: (1) the choice is, in fact, perceived as a choice; (2) no obstacle is seen to it on grounds of physical processes, available technology, economic efficiency, and wider spatial impacts; and (3) social institutions do not block its adoption.

The Many Faces of Gilbert at Work

Top: In this 1960s meeting of the High School Geography Project, Gilbert uses the conference recess for "consensus building."

Bottom left: Gilbert at work in the president's office, Haverford College

Bottom right: Gilbert, the globe-trotting chair of the Geography Department at the University of Chicago. During his fifteen years at Chicago he made several dozen trips abroad.

Top: One of Gilbert's many impromptu chats with students on the campus of the University of Colorado

Middle: Gilbert with Mohamed Kassas and Martin Holdgate, co-authors of The World Environment, 1972–1982: A Report by the United Nations Environment Programme.

Bottom: U.S. Forest Service Advisory Committee field trip, 1968

7 The Battle over Floodplain Management

When I asked if they had ever considered looking into a floodplain
to see what happened there, as distinct from computing the losses that
would be experienced or averted, they said they weren't interested
in that.

—GFW

T HE WHITES' FIFTEEN YEARS IN CHICAGO, from 1955 to 1969, were pivotal both for Gilbert's career and for floodplain management in the United States. In 1966 he chaired a federal task force under President Lyndon Johnson that made floodplain management a priority within the federal government and contributed to the 1968 legislation establishing the National Flood Insurance Program (NFIP), probably the most important—and most contentious—legislation with which Gilbert was ever involved. How the nation decided to undertake this ambitious and problematic flood loss mitigation program and how Gilbert, after being away for two decades from the issue of federal involvement in river and floodplain management, reentered the debate in a leadership role, are the focus of this chapter.

A Return to Floodplain Management

The Flood Control Act of 1936 was both the evolutionary outcome of various attempts at flood control legislation over the previous decade and an immediate response to severe flooding in many locations in the United States in 1935 and in the northeastern states in 1936. The act and its subsequent amendments established structural adjustments (i.e., dams, levees, seawalls, etc.) as the principal federal approach to the management of floods. These sometimes ambitious and often expensive programs were undertaken primarily by the U.S. Army Corps of Engineers and the Soil Conservation Service. The Corps alone would build 300 dams and their reservoirs in the following years. By midcentury, federal expenditures for dams and levees under construction or authorized since 1936 had surpassed the prior total federal outlay for such structures since 1776. By 1960 the Corps had expended $3.8 billion, and another $5 billion had been authorized. Despite massive engineering efforts to control rivers, however, property losses due to flooding had not abated. Accordingly, in 1961 the Corps requested an additional $6 billion for river flood control and $500 million for coastal hurricane mitigation. The dilemma was heightened by the

National Resources Planning Board having lost its battle to implement coordinated, unified mitigation efforts among federal agencies. Even the NRPB's modest goal of persuading the National Weather Service, Soil Conservation Service, and Corps to adopt uniform modes of obtaining flood damage data had failed.

Unfortunately, two things would have to occur before the controversy regarding the best approach to floodplain management would be renewed: (1) floodplains below the new dams and their reservoirs or along levees would have to become occupied with homes and businesses assumed safe from flooding; and (2) one or more of those structures would have to fail, resulting in costly flooding on the resettled floodplains. In other words, a disastrous rainfall—while unlikely in the short run, a virtual certainty in the long run—had to occur. Sadly, every significant advance toward unified floodplain management has come at the cost of lives and property. Fortunately, by the 1960s improvement in early warning systems had led to a steady decrease in loss of life, even as property losses continued to increase at a disturbing pace.

As implied, the security generated by dams and levees was, and remains, an illusion. In planning such structures, the designers have to make decisions regarding the severity of flooding to be controlled. Over time, planning agencies generally agreed that the standard for such engineering projects would be the containment needed to handle the maximum rainfall and flow recorded in a given river basin during the previous 100 years. In at least two respects the resulting structures supported unwise occupancy of floodplains. First, the standard resulted in maps that established boundaries of maximum projected flooding outside of which human occupancy was deemed safe. Since this mapping was done on the basis of flooding events that occurred on average once per century, they were, at the least, of limited use and, at the most, disastrously misleading when flooding occurred greater than the projected 100-year flood. Moreover, an illogical (but not uncommon) assumption regarding a 100-year flood was and is that such a flood will occur only once in a century. In fact, the 1-in-100 probability remains the same every year, meaning that a city could experience two floods of that magnitude in consecutive years (or even in one year!) as likely as it could experience them a century apart. The probability in any given flood season remains 1 in 100, regardless of prior occurrences.

Second, precision in mapping floodplain vulnerability to any given magnitude of precipitation (e.g., a 50-, 100-, or 500-year flood) depends on the analysis of the entire drainage basin's absorption and runoff potential. Such analysis must consider soil types and vegetation, erosion and consequent impairment of runoff (silting of rivers and reservoirs), wetlands or other temporary overflow catchments, and interference with natural absorption due to human changes in the landscape (e.g., agriculture and associated drainage systems, highways, and paved urban areas). Obviously, maps of floodplain vulnerability must be regularly updated if they are to provide any reliability, particularly when humans encroach on the floodplain—the more development, the less soil absorption and the more rapidly runoff swells creeks and rivers. Perhaps less obvious, the effects downstream are only compounded by changes upstream. Keeping floodplain maps current and in the hands of municipal officials, planners, builders, insurance companies, and present and potential property owners is an enormous challenge, requiring local, state, and national cooperation if this approach is to be successful in managing the nation's floodplains and flooding.

Two serendipitous events coincided with Gilbert's return to Chicago and his renewed interest in this problem. First, apart from flooding on the Columbia River in 1948 and the Kansas and Missouri Rivers in 1951, there had been few disastrous floods in the United States since White left Washington in 1941, compared to the decade before and the decade ahead. Hence, while Gilbert was in Europe and at Haverford, the continued dominance of the structural approach to flood control had not been seriously questioned. When disastrous flooding recurred, beginning in 1954 in New England due to hurricanes, public doubt about that approach returned, just as Gilbert was resuming his academic career in geography. In a sense, with respect to his scholarly interests and career, he had chosen probably the most expendable fifteen years to work with the American Friends Service Committee and Haverford College.

Second, with the dissolution of the National Resources Planning Board shortly after Gilbert's departure from Washington, the government had come to rely less and less on academic expertise and consultation concerning natural resources. No other discipline or organization had assumed the leadership roles that geography and the University of Chicago held in the 1930s. When, in the late 1950s and 1960s, governmental agencies again began seeking scholarly advice, Gilbert White and the University of Chicago Geography Department were not only available but supplied with an agenda.

At the same time, other scholars and universities also became significantly involved. In particular, Harvard University political science professor Arthur Maass also worked with the Corps and related federal agencies on natural resources management. Maass's influential 1951 publication, *Muddy Waters: The Army Engineers and the Nation's Rivers,* incorporated and disseminated widely some of the ideas Gilbert had set forth in his dissertation, *Human Adjustment to Floods* (White 1945). That dissertation had been circulated in limited quantities by the Geography Department during the 1940s and did not receive wide distribution until its republication in 1954. Arthur Maass's choice of Harold Ickes, the former Public Works Administrator under FDR and long-time opponent of the Corps, to write the introduction to *Muddy Waters,* may in part explain the mixed, sometimes cold reception within the Corps of Maass's seminal publication. Ickes could not conceal his antipathy for the Corps, placing an unnecessary hurdle in the way of the Corps' consideration of Maass's ideas.

To historian Marty Reuss, Gilbert summarized his own reservations:

I remember once meeting with the Harvard group for an examination of the way in which they were treating the economic analysis of flood loss reduction. . . . When I asked if they had ever considered looking into a floodplain to see what happened there, as distinct from computing the losses that would be experienced or averted, they said they weren't interested in that; that wasn't a part of the kind of analysis that they were pursuing and that they were training people to pursue. That was typical, I would say, of the economic analysis that was going on. You didn't, for an irrigation project, go in and look at the quality of life of the farmers. You looked at what you could tally up on returns from crop production or sales. . . . This is significant but one would also like to know what the production has been on that field year after year, how this production may have been affected by flooding, not only in terms of crops lost but yields gained. And one would then want to know what sort of measures the farmer takes to optimize his returns from that field, including cultivation practices, the kind of seed he uses, any technical measures that he may take within the field to, for example, minimize scouring by stubble in the post-harvest season, and so on. This requires a different mode of examination than just collecting flood damage data (Reuss 1993a).

Following Gilbert's lead, two other hydrologists used their book, *Floods,* to move beyond conceptualization of disaster research as primarily measurement of flood events, their projected damage, and the potential reduction in flood losses (Hoyt and Langbein 1955). White judged Langbein in particular to be, at the time, the most original thinker regarding flooding. Happily, *Floods* also impressed Corps engineers and reinforced confidence in Gilbert's work. And ultimately the thinking of Maass and White converged a bit, both men significantly changing the way the Corps of Engineers addressed the problem of flooding.[1]

In the mid-1950s, however, the nation did not regularly incorporate nonstructural adjustments to flooding, such as flood-proofing, relocation, and insurance, within a broad program of floodplain management. Before that could happen, scientifically sound, user-friendly community floodplain studies that included accurate, regularly updated maps of at-risk areas had to be carried out. And, again, even before that, agreement had to be reached on the magnitude of flooding upon which to base such maps (i.e., the magnitude within which development would be restricted) and on the level of projected water rise on the margins of flood-zoned areas that would be deemed manageable through flood-proofing of structures in those areas. Finally, but perhaps most critically, the many agencies with vested interest in floodplain management needed to be in general agreement on approaches, priorities, and necessary legislation.

The agencies in the best position to take the lead on these issues and establish such criteria with community leaders and policy makers were the Corps of Engineers, which had regional offices in all major river basins of the nation, and the

Tennessee Valley Authority, which had been responsible since 1933 for 40,000 square miles of the Tennessee River basin in seven states. As discussed earlier, there had been considerable competition between these two agencies since the founding of the TVA. Harold Ickes, secretary of the interior when the TVA was established, was suspicious of the Corps' influence in Congress, and Arthur Morgan, director of TVA, was so hostile toward the Corps that he publicly opposed even Gilbert's efforts to mediate (Reuss 1993a). Morgan's intransigence and opposition to a growing emphasis on hydropower production led to his dismissal. In contrast, Gilbert was convinced early in his stay in Washington that cooperation not only with these agencies, but also with the Bureau of Reclamation and the Soil Conservation Service, was essential for any effective program of river basin management. Once he had settled into his role as chair of the Geography Department at Chicago, he began looking for opportunities to promote interagency dialogue and to enlist support for his research agenda.

Because of his many contacts within the Corps and TVA, Gilbert gained the assistance of both. The TVA, like the Corps, had relied heavily on dams and levees for flood control whenever economically feasible. Fortunately, with its regional planning group of roughly thirty scientists, including geographers, TVA had gathered extensive data on past floods in the basin and investigated the potential magnitude of future floods. Moreover, TVA personnel had good working relationships with state and local governments. Gilbert saw the opportunity to enlist TVA assistance in developing for the Tennessee basin the kinds of community data that would ultimately be needed for all basins in the United States. Aldred (Flash) Gray, director of the TVA Regional Studies staff, knew Gilbert's writings and as a geographer understood his ideas. However, to complement Gilbert's social science approach, the TVA (and Gilbert) needed an engineer to manage the technical issues involved in defining local flood problems. Gray hired James Goddard, a TVA engineer trained in both hydraulics and mapping who also was a believer in nonstructural mitigation.

Goddard directed TVA's Community Flood Damage Mitigation Assistance Program. The program identified 150 communities in the basin with known flood problems and helped them compile the local flood hazard information needed to develop floodplain maps and, ultimately, floodplain management plans. The endeavor represented several giant steps toward more effective mitigation of flood losses, and it was the first to use the term "floodplain management." It established the size flood to be protected against: initially a 50-year but ultimately, by the mid-1970s, a 100-year event (with some pressure from Gilbert White and a few others to consider 500-year floods as well). Additionally, 1 foot of floodwater at the margins of zoned floodplains was judged to be the maximum acceptable depth for purposes of mitigation planning. Early in the 1960s Goddard and White arranged for White's University of Chicago graduate student, Jack Sheaffer, to conduct dissertation research on the "flood-proofing" of marginal properties where up to 1 foot of flooding could be anticipated. Flood-proofing mitigation strategies included blocking openings into structures, raising structures, or moving the control systems of heating/cooling and related electrical systems to higher levels within buildings (Sheaffer 1960). Working at this nuts-and-bolts level of planning, Goddard and White became close friends, with Goddard continuing as an ally in promoting their shared belief in nonstructural floodplain management the remainder of his career.[2]

To further strengthen his own relationship with the Corps of Engineers, White suggested that the Corps allow a senior technical staff member to conduct research in the Geography Department at Chicago. His objective was to have a knowledgeable Corps member check at an early stage the department's findings and methods and thereby to increase the credibility of those findings within the Corps (Reuss 1993a). The Corps selected Francis Murphy from their Seattle District, a flood control engineer for twenty years who had been impressed with White's dissertation. In his book-length report following his year of study, Murphy told his Corps colleagues exactly what Gilbert had hoped: that 2,000 communities needed flood-risk maps that delineated hazard areas, plus standards and guidelines for building codes. The maps, he asserted, could be prepared at an average cost of $10,000. Murphy's detailed recommendations, while received with some ambivalence within the Corps, were incorporated in draft legislation for Congress submitted in October 1958 by the Corps' Civil Works Directorate.[3]

These recommendations were mirrored in most respects by the TVA's parallel draft legislation submitted to Congress five months later. A notable difference was Murphy's and the Corps' endorsement of federal subsidization of any flood insurance program. Goddard and White believed that federal financial support would only hasten encroachment into floodplains and exacerbate the dilemma of increasing flood losses. This disagreement continues to this day.

To promote congressional action on these recommendations, Gilbert persuaded the Council of State Governments to hold a conference in Chicago before the end of the year on flood legislation. The council recommended that Congress direct one federal agency to take the lead but to cooperate with other agencies and state governments to produce evaluations and maps providing basic data on flood magnitude and frequency for flood risk areas. The General Assembly of States endorsed the council's recommendation, and under the Flood Control Act of 1960 the Corps was assigned this coordinating responsibility.

White then arranged concurrent publication by the Geography Department of Murphy's *Regulating Flood Plain Development* (Murphy 1958) and Chicago geographers' review of land-use histories of seventeen urban areas (White et al. 1958). This research, funded by Resources for the Future, examined what had happened in the nation's floodplains since the Flood Control Act of 1936 and Gilbert's dissertation research in those communities. Why—after twenty years and $4 billion in expenditures—had urban flood losses declined little, if at all? The concurrent publication of the two related books insured that those in a position to influence congressional action on the parallel Corps and TVA legislative initiatives would have plenty of documentation regarding the limitations of structural flood control and the need for broader, more comprehensive management of floodplains.

A workshop held in Chicago late in 1958, also funded by Resources for the Future, brought together representatives from the relevant federal agencies to discuss the findings of both the White and Murphy books. The participants learned that because of land-use pressures and the lack of incentives to stay out of floodplains, floodplain occupancy was increasing, even in areas where population was declining. The statistics were sobering. Although heavy investment in structural adjustments by the Corps was lowering property losses at the rate of about 3 percent annually, the potential for damage was growing at 2.7 percent because of encroachment on urban floodplains. The result was a negligible net decrease in annual losses. Each year, for every $6 of potential flood damage reduced by new flood protection measures, at least $5 in potential flood damage was added. The study concluded that the Corps of Engineers had become, despite its intentions, one of the major real estate development agencies in the country. On more than 650 urban floodplains, the Corps was encouraging occupancy as a result of dam and levee construction (reviewed in Moore and Moore 1989).

To gain detailed data on perceptions surrounding flooding and floodplain management, another team of Chicago graduate students fanned out across the United States in the early 1960s. They focused on six urban floodplains and were led by Gilbert's student Robert Kates and White himself, who worked in LaFollette, Tennessee (Kates 1962; White 1964b). The team included psychologists and sociologists who explored competing optimizing and subjective utility models, popular at the time, for predicting behavior. But those models proved of little use in predicting the seemingly irrational behavior surrounding flooding that the students observed in the field. Why would people, while recognizing differences in the hazard vulnerability of different parts of a floodplain, not incorporate those differences when assigning property values in the floodplain? Why would people often return to property severely damaged by flooding, when it was clear that after making repairs, they could well incur the same losses again? Moreover, since these perceptions differed from person to person, what factors accounted for the differences?

Economic loss and gain were salient factors, yet they did not adequately predict behavior unless personal experience and the quality of information available to individuals concerning hazard potential were also taken into account. Perhaps the most sobering finding was that the perceptions and judgments of resource managers at the local level could easily outweigh the judgments of scientists in the minds of citizens making private decisions about where and how to build in floodplains.

The increased understanding of why people were exposed to flooding provided by this study resulted in an increased realization of the need for collaboration and cooperation among local, state, and national agencies and institutions—of the need for truly unified national floodplain management. For such a program to be realized, Congress had to recognize the need for legislation and to allocate the requisite funds.

The Senate Select Committee on National Water Resources

A devastating series of floods, primarily caused by hurricanes, in seven of the twelve years from 1954 to 1965 resulted in several billion dollars in property damage, took more than 1,000 lives, and increased federal disaster assistance from $52 million in 1952 to $374 million in 1966. In part due to this string of floods, in 1959 the Senate established a Select Committee on National Water Resources, which for two years was the conduit to Congress for ideas and legislation regarding floodplain management. Theodore Schad, the committee's staff supervisor, brought Gilbert in as a consultant for informal conversations with the committee chair, Senator Robert Kerr of Oklahoma, to ascertain the contentious issues and opposing voices and what information would be most helpful to the committee. Gilbert then arranged workshops to facilitate the discussion among politicians, agency personnel, and scholars, building on friendships forged through years of informal discussions of ideas whose time appeared to have arrived.

The first legislation resulting from these deliberations was the Flood Control Act of 1960, which authorized the Corps to compile and disseminate information on floods and flood damage at the request of a state or local government agency. Up to $1 million annually would be available to compile and distribute these data, related engineering advice, and other technical assistance. Intended to encourage optimum use of river valleys, these Floodplain Information Studies would provide a basis for reducing damage and mitigating flood hazards through local regulation, land-use planning, and other means, including structural projects. The legislation clearly avoided committing the Corps to planning floodplain land use or regulation but strongly supported local community initiatives. Heeding Francis Murphy's advice, the designers of the studies chose to inform users through easily understood, nontechnical language and simple maps, charts, and carefully selected photographs. Moreover, reflecting Gilbert's penchant for distinguishing between cognitive and evaluative judgments, the reports were to state clearly what were matters of fact or observation and what were the judgments or estimates of those preparing the reports.

One of Gilbert's objectives in consulting with the Select Committee was to ensure that the TVA had an opportunity to share its experience in floodplain management. He clearly achieved that goal. The information supplied by the Corps borrowed substantially from the works of Goddard and White. Gilbert made sure

U.S. Senate Select Committee on National Water Resources, 1961. Gilbert is far right, staff supervisor Ted Schad is center rear, Abel Wolman is to Schad's right, and chairman Senator Robert Kerr is standing, left.

that copies of the University of Chicago research papers dealing with various aspects of floodplain regulation were sent to all Corps internal divisions and district offices. The bibliography in the Corps engineering manual, which described the Floodplain Information Studies program and directed its implementation, listed eighteen references: seven were products of Goddard's TVA work, and five came out of White's Chicago program. For legislation drafted largely by Corps personnel, such generous acknowledgment of TVA work was unprecedented, salutary, and a tribute to Gilbert's efforts to foster cooperation.

Gilbert assisted in drafting the Select Committee's final report, submitted in January 1961. Its recommendations included completing basinwide studies, establishing a grant program to states for water planning, creating a research program on water, conducting a biennial national water assessment, and taking steps to enhance water efficiency, including regulation of floodplain use and determination of flood hazards. In January 1961, John F. Kennedy was inaugurated, and unfortunately—in Gilbert's opinion—the new president promptly asked his cabinet secretaries involved with water resources to come up with a new plan for coordinated water development. The Select Committee's report was quickly superseded by

Senate Document 97. Compared to the Select Committee's report, Gilbert considered the Senate's substitution "pedestrian and unimaginative . . . a series of moderate adjustments of what had been the prevailing policy" (Reuss 1993a).

Perhaps because of the change in administration with Kennedy's death or because of opposition from competing agencies, one of the Select Committee recommendations closest to Gilbert's heart was painfully slow to be realized. Annually beginning in 1961, a Water Resources Council (WRC) to coordinate the work of all federal agencies involved in water management had been proposed, but the council was not established until 1965. The WRC consisted of the secretaries of the Army, the Department of Agriculture, the Department of the Interior, and the Department of Housing and Urban Development (HUD), and the chair of the Federal Power Commission. With the president's approval, the WRC could establish river basin planning commissions that would include representatives from federal agencies, states, and commissions involved in each basin. While opposition from various agencies and individuals to establishing TVA-like authorities for other major basins again prevented full realization of this goal, the WRC was empowered to establish the principles, standards, and procedures for developing comprehensive regional river basin plans.[4] Four years of congressional infighting had somewhat corrupted the original intent of the Select Committee's recommendations, but the fortuitous provision for state representation in river basin planning would have far-reaching benefits.

Perhaps most discouraging to Gilbert and many others who followed these legislative initiatives in the early 1960s was Congress's failure to address the critical issue of cost sharing. After the effort was abandoned to require project beneficiaries to pay half the cost of projects that raised land values, Gilbert became even more concerned that the flood control program, even under the WRC, would continue to be a program of land development through flood protection construction. The more things were changing, the more they remained the same.

Floodplain Management on a Local Scale: Chicago

Concurrently with these often discouraging federal efforts in the early 1960s, Gilbert was involved more encouragingly in local and international floodplain management. The Northeastern Illinois Metropolitan Planning Commission, created in the 1950s to plan Chicago-area growth, was persuaded by Gilbert to develop the first major metropolitan floodplain management plan, including comprehensive mapping of area floodplains. In the early 1960s he cochaired with Harold Gotaas the resultant planning committee and arranged for the technical assistance and funding needed for this ambitious undertaking. Several geography students (notably Jack Sheaffer and Shue Tuck Wong) were attached to the committee as research assistants. The Cook County Forest Preserve supplied financial support when they determined that they could advance their preservation goals once the mapping determined which land in hazardous areas should not be occupied. The U.S. Geological Survey provided technical assistance. Indeed, the survey team was eager to tackle this large project, since, with Gilbert's encouragement, it had recently completed mapping the much smaller Topeka, Kansas, floodplain. The Chicago regional project became a noteworthy example of using flood-prone lands to protect wildlife habitat and provide recreational opportunities and aesthetic pleasures, purposes beyond the traditional aims of residential and commercial development.

Gotaas and White's committee, with Sheaffer's assistance, also became involved with an interstate controversy between the State of Illinois (and the Metropolitan Sanitary District of Greater Chicago) and the States of Michigan, Minnesota, New York, Ohio, Pennsylvania, and Wisconsin, all of which share the water of the interconnecting Great Lakes. Chicago had sought the legal right to increase its diversion from Lake Michigan above the 1,700 cubic feet per second authorized by Congress in 1930 for Chicagoans' domestic use. The committee's report concluded that the 1,700 cubic feet per second would still meet Chicago's needs if leakage from pipes and faucets badly in need of repair was stemmed and if available ground and surface water in the region was properly treated and managed. The report, based on meticulous studies (some involving Chicago graduate students in geography), was accepted by the Northeastern Illinois Metropolitan Planning Commission, and the judge ruled in favor of the complainant riparian states (Gotaas and White 1966).

Floodplain Management on an International Scale: The Lower Mekong River Basin

Concurrently with his involvement with the Northeastern Illinois Metropolitan Planning Commission, Gilbert was invited to test in a much larger Southeast Asian context the thesis that guided Chicago's floodplain planning: that flood control as a principal goal should be supplanted by comprehensive floodplain management in order to achieve broader benefits for both society and the entire floodplain ecosystem. As mentioned in the previous chapter, he was invited in 1961 to chair a Ford Foundation mission, with representatives from the United States, United Kingdom, and Netherlands, to advise a United Nations Mekong River Committee. The U.N. committee comprised representatives from the four principal nations sharing the lower Mekong drainage basin: Laos, Cambodia, Thailand, and Vietnam. Roughly half of the 27 million people in these countries at that time lived in the river's drainage region.

The United Nations Economic Commission for Asia and the Far East (ECAFE) was concerned primarily with flood control when, in the early 1950s, it selected the Mekong from among East Asia's major rivers for detailed study. Research showed that the river had great potential to support hydropower generation and irrigated agricultural production if flooding could be controlled—a major "if," given the size and power of this, the third-largest river in Asia. The Mekong flows 2,625 miles

(Above) Gilbert with ECAFE director U Nyn in Bangkok and (left) at the Department of the Interior, Washington's liaison agency with both ECAFE and the Ford Foundation Lower Mekong Committee, 1960s. Photos courtesy of the Department of the Interior.

from its headwaters in the Tibetan Himalayas; its lower drainage (below the borders of China and what was at the time Burma) covers an area larger than France or Texas; and its minimum annual flow into the South China Sea at midcentury was 400 million acre-feet. Even at Phnom Penh, 190 miles from its mouth, the minimum annual flow was more than double the flow of North America's Columbia River at its mouth. Only about 3 percent of the lower Mekong's 235,000-square-mile basin was irrigated, no bridges crossed the river, and no dams spanned the main river or its principal tributaries.

Against this background, the Japanese government offered to do the reconnaissance requisite for potential dam construction on thirty-four tributaries in the lower Mekong River basin. In addition to outlining the possible hydroelectric and irrigation options, secondary considerations for flood control and navigation were included as well. "This report caused quite a sensation, and the governments of the four countries of the lower basin were extremely happy with the massive scale of the vision which had been outlined for the development of the lower Mekong and its tributaries" (Hori 2000). This comprehensive plan, emphasizing structural adjustments, was presented to Gilbert's Ford commission as they began their study.

White's commission was asked to assess the economic and social effects of that kind of Mekong development before a final plan for flood control and floodplain management was adopted. Very early, the commission became convinced that lessons from the United States and Europe would help the U.N. Mekong River Committee and ECAFE's Bureau of Flood Control (responsible for all East Asian waterways) avoid the more obvious mistakes made in North Atlantic river basin development. Subsequently, the commission was instrumental in convincing the U.N. Mekong River Committee that the construction of major dams for hydropower, especially on the main stem of the Mekong, should be preceded by cautious experimentation with smaller dams on one or more tributaries. This argument was well received, particularly since one of the goals of the U.N. Mekong River Committee was to extend navigation for commercial vessels from the lower 276 miles of the river to Luang Prabang, 1,000 miles inland. Increasing the navigable portion of the river would greatly stimulate foreign commerce with Laos and inland Thailand. Damming the Mekong would complicate such navigation.

The commission's other recommendations, which addressed planning to enhance opportunities for the poor and reforming education, were also well received. These challenges—poverty and education—were far different from those Gilbert and his colleagues had dealt with in North America and Europe. The poor were largely illiterate farmers whose greatest needs with respect to river development were engineering projects to desalinate and irrigate enormous expanses of waterlogged soils that had passed out of production. Even in Thailand, the most economically advanced of the four countries, the annual per capita income was less than $100. The great majority of the 20 million people who potentially would be affected by international management of the Mekong were agriculturalists living close to the margin of subsistence. The challenge in improving crop yields, and especially the overall production of rice, was to raise the standard of living not only for existing populations but also to keep pace with an annual population increase averaging 3 percent.

This challenge was considerable; increases in rice production averaged only 2 percent annually over the years immediately prior to the Ford Commission study. In reality, agriculture, including fishing, would provide only a partial solution. Other approaches, including the extraction and use of natural resources such as minerals and the development of small industry, would have to be included in any comprehensive program of meaningful development. Major changes would also have to be made in institutions and habits to effect a transition from an essentially agrarian society to one in which manufacturing played a significant role. With adult literacy at about 50 percent in Thailand and 20 percent in the other three nations (with comparable percentages of children in school), the needed transformation in educational institutions was daunting.

Inexpensive power was a basic requirement of all projected economic development, with hydroelectric energy the obvious solution. The Plain of Reeds project, involving a million hectares (2,470 million acres) in Vietnam and Cambodia, demonstrated the potential. Annually, in this region, soils were waterlogged for several months and then subject to drought when alum salts rose to the surface by capillary action and made growth of anything except marshy reeds impossible. However, with cheap electric power from Sambor, Cambodia, the Plain of Reeds could be pumped free of water during the waterlogged period. Then in dry months, fresh water from the Mekong River could be pumped into the area to keep the soil moist, thereby preventing the rise of alum salts and enabling the growth of rice and other crops.

The Ford Commission's recommendations on almost every front benefited from Gilbert's involvement with floodplain issues in the United States and from his 1950s leadership of a U.N. review of Africa's arid regions and soil degradation due to poorly managed irrigation. To the credit of the Japanese government, it accepted the judgment of the Ford Commission (and the decision of ECAFE) not to implement the Japanese recommendations for grandiose dams construction. In fact, Gilbert was invited to write the foreword for the resultant Japanese publication reviewing the Mekong's environment and history of development (Hori 2000).

By the beginning of the twenty-first century, there still had been no large dams erected on the lower Mekong. Instead, the primary flooding adjustments have been basinwide flood forecasting and warning systems based on a network of hundreds of hydrological and meteorological stations. Flood control has yielded to a much broader program of water management, including water quality monitoring, small-scale salinity control structures, and comprehensive ex post facto evaluations of multipurpose dams and reservoirs erected in northeastern Thailand in the 1960s and 1970s (Binson 1965). These postaudits were conducted using Gilbert's network of contacts (Wescoat and Halvorson 2000).

Gilbert was generally satisfied with the Ford Commission's report and his continuing involvement as consultant to the U.N. Mekong River Committee through 1970. As discussed in Chapter 6, however, he remained profoundly dissatisfied with the commission's efforts (too little, too late) to convince the United Nations to intervene and try to reduce the tensions between the governments of South Vietnam/Laos and guerrilla forces of the Vietcong/Pathet Lao. During the years Gilbert consulted with the Mekong Committee, the guerrillas never interfered with research or construction projects. By the early twenty-first century, the U.N. Mekong River Committee had survived forty years of recurring divisiveness among the participating governments, with only one interruption in plenary sessions in 1976–1977 when Cambodia temporarily withdrew.

Resources for the Future

In 1952 Gilbert attended a Ford Foundation conference that led to creation of an innovative research institute focusing on natural resources. With Ford Foundation financing, the experimental Resources for the Future (RFF) commenced conducting its own research (and facilitating related research by others) on primarily U.S. public policy concerning natural resources. With this mandate, RFF rapidly became an important source of personnel and funding for much of the work and conferences organized at the University of Chicago to promote wise floodplain management. Earlier in this chapter, such assistance was acknowledged in two contexts. In addition, economist John Krutilla was loaned by RFF to Gilbert's Mekong River Coordinating Committee.

In 1967 White joined the RFF Board of Trustees, becoming board chairman in 1974. During his five-year tenure as chair, the Ford Foundation decided to reduce its funding for environmental research. Ford proposed that RFF become a subunit of the Brookings Institution, and the foundation was willing to contribute $8 million to Brookings to help with the transition. But Gilbert and the board wanted to maintain RFF autonomy and opted to try to raise the $20 million endowment needed to establish RFF as a freestanding institution. Gilbert suggested that the Ford Foundation give RFF the same $8 million that would have gone to the Brookings Institution on the condition that RFF staff raise another $8 million to add to $4 million still available from Ford's previous five-year grant. The foundation agreed, and Gilbert spearheaded the successful acquisition of the matching $8 million, primarily from the Andrew W. Mellon, Rockefeller, Mott, and MacArthur

Foundations. That success enabled RFF, still autonomous, to celebrate in 2002 its fiftieth year of national and international research on natural resources.

In recognition of Gilbert's contributions to the legacy of RFF, a Gilbert F. White Postdoctoral Fellowship Program was endowed to enable social as well as natural scientists interested in policy-relevant interdisciplinary research to spend a year with RFF. A number of Gilbert's former students and colleagues have benefited from this opportunity.

The 1966 Task Force on Federal Flood Control Policy

In 1966 the Bureau of the Budget under President Lyndon Johnson, concerned about the inadequacy of federal flood control policies and programs, had requested a review of existing policies and an assessment of the feasibility of embarking on a federally managed flood insurance program. The BOB initially turned to RFF to conduct the study, but because RFF president Marion Clawson was already chairing a parallel Department of Health, Education, and Welfare task force requested by Congress, the BOB turned to White. Gilbert briefly considered a BOB proposal that he single-handedly prepare a report on the status of flood control before concluding that it would be a sterile enterprise with minimal influence. He then suggested that a task force be convened comprising representatives of the relevant federal agencies, plus a few experts on selected aspects of the complex undertaking. If the bureau agreed to that suggestion, he would select the personnel and serve as chair. The task force recommendations would go first to the BOB and from there to the agencies for comment. The BOB agreed to all points (Reuss 1993a).

This project was an optimal situation for Gilbert. He had the ear of the president through the BOB, a direct conduit to Congress through the associated task force chaired by close friend and like-minded Marion Clawson, and freedom to select his own task force. He asked a BOB officer, John R. Hadd, to serve as staff director for the task force and coaxed his friend Jim Goddard at the TVA to join the endeavor and assist in the selection of other members. They invited leaders from the U.S. Army Corps of Engineers, U.S. Geological Survey, Housing and Urban Development (HUD), and Department of Agriculture. Of these, the Corps was particularly important, and they selected Richard Hertzler as their representative, a man with whom Gilbert had worked in the 1930s. For a state government representative, White and Goddard turned to Irving Hand of the Commonwealth of Pennsylvania. Gilbert again invited RFF economist John Krutilla's participation, who joined Gilbert as the task force representatives from academia.

Between them, White and Goddard knew every member of the team. All were secure and respected in their agencies but not bound by agency loyalty or bureaucratic mindsets. (White was determined not to be impeded by agency loyalties as Harlan Barrows had been while chairing National Resources Planning Board committees in the 1930s.) Agency representatives would present the final draft of the task force's finding to their agencies and obtain official comments, but apart from that they were specifically instructed not to be constrained by their agencies' policies or biases. The group worked congenially and assiduously for almost a year.

When they completed their assignment, Gilbert arranged for a dinner of task force members and BOB staff to discuss the report's implications and probable effects. Gilbert then polished the final report (White [with the task force] 1966a) before its submission to the BOB for transmittal to the president and finally to Congress.

Gilbert's principal authorship of what became House Document 465 was apparent to anyone familiar with his ideas and his articulacy. For Gilbert's part, few accomplishments in his career brought as much satisfaction as this monumental step toward integrated floodplain management involving federal, state, local, and private cooperation. The first consequence of House Document 465 was Executive Order 11296 that mandated, for the first time, that federal agencies formally incorporate flood planning into their programs. Executive agencies were to take into account flood hazards when planning construction of new federal buildings, structures, roads, or other facilities and to apply flood-proofing measures whenever practical and economically feasible. Agencies responsible for federal grant, loan, or mortgage insurance programs were to evaluate flood hazards in order to minimize potential flood damage. The Corps was to prepare all flood hazard information reports except those within the Tennessee River basin, where the TVA would conduct the studies. The Corps obtained authorization to spend up to $7 million per year to prepare these reports (J. Wright 2000).

The title of the task force report, *A Unified National Program for Managing Flood Losses: Report by the Task Force on Federal Flood Control Policy,* was a subtle shift from the task force's original mandate from the Bureau of the Budget to assess flood control. Gilbert's personal preference was to avoid mention not only of flood control but of flood losses as well, emphasizing instead making the best use of floodplains. However, he acquiesced to colleagues' conviction that Congress and the public would want to see a focus on reducing the human costs of flooding. As it turned out, his preferred title would have been a misnomer, given subsequent developments.

Gilbert assumed that the nation would see some substantial changes in federal management of floodplains because the WRC now had President Johnson's support for a flood insurance program. Unfortunately, the very Bureau of the Budget that sought Gilbert's assistance was unable to let go of responsibilities the WRC had been created to centralize. Gilbert never got to the bottom of the problem, suspecting that someone within the bureau was obdurately resisting relinquishing authority to the WRC while unwilling to promote the report's recommendations himself. The result was halfhearted, intermittent activity within the BOB. White talked with bureau staff and even the director but never learned exactly why the WRC was denied the authority to promote its recommendations. Part of the answer, but only part, may have been BOB dissatisfaction with the WRC's penchant for costly and often unproductive "framework studies."[5]

Notes

1. Their contributions have been documented by Martin Reuss, a senior member of the Corps' Office of History. Reuss conducted lengthy interviews with both men (Reuss 1989, 1993a) and subsequently asked them to contribute their professional correspondence, papers, and extensive libraries of natural resources literature to the office when they retired. Both agreed, and in April 2001 a symposium was held in their honor, and the Maass-White Reference Room was inaugurated at the Corps' Institute for Water Resources at the Humphreys Engineer Center in Alexandria, Virginia. Their personal papers were stored and catalogued by the Office of History; the adjacent Institute for Water Resources contributed the Reference Room for their publications. White's papers alone fill shelves 6 feet high and 25 feet long.

2. In 1984 the Association of State Floodplain Managers (ASFPM) established the Goddard-White Award to honor outstanding contributions to floodplain management. As the ASFPM states on its website, "It is an indication of the level of esteem the Association holds for the two namesakes as well as the recipients, and is the Association's highest award." In 2002 it was bestowed on Jack Sheaffer for his lifelong commitment and contributions to nonstructural floodplain management.

3. Murphy warned, "There are indications that if the Corps of Engineers does not step forward and volunteer to assume this function, federal agencies much less capable of doing so will initiate programs that will prove wholly inadequate, yet preclude a subsequent adequate effort by the Corps" (Murphy 1958, quoted in Moore and Moore 1989). In a follow-up memorandum for internal Corps use, Murphy stated bluntly, "I was given the impression that Corps relations with local communities leave something to be desired. . . . There is a definite feeling that we are too dogmatic in our general attitude and in our presentation of engineering solutions. . . . We do not give local officials choices of alternative answers to problems but exhibit a 'take-it-or-leave-it' attitude" (Murphy 1959, quoted in Moore and Moore 1989).

4. "In principle, the Council had authority to establish uniform standards for evaluation and formulation of water projects by all federal planners, review plans from river basin commissions, and recommend changes in the entire federal water resources program. In practice, because the act specified that any institutions the Water Resources Council created would not replace or supersede the authorities of federal water resources agencies, final authority over water projects remained with Congress and the executive branch. In dealing with questions in the areas of cost allocation, cost sharing, and repayment for projects, therefore, the Water Resources Council could function only as a coordinating agency charged with the difficult task of reconciling longstanding interagency differences" (Moore and Moore 1989).

5. In 1985, when recalling his long involvement with the Bureau of the Budget, Gilbert observed, "I was unsympathetic with any effort to make the Bureau of the Budget more of a managerial agency because I was and am more traditional in the view of what the function of the Bureau office should be. I thought the Bureau office should be a very powerful group within the government, but that it should not be a genuinely managerial group" (Reuss 1993a).

8 The National Flood Insurance Program and the Natural Hazards Center

A flood insurance program is a tool that should be used expertly or not at all. Correctly applied, it could promote wise use of flood plains. Incorrectly applied, it could exacerbate the whole problem of flood losses.

—GFW

THE DRAFT OF GILBERT'S 1966 REPORT by the Task Force on Federal Flood Control Policy was reviewed favorably by all eighteen agencies with a vested interest in its recommendations, a tribute to the sense of ownership that the task force members had created in their respective agencies. Yet in achieving this broad consensus, Gilbert sacrificed few if any of his principal aims. The final report, *A Unified National Program for Managing Flood Losses,* which became House Document 465, was clearly his work, with gentle condemnation of past uneconomical uses of the nation's floodplains and cautionary observations regarding federal flood insurance.

Unquestionably, the political and social climate was more open to the implementation of a flood insurance program than ever before; a decade of severe river and particularly hurricane flooding compelled the government to do something to curb losses. Nonetheless, Gilbert strongly doubted that the nation was ready for the legislation that Congress finally enacted in 1968—the National Flood Insurance Act. That may appear paradoxical, given that the legislation flowed from the work of his own (BOB) as well as from the Clawson (HUD) parallel task forces. More to the point, Gilbert feared that sudden attention given nationally to federally subsidized flood insurance would divert attention from the broader goal of his task force recommendations: a "unified national program" for managing not only flood losses/flood control but also floodplains as ecosystems. Gilbert had acceded to the BOB's request for assistance because of his preoccupation with this overarching objective. With the less cautious advocacy for moving ahead with flood insurance contained in Clawson's parallel task force report to HUD, Gilbert feared that the cart had gotten ahead of the horse.

But who could know what lay ahead? There had been no such comprehensive experiment anywhere in the world. No one in 1968, including Gilbert White, could foresee all the ramifications of and obstacles to implementing a national flood insurance program. Nor could anyone fully grasp the magnitude of even greater challenges to achieving a unified, national program of floodplain management. And more encompassing yet would be wise management of river basins, the overly ambitious mandate of the Water Resources Council established several years ahead of the National Flood Insurance Program (NFIP). Therefore, before focusing on the NFIP in this chapter, the broader question of "what constituted integrated floodplain management in the mind of Gilbert White?" needs to be examined.

Admittedly, Gilbert's task force had addressed its mandate haltingly, given scientists' limited experience to that date in looking so holistically at nature's ecosystems. Accordingly, one must jump ahead from 1966 to 2003 for perhaps Gilbert's most succinct definition of what constitutes integrated floodplain management. The final book-length publication of Gilbert's career (with coauthor James Wescoat), *Water for Life,* has previously been mentioned. In it they list the seven major elements of comprehensive management of floodplain use. Some of them were well understood by Gilbert when chairing the 1966 task force and have been alluded to and elucidated in varying degrees earlier in this book. A few others become new topics later in this book. Briefly for now, the seven are:

> (1) mapping the estimated frequency and magnitude of flooding; (2) planning and regulation of use of vulnerable areas and of areas contributing to flood flows; (3) government support of insurance against flood losses; (4) improvement of flood warning systems and advice and training as to how to respond effectively to warning; (5) research and education as to how to floodproof property against damage; (6) extending the federal program of financial assistance to victims of flood damage, to include support for buying out damaged property to support abandonment of severely affected property and movement to lands beyond the reach of floods; and (7) taking explicit account of the costs and benefits to ecosystems and human recreation of leaving a floodplain completely open to water and silt from natural overflow (Wescoat and White 2003).

A federally managed insurance program is but one of the above seven, and accordingly Gilbert's task force addressed it only in passing in view of the centrality of insurance in the mandate of the Clawson task force. Gilbert's task force did support the conclusion that subsidized insurance was a necessary compromise between private risk bearing of flood losses and total assumption of losses by government. And the Clawson report proposed, as Gilbert hoped it would, that any such program be initiated on a limited trial basis in selected locations to determine its feasibility and consequences. An introductory statement of the White task force report offered the same caution:

> A flood insurance program is a tool that should be used expertly or not at all.
> Correctly applied, it could promote wise use of flood plains. Incorrectly applied, it

could exacerbate the whole problem of flood losses. For the Federal Government to subsidize low premium disaster insurance or provide insurance in which premiums are not proportionate to risk would be to invite economic waste of great magnitude (White 1966a).[1]

In the end Congress adopted the Clawson report's more ambitious recommendations regarding flood insurance, despite Gilbert's counsel. Congress established the NFIP, creating a Federal Insurance Administration (FIA), initially under HUD for its implementation. The NFIP's dual objectives were (1) to distribute flood losses among all occupants of hazardous floodplains through a program of federally subsidized insurance offered through the private sector and (2) to reduce losses by discouraging new development in floodplains. The latter would be achieved through state and local zoning ordinances, higher premiums for new construction than for old in floodplains, and eventually through selective acquisition of flood-prone property and relocation of the inhabitants of flooded property to homes and businesses on higher ground. The program would offer a quid pro quo: affordable flood insurance in return for community commitment and action to mitigate flood hazards (for example, enacting land-use controls). Losses presumably would thereby be reduced.

Congress did not altogether ignore the cautions mentioned in Gilbert's task force report. Congress attended to the recommendations that (1) communities be required to follow all floodplain management guidelines established by the FIA before being allowed to enroll in the insurance program and (2) that the cost of insuring any new construction in floodplains be actuarially based on the losses predicted for the new structure's location and elevation. However Gilbert's (and Clawson's) suggestion for an initial limited experimental program fell on deaf ears. The first administrator of the Federal Insurance Administration, George Bernstein, proceeded immediately to establish regional offices for a nationwide program. But lacking the maps needed to institute appropriate local regulations and with no established rates for the range of possible losses, in the first year only 4 of the estimated 20,000 at-risk communities enrolled in the program. Only twenty policies were sold.

Sorely disappointed, Gilbert described the program of studies that ensued as "a trough in which a number of engineering outfits fed. In my opinion [instead of hiring private engineering firms] they might have done much better to carry on a more modest program using, as was first envisioned, the Corps and Geological Survey for that purpose" (Reuss 1993a). He also faulted Bernstein for working almost exclusively through the regional offices that the FIA immediately established, rather than with preexisting state organizations that had ties to local communities and governmental bodies. Beyond these problems, the primary pitfall, in Gilbert's opinion, was a lack of appreciation for the need for individualization of community floodplain management programs, including the establishment of truly actuarial insurance rates based on the distinct flooding risks in each locality. A related problem was that all locations relied on one criterion—the 100-year flood—as the FIA pushed to make the program available as rapidly as possible. A monolithic national policy discouraged communities from looking at their unique flood problems and coming up with appropriate solutions suited to their individual issues, conditions, and history. Gilbert felt so strongly about this problem that he tried to meet with Bernstein to argue his point, but to no avail (Reuss 1993a).

By the second year, both Gilbert and the program had to accept that many communities would have to be given a temporary "emergency" exemption from the requirements of the program while flood hazard rate maps were developed. The maps would serve the dual purposes of identifying 100-year flood hazard areas that would require local management through land-use and building regulation and providing the information needed to calculate insurance premiums. Within five years, emergency enrollment in the NFIP mushroomed to over 2,000 communities. However, new construction was insurable at subsidized rates—setting the precedent Gilbert had most feared. Further, participation unfortunately remained voluntary until 1973; communities did not have to enroll in the NFIP, and individuals did not have to purchase insurance. But then in 1972 and 1973 hazard losses soared. Forty-eight presidential disasters were declared in 1972, all but three involving flooding. In 1973, tropical storm Agnes and flash flooding in Rapid City, South Dakota, resulted in $2.5 billion in federal disaster assistance for the year. Congress responded by passing the Flood Disasters Protection Act, which mandated county or community enrollment in the NFIP and the acquisition of insurance by owners of flood-prone property purchased using any kind of federal financing.

With these modifications in the program, NFIP enrollment accelerated. By mid-1984, 17,629 communities had joined, and almost two-thirds had graduated from "emergency" to "regular" status after mapping their floodplains and establishing actuarial rates tailored to their unique hazard profiles. Within those 17,629 communities, nearly 2 million policies were sold covering nearly $100 billion of flood-prone property. But claims for losses due to flooding throughout the 1970s were unexpectedly high, with payouts three times higher than income from premiums in 1979. In 1981, insurance rates went up and almost closed this gap. But at the same time, the mapping of the 10,000 communities that had requested this service was barely half complete, and the average cost per community study was $62,000, compared to just $27,000 three years before. Clearly, there was a great need to find more efficient ways to map flood-prone communities and then to update the maps.

The 1970s were a roller-coaster of successes and setbacks in pursuit of the 1968 legislative objectives. In 1975, in Minnesota, Gilbert presented a detailed "National Perspective" to a National Forum on the Future of the Flood Plain (White 1975b). Since many in the forum audience were already convinced of the problems, his remarks were considerably more blunt than those he offered later to a Senate committee reviewing the flood insurance program.[2] His strongest criticisms were directed at the Office of Management and Budget (formerly the Bureau of the Budget) and the

Water Resources Council, whose mandate since its founding a decade earlier had been to orchestrate river basin management. He noted that the WRC's anticipated report had been pending for six years because of the inability of the member federal agencies to reconcile their differences. He was less critical of the Corps of Engineers, noting that it was pursuing some alternatives to structural flood control. Additionally, the Council on Environmental Quality had taken a vigorous, positive stand regarding floodplain management, although it unfortunately had little influence on day-to-day management decisions. Gilbert had nothing positive to say, however, about the performances of the Soil Conservation Service and the Department of Housing and Urban Development, which oversaw the NFIP.

Even worse, all this foot-dragging went on while local land-use planning and development in potential flood areas was increasing at an unprecedented rate in response to the requirements of the insurance program. Technical assistance from state and federal agencies failed to keep pace. Not more than twenty states provided significant services to support the thousands of communities involved in the NFIP. Communities particularly needed sophisticated projections that plotted the likely costs and benefits of various flood adjustments. Gilbert's and Haas's own research, published that same year (White and Haas 1975), suggested several generalizations that warranted refinement. Their preliminary findings suggested that structural protection projects alone would foster net benefits in the short run while increasing the catastrophe potential. By comparison, relief and insurance alone would promote both increased net losses and catastrophe. Properly managed land use, however, had the potential to promote increased benefits while reducing the disruptive impact of the rare catastrophic event.

Whether talking to the private sector or to government, Gilbert never passed up an opportunity to decry government subsidies of insurance premiums; their size—90 percent on existing structures in 1975—only encouraged the maintenance of existing buildings in floodplains, even though the FIA was promoting abandonment and relocation of such structures. Looking ahead, Gilbert always reminded audiences that unless the FIA continually updated its maps of flood hazard areas to reflect development within and bordering floodplains (which, as suggested above, FIA procedures then encouraged), losses would never subside. He was optimistic that the costs of mapping could soon be reduced to one-fifth of their current price and therefore that mapping could increase fourfold with no increase in that budget allocation (White 1975b).

For the remainder of his career, Gilbert was both a critic of and cheerleader for the NFIP, a program for which he felt responsible. Still, Richard Krimm, an official with the FIA and Federal Emergency Management Agency for over three decades, from the birth of the NFIP until his retirement in 2000, observed that "despite the slow endorsement and implementation of available non-structural mitigation adjustments, we are less poorly off in these regards than would be the case had Gilbert White not made floodplain management his career goal these past seven decades. Losses in property, if not in lives, have steadily increased unfortunately, but were it not for Gilbert's commitment those losses in all likelihood would be substantially greater" (Krimm 2001).

In the late 1970s Gilbert participated in a small panel that recommended that the flood insurance program be transferred from HUD to the new Federal Emergency Management Agency within the executive branch. FEMA was established in late 1978 by Congress during the Carter administration, effectively merging by early 1979 the five agencies most concerned with national defense and disasters. In a related move to consolidate disaster mitigation efforts and postdisaster assistance, twelve federal agencies signed an interagency agreement to promote hazard mitigation under FEMA's leadership. President Jimmy Carter also asked Congress to authorize $35 million, to purchase more than 1,000 properties that had experienced repetitive flooding. In Gilbert's opinion, that was one of the most hopeful developments of the decade, building on the earlier 1974 Water Resources Act that had authorized the Corps of Engineers to protect the natural valley flood storage capacity of a watershed near Boston by buying several thousand acres of wetlands instead of trying to control the river. These precedents would not be widely emulated, however, until the 1990s.

International Collaboration and the Natural Hazards Center

Following the Whites' move from Chicago to Boulder, Colorado, in 1970, Gilbert's further involvement in floodplain management and the flood insurance program was closely tied to the Natural Hazards Research and Applications Information Center (NHRAIC, or Natural Hazards Center), which he founded at the University of Colorado in 1974. The center was created to ensure that academic research findings and other information about human adjustments to hazards, including the National Flood Insurance Program and integrated floodplain management, were transferred to the people who could use and benefit the most from that information (e.g., emergency managers, public officials, planners, and agency staff). The Natural Hazards Center was one more extension of White's agenda, reflecting his belief in the need to introduce applied research into the policy arena, and it broadened his influence greatly.

Leading up to his founding of the Natural Hazards Center, Gilbert was increasingly involved in interdisciplinary and international exploration of the interrelationships between human management of natural resources and the sustainability of those ecosystems. From 1966 to 1971, he chaired a United Nations Development Programme (UNDP) task force that examined a number of major water storage projects in the African Nile, Volta, Senegal, and Zambezi River drainages. In each case Gilbert headed an international mission to establish an action plan between the countries involved and UNDP to salvage large dam and reservoir projects that had been undertaken without adequate understanding of deleterious side effects.

The Soviet engineer in charge of constructing the High Aswan Dam in Egypt, for example, had once explained that his job was to build effectively, not to look at the dam's effects. White's task force recommended that a new research institute be established to study the likely problems posed by and for aquatic life in the lake being created by that dam (White 2002). This work led to Gilbert's ongoing consultation in the 1970s on the downstream effects of damming the Nile, and again in the 1980s on domestic water quality and quantity in developing countries (collaborating with Anne White in the case of Egypt).

৽

NATIONAL ASSOCIATIONS of geographers have their own association, the International Geographical Union (IGU). The IGU in turn participates in a number of other international, interdisciplinary associations, including the International Council of Scientific Unions. After serving in the early 1960s as president of the Association of American Geographers, Gilbert became involved with the IGU and ICSU, most notably with the IGU's Commission on Man and Environment, which he chaired from 1969 to 1976, and ICSU's Scientific Committee on Problems of the Environment, which, as mentioned earlier, he served as president from 1976 to 1982. His initial involvement with SCOPE and eventually its committees resulted from a decision by the IGU to designate its Commission on Man and Environment (and thus its chairman, Gilbert White) as IGU's liaison with SCOPE. Gilbert welcomed the assignment, which promptly led to his participation in a review of the environmental effects of human-made lakes and his organizing, with Chicago colleague William Ackermann, an international symposium on those issues.

A number of other colleagues and students at Chicago and later at Colorado became his associates in this international work. The first was his former student Ian Burton, of the University of Toronto, who, with scientists from Israel, the Soviet Union, Poland, and Japan, joined Gilbert on the Commission on Man and Environment. In addition, there were sixty-nine corresponding members from twenty-six countries involved peripherally. Gilbert felt that a principal purpose of the IGU was to apply geographic knowledge, experience, and analysis to understanding changes that humankind causes in the environment, avoiding deleterious changes, and improving the environment for the collective welfare of all life forms. The Commission on Man and Environment selected a few problems that could benefit from relatively prompt analysis by geographers working with scientists in other fields, using the following criteria: problems should relate to human use and misuse of the environment; geographic experience and analysis should apply directly; and geographers should be available to take the lead in bringing together and disseminating the relevant research.

The commission selected eight issues to examine: technology's impact on the environment, national nature reserves, environmental changes on the urban fringe, environmental constraints on economic development, natural hazards research,

Chicago students Robert Kates (left) and Ian Burton (right) with Gilbert outside Rosenwald Hall, home of the Geography Department in the "windy city," 1990s.

mapping of environmental perturbations (including the mapping of environmental hazards), river basin development, and man-environment theory. Gilbert's former student Robert Kates from Clark University in Massachusetts cochaired the subcommittee working on the last issue, which underlay all the other problems.

Kates, Burton, and their mentor Gilbert White became an abiding triumvirate in hazard research over the next three decades. Gilbert often led the trio, with his broad perspective and ability to secure the resources needed to tackle significant problems, including both funding and able, committed students. Indeed, Gilbert was renowned for his recruitment and especially his training of these young people. He sought out the best and then elicited their best through his extraordinary example, friendly persuasion, and high expectations. For Gilbert, science involved both discerning what is worth doing and finding people equal to the task. "One of the common and commonly destructive questions about research runs, 'But is it geography?'" he once said. "I would like to see us substitute, 'Is it significant?' and 'Are you competent to deal with it?'" (Kates and Burton 1986, vol. 1).

With funding from the Commission on Man and Environment, in 1969 Kates, Burton, and White launched the first comprehensive scientific review of local, national, and global hazards. With the help of students and associates, they initiated field studies in thirteen nations, which examined cyclone response in two countries, floods in five, drought in seven, snow problems in three, frost in two areas of the United States, volcanic eruption in Hawaii, and earthquakes in California. Two major publications resulted from this research: *Natural Hazards: Local, National, and Global* (White, ed. 1974) and *The Environment as Hazard* (Burton, Kates, and

White 1978). The latter provided the philosophical basis and model for interpreting the case studies of the former. The royalties from both were assigned to the IGU. A separate set of studies, headed by Burton, dealt with responses to air pollution in the urban environments of five countries.

The five questions that White had raised initially with respect to flooding in the United States were now asked regarding the whole gamut of natural hazards globally: What is the nature of the physical hazards involved in extreme events? What types of adjustments has humankind made to those hazards? What is the total range of possible adjustments that people theoretically could make? What accounts for the differences in adoption of adjustments from place to place? What would be the effect of changing public policy insofar as it constitutes a social guide to the conditions in which individuals or groups choose among adjustments?

To address this ambitious agenda of interdisciplinary and international work, which had outgrown any one departmental affiliation, Gilbert needed a congenial academic base. Serendipitously, the ideal home was looking for occupants.

The University of Colorado

A decade earlier, the University of Colorado had launched the interdisciplinary Institute of Behavioral Science (IBS) and had obtained funding from the National Science Foundation's Center for Excellence program to recruit eminent scholars. The renowned economist Kenneth Boulding was one of the first academicians to relocate (from Michigan), and he suggested that Gilbert be invited to join to succeed the outgoing IBS chairperson.

Two years after joining IBS and assuming a professorship in geography at the University of Colorado, Gilbert and sociologist Eugene Haas proposed a national assessment of natural hazards research to provide "a more nearly balanced and comprehensive basis for judging the probable social utility of allocation of funds and personnel of various types of research ... and stimulate, in the process, a more systematic appraisal of research needs by scientific investigators in cooperation with the users of their findings" (White et al. 1975). They received funding from the National Science Foundation's new program for "research applied to national needs" (RANN) and embarked on an ambitious review of available knowledge about avalanche, coastal erosion, drought, earthquake, flood, frost, hail, hurricane, landslide, lightning, tornado, tsunami (tidal wave), urban snow, volcano, wildfire, and wind hazards.

The timing was propitious; the assessment's national visibility and potential to influence public policy were assured because of ongoing congressional debate and a 1973 White House "Report on Federal Disaster Preparedness and Assistance" that followed the coastal and inland flooding brought on by tropical storm Agnes and flash flooding in Rapid City mentioned earlier. Not surprisingly, the principal question the assessment would address was, again, why economic losses from disasters continued to rise despite massive federal expenditures on hazard reduction programs. Echoing Gilbert's thesis that federal disaster aid was as much a problem as a solution in this regard, the 1973 White House report complained that federal disaster assistance had become counterproductive because it replaced rather than supplemented nonfederal state and local efforts.

The RANN funding supported a host of master's theses and doctoral dissertations. Students teamed with experts, both scholars and practitioners, and their work resulted in a series of monographs spanning the entire range of natural hazards. In all, thirty investigative staff (primarily graduate students) were involved, with both Ian Burton and Robert Kates serving as regular consultants. In addition, the study relied on an advisory committee of fourteen representatives from relevant federal agencies, the National Science Foundation (NSF), and other universities with hazards research programs. Notable among the latter were the programs at Ohio State University and the University of Delaware, directed by E. L. Quarantelli and Russell R. Dynes, respectively. The assessment project conducted workshops to address each hazard, and for his three-day workshop on flooding, Gilbert invited eight additional consultants from the public sector.

One of the assessment's primary recommendations was to improve the mechanisms for disseminating scholarship useful to public officials, including the creation of a clearinghouse of natural hazards information. When assessment graduate students first came up with this idea, they urged that the clearinghouse be housed at the University of Colorado. Gilbert had not considered this possibility. His international work at the time was leading him away from a specific, heavy emphasis on natural hazards. He considered the suggestion for some time before finally endorsing the idea, but he resolved not to become centrally involved. Events would have it otherwise.

The clearinghouse idea rapidly gained support, and Gilbert and his colleagues gained funding for it primarily from federal agencies because some of them recognized that it would be difficult for such an interdisciplinary venture to gain support from regular academic funding sources. The Natural Hazards Research and Applications Information Center was launched in 1974, as part of the IBS Research Program on Environment and Behavior. Eugene Haas, Gilbert's co–principal investigator in the original assessment, was appointed director, and Gilbert became a center associate while continuing as IBS director and a member of the Geography Department. Almost from the outset of Haas's tenure with the Natural Hazards Center, his leadership was compromised by university censure for misuse of public funds. To salvage the fledgling center's reputation, White led the center from 1976 to 1984, with assistance briefly from geography colleague Risa Palm, until a young geographer, William Riebsame, became director. Gilbert accepted no increase in salary for this addition to his responsibilities as director of IBS. When Riebsame resigned eight years later, Gilbert stepped in again as director from 1992 to 1994, well after his retirement from the university in 1978, until sociologist Den-

Gilbert with Boulder Natural Hazards Center's codirectors, Mary Fran Myers (left) and Dennis Mileti (right), mid-1990s. Photo courtesy of CU-Boulder Publications & Creative Services Photography Department.

nis Mileti was hired as director. Mileti had participated in the original assessment as a graduate student with White and Hass. His interests focused on earthquakes, floods, and hazard warning systems.[3]

Throughout its history the Natural Hazards Center has explored the links between sustainable development and mitigation of natural (and, to a lesser degree, human-caused) hazards. Because 90 percent of natural disaster losses in the United States were flood-related during this time, Gilbert's expertise in flooding enhanced the center's reputation for excellence. Until Mileti was appointed center director in 1995, "human-made" technological disasters received less attention. However, over the years the center came to recognize that human response and adaptation to various hazards were often similar, no matter what the precipitating event. Moreover, part of the center's fundamental philosophy and message has always been that extreme events of nature do not constitute disasters unless humans are in their way. Hence, many natural disasters are, at base, human-caused because of poor decisions, social and economic forces, and other human factors. Thus, when Dennis Mileti assumed directorship of the Natural Hazards Center, he broadened the center's focus to include technological hazards.

Perhaps more significantly, he orchestrated a second national assessment of natural hazards in conjunction with the twenty-fifth anniversary of the first assessment and also in conjunction with the United Nations International Decade for Natural Disaster Reduction, spanning the 1990s (Mileti 1996). The second assessment resulted in a landmark volume, *Disasters by Design: A Reassessment of Natural Hazards in the United States* (Mileti 1999). Mileti retired as center director in 2003, to be succeeded by Kathleen Tierney (formerly with the University of Delaware's Disaster Research Center).

The Natural Hazards Center's staff (ranging from six to eight employees) work in four complementary areas: information dissemination, information services, an annual workshop, and "quick response" research. In information dissemination, the center's most visible publications are a bimonthly newsletter, the *Natural Hazards Observer,* initiated in 1975 and now serving 15,000 readers in the United States and overseas; an email publication, Disaster Research, added in the early 1990s and now going out to about 3,000 recipients; a series of "Natural Hazards Informers" that address specific hazards and hazard issues; and scores of monographs, working papers, and other publications. In 2000, in association with the American Society of Civil Engineers, the center also launched a professional journal, *Natural Hazards Review.*[4]

With more than 22,000 items, the Natural Hazards Center Library, the basis of the center's information services, may comprise the world's largest collection on human adjustment to hazards. The center's research program, however, is limited primarily to supporting "quick response studies" immediately following disasters. The program, funded by NSF and administered by the center, enables researchers throughout the nation to pre-apply for financial support (thus avoiding time-consuming paperwork) and travel quickly to a disaster site to gather information about the disaster's immediate impact, response, and recovery. On average, the center funds about ten such studies annually.

The center probably is best known for its annual invitational workshops, held each July in Boulder, which bring together several hundred academicians; federal, state, and local government officials and employees; nonprofit agency representatives; business professionals; and students involved with hazards and hazard mitigation. Mary Fran Myers, center codirector, was in charge of these ambitious conferences during the last decade of White's involvement with the center.[5] Among other things, she made sure that roughly one-third of the participants each year were new to the workshop. Additionally, over the years, she invited a steadily increasing number of participants from abroad. The workshops offer dozens of sessions that examine hazards from myriad perspectives. In contrast with single-discipline, professional conferences, the workshops promote dialogue and networking and eschew the reading of formal papers. They have become an ideal environment in which staff of federal agencies, such as the Corps of Engineers, FEMA, and the FIA, can present their latest program developments, air their concerns, and also participate in sessions bearing directly on their federal mandates. In the workshop's informal setting beyond the high visibility in Washington, communication across agencies, across federal, state, and local jurisdictions, and between scholars and policy-making officials can occur more easily and effectively. Agency representatives feel very much at home; after all, many of them belong to agencies that contribute the funds that support the center itself.

White's personal style—informal but attentive—set the tone for the workshops from their beginning. For many participants, especially those not from academia, returning to Boulder (and talking with Gilbert) became an annual pilgrimage. Of course, Gilbert never dominated these meetings. In fact, he typically observed proceedings from the rear of the room, moving from session to session and participating formally only rarely. When he served as center director, he did offer a welcome and introduction, and he chaired the closing session, always giving, without notes, a succinct summary of the salient ideas from the four-day meeting. A picnic on the last evening of the workshop was always held at the Whites' Sunshine Canyon home until the Whites moved into Boulder in the late 1980s. Attendees in the early years recall the burro rides before the barbeque.

In the next chapter, which examines floodplain management and the NFIP in the last quarter of the twentieth century, the importance of the Natural Hazards Center and its workshops for advancing Gilbert's ideas and agenda will become obvious. Gilbert has said that his students' contributions would prove to be his greatest legacy, and it is difficult to argue with that assessment. Many of today's senior hazards scholars once studied with Gilbert. But the center has also strongly influenced and shaped how hazards are considered and dealt with both nationally and internationally. It has been used as a model for a dozen similar institutions overseas. Indeed, by the end of Gilbert's career, the center may have conveyed Gilbert White's legacy as much as his students.

White's move to the University of Colorado and its Institute of Behavioral Science in 1970 marked roughly the midpoint of his career. His formal involvement with the Natural Hazards Center spanned its first two decades (1974–1994), although he continued to attend annual workshops thereafter through 2005, when his services to the hazards community were honored in conjunction with celebrating the thirtieth anniversary of the workshop. It is fair to say that the hazards community, even internationally, was by 2005 encouragingly unified in philosophy and priorities to be addressed. But it was not always so.

A Storm Cloud of Dissenting Views

Before reviewing the last half of Gilbert's career, in particular his commitments and accomplishments beyond water issues and floodplain management, it will be instructive to examine the dissent among some geographers, sociologists, and related behavioral scientists to White's (and his colleagues') "dominant view" regarding what constitutes natural disasters and what most adequately explains human losses therefrom. In particular, the two publications of White, Burton, and Kates in the 1970s mentioned earlier—*Natural Hazards: Local, National, and Global* (White 1974) and *The Environment as Hazard* (Burton, Kates, and White 1978)—drew a spate of critical reviews. Subsequently much of that criticism was addressed and incorporated into the thinking of disaster researchers, including those associated with the Boulder Natural Hazards Center and other academic disaster centers. This synthesis of views that originally competed during the 1970s and 1980s has helped clarify the problem of rising property losses due to natural disasters. Indeed, the sharing, synthesis, and evolution of ideas that the center and especially its annual workshops encouraged perhaps demonstrated White's original biases resulting from his education in geography at the University of Chicago and from his work in the policy arena during the New Deal. In particular, several cultural geographers, sociologists, and anthropologists who examined disasters in rural, often indigenous, communities of "developing" nations questioned assumptions in the dominant view of White and his colleagues that were based on experiences in technologically "developed" nations.

White, Burton, and Kates (and, indeed, the first assessment that preceded the establishment of the Natural Hazards Center) hypothesized that increasing losses were basically a result of increasing population densities in hazard-prone locales, for example, where land meets water, one tectonic plate meets another, or economically marginalized people are forced to live and farm deforested, landslide-prone hillsides. "The corollary of such an argument is that adjustments should be directed at changing the population's perception and behavior with respect to hazards. It is not surprising, therefore, that much traditional research has advocated policies aimed at affecting the human occupancy of hazardous areas" (Marston 1983a). Anthropologists as well as geographers responded that in marginalized societies where not only loss of property but also loss of life was escalating, such "policies" often do not exist or cannot be implemented. Different political and economic systems, especially in regions of the world less familiar to disaster researchers from wealthier, culturally more homogeneous North Atlantic nations, clearly influenced and probably amplified the human costs due to extreme natural events. "It is not only that disasters occur and affect particular populations but, more importantly, that hazardous conditions exist in the day-to-day context of a population and that extreme events accelerate the crisis" (Marston 1983a). As for changing such marginalized populations' perception and behavior with respect to hazards,

> Are people unaware and poorly prepared because natural extremes are rare and unpredictable? Are they indifferent to the possibility of flood or earthquake because preoccupied with "present gratifications"? Or is it because the everyday conditions of work, life support, social and mental security or the artificial environment require all of their risk-avoiding and risk-taking energies? (Hewitt 1983, p. 26)

Kenneth Hewitt suggested that the marginalized poor appear ill-adapted only to the "socially narrowed world of technocratic or academic specialists" who lack understanding of the realities of existence in poverty. Worse, "in the interests of saving people from their own folly, the politically and economically most vulnerable may get further disadvantaged. . . . The eco-crat operating in the name of sustainable development and environment survival may be destroying locally adaptive responses that are the last refuge of the most threatened" (O'Riordan 1997).

According to the critics, the traditional/dominant focus paid insufficient attention "to how choice, perspective, and adaptation to hazards may be constrained and mediated by the cultural and economic values of a particular society. ... All of the (alternative) approaches advocate either institutional reform or fundamental social and economic change as the way to a less hazardous environment" (Marston 1983a).[6]

Interpretations of Calamity, edited by Kenneth Hewitt (1983), cited several of these "alternative approaches." The book was less polemic than were some of the reviews of the 1974 and 1978 publications of White and colleagues. (In particular, William I. Torry published a critique in 1979 to which Burton, Kates, and White uncharacteristically felt constrained to respond [1981]). Hewitt acknowledged that most critiques of the dominant view were still basically in the tradition of human ecology. These wide-ranging critiques went to the heart of a dilemma that White faced throughout his career: he placed great faith in the use of science and technology by enlightened corporate and political leadership. Knowledge in the right hands would slow, if not reverse, losses from disasters. Hewitt and the contributors to his edited collection, by contrast, argued that this "dominant view," even when informed by cross-cultural and international perspectives, remains a basically flawed, technocratic worldview

> that subordinates other modes and bases of understanding or action to those using technical procedures. More precisely, technocracy gives precedence in support and prestige to bureaucratically organized institutions, centrally controlled and staffed by or allocating funds to specialized professionals. For social scientists it is important to recognize that technocracy is not only or necessarily an obsession with technology in the narrow sense of engineering structures and machines. ... The social, economic and political "people" factors involved in hazards reduction, that White and Haas (1975) emphasize, also can be and usually are approached technocratically. ... Moreover, science and research themselves, however practical in orientation, tend to be determining factors only at certain levels in these institutions—rarely the highest—and only in the outlook of a certain class of persons within them—rarely those with the main powers of decision (Hewitt 1983, p. 7).

Given the extent to which the Natural Hazards Center relies upon funding from the "centralized, official, and bureaucratically organized" world of the U.S. government and the extent to which Gilbert White never lost faith in government's potential to provide the sort of meaningful public service that he engaged in during FDR's New Deal administration, one might ask: How did White manage to free himself as much as he did from the technocratic bias of the dominant view described by Hewitt? How has the center, still under White's influence, continued to provide leadership in forging new perspectives and a new synthesis among the increasingly diverse international natural hazards community, even into the twenty-first century?[7] To those questions Hewitt himself supplies much of the answer: "I suggest that in the international system . . . the social and intellectual debates raging in the most powerful states, themselves challenge the effectiveness as well as the truth of the dominant view" (Hewitt 1983). Gilbert (and the Natural Hazards Center) never stopped listening, and increasingly from the 1970s forward, he listened to the leading environmentally concerned scientists around the world and the alternative views (see Chapter 12).

From listening to these voices, perhaps the most important lesson Gilbert learned during the last three decades of his career was the essential role of grassroots, bottom-up advocacy in creating a sustainable world. If the corporate state in technologically "developed" societies is a problematic ally of the socially responsible science for which White and the natural hazards community stand, in the poorer nations the situation is far worse. What happens in the least developed societies to promote sustainability overwhelmingly flows upward from small-scale local initiatives.[8] In a 1997 article discussing the significance of Gilbert's doctoral dissertation, Timothy O'Riordan cited the importance of "empowerment" in coping with the risks associated with natural hazards (in the most as well as the least technologically "developed" societies) and elaborated at length on the support for this thesis in the dissertation:

> This community empowerment mediation approach to strategic resource decision-making is beginning to happen all over the western world, though it has many counterparts in local decision-making in the developing world. . . . Such an approach is triggered by the White philosophy of economic gain, social equity, and environmental fit: simple to say, enormously problematic to achieve (O'Riordan 1997).

Notes

1. Recommendation Eleven of the report reflected Gilbert's effort to anticipate the many potential problems and his desire for a limited feasibility study:

   "The following stages must be completed before solid judgment can be reached on the design of a national flood insurance program:

   a) Hydrological and statistical studies should be made to evaluate average annual damages and their variance, geographic distribution, and required rates. These also should investigate differences in land use, age of structures, type of hazard, local planning, and other factors as they affect the feasibility of insurance coverage.

   b) A limited experimental test program should be designed, taking into consideration the results described in stage 'a'.

   c) The experimental program should be tried with a range of areas, types of structures and other conditions that constitute a stratified sample of the national situation. It would include alternatives with respect to partial, compared with complete, participation among flood plain occupants and with respect to different rates for new versus existing developments.

d) Results of the experimental program should be evaluated.

e) A course of action then should be recommended with respect to a national program of flood insurance with whatever coverage and features seem warranted by the experimental program.

2. Testifying before Congress, Gilbert accented the positive wherever possible. "I am impressed by the relatively small number of complaints I hear reported in the past two years from the more than 65,000 property owners who are paid even though the volume is very high. . . . [Evidence shows] that the current number of policy holders— 1,800,000—is about 35–40 percent of the potential insurers in high frequency zones. . . . Increasingly the insurance is sold for the most part in communities which are taking on the responsibilities of the regular program to curb those unwise encroachments which generate subsequent calls for Federal insurance. . . . FIA is beginning to find ways of coping with . . . communities with zoning regulation on the books, but with so many exceptions that it is meaningless. . . . Two years ago I was doubtful that FIA would be able to respond effectively to the range of issues I have noted. It seemed more wedded to selling policies and approving paper regulations than to the improvement of flood plain conditions. During the past year it has made remarkable progress in confronting these issues and in working out solutions. . . . I think it would be against the public interest to make any radical changes in policy until the present new and promising administrative practices have been given a chance to demonstrate their strengths and weaknesses" (White 1980a).

3. Securing annual funding for the Natural Hazards Center has been a time-consuming and often difficult task for every center director. Yet, ultimately, funds have always been provided by a frequently changing consortium of organizations and agencies. Those dependably have been the U.S. Army Corps of Engineers, U.S. Department of Education, U.S. Environmental Protection Agency, Federal Emergency Management Agency, U.S. Geological Survey, Institute for Business and Home Safety, National Aeronautics and Space Administration, National Science Foundation, National Weather Service, and Public Entity Risk Institute.

4. Almost all the Natural Hazards Center's products and services, including its newsletters and library database, are now available via its website: http://www.colorado.edu/hazards.

5. Sadly, not only for her friends, coworkers, and family but also for the entire hazards community, Mary Fran passed away due to cancer in 2004.

6. Marston's 1983 review essay, "Natural Hazards Research: Towards a Political Economy Perspective," after succinctly summarizing the "traditional approach" (termed the "dominant view" in Hewitt's summary, also published in 1983), usefully distinguishes among the "liberal/radical" approaches discussed in this chapter; "managerialism," with its thesis that institutional reform, involving "urban managers," can lead to the removal of some of the constraints that contribute to disaster vulnerability; "materialism," focusing on cultural socioeconomic differences in meeting material needs that

can produce seemingly irrational and environmentally destructive practices explainable only by identifying the deep structures and often unconscious motivations influencing perception and behavior; and "human ecology–political economy" wherein societal cultural context is not neglected in linking analysis to local, regional, and global economic and social forces. Her own research on earthquake vulnerability in California (Marston 1983b) elucidated how state intervention in the economy (e.g., providing for disaster loans following flooding, earthquakes, and landslides) can counterproductively undermine policies made at the national level by encouraging location in hazardous locales and a disinclination to insure privately against disaster loss because of expected forthcoming state aid.

7. William Anderson, now with the National Research Council but formerly with by the National Science Foundation (where he was involved with the major hazards research centers in the United States since the 1960s) cited Gilbert as a leader in integrating the parallel (sometimes competing) foci of sociologists and geographers involved in disaster research. As an African American, Anderson also credits Gilbert, through the Natural Hazards Center, with involving an increasing number of minority researchers in the U.S. hazards community (Anderson 2001).

8. Jacques Leslie's four case studies of grassroots efforts around the world to confront and mitigate the risks posed by construction of a large dam are illustrative. He sets these case studies within the global context of impacts of dams constructed during the twentieth century (Leslie 2005).

9 Toward Unified Floodplain Management, 1975–2000

The Unified National Program is neither unified nor national.
—GFW

The Floodplain Management Challenges of the 1970s and 1980s

Throughout the latter part of the twentieth century, the progress toward a unified floodplain management program required leadership at the national level in both government and science. Increasingly, this effort also depended upon comparably dedicated leadership at the local and state levels. Gilbert's contributions locally are the subject of Chapter 10. This chapter includes a review of his state-level initiatives, foremost among them the Association of State Floodplain Managers (ASFPM). His national involvements understandably declined with advancing age, but given the importance to Gilbert of the nation's quest for integrated floodplain management, this chapter follows that history to the end of his twenty-first century involvements.

As mentioned in Chapter 8, Gilbert was disappointed with the establishment in 1969 of regional offices by the Federal Insurance Administration, which, he thought, reflected the FIA's underestimation of the human resources and community experience already available locally, especially in the states of the upper Mississippi and Missouri/Ohio River drainages. Illinois, Indiana, Michigan, Minnesota, Ohio, and Wisconsin all had active floodplain management programs, some with statutory authority, whose work predated and helped shape the FIA's flood insurance studies. Initially, those state floodplain managers (some were volunteers and others public employees) met independently of the FIA's district and national meetings. To its credit, the FIA paid increasing attention, first to community complaints and then to offers of assistance from public and private sector practitioners, whose experience the district offices of FIA would find indispensable.

The immense challenge in the 1970s, to both the FIA and local communities, was to develop accurate community floodplain maps, viable land-use plans, and accurate actuarial flood insurance tables. One of the first requests that the FIA made to state floodplain managers was to develop a process for state approval of agency plans affecting local communities prior to those plans actually being submitted to community officials. These plans resulted from FIA studies as well as those conducted by cooperating agencies, such as the U.S. Army Corps of

Engineers, Soil Conservation Service, and U.S. Geological Survey. The FIA had become frustrated with delays caused by state reviews and had decided to circumvent state involvement. However, states with statutory authority in this domain countered by refusing to allow use of any studies for local regulation of floodplains that had not been state-approved. At an impasse, in 1977 the FIA met with the floodplain managers from those upper midwestern states. FIA agreed to reverse its decision and to involve state coordinators in national and regional meetings of the FIA. Shortly thereafter, state officials formed the ASFPM, held their first meeting in 1979 (with fifteen states represented), and elected Larry Larson, a floodplain manager from Wisconsin, to be their chair. (Larson became the executive director of the ASFPM in 1982 and has held that position ever since.)

Gloria Jimenez, FIA administrator at the time, invited ASFPM members to the first joint FIA-ASFPM meeting in Washington, D.C., later that year. By 1982, this mostly volunteer movement had graduated from simply monitoring and advising federal agencies to providing technical training in local floodplain management. In the following years the ASFPM added state branch associations as chapters with their own volunteer boards, training, and regional meetings supplementing the national annual ASFPM meetings, which by 2005 involved 1,000 participants. The organization decided in 1983 to include professionals involved in floodplain management at the national as well as at the state level. Voting membership is vested in individual members, not states, agencies, or companies. For its part, the FIA created a State Assistance Program to support and complement these efforts.

Larry Larson, who presided over this mushrooming network of public and private floodplain professionals, consulted with Gilbert and Natural Hazards Center staff, beginning with the center's first summer workshop in 1975. Together they used the supportive environment of the summer workshops to present and debate candidly state and federal perspectives, particularly regarding the National Flood Insurance Program. The organizations involved in these discussions, both at the workshops and increasingly at the national ASFPM meetings, expanded greatly over the years to include the Council of State Governments, the National Governors Association, the National Wildlife Federation, the Association of State Wetland Managers, as well as the agencies that financed the Natural Hazards Center (listed in Chapter 8). Through these meetings, both ASFPM and Natural Hazards Center staff developed close working relationships, indeed close friendships, with staff and administrators of first the FIA and subsequently FEMA. In fact, these agencies have participated in all Natural Hazards Center workshops, thus insuring that they are at least familiar with the researchers and practitioners, the research and practice, in the evolving discipline of floodplain management.

Those involved generally agree that Gilbert was the behind-the-scenes father of the four organizations most responsible for floodplain management in the United States in the last quarter of the twentieth century: FIA, FEMA, ASFPM, and the Natural Hazards Center. That many individuals now involved in the first three may never have heard of Gilbert White is as the self-effacing scholar would want it.[1] ASFPM executive director Larry Larson observed, "Frankly, without Gilbert encouraging us and giving us credibility, I'm not sure we would have survived. After all, we did not have money . . . only enthusiasm, a cause, and a vision. Gilbert continually encouraged and promoted the ASFPM at the center workshops, in national policy circles and elsewhere" (Larson 2005).

In addition to the aforementioned Goddard-White award, in 2004 the ASFPM Foundation inaugurated an annual National Flood Policy Forum to develop

Gilbert with James Goddard of the TVA. The ASFPM Goddard-White Award is given to individuals who have been instrumental in carrying forward the goals and objectives of floodplain management throughout the United States.

policy recommendations and establish an ongoing record of flood policy issues and directions for the future. At the suggestion of former ASFPM president Douglas Plasencia, this forum bears Gilbert's name, a tribute to his work as "the most influential floodplain management policy expert of the 20th century . . . and in recognition of the success of his deliberative approach to policy analysis and research" (ASFPM Foundation 2004).

If Gilbert was the father of unified floodplain management, its mother was clearly adversity. Only repeated coastal flooding in the late 1950s and 1960s led the Johnson administration to act on the recommendations of the 1966 Federal Task Force on Flood Policy Management that Gilbert had chaired, and only costly flooding in 1972 and 1973 again provided Gilbert access to the White House. He participated in yet another task force that led to congressional legislation tightening the conditions (especially requiring mitigation planning) under which subsidized flood insurance would apply and disaster assistance would be forthcoming. Yet it was only in response to extreme destruction and flooding in the gulf states brought on by Hurricane Frederic in 1979 that the federal government adopted some of the recommendations of Gilbert's University of Chicago graduate student and flood-proofing pioneer, Jack Sheaffer (see Chapter 7).

Gilbert worked with Congress to secure support for the 1973 White House policy paper recommendations. Again, he was the right person in the right place at the right time. The FIA had recommended that community enrollment and individual insurance for floodplain property purchased or developed with federal assistance be mandatory. The recommendations had passed the House after much debate, but in the Senate Banking Committee, chaired by William Proxmire of Wisconsin, making enrollment and insurance mandatory was not acceptable. Committee member Bennett Johnson of Louisiana was particularly opposed. In this confrontation he had the support of the National League of Cities, the National Savings and Loan Association, and the Associations of Bankers, Realtors, and Home Builders. In fact, the only groups lobbying for the recommendation were comparatively powerless environmental organizations. Richard Krimm of FIA was shepherding the legislation through Congress and in frustration asked for Gilbert White's "friendly persuasion." Gilbert took Senator Johnson to lunch, and the Banking Committee subsequently joined the House in passing the crucial 1973 Flood Disasters Protection Act.

The 1973 act added mudslides and coastal erosion to hazards covered by the National Flood Insurance Program. Coastal storm surge and frequent costly losses for people able to afford prized ocean views had, from the inception of the NFIP, resulted in a greatly disproportionate amount of FIA payouts going to coastal areas. After Hurricane Frederic in 1979 devastated a highly developed region of coastal Alabama, FEMA commissioned a study by Jack Sheaffer that documented that federal subsidies, including flood insurance, encouraged development, as did federal reimbursement for the heavy losses due to the storm.[2] Two resulting pieces of legislation, the 1981 Omnibus Budget Reconciliation Act and the 1982 Coastal Barrier Resources Act, effectively limited development of undeveloped coastal property but left unaddressed the dilemma of reinsuring multiple damaged properties. Reinsuring structures following their repair or reconstruction, only to have them damaged again by flooding, was a problem that would continue to haunt the FIA. In some cases, payouts over time far exceeded the value of the property insured. Even with the 1982 legislation, at the end of the century over 50 percent of the 4.1 million policies in force and over 60 percent of the $482 billion in insured property were in communities bordering on coastal waters.

One salutary NFIP achievement of the 1980s was solvency. Initially, the FIA required participating private insurance companies essentially to sell flood policies with the FIA name and format. However, in 1983 a "Write Your Own" (WYO) experiment allowed companies to market policies under their names (but with FIA still assuming the financial risk). Participation climbed, and thereafter the FIA was fully self-supporting.

In 1975 the Ford administration established the Interagency Floodplain Management Task Force (initially under the Water Resources Council and later under FEMA) to carry out the task of preparing for Congress the unified national program for floodplain management as required of the executive branch by the Flood Insurance Act of 1968. Subsequently, in 1978 the Carter administration created FEMA and supported a 1979 Water Resources Council study of nonstructural flood mitigation. However, because there were few major flood disasters in the United States in the decade between hurricanes Frederic (1979) and Hugo (1989), these developments were almost anticlimactic. Gilbert was particularly frustrated with the interagency task force, which first issued a report in 1979 (updating a 1976 WRC report) and then another update seven years later (FEMA 1986) and only in 1987 finally commissioned the first broad assessment of floodplain management since Gilbert's 1966 task force report.

The TVA was asked to manage this latter assessment of floodplain management in the United States, and one of its staff members, James Wright, in turn assembled a special National Review Committee, chaired by Gilbert, to make its own summary evaluation of the status of floodplain management and to critique the task force report.[3]

Given the magnitude of the effort expended (the final report, *Assessment Report of Floodplain Management in the United States* [L. R. Johnston Associates 1992], is over 600 pages long) and the opportunity afforded by this project, Gilbert and his colleagues on the review committee found the study disappointing, although even-handed. The authors had not sufficiently documented existing conditions to permit recommendations regarding future directions (Kusler and Larson 1993). Moreover, this product of the interagency task force mostly supported the agencies' status quo (Platt 1999). Gilbert was particularly disappointed in the missed opportunity to conduct a thorough empirical assessment of the effects of the National Flood Insurance Program on flood losses. His National Review Committee concluded that

> the present status of floodplain management does not encourage complacency. The record is mixed. There are encouraging trends, as with the number of communities having some form of floodplain regulations, but the rising toll of average annual flood losses has not been stopped or reversed. Some activities look more productive on paper than on the ground or in the real vulnerability of people. On balance, progress has been far short of what is desirable or possible, or what was envisaged at times when the current policies and activities were initiated (White, for the Task Force, 1992a).

"The rising toll of losses" was not what many government officials wanted to hear, and a debate ensued over whether those cost increases were real or simply reflected expanding population and development. Some argued that on a per capita basis, losses may have been stemmed.[4] Gilbert and Natural Hazards Center associates researched the data thoroughly and concluded that undoubtedly losses were steadily outstripping investments in mitigation. White's opening address to the 1993 Silver Anniversary NFIP conference stated the dilemma unequivocally:

> Taking the total damages on a five-year average ending in 1990, and using 1985 dollar values, the record of losses for the United States as a whole does not encourage the belief that great reductions in the net cost of flooding to the nation have been achieved since the mid 1960s. After reaching new heights in the 1970s, they have persisted at levels as high or higher than previous years. A few studies and random observations suggest that the severity of flooding in many urban areas has increased and that invasion of floodplains by uneconomic land uses has continued in numerous areas (White 1993a).

Those conclusions were based on data through the 1980s. In 1996 FEMA would report that hazards losses had quadrupled from 1985 to 1995.

Given the general complacency and lack of major disasters during the 1980s and the consequent unwillingness in Washington to assess the effects of federal policies in selected communities, White decided to address the issue himself. A logical agency to initiate such research (again, a "postaudit" in Gilbert's terms) was the Tennessee Valley Authority, given its experience and experimentation with floodplain management in over 150 communities, almost two-thirds of which had adopted zoning regulations in cooperation with the FIA. Gilbert suggested to the chair of the TVA board of directors "that many who might benefit from the agency's example had insufficient information about the TVA's approach to working with state and local officials." The TVA promptly issued a report on its thirty-year floodplain management history.

But Gilbert and Jim Wright of the TVA had something more ambitious in mind. The Natural Hazards Center formed a nationwide advisory committee, developed a research design, and, after a pilot test, oversaw surveys in a sample of 18 of the 150 TVA communities.[5] The most useful finding was that citizens and local governments relied heavily on assistance provided by federal agencies to local planners and decision makers. If they did not receive assistance in interpreting sophisticated technical information, communities did not use that information. Further, the frequent turnover of officials at the local level meant that such assistance was needed repeatedly. The TVA provided this kind of technical assistance about 400 times annually. Although unsurprised, Gilbert welcomed these hard data on the importance of educating and involving local leadership in planning and implementation. He advocated this approach at every opportunity.

These results (Boggs 1986) served as a guide to other agencies, and subsequently an Interagency Floodplain Management Task Force seminar was held in Washington, D.C. It was chaired by Jon Kusler, an adviser to Larson on the formation of ASFPM, a national leader in wetlands preservation, and founder of the Association of State Wetland Managers. The seminar results were in turn published by the Natural Hazards Center. Earlier, the center had also published Kusler's extensive two-volume update of his pioneering research on regulation of flood hazard areas to reduce flood losses, which was begun the year the National Flood Insurance Program was created (1968). TVA then published a third volume by Kusler in 1982 (ironically the same year that President Ronald Reagan abolished the Water Resources Council that had commissioned Kusler's work in 1968).

The demise of the WRC was traceable to the relative paucity of presidentially declared disasters during the Carter and Reagan administrations. Reagan concluded that the WRC was no longer needed and in fact questioned if much of the hazards bureaucracy was not dispensable. As Jim Wright said, "Generally, the concerns expressed by the Reagan administration were the cost, but not the benefits, of compliance with the Executive Order (of President Carter's administration) and impacts on affordability of housing" (J. Wright 2000). White and others suggested to then director of the Interagency Floodplain Management Task Force, Frank Thomas, a less generous reason for President Reagan's terminating the council: Was the WRC's demise so early in Reagan's presidency retaliation for the WRC's identifying for President Carter federal *structural* water projects that he should oppose?

Reagan asked for a FEMA review of NFIP policies generally and specifically of the need to hold stringently to the 100-year flood standard. Relaxing the scope of floodplain protection would permit increased development. FEMA conducted the review but fortunately recommended no weakening of FIA guidelines.

Frank Thomas had been the champion (and lightning rod) for federal agency efforts to collaborate and unify floodplain management since the Water Resources Council had launched the Unified National Program of Floodplain Management in the early 1970s. After WRC's termination he moved to FEMA, where he became perhaps Gilbert's staunchest agency ally advocating comprehensive floodplain management, as opposed to simple flood loss reduction.

Both Thomas and Jim Wright of the TVA were more charitable in their assessments of the Unified National Program accomplishments through the 1970s and 1980s than was Gilbert. For example, in 1992 in their evaluation of the *Assessment Report of Floodplain Management in the United States,* White's National Review Committee stated:

> While considerable progress has been made over the past two decades, the Unified National Program is neither unified nor national. In several respects it falls short of achieving the goals set out for it by the Congress and previous administrations. It does not integrate adequately either the numerous program aims that have been set forth or the efforts of those charged with implementing them (White 1992b).

Both the voice and substance are clearly Gilbert's.

Yet Gilbert in turn was more charitable than were some of his students and associates. Successive Unified National Program reports, reflecting Gilbert's wording of President Johnson's Executive Order 11296 in 1966, have voiced a commitment to floodplain management, as opposed to river control. However, Rutherford Platt, a historian of floodplain management, suggests that there has been a subtle shift away from that executive order's insistence on "intelligent planning for and state and local regulation of the use of lands exposed to flood hazard." Increasingly in the 1976, 1979, 1986, and 1994 reports, land use regulation was more implied than explicitly emphasized in the broad range of possible structural and nonstructural adjustments (Platt 1999). As discussed later, by the 1990s pressure was increasing at the federal and local levels to weaken land-use regulation prescribed by the National Flood Insurance Program. This battle continues today.

The International Decade
for Natural Disaster Reduction

Another disappointment for Gilbert in the late 1980s was his and several associates' diminishing influence within the National Academy of Sciences (NAS) as disagreements developed in the NAS preparations for the International Decade of Natural Disaster Reduction (IDNDR) in the 1990s. NAS president Frank Press strongly endorsed (and perhaps conceived) the idea of launching a global initiative to significantly reduce the global costs of natural hazards. James (Ken) Mitchell, former Chicago student and research associate of White's, agreed to chair an ad hoc committee on the subject under the National Research Council of NAS. The committee's draft reports focused on improving the use of existing scientific information rather than on the development of new research and development initiatives. Mitchell also wanted the decade to have a simple focal task that would be pursued in every country, perhaps a survey undertaken to obtain comparable international data concerning what could be done to reduce the danger and cost of disasters. Not long before, Gilbert had joined a short-term study in the Yucatan, Mexico, on attitudes and approaches regarding hazards and their mitigation. An example supplied by Yucatan schools impressed Gilbert with its ingenuity and simplicity: rehang the doors of schools to open outward rather than inward, as was the custom, so that earthquake rubble within the room would not prevent the occupants from opening the doors and escaping from the building. From this suggestion, Mitchell's ad hoc committee agreed that increasing the safety and security of schools would be an appropriate theme, since school personnel are readily available in any country and represent comparatively comparable samples, at least in terms of socioeconomic status.

All but one member of the committee concurred, with the dissenting vote of George Housner duly noted in submission of the recommendation to NAS president Frank Press. In Gilbert's recollection, Press was so distressed with the idea of using elementary schools, rather than scientific organizations, to garner such important opinions that he dismissed the committee and appointed a replacement group. The only holdover was George Housner, who agreed to chair the new committee. Dutifully, the replacement committee recommended calling for national conferences of distinguished scientists to address the issue.[6] "The new committee that replaced us took off in a quite different direction that emphasized a large number of specialized technical projects (around 80 if memory serves) along lines that the Academy felt more comfortable with. It was this Housner Committee report that was sent to the United Nations to act as a starting point for the Decade" (Mitchell 2005).

But early into the 1990s, it became clear that a program favored by the NAS-NCR in the United States was at odds with needs as perceived by many other nations. Following an international conference at Yokohama in 1994, the agenda of the IDNDR was revamped along lines more sensitive to the needs of hazard information users to which Mitchell's ad hoc committee and Gilbert White were more sympathetic. But in

Gilbert in the early 1980s, with Shona, without whose prescient aid he might well have preceded Anne in death

part due to the reorientation, momentum waned, and the IDNDR failed to realize its potential. "The U.S. government was never really enthusiastic about the proposed Decade and never threw its full weight behind the effort. The Academy remained very quiet about the whole experience" (Mitchell 2005). From the outset, Gilbert had been rather skeptical of the NAS's leadership role in the IDNDR experiment, citing instead the model adopted the preceding decade (1981–1990) for the International Decade for Clean Drinking Water. At the close of the IDNDR, Gilbert observed,

Anne in the late-1980s.

> One possibly negative effect of the Decade effort is that its emphasis may have led key public officials to feel that in promoting the agreed cooperative scientific and technical programs, they were making genuine progress in dealing with hazards. Thereby, they may have neglected other more positive prevention and mitigation measures. Lacking thoughtful assessment of representative programs, it has been difficult to know if the net effects have been positive or negative (White 1999a).

Gilbert's fear of the IDNDR's potential counterproductivity was reinforced by the announced goal at the outset of the decade, by the U.S. Committee for the Decade, that losses from disasters would be cut in half nationally by 2000, a patently unrealistic and misleading expectation.

But the 1990s carried a far greater disappointment and sadness for Gilbert than these developments in hazard policy and management. Anne's health began to decline following a trip to China with Gilbert, and she was diagnosed with cancer. She died in 1989 (see Chapter 13). The blow to Gilbert was severe, and he was little inclined to become deeply involved in the political debates that reemerged when a spate of costly disasters, beginning with Hurricane Hugo in 1989, gained national attention.

Mitigation as Policy

In recent decades perhaps the key concept in national policy to reduce disaster losses has been mitigation. In the final analysis, reduction in vulnerability to hazards and hence in losses due to disasters depends on federal directives as well as steps taken by communities and individuals to avoid or lessen damage and suffering. In turn, these steps depend on property owners' knowledge and perception of the hazard risks they face and of the costs and benefits of the options available to mitigate those risks. Gilbert and several University of Chicago students had conducted initial interdisciplinary research on these questions of perception in the 1960s. Subsequently, this circle widened to include, among others, Howard Kunreuther and Paul Slovic, two highly regarded scholars in economics and psychology, respectively (Kunreuther, Slovic, and Slovic 1986). Their studies became increasingly important to Gilbert as mitigation became increasingly salient in federal policy during the Clinton presidency (Kunreuther and Slovic 1986).

Earlier, the Carter administration had similarly endeavored to make mitigation central to its disaster management initiatives, particularly when it created FEMA. There, mitigation teams had been authorized for rapid deployment following disasters, when motivation is greatest to prevent future losses. Subsequently, with the comparative absence of major disasters during the Reagan years, priorities shifted, and commitment to proactive measures requiring time and money waned. But in the early 1990s, that attitude dramatically changed. Massive losses between 1989 and 1993 from five major hurricanes, earthquakes, and river floods resulted in mitigation making more sense to more people than at any time previously.

Despite this new perspective and efforts to develop more comprehensive plans to address hazards, by the latter part of the twentieth century the agencies' programs and rhetoric had not significantly altered behavior to reduce losses. Gilbert and his colleagues felt that the explanation had to lie in misperceptions of the risks at the grassroots level. Failure to mitigate hazard vulnerability in the face of overwhelming evidence and increased knowledge of that vulnerability made sense only if the perceived benefits of action were outweighed by their perceived cost. Inescapably, many students of disasters concluded that Americans had become so accustomed to government assistance following disasters that they considered such help an entitlement. In other words, the costs of mitigation are undeniable, but the benefits of official inaction appear to individual homeowners to be that assistance following a disaster is virtually guaranteed. Clearly, such a perception can result in complacency and underestimation of the risks associated with an extreme event.

A disturbing question necessarily followed—the question that, in one form or another, plagued Gilbert throughout the history of the National Flood Insurance Program: could the FIA's well-intentioned efforts have become as much the problem as the solution? Gilbert's primary focus in the 1990s was this haunting question, and he remained convinced that empirical study of the effects of federal policies and resultant floodplain management programs in a sample of communities must be federally authorized, funded, and conducted.[7]

Progress in the 1990s

In 1988, under President George H. W. Bush, all previous legislative initiatives dealing with federal disaster response (emergency aid and reconstruction) dating back
to the federal Disaster Relief Act of 1950 were reviewed and amended to underscore
and reiterate the need for mitigation. Section 404 of the resultant 1988 Stafford
Disaster Relief and Emergency Assistance Act created a new hazard mitigation
grant program under FEMA to assist states in conducting cost-effective projects
that would substantially reduce the risk of future damage, hardship, loss, or suffering in any area affected by a major disaster. The percentage of funding assistance
to a community, following a president's declared disaster, that could be allocated
to such mitigation was set initially at 10 percent and raised to 15 following the great
midwestern floods of 1993. Gilbert was especially pleased that the *federal* share of
such mitigation initiatives could not exceed half, with the remaining portion being the responsibility of state and local governments. But perhaps predictably, in
Bush's bid for reelection in 1992 the *federal* share of total disaster assistance following Hurricane Andrew (the nation's most costly hurricane to that date) skyrock-
eted to almost 100 percent. Similarly, President Bill Clinton succumbed to pressure
from Congress to raise the federal share for mitigation from 50 to 75 percent
following the 1993 floods in the Midwest.[8]

Hurricane Andrew was pivotal in turning national attention to mitigation. The
cost to the insurance industry and federal government was $17.5 billion, with
roughly one-quarter of the losses attributable to substandard construction due to
poor workmanship or inadequate enforcement of building codes. Flood-proofing
and hurricane prediction measures alone could have substantially reduced the
losses. But the widespread criticism regarding delayed and ineffectual response by
the agencies to the tragedy was even more damaging to FEMA/FIA. The delayed
response occurred despite Andrew being the first disaster experienced after the
federal earthquake response plan (coordinating the efforts of twenty-six federal
agencies and the American Red Cross) had been extended to include hurricanes.
In 1993, with a new administration in the White House, the entire structure of federal response came under scrutiny by a host of congressional and administrative
offices. In particular, a National Academy for Public Administration (NAPA) study
focusing on FEMA led to substantial reorganization of that agency and creation of
a Mitigation Directorate.[9]

The National Performance Review of selected agencies chaired by Vice President
Al Gore highlighted serious mistakes in FEMA's past performance, including lack of
clear criteria for presidential disaster declarations. The broad presidential discretion
in declaring disasters (and thus in providing funds to local jurisdictions) and the
parallel temptation in Congress to be generous were yet additional disincentives to

mitigation and preparedness and, ironically, potentially contributed to the increasing losses due to disasters (Platt 1999).

Disaster management gained a high profile in the Clinton administration. Clinton's FEMA director, James Lee Witt, was the first agency director to become a member of a presidential cabinet, and he refocused FEMA's efforts on mitigation. The Mitigation Directorate under Frank Thomas assumed responsibility for mitigation programs involving floodplains and earthquakes, and in 1995 FEMA published *National Mitigation Strategy,* in which Witt announced an ambitious goal: "To change public attitudes about the risk of natural hazards and, in so doing, to reduce the loss of life, property, and the environment by 50 percent over the next 25 years" (FEMA 1995). One-third of the way through those twenty-five years, only one of those objectives seems to have been realistic: loss of life from natural disasters has shown a gradual decrease over the past half century. Meanwhile, property losses have continued to escalate. On the third point, so far no one has determined the long-term impacts on the environment of our adjustments to hazards.

In terms of losses from natural disasters, 1992 had been the most costly year in the nation's history: Hurricanes Andrew and Iniki (in Hawaii) cost $30 billion, contributing to the four-trillion-dollar national debt the Clinton administration inherited. Then, early in the Clinton presidency, another megadisaster struck, rivaling Hurricane Andrew in total damage and doubling from two to over four billion dollars the federal portion of the losses. Indeed, with the great midwestern floods, 1993 surpassed 1992 in total losses to disaster. A record 525 counties in the basins of the upper Mississippi and lower Missouri were declared disaster areas by Clinton. One hundred thousand homes were affected, and FEMA used the newly increased percentage of federal assistance available for mitigation (from 10 to 15 percent) to purchase and remove from floodplains 8,000, or 8 percent, of those properties—the largest buyout in U.S. history.

The 1993 floods were particularly disappointing to the Federal Insurance Administration: "In this, the largest inland flood since the advent of the National Flood Insurance Program in 1968, flood insurance played a very minor role. Total claims amounted to $293 million on 16,167 claims. This was the third largest payout under the NFIP, but it comprised only about 2 percent of the total damage estimate of $12 billion and about 14 percent of total federal disaster outlays" (Platt 1999). At that time, estimates of those at flood risk nationally (i.e., those owning insurable buildings) who were insured under the NFIP ranged from 20 to 30 percent; initial estimates of that percentage for the flood zones struck by the Midwest floods ranged from only 10 to 20 percent, or about half the national average.

President Clinton appointed a special Interagency Floodplain Management Review Committee to assess the nature and magnitude of losses from the great midwestern floods and to recommend changes in federal policies to reduce future losses. The high-level committee of thirty-one people was chaired by Brigadier General Gerald Galloway, dean of the faculty and professor of geography at the U.S. Military Academy, West Point, New York, whose involvement with the Corps of Engineers and acquaintance with Gilbert's commitment to nonstructural adjustments to flooding dated back to the New Deal era. The "Galloway Report," officially entitled *Sharing the Challenge: Floodplain Management into the 21st Century—A Blueprint for Change* (Galloway 1994), was a comprehensive assessment and set of recommendations that addressed environmental, agricultural, and engineering issues. The report tactfully advised against replacement or expansion of levees (which had widely failed) and for restoration of natural wetland storage, even at the cost of selective abandonment of agricultural lands. The report was cautious and tactful, anticipating furor among farmers owning floodplain land made highly productive by periodic flooding but protected to varying degrees by a host of privately constructed levees. "Land use control . . . ," the report said, "is the sole responsibility of state, tribal, and local entities. . . . The federal responsibility rests with providing leadership, technical information, data, and advice to assist the states" (Galloway 1994).

Echoing Al Gore's National Performance Review, the Galloway Report warned against allowing federal disaster assistance to lessen incentives for individual mitigation. (In the insurance industry the analogous problem had been labeled the "moral hazard" of subsidized insurance.) From 1989 to 1993, over $27.6 billion had been paid out in federal disaster assistance. Especially worrisome to Gilbert was that a growing proportion of that federal assistance came from unbudgeted special appropriations, which totaled $22 billion just between 1992 and 1994. In total, the 578 presidential disaster declarations during the previous fifteen years had resulted in over $120 billion in direct grants, low-interest loans, and insurance payments. Moreover, in fifteen instances since 1985, communities and states had received waivers for the 25 percent of disaster costs that they were required by law to contribute to qualify for federal assistance.[10]

White enthusiastically began working with both Galloway and James Lee Witt, applauding and critiquing the federal agencies, lobbying members of Congress, networking and sharing new ideas through Natural Hazards Center workshops, and helping to promulgate research findings through center publications. Perhaps he had found renewed enthusiasm. Certainly the mid-1990s were happier years than he had just been through; he had begun to heal following the loss of Anne and had even found a new companion, a nurse named Claire Sheridan (see Chapter 13). He also was ably assisted by Mary Fran Myers, the center codirector, who had joined the center after working in floodplain management for the state of Illinois. The Natural Hazards Center workshop of 1993 provided a platform for FEMA director James Lee Witt to rally practitioners and researchers behind the new Mitigation Directorate agenda. In his prepared remarks, he set forth objectives that would guide FEMA's future: creating a unified partnership among all federal, state, and local governmental and private organizations to develop an all-hazards emergency management system; establishing mitigation as the foundation of that national system; and strengthening disaster response capability, especially by strengthening state and local emergency management programs. He asserted, "Such an approach will put the focus back on our communities and establish a 'bottom-up' approach to emergency management and public safety that is responsive to the people's needs"(Witt 1993).

Although Witt did not mention auditing past performance, Gilbert applauded the renewed attack on the inefficiencies of the Washington hazards bureaucracy and the determination to adopt a grassroots "bottom-up" program. In their "Invited Comment" article in the center's newsletter, the *Natural Hazards Observer,* Gilbert and Mary Fran Myers seconded the challenge to administrators "to adapt their single-focus programs to broader, multi-purpose aims that integrate and resolve competing goals.

> At a minimum, action should be taken immediately to promote comprehensive statewide floodplain management planning; strengthen the coordination of federal agency floodplain management activities and their compatibility with state programs; establish priorities for wetland restoration; and integrate the nation's disaster response, flood insurance and relief policies more closely with broader environmental and economic aims (Myers and White 1993a).[11]

Gilbert was always looking for opportunities to promote increased cooperation vertically among local, state, and federal decision makers and practitioners and horizontally among states sharing rivers and federal agencies sharing jurisdictions. Indeed, he ended his plenary address to the twenty-fifth annual meeting of the National Flood Insurance Program with a plea for "genuinely positive collaboration . . . a thoroughly complex task." Later in 1993, testifying before the House Committee on Public Works, he delivered a succinct and eloquent summary of his concerns:

> There is now a widely-held recognition among diverse sectors of the nation that a lasting economical, and sustainable solution to the flood problem preventing future catastrophes of the magnitude of 1993 can and must be achieved through integrated action. Experience has shown that it is not sufficient to depend upon engineering works alone, or flood proofing of structures, or improved warnings, or emergency disaster assistance, or indemnification through an insurance system, or changes in land use, or restoration of once-low-lying wetlands. There are now enough places around the country to demonstrate that different combinations of those types of measures may be right for one landscape or community but not others. Primary reliance on any one set of measures throughout the country will be inadequate. . . . In the Midwest there are approximately 200 communities [affected by the Mississippi flood] that are seriously canvassing possible

alternate ways of coping with flood threats. The major obstacle to working out reasonable, sustainable answers to the problems posed by these communities is the habit and convenience of agencies working separately on their own narrow missions. It is easy to give lip service to working out community problems. It is more difficult to do so in practice.... What seems needed is resolve, a sense of constructive direction, and flexibility in tackling in a unified fashion the complex of government procedures required for effective floodplain management. To achieve this will require strong administration from the Executive Branch. It will need to be based on Congressional authorization for joint activity by the Federal agencies involved, and for flexibility in using appropriated funds to carry out designated activities on an experimental basis (White 1994e).

The 1994 Natural Hazards Center workshop followed on the heels of the Galloway Report, and Galloway was on hand to summarize the findings. Gilbert's correspondence with Galloway following the workshop is instructive. While congratulating Galloway both for the report and his role in the workshop discussion of implementation strategies, Gilbert recalled his own disillusionment following the enthusiastic reception of his 1966 task force report and the resultant executive order from President Johnson. Gilbert likened the upbeat center workshop just concluded to the comparably optimistic 1968 Floodplain Seminar held in Chicago by HUD following passage of the act that created the flood insurance program.

[Congressional] recommendations were clear, unanimous, and far-seeing. However well-intentioned the administrators [subsequently appointed], most recommendations were not followed by FIA. Because no thorough prior studies and post-audits were supported by FIA it is impossible to make a solid assessment of the consequences. My personal opinion based upon 24 years observation is that had those recommended criteria, practices, and studies been adopted, the situation in the Midwest last year would have been far less serious, and your report, if any, would have been quite different. Indeed, FIA practice may have exacerbated the situation. The basic lesson, I believe, is that with plain Congressional directive, strong Presidential blessing, and widespread, local and state support, a far-seeing policy in this complex field is not likely to be translated into positive action unless the Executive and Legislative branches are assiduous in seeing to it that there is serious oversight and post-audit following adoption of a general policy (White 1994c).

Gilbert sent copies to James Lee Witt at FEMA, the Association of State Floodplain Managers, congressional staff, and Elaine McReynolds, the administrator of the Federal Insurance Administration. McReynolds promptly responded (McReynolds 1994), understandably defensive and ready to contest the suggestion that FIA had been a counterproductive enterprise. The statistics she offered, accomplishments she reviewed, and proposals for improvement she advanced—while impressive—missed the mark as far as Gilbert was concerned. He replied:

My concern in writing earlier and in replying as I do now is based on the conviction that you currently have a remarkable opportunity to achieve major improvements in the program as it relates to FEMA's new emphasis upon mitigation. One difficulty with judging proposals for improvement is that there is so little solid information as to precisely what has happened as a result of national flood insurance. Statistics on policies sold and claims filed, for example, do not answer questions of who didn't purchase insurance, and what mitigation measures might have been undertaken with different premium and education policies. While policy sales may be spurred by greater emphasis on mandatory purchase and lender compliance, as provided in the 1994 NFIP Reform Act, I suspect that greatly broadened marketing is unlikely to be successful until there is better understanding of the whole range of factors affecting flood insurance purchase, including accompanying land use (White 1994d).

Gilbert shared the McReynolds correspondence with Howard Kunreuther, with whom he was writing a review article entitled "The Role of the National Flood Insurance Program in Reducing Losses and Promoting Wise Use of Flood Plains." It was in part a critique of the FIA's self-assessment during the proceedings of the silver anniversary meetings the previous year, but it was also positive, at least insofar as it proposed hypotheses worthy of study regarding why the NFIP had not met its original objectives. But McReynolds's reaction to Gilbert's letter only emboldened Kunreuther, if not White as well, and the draft of their review article was blunt, charging that the flood insurance program "has fallen far short of achieving either of its goals" (wise use of floodplains and reduction of losses from flooding).

They shared the draft with Frank Thomas and Frank Reilly of FEMA, and Reilly's hand-written reply to Gilbert was equally blunt:

Although I agree with what is said in IV—Modest Proposals for Improving the NFIP—I am troubled by the rest of the article. . . . I am very concerned that if you and Howard join in the condemnation of the NFIP by the use of pejorative phrases such as "why the program has failed," it will play into the hands of those who want to maintain the status quo or eliminate the NFIP. The current distrust of federal regulatory programs makes these outcomes very realistic (Reilly 1994).

Gilbert had been "eldered," the Quaker term for admonished (albeit tenderly), very few times in his life, but this was one of them. Despite a more favorable review of the draft by Frank Thomas, White and Kunreuther concluded that Reilly had a point and took his criticisms into account in the version of the paper (Kunreuther and White 1994) published in a special issue of *Water Resources Update,* edited by Gilbert and Mary Fran Myers.

The following year the *Update* carried an even more disputatious article by Gilbert, "Decision or Procrastination in Floodplain Management." Although another year had elapsed, little action had been taken on the Galloway report. White's appraisal in the article was negative: the ten or more agencies sharing the responsibility for federal disaster relief were still far too autonomous, still too out of touch with state agencies and officials, and still inattentive to the "over-arching but as yet inchoate aim of mitigation." Insurance against flood losses still needed reform and more coherent administration despite the changes of the previous year. The natural and aesthetic values of wetlands and floodplains were still underappreciated and largely ignored in floodplain planning. Finally, Gilbert concluded, "None of these improvements can be achieved over time without a more discerning and continuing executive and legislative audit of how well policy directives are translated into action" (White 1995). Gilbert continued to speak truth to power, whether or not those at the top were listening.

But White seldom used the Natural Hazards Center's *Natural Hazards Observer* to promote his personal views. He sought other avenues, leaving the Natural Hazards Center platform for colleagues in the common cause. One of these was former University of Chicago graduate student Rutherford Platt. Platt, a geographer and legal scholar, contributed a detailed history of the National Flood Insurance Program to Volume 2 of the festschrift in Gilbert's honor (Kates and Burton 1986), and, as mitigation became a more and more salient subject, provided an update in his book *Disasters and Democracy* (1999). Platt served as a consultant to FEMA on coastal flooding issues, and his perspective usefully complemented Gilbert's expertise concerning river basin flooding. Platt was increasingly outspoken during the 1990s regarding hazard problems along the nation's coasts, where abuses of the NFIP were most grievous. In September 1996, he provided the cover article for the *Natural Hazards Observer*. In "Hazard Mitigation: Cornerstone or Grains of Sand?" he applauded the foundation provided by *National Mitigation Strategy* but pointed out the vagueness of the program, which often failed to specify who was being required to do what, and attacked some of the fundamental premises upon which the program was established:

> The strategy assumes that, provided with adequate information about hazards, nonfederal authorities and private property owners will do the right thing, e.g., avoid unsafe building locations and/or practices. But recent experience along the nation's coasts and in areas subject to wildfire suggest that local governments and owners are eager to rebuild and expand housing in areas of high amenity value, despite the risks involved. If persuasion fails, will regulation take over? The strategy shuns the "R word" and in fact scarcely mentions existing regulatory requirements of the National Flood Insurance Program, which arguably need to be strengthened in certain respects.... Meanwhile, Congress and the president may be creating disincentives to nonfederal mitigation through overly generous disaster assistance policies.... A common concern ... is that the federal government is itself fostering the perception among states, local governments, and private interests that the costs of disasters will be predominantly absorbed by the nation through grants, subsidies,

insurance declarations, the waiver of nonfederal cost shares in a number of disasters, and the willingness of Congress to fund disaster assistance through off-budget supplementary appropriations (Platt 1996).

Platt was quick to acknowledge that FEMA is not the culprit in many of these issues. Supplemental appropriations were the province of Congress; presidential declarations were the province of the White House (with FEMA in an advisory/administrative role); and the waiver of nonfederal cost sharing was likewise a political act beyond FEMA's purview. In conclusion, he cautioned, "If these adjustments in the larger context are not made, FEMA's mitigation efforts will not be a 'cornerstone' but merely grains of sand scattered by the winds of political and private expedience" (Platt 1996). Those who make and enforce our laws, Platt pointed out, have found it increasingly expedient to support voluntary rather than mandatory regulation in floodplain land use.

Gerald Galloway also used the *Natural Hazards Observer* to good advantage in reviewing what had transpired nationally in the five years since the 1993 Mississippi flood (Galloway 1998). In addition to the Natural Hazards Center, the ASFPM has faithfully monitored and reported year-by-year FEMA and FIA achievements, or the lack thereof, through the published proceedings of annual ASFPM conferences. Gilbert White last contributed in this fashion at the twenty-first annual conference in Little Rock, Arkansas (ASFPM 1996).

"No Adverse Impacts"

Many communities have used the NFIP constructively to improve river corridors, meeting recreational, open-space, and environmental needs while lessening the flood risk to property and people. The former provide exemplary models of coordination horizontally within the local community, vertically at the state and national level, and regionally where mitigation efforts in one community can have unintended consequences for a sister community. As it became clearer that mitigation measures adopted by one community could increase the flood hazard for downstream communities sharing that river basin, the ASFPM promoted a policy of "no adverse impact" (NAI) and began publishing case studies of communities' experiences with integrated programs of "wise use" (ASFPM 2002).

Somewhat to the surprise of ASFPM leadership, White urged caution in promoting NAI, based in part on the contentious experience of reconciling City of Boulder and Boulder County development goals with an affordable mix of structural and nonstructural adjustments to mitigate flooding losses (see Chapter 10). Gilbert argued that allowing development in floodplains, even with a commitment to no adverse impacts, "fails to recognize adequately a variety of possibly positive measures such as improved flood warnings, flood-proofing, and ecosystem restoration." In short, because all development had some adverse impacts, Gilbert feared that touting NAI set too strict a standard. Relaxing on the development issue risked undermining the encouraging forces of change. In his letter to Larry Larson and Donald Vogt, chairman of the ASFPM Foundation (White 2001), Gilbert enumerated those promising developments: a new "white paper" from the Corps of Engineers Institute for Water Resources on incorporating environmental considerations into floodplain management (Stakhiv et al. 2001); the increasing interest by environmental groups (such as the Association of Biodiversity Information) in examining the natural functions of floodplains; and the independent initiatives by Jack Sheaffer in northern Illinois and by Rutherford Platt in Massachusetts, who with his Ecological Cities Project was appraising the interrelationships of large urban developments and floodplain management. But heading Gilbert's list of hopeful initiatives was FEMA's decision *finally* to mount a full-scale assessment of the National Flood Insurance Program's positive and negative effects (White 2001).

The credit for this courageous decision went to the FIA administrator during the closing years of the Clinton administration, JoAnn Howard, who was gratifyingly open to Gilbert's counsel and the advice of the natural hazards community generally. At her initiative, in 1998 the FIA contracted with researcher Dixie Shipp Evatt, assisted by Natural Hazards Center staff, for an assessment of selected aspects of the NFIP. Then, in 2000 Howard launched the expanded assessment of the NFIP. In two phases, over a projected two-year period, a postaudit research endeavor was commissioned from the American Institutes for Research, the Pacific Institute for Research and Evaluation, and Deloitte and Touche. Initially, the team reviewed the literature, chronicled the principal events affecting the NFIP since its inception, determined the key issues to evaluate, and planned an implementation schedule. Gilbert, Larry Larson, and Dennis Mileti (as director of the Natural Hazards Center) were appointed to the steering committee. Shortly after this endeavor was launched, President Clinton was succeeded by the George W. Bush administration, and JoAnn Howard and James Lee Witt were replaced as directors of FIA and FEMA, respectively. In the subsequent reorganization of FEMA, the FIA became part of the Flood Insurance and Mitigation Administration (FIMA). And in the aftermath of the attacks of 9/11/2001, all FEMA-related offices were subsumed under the Department of Homeland Security. To their credit, the succession of leaders over five years in this massive reorganization have not dropped the NFIP study.

That said, Larson and White have become steadily more discouraged with the committee's lack of integrated study. They, along with Mileti and several other committee members, pushed for studies not only of flood loss reduction but also for how the NFIP has affected disaster costs in the United States.

> Too often that link is forgotten. As the study is drawing toward conclusion, I am quite concerned that it will not pull the various studies together into the big picture for the nation. It is like the national assessments of hazards that

first, Gilbert, and then Dennis did—if each of them had not pulled the various pieces together, no one would have been able to understand the big picture of hazards, and how the nation was or was not dealing with them. At the critical point in the study, the study leader Rich Tobin left for another job. I see no one left there who is capable of pulling it all together. As such, it is possible that five years and $35 million may have been wasted (Larson 2005).

Gilbert became so discouraged that he threatened to complain to the authorizing congressional committee. This FEMA assignment, plus chairing the FEMA Steering Committee on Flood Loss Data, a project to develop databases and computerized maps of the entire nation's potential losses from earthquakes and flooding, constituted Gilbert's only remaining official involvements with the federal government into the twenty-first century.[12]

During the five years following ASFPM's decision to advocate for "no adverse impacts," the concept strengthened within the lexicon of the major federal agencies involved in floodplain management. Among local and state initiatives, Connecticut adopted NAI principles in its floodplain management law, and Ohio developed a model floodplain management ordinance showing communities how to incorporate NAI. Although not disagreeing with Gilbert White that any development usually has some adverse impact, Larry Larson of ASFPM argued that NAI represents a fundamental shift in how Americans deal with development in communities. For the past forty years and more, communities merely looked at

> how to build that structure in the floodplain to reduce its risk. NAI changes the community's view to how development impacts both existing and future homes and businesses. That generates a whole new balanced set of considerations before development occurs. Property owners downstream, upstream, across town and in the next town suddenly become aware that they may be adversely impacted by a proposed development. The key to the concept is that development is not stopped because it causes adverse impacts, but that those impacts are mitigated before the development occurs. It is a "do no harm" idea that citizens see as a good neighbor policy (Larson 2005).

National Honors in 2000

The National Academy of Sciences figured prominently in White's career as a geographer, and he in turn was responsible for significantly increasing geography representation in the academy. There were no geographers in the academy in 1973 when Gilbert was inducted. Unbeknownst to him, NAS members who participated with him on the congressional task force established in the aftermath of tropical storm Agnes in 1973 sponsored his candidacy. He was only the fourth geographer ever elected. Upon being inducted, Gilbert promptly looked into the election process, and, beginning in 1975, geographers were voted into the academy regularly. By the end of the century there were ten, including several former colleagues and students of White's.

The NAS sponsors and evaluates research through its National Research Council, in addition to addressing such concerns as human rights through NAS committees. Gilbert served on fourteen NRC research committees, chairing four. Perhaps his greatest legacy with respect to this academic fraternity was his continued insistence that findings of science be applied to the public welfare. This conviction was acknowledged fittingly when, on May 1, 2000, at its 137th meeting, the National Academy of Sciences bestowed its Public Welfare Medal on Gilbert White. This medal, presented periodically since 1914, was the inspiration of George F. Becker, who would have been pleased to know that one of its recipients would be the husband of his great-niece by marriage, Anne Underwood White.[13]

The National Medal of Science is presented annually to a number of distinguished scientists dedicated to research in the national interest. One of President Clinton's final official acts, in December 2000, was to confer the medal on Gilbert at a White House ceremony.

Notes

1. A Coloradan involved in state floodplain management and the National Flood Insurance Program since its inception and one of ten regional NFIP managers from 1978 to 1988 published a history of the NFIP in 2000 without mentioning Gilbert White (Quinn 2000).

2. "Sheaffer and Roland estimated that it would be cheaper for the federal government to buy the remaining undeveloped coastal barriers than to subsidize their development and then bear the costs of rebuilding them after a disaster. This concern was reinforced by a 1982 GAO report that found federal flood insurance to be at least a 'marginal added incentive for development in coastal and barrier island communities.' And a 1981 position paper by 'Concerned Coastal Geologists' urged retreat from eroding shorelines in place of government-sponsored efforts to stabilize coasts and beaches" (Platt 1999).

3. The TVA contracted with Larry Johnston and Associates to conduct the full assessment. However, Johnston died suddenly in 1990 before the work was completed. Subsequently, through the Natural Hazards Center, the TVA contracted with Jacquelyn Monday—a Natural Hazards Center editor, former FEMA employee, and long-time associate of the ASFPM—to help finish the large report, *Assessment Report of Floodplain Management in the United States* (L. R. Johnston Associates 1992) and to prepare the Review Committee's Summary Report, *Action Agenda for Managing the Nation's Floodplains: An Assessment Report* (White 1992b).

4. White's University of Chicago graduate student, Jack Sheaffer, has argued that the most sensible longitudinal measurement of property losses will also factor in gross

national product (GNP). Annual per capita GNP has, with few exceptions, steadily declined since World War II (while population doubled by 2000). When per capita annual losses from natural disasters are compared with per capita GNP in 2000, against those comparisons at midcentury, annual per capita losses decreased by roughly 30 percent (Sheaffer, personal communication).

5. Jacquelyn Monday was instrumental in much of this work.

6. For the next several years, until Frank Press stepped down from the presidency of NAS, neither Gilbert nor Ken Mitchell received invitations to assist the academy.

7. Even without federal authorization and funding, a few scientists have proceeded on their own with such postaudits, occasionally with the help of the Natural Hazards Center. A sophisticated and ambitious research design to compare diverse coping strategies regarding floods in United States and Canadian communities was developed over several years by Gilbert's former students Burrell Montz and Graham Tobin. The two sought funding from various public and private sources, and the Compton Foundation agreed to support a pilot study. Other researchers secured additional funding for evaluation of the research design and the pilot study, but despite a positive evaluation, the research never took place because no one would fund the actual study. Prior to that, Gilbert had been successful in raising funds for worthy scientific work at all levels, and the lack of support for this particular enterprise was especially troubling to him.

8. In 1996 a research team at the University of North Carolina reviewed the consequences over the previous eight years of making 10 to 15 percent of federal disaster relief available for mitigation planning. They found that most states had some communities with mitigation plans in force. These plans at a minimum described the local hazards and their histories, but they were "weaker in assessing vulnerability of people and property to those hazards and in assessing 'risk' in any systematic manner. . . . Mitigation action proposals tend to stress measures that are easiest to implement (promoting awareness, technical assistance) rather than actions that are more effective but require greater political commitment, cost more, and intervene more directly in the development process" (Kaiser and Goebel 1996, quoted in Platt 1999).

9. "FEMA has not had the visibility, leadership or political clout to bring about the integration of programs or of the investments in mitigation and preparedness" (NAPA 1993).

10. A Senate task force in 1994, seeking to stem this ever-increasing flow, recommended more stringent criteria for presidential disaster declarations, new incentives for mitigation, and increased reliance on insurance but stopped short of providing instructions for implementation of these recommendations. Nor did the Senate committee endorse extension of the flood insurance concept to an omnibus hazards insurance program that a parallel House task force had recommended.

11. Their coauthored contribution to *Environment* later that year expanded on these themes, integrating detailed findings and lessons learned from the midwestern floods with the assessment recommendations finally published the year before (Myers and White 1993b).

12. Charles Scawthorn, serving with Gilbert on the FEMA Flood Loss Committee from 1997 to 2003, was technical project manager on the development of the flood model for the committee. Scawthorn credits Gilbert with providing "the moral compass and conscience of the Committee. ... As the Project Manager I was particularly mindful of time and schedule. Gilbert also had that perspective, and gently but consistently kept that perspective before the entire team. ... This was particularly important, as at times the rest of the team was ready to compromise, but Gilbert would not give up. Others did most of the talking, but Gilbert was the backbone of the Committee, never losing sight of what was really needed. I very much appreciated his quiet leadership, and his attendance at all meetings despite his being well on in years" (Scawthorn 2005).

13. The one other Quaker citizen scientist to receive the NAS Public Welfare Medal was Herbert Hoover, a mining engineer before he embarked on his political career. With his wife, Lou Henry, Hoover translated Georgius Agricola's monumental 1556 opus on location and mining of minerals, *De Re Metallica*. Among Gilbert's most prized possessions is one of the few extant copies in the original Latin of this book, as well as a copy of the Hoovers' English translation.

10 *Floodplain Management at the Local Level: Tulsa, Oklahoma, and Boulder, Colorado*

It's obvious that you're the backbone of a movement and that you more than anyone else have answers to the questions I've been pursuing.
—**Ann Patton (in a letter to Gilbert White)**
Floodplain Manager, City of Tulsa, Oklahoma

T
O SOME DEGREE, GILBERT WHITE pursued integrated floodplain management throughout his career, but it became central to him on the national level in the 1960s and, through the Natural Hazards Center, at regional and local levels beginning in the mid-1970s. In many ways, floodplain management is most complex at the local level, where government officials, planners, developers, and individual citizens must deal with the problem of flooding itself on the one hand and the complex organization of institutions, laws, regulations, and potential solutions available on the other. Indeed, the resulting uniqueness of individual local situations raises a fundamental question: Is the goal of integrated floodplain management overly ambitious in a democracy such as the United States?

Throughout his academic career, Gilbert was committed to ensuring that the communities in which he lived practiced wise management of their floodplains. In this regard, Boulder, Colorado, which became the Whites' home in 1970, proved a persistent challenge. In fact, Boulder was not unlike most of the 21,600 U.S. communities founded along rivers and coasts. It seldom experienced heavy flooding, and the mitigation of losses from flooding was not a high priority in community planning. Despite Gilbert's efforts to apply his knowledge and despite Boulder being (by mid-century) Colorado's community most at risk of disastrous flooding, it was an uphill battle throughout the Whites' years in Boulder to mitigate adequately against a flood of even the 100-year magnitude. His own university stubbornly pursued an agenda of development on its property in the city's floodplain. (Some of his friends jokingly attributed Gilbert's longevity to his determination to witness long overdue flooding that would vindicate his unrelenting insistence that Boulder development be restricted in even the 500-year floodplain.)

Not surprisingly, cities at the confluence of two or more rivers or tributaries that experience regular flooding have some of the most dramatic flood histories—and, occasionally, the most exemplary flood mitigation programs. In the United States in the latter half of the twentieth century, one of them was Tulsa, Oklahoma. During the last quarter of the century, White and the Natural Hazards Center helped Tulsans turn around the city's reputation from being the nation's worst to one of its best communities in managing stormwater. From there, Tulsa soon emerged as a leader in integrated management of floodplains. The city developed and carried out management plans, not only for the Arkansas River flowing through Tulsa but also for the river's dozen tributary streams and the resultant thirty microdrainage basins in the metropolitan area.

In the latter part of the twentieth century, a handful of communities, including Tulsa, provided national leadership and helped maintain morale (including Gilbert's) and interest in the nation's progress (albeit slow and difficult) toward the goals embodied in the report of the 1966 Task Force on Federal Flood Control Policy, prepared for President Lyndon Johnson and Congress. No one anticipated the myriad planning, engineering, legal, and funding challenges that the National Flood Insurance Program would entail. Such a program requires persistence and political will among the highest leaders and a resulting commitment to long-term mitigation planning—all this despite the relatively short life of any one administration and the vote-getting popularity of short-term solutions and quick gratification (e.g., disaster relief). Consequently, the movement toward comprehensive floodplain management has involved grassroots efforts opposing both the powerful interests of those wishing to capitalize on the development of floodplains and those not wanting to restrict such development for political reasons. At the same time, integrated management has required coordinated planning, state-of-the-art science and technology, and coordination among communities sharing any river.

Indeed, coordination is perhaps the most difficult requirement, since not only community but also county, state, and national officials, as well as local organizations and businesses, must be involved or at least apprised of developments. The Natural Hazards Center and, subsequently, the Association of State Floodplain Managers, which the center nurtured, have been central in achieving whatever success the nation has realized, either horizontally among jurisdictions or vertically from the local to federal level. This integration is one of Gilbert's strongest legacies, regardless of whether the steadily increasing costs of flooding are ever reversed.

Beyond his focus on human occupancy of floodplains, Gilbert's broader vision as a geographer encompassed wise stewardship of all the ecosystems dependent upon healthy and well-managed floodplains. Although floodplains constitute no more than 10 percent of the land area of the planet, they are generally more biologically diverse than upland areas and can provide habitat for up to 80 percent of a region's wildlife species. Hopefully, White's legacy will also include helping to slow the decline in the earth's diversity of life forms.

Below: Projected flood-plain for a 500-year flood in the city of Boulder. (Images courtesy of Marshall Frech)

Boulder, Colorado
Flood Hazard Zones

Downtown

University of Colorado Student Housing ——— ——— **Boulder High School**

"100-year floodplain"   "500-year floodplain"   High Hazard Area

www.floodsafety.com/colorado

White Family Residences

5607 Dorchester Avenue, Hyde Park, Chicago. This house was in the White family for three generations, commencing when Gilbert was one year old.

Washington, D.C. Top-floor apartment at the corner of 16th and I Streets, shared with George Vanderhoef from 1933 to 1942.

Corner of Mole and Cherry Streets, in downtown Philadelphia,. It was Gilbert and Anne's first home, from 1944 to 1946, and the birthplace of their son, William.

The president's residence at Haverford College, at 101 College Circle, the birthplace of daughters Mary and Frances.

Year-round mountain cabin in Sunshine Canyon, Boulder County, Colorado, constructed in 1970. It was the family residence until Gilbert and Anne joined other Boulder university and Quaker friends in the communal apartment complex at 624 Pearl Street in 1984.

"The Meadow" cabin south of Allenspark, Colorado, twenty-five miles northwest of Boulder, that replaced the mountain home in Sunshine Canyon for mountain retreats.

Gilbert and Anne Globetrotting

Nairobi, Kenya, with Russian SCOPE colleague, Vassily Smyryagin, 1978

Egypt, 1977

Sunshine Canyon, 1980s

Stockholm, Academy of Sciences SCOPE meetings, 1979

Paris, 1980

Grand Canyon (n.d.)

Award Ceremonies

National Academy of Sciences Public Welfare Award, 2000. From left: Ian Burton, Mary White, Ellie Kates, Jerry Sears, Will White, Anne Chapin, Frank Traylor, Claire Sheridan, Gilbert White, Frances White Chapin, Susy Traylor, Olivia White

National Medal of Science, 2000, presented in the Oval Office, White House. From left: Claire Sheridan, President Bill Clinton, Gilbert White

National Geographic Society Hubbard Award, 1994. From left: Frances White Chapin, Mary White, Gilbert Melville Grosvenor, Gilbert White, Olivia White, Will White

Volvo Environment Prize, 1995. Presented to Gilbert in Gothenburg, Sweden

Gilbert in his office at 624 Pearl Street. Photo courtesy of CU-Boulder Publications & Creative Services Department of Photography.

But before examining Gilbert's contributions to global education regarding this and other central issues of geography and human ecology, it will be illuminating to examine in depth the experience of two communities, Tulsa, Oklahoma, and Boulder, Colorado, in dealing with a common, specific problem—floods.

Tulsa, Oklahoma

Tulsa is exceptionally vulnerable to nature's extremes, not only because it spans many waterways but because the meteorological patterns of the eastern Great Plains generate severe thunderstorms and tornadoes almost every spring and autumn. To keep these natural hazards from becoming human disasters, Native Americans for centuries occupied the high ridge bisecting Tulsa that divides the drainages of the Arkansas and Verdigris Rivers. Early European settlers wisely followed that example, but once oil was discovered in the area in the late nineteenth century, the city's population mushroomed from 7,000, when Oklahoma became a state in 1907, to 72,000 in 1920. In 1905 the world's largest oil deposit to date was discovered at Glenn Pool, south of Tulsa, and the city began to call itself the world's oil capital. By 1920, Tulsa's floodplains contained both homes and businesses, and the city incurred increasingly heavy losses due to repetitive flooding. The problem became sufficiently severe that the U.S. Army Corps of Engineers (with a district office in Tulsa) undertook a levee-building program along the Arkansas River that was completed in 1943. Twenty years later, in response to continued catastrophic flooding, the Corps undertook its second structural control measure, damming the Arkansas at Keystone 15 miles above Tulsa. With each Corps project, real estate development expanded east and south of Tulsa's center, and with that development, both the city limits and the percentage of the developed city occupying floodplains increased. By 1966, two years after completion of Keystone Dam, Tulsa's 300,000 residents occupied 160 square miles, 15 percent of which were in floodplains of various drainage basins.

Until 1970, the city had no ordinances regulating development in those floodplains. Zoning was too controversial to be enacted, and building regulations did not address flood hazards. In addition, there were no regulations governing land grading, soil erosion, and sedimentation, or, consequently, any regulations addressing water pollution. The system of underground and surface stormwater drainage that did exist to mitigate residential flooding losses was poorly maintained because no master map of the underground watershed drainage components existed, and there was poor access to many surface components. Despite a ruling in 1935 by the Oklahoma Supreme Court holding that municipalities could not discharge stormwater that would increase water velocities and volumes on downstream property owners, Tulsans showed little concern for the downstream impacts of their own development. In fact, a lumberyard owner and real estate developer, while Tulsa's mayor, initiated extensive subdivision development on floodplains before flooding in 1957 and 1959 inundated over 500 new homes.

Tulsa, Oklahoma, mitigation efforts during the late 1980s included clearing more than 900 buildings from its floodplains. Lands cleared after Mingo Creek floods (above) now serve as picnic grounds (below). Photographs courtesy of the City of Tulsa.

By 1960, the city finally crafted a comprehensive plan requiring land development on a basin-by-basin basis that acknowledged downstream impacts of upstream development. But even this comprehensive plan was largely ignored, and piecemeal development continued unchecked. In 1968 J. D. Metcalfe, a businessman, arranged for Ian McHarg, an expert on urban open space recreation and parks development, to survey the problem. McHarg observed that Tulsa was irresponsibly building homes in the floodplains while locating parks on high ground. Since the norm in the United States is for 10 percent of a community's land to be devoted to parks and open space, and since at least 10 percent of Tulsa was in floodplains, McHarg advised reversing the uses—turning the floodplain acres into parks and recreation areas and relocating houses to the higher elevations. Nothing came of this recommendation. Because the Disaster Relief Act of 1950 provided assistance to victims of flooding and tornadoes, "officials and agencies say they lost the ability to require and/or provide adequate controls or facilities to prevent flooding problems" (Poertner 1988).

It was to help the city of Tulsa and the thousands of other communities in similar dilemmas that, as discussed earlier, the federal government asked for Gilbert White's assistance in 1966. After the National Flood Insurance Program was enacted in 1968 and Tulsa experienced serious flooding in 1970, the city opted to join the NFIP, and the situation quickly changed. One of the first requirements for participation in the program was a zoning ordinance to reduce floodplain occupancy. The following year the NFIP's first maps were issued, and by 1972 floodplain maps had been adopted for the city's Arkansas River floodplain. With the new regulations and maps, city officials and developers could no longer pretend that the Keystone Dam would protect development on the floodplains below.[1] However, joining the NFIP had not forced Tulsans to reach consensus on the most appropriate local strategies to control floods, and, moreover, there was little public interest in the first place. Indeed, a Tulsa planner's farsighted proposal that repeatedly flooded homes be purchased with $18 million in urban renewal funds was rejected out of hand as too radical by city commissioners.

Then came 1974, the "Year of the Floods" in Tulsa. Flooding occurred in April, May, June, September, and November. Some homeowners along Mingo Creek, which drained one-third of the city and caused two-thirds of the flood damage, evacuated and repaired their homes three times that year. "Victims waded out of the [September] flood, drenched, stormed a city meeting, and demanded action by the city" (R. D. Flanagan 1994).

A community debate ensued. It raged vigorously immediately following floods and cooled predictably between events, but it did not stop. Tulsans for a Better Community (TBC), a group founded by repeatedly flooded homeowners, joined other neighborhood organizations in a Tulsa Homeowners Coalition. Carol Williams, a coalition activist, demanded that the city commissioners comply with federal standards and stop upstream development until the city had dealt responsibly with the existing problems caused by unbridled development. Following citizen flood hearings organized by Congressman James R. Jones and the consequent creation of a task force on flood control by Oklahoma governor David Boren, Congress authorized a Tulsa study by the Corps of Engineers. The 1974 study came none too soon; later that year heavy rains filled the Keystone Dam reservoir to capacity for the first time in its ten-year history.

The city commissioners were again asked to consider the option of purchasing and removing repeatedly flooded and repeatedly rebuilt homes. On his own initiative, one citizen, Bob Miller, even visited Rapid City, which had undertaken such a relocation project following a disastrous flash flood in 1972. Tulsa city engineers responded by proposing a Mingo Creek floodplain modification project that called for the clearance of thirty-three homes.

　　　　⁊

FRUSTRATED WITH POLITICAL INFIGHTING locally and nationally and recognizing the lack of agreement on what local solutions to flooding would make most sense for Tulsans, a reporter for the *Tulsa World* set about educating herself and the community regarding the resources available. Ann Patton's research led her to the Natural Hazards Center and Gilbert White.

Patton attended the center's first annual workshop in July 1975, and two months later she and five other Tulsans attended the National Forum on the Future of the Floodplain in Minnesota, where Gilbert White was a featured speaker. As mentioned in Chapter 9, because he was speaking to a like-minded audience of deeply frustrated practitioners, Gilbert was outspoken regarding the lack of federal leadership in dealing with both federal agency inflexibility and local land development interests that were undermining nonstructural approaches to floodplain management, including the National Flood Insurance Program. The previous year the Water Resources Development Act had recognized the importance of nonstructural solutions with a provision for 80 percent federal funding of such local innovations. However, the Office of Management and Budget (OMB) was holding up the legislated funding. It had been seven years since the Water Resources Council had been mandated to develop a Unified National Program of Floodplain Management in the wake of the report of the 1966 Task Force on Federal Flood Control Policy.[2] The ongoing debate at the national level was raging as well in Tulsa. Was the ultimate goal of floodplain management to maximize reduction of flood losses or to optimize use of floodplains?

White was frustrated, and he decried the WRC's disregard for the legislation of the past six years, which presumably had settled that debate by saying that both questions were of national concern (Patton 1975). His appeal for grassroots citizen activists to proceed with local mitigation efforts, regardless of the quality and quantity of federal assistance, galvanized the Tulsa delegation.

By the end of that year, Tulsa had allocated $8 million from the city's 2 percent sales tax revenues, federal revenue sharing funds, and community development block grants for several structural mitigation projects. Subsequently, the voters became much bolder, approving early in 1977 a $22 million bond package for emergency street, bridge, and drainage improvements. Flood control became the city's highest priority in submitting applications for federal funding for jobs and public works. Workers paid through the Comprehensive Employment and Training Act (CETA), augmented with local funding, launched a drainage-way maintenance program.

However, Tulsa's developers were similarly well organized, and after no flooding occurred from the end of 1974 through April 1976, two city commissioners who were strongly in favor of floodplain management were replaced by development advocates, fueling what became known as Tulsa's Floodplain War. As providence would have it, two weeks after the new commissioners were sworn in, 10 inches of rain fell in three hours, resulting in Tulsa's first Memorial Day flood, the record flood to that date. Three thousand structures were flooded, and an enraged citizenry confronted the pro-development city commission. They also confronted officials of the federal government, which had failed to fund the section of the flood insurance legislation that would allow damaged homes to be removed or relocated from the floodplain. Carol Williams and other victims of repeated flooding (some had been flooded five times in six years) begged to use their flood insurance checks or Small Business Administration loans to help them relocate and petitioned the city to allow them to remain in temporary housing until the federal government's responsibilities and a solution could be determined. Their petitions fell on deaf ears.[3]

Patton and her colleagues countered by inviting the open space consultant Ian McHarg to be the keynote speaker at a symposium on local flooding held at the University of Tulsa and funded by J. D. Metcalfe. The city's inaction on his recommendation in the 1960s to swap floodplain development with hilltop parks resulted in a scathing denouncement by McHarg: "Mingo Creek [development] should be enshrined in the Smithsonian Institution as a case study in stupidity." Another invitation went to Don Barnett, Rapid City's mayor at the time of its 1972 flood. Ron Flanagan, a local planning consultant who was advising citizen groups at the time, recalled Barnett leaning across the table at a meeting with the city commission and proclaiming, "Sometime, Mayor, you have to bite the pickle. Sometime you've got to really recognize that this house by this crik is a mistake!" (R. D. Flanagan 1994).[4]

Frustrated, Patton again turned to Gilbert White in an interview for the *Tulsa World.* He observed that when a community makes land-use management decisions, citizens line up behind either real estate development or environmental conservation. When this confrontation takes place, technical support available to the environmentalists plays a critical role in determining the outcome. The battle was being lost where well-intentioned local people lacked requisite technical support. Upon returning home, Patton wrote, "It's obvious that you're the backbone of a movement and that you more than anyone else have answers to the questions I've been pursuing." Gilbert was similarly impressed by Ann and responded, acknowledging the inadequacy of professional efforts to educate the public: "This makes it all the more important that people like you continue to put in understandable and plain speech what some of us try to say much less effectively." The interview and correspondence were the beginning of both a personal friendship and a commitment to Tulsa by the Natural Hazards Center that led to Gilbert's receiving a "Key to the City" from the mayor of Tulsa in the 1980s.

In the end, however, flooding was again the stimulus for significant change. The disastrous Memorial Day flood of 1976 forced the pro-development city commissioners to pass Tulsa's first floodplain building moratorium later that year. But as chance would have it, no significant flooding immediately followed, the pro-development interests strengthened their majority in 1978, and the commission rescinded the moratorium and reduced the floodplain management staff. Further, an earlier stormwater detention ordinance, calling for builders to ensure that new construction not add to surface runoff downstream, was amended to permit payment of a fee in lieu of providing detention. One bright spot in this era of backsliding was the naming of city planner Stan Williams to help head the Federal Emergency Management Agency's federal Interagency Hazard Mitigation Task Force. His assignment was to draft a manual of procedures for identifying needed hazard mitigation following federally designated disasters.[5]

Tulsa made good use of Stan Williams's efforts in 1984, following another Memorial Day flood, which "made the previous record flood on Memorial Day 1976 look like a drizzle" (Patton 1993). The second flood left 14 dead and 288 injured and resulted in $180 million in damage to nearly 7,000 buildings. Nineteen days before, Tulsa had elected Terry Young mayor and J. D. Metcalfe city commissioner. Metcalfe and Young's respect for Ann Patton led to her being appointed director of a hazard mitigation team convened at daybreak following six hours of precipitation that produced 15 inches of rain. Three experts were hired to undertake planning for the team, all veterans of many years of coping with Tulsa's seemingly intractable flood hazards: Charles Hardt, formerly the city's first hydrologist and a consultant with nationally recognized Wright-McLaughlin Water Engineers of Denver; Ron Flanagan, who also had worked with Wright-McLaughlin; and Stan Williams, recently with FEMA. Within seventy-two hours, with volunteer help from the city's engineering community, the team prepared maps showing the extent of flooding. They identified target buyout areas by the following week, eager to have their own recommendations drafted by the time a federal interagency hazard mitigation team came to town to conduct an independent assessment of Tulsa's needs, as required under a presidential disaster declaration.

Patton and her colleagues knew, based on their disheartening past experience, that they had three days at most to alter victims' expectations when they filed claims with the Federal Insurance Administration to rebuild their flooded homes. The federal and local bureaucracies of FEMA and the National Flood Insurance Program were geared to help victims rebuild their homes and lives as rapidly as possible—despite federal regulations requiring local authorities to abide by salvageable guidelines laid down by the NFIP and not to rebuild "substantially damaged" buildings that did not comply with mitigation requirements. Regarding this regulation, Ann Patton said, "We intended to comply with that requirement, even though FEMA was not then enforcing it" (Patton 1993).[6] In the end, the city purchased 306 homes using federal and local funding.[7] Two years later, a large mobile home park was flooded and purchased by the city for $2 million, again in lieu of rebuilding. The park was turned into an open space recreational area instead.

To institutionalize such pre- and postflood planning and response, in 1985 Tulsa created a stormwater management department and charged the department with formulating a master drainage plan for the city. To ensure a dependable source of future funding for acquisition of flooded or flood-prone properties, a city ordinance was adopted that required residents to pay a flat $2.95 per month and businesses to pay proportionally according to their stormwater runoff. This assessment is supplemented by capital funds set aside annually for acquisitions. Further, in 1991 Tulsans approved $600,000 in sales taxes specifically for floodplain acquisition or flood-proofing of endangered structures. In the decade following the 1984 flood, Tulsa invested $200 million in structural, nonstructural, and related flood projects, only $80 million of which were federal funds. By 2004, over 1,000 homes had been purchased for demolition or relocation to higher ground, not one of which has since been flooded. In addition, on average $700,000 is allocated annually from the city utility fee to support small flood mitigation projects based on a citywide master plan that ranks and prioritizes hundreds of projects on the bases of objectives, costs, and benefits.

Enhancement of the surrounding environment is a consideration in every project and proposal. Enhancements include establishing open space for recreation and wildlife (e.g., parks with playing fields that can accommodate stormwater during floods, small fish-stocked lakes for stormwater detention, and wetlands that support migrating birds and small animals); planting trees to retain soil; and constructing trails for biking, walking, and jogging that also permit easy access to and maintenance of mitigation structures.

In 1992 Tulsa received FEMA's Outstanding Public Service Award for its national leadership in floodplain management. That year the city's flood program received the highest ranking in the NFIP's Community Rating System, thus giving Tulsa residents the lowest flood insurance rates in the nation. In 1994 Patton edited a document describing Tulsa's approach to floodplain and stormwater management, *From Rooftop to River,* and dedicated it "to two gifted leaders," Gilbert Fowler

White and Joseph Davis Metcalfe—"one national and one local . . . Both epitomize the many pioneers whose contributions leave the city and the nation immeasurably enriched." Patton retired from Tulsa's public works department in 2004, following thirty years of promoting successfully in one community the range of nonstructural as well as structural adjustments to flooding that Gilbert White had advocated throughout his career.

Boulder, Colorado

In contrast to his work with Tulsa, where his influence was indirect, in Boulder Gilbert White was central to a half-century struggle to determine and reconcile city, county, and university interests regarding the use of the floodplains created by thirteen creeks that drain runoff into the city from the foothills of the Rocky Mountains to the west. Boulder Creek is the largest watercourse in the county, draining 155 square miles. It flooded seriously in 1894, now considered to be the 100-year flood of record. As in Tulsa, foresighted citizens invited a consultant early on (in 1910) to provide advice on how to mitigate Boulder's flood risk. As did McHarg in Tulsa, the renowned landscape architect Frederick Law Olmsted, Jr. (son of the designer of New York's Central Park), recommended keeping the floodway completely free of residential and commercial development. He advocated using the space for parks and other recreational uses, such as the Boulder Creek greenway trail system that travels along the entire length of the creek through the city today. He further pointed out that this probably would be the cheapest way to address the flood problem presented by Boulder Creek. However, Boulder city officials at the time ignored this advice because only minor flooding occurred in subsequent decades.

In the late 1950s, Gilbert White visited Boulder as part of his University of Chicago restudy of the nation's vulnerability to flooding two decades following the Flood Control Act of 1936. On the occasion of Gilbert's ninetieth birthday, Janet Roberts, a Boulder community activist and political leader over several decades, reminisced about that 1950s meeting of the League of Women Voters when Gilbert issued his first public warning regarding the city's extreme vulnerability. Until then she, like most Boulderites, had no idea that Boulder "was the most vulnerable city in Colorado." A few years later, as a member of the Boulder City Planning Board, Roberts again heard Gilbert warn of the potential risks created by indiscriminate building in floodplains. At the time regulations did not require that flood hazards be disclosed in any way in the plats of new subdivisions. "Indeed," she said, "the developers were vehemently opposed to any such adverse public notice" (Roberts 2001). Janet Roberts subsequently ran for city council in 1959. On the same ballot was a question regarding building a new public library. The chosen location was directly in the 100-year floodplain. White, Roberts recalled, objected passionately to the location, but even she was persuaded by city staff that the building had been designed so that the first floor

Boulder flood of 1894 as seen from the top of the flour mill looking westward. Photo courtesy of the University of Colorado at Boulder library archive.

would be above a 100-year flood. The location was not changed. As the years went by, experts modified the floodplain map many times to reflect new information, each time increasing the threat of flooding to the library.

Gilbert returned to Boulder in the 1960s, reiterating Olmsted's counsel a half-century earlier to avoid the suffering and incalculable costs of flooding by respecting the river's "right" to its floodway. White urged zoning to reserve as much of the floodplain as possible for open space and recreation. Boulder had had improbable good luck with no serious flooding in over sixty years.

Still, the city remained complacent until the South Platte River flooded in the Denver Metro area in 1965. Following this event, city staff presented recommendations to the Boulder City Planning Board concerning possible minimization of flood damage potential in Boulder. In 1966 Gilbert White prepared a report for the city titled "Flood Hazard Reduction and Floodplain Regulations in Boulder City and County, Colorado." The report addressed concerns regarding the increasing encroachment of the floodplain, growing issues about life safety and victimization of new property owners, and the need for wise land use regulations to avoid flood losses.

The city did not act on these floodplain recommendations until after Congress established the National Flood Insurance Program in 1968. Boulder residents Ken Wright (of Wright-McLaughlin Water Engineers) and his attorney-wife Ruth knew of and concurred with Gilbert's advice and admonitions. In the late 1960s Wright had sought Gilbert's help in developing the comprehensive *Denver Metro Urban Drainage Manual* (the effort that brought Wright-McLaughlin Water

South Boulder Creek flood mitigation. Top, 1972 aerial of Boulder High School; bottom: 2000 aerial of Boulder High School following removal of many residences in the floodplain. Photographs courtesy of the City of Boulder.

Engineers to Ron Flanagan's attention in Tulsa). White in turn invited Ken to participate in the Chicago NFIP implementation conference in 1968. Gilbert's prominence as a floodplain management expert then led the Boulder City Council to ask him to provide suggestions regarding a zoning ordinance, while at the same time the Boulder County commissioners hired Wright to recommend regulations for countywide floodplain management.

Then Boulder's luck finally turned. In 1969 a significant storm event produced Boulder Creek flows of approximately 3,000 cubic feet per second, equivalent to 25 percent of the 1894 flood discharge. The flood took no lives but inflicted enough property damage ($5 million) that the city adopted its first floodplain ordinance on August 19, 1969, as set forth in Ordinance No. 3505. The ordinance called for the first land use regulation of Boulder's major drainage-ways, established flood-proofing requirements, defined a floodway for Boulder Creek (that later prohibited residential development therein), and mandated floodplain mapping according to NFIP guidelines. These nonstructural measures complemented a Corps of Engineers' plan for structural improvements, such as streamlining the creek's channel for more rapid discharge (Birch and Wheeler 1987).

The community provided partial support to implement these measures, but, when most of the funding was still wanting in 1973, the city passed an ordinance creating a Storm Drainage and Flood Control Utility (now designated the Storm Water and Flood Management Utility). The legislation established a tax of $1 per month for single-family residential properties and more for other properties, based proportionally on drainage conditions that exceeded that of the average single-family residence.[8] In 1986 the utility fee was raised to $1.67 for residences, producing $860,000 in annual revenue. However, at the same time the revised master plan price tag had risen to $40 million, while the 1969 objectives remained largely unrealized.

The Whites and the Wrights remained allies on assorted fronts during the last quarter of the twentieth century and into the twenty-first. In 1979 Anne White hired on as a consultant to Ken Wright, to stage a statewide floodplain emergency exercise to assess state agencies' preparedness. Gilbert had helped organize a flooding response workshop for county and city officials two years earlier that identified the utility of such exercises statewide. A member of the state legislature for fourteen years, Ruth Wright was a natural resources management advocate and chaired the state's Great Outdoor Colorado Board of Trustees, which was established to oversee the use of state lottery proceeds allocated for protection of open space, wildlife habitat, and parks and recreation. Anne joined in this effort, serving from 1976 to 1982 on the Boulder County Parks and Open Space Advisory Committee. Earlier, she and Gilbert alternated serving on the joint city-county Boulder Area Growth Study Commission, and for several years prior to her death she alternated serving on the successor board of PLAN Boulder, a citizens' group addressing such local issues as growth and expansion of open space. Gilbert received PLAN Boulder County Achievement commendations in 1984 and 1994, as well as a Boulder City Council commendation in 2001.

Gilbert and Ken Wright served on numerous independent review panels, in part to ensure that city and county officials were aware not only of the city's 100-year floodplains but also of the 500-year flood potential to inundate much larger areas of the city. On October 8, 1973, the Boulder Creek Subcommittee of the Corps of Engineers Committee on Environmental Planning (CECEP), on which both Gilbert and Ken were instrumental participants, presented Boulder's City Council with a Boulder Creek nonstructural improvements policy. The recommendations of the subcommittee resulted in a local resolution that set forth policy guidelines relating to flood control activities for Boulder Creek. It included an inventory and evaluation of the existing floodplain, development of criteria for flood-proofing buildings, implementation of floodplain land use management, creation of an early warning system, and preservation of unoccupied areas of the floodplain for parks and recreation. The landmark resolution provided the basis for enhancing Boulder's floodplain management program, only later to be realized.

Gilbert and Ken's work was aided, sadly, in 1976 by a flash flood in the Big Thompson River canyon north of and parallel to Boulder Creek. The disaster, resulting from a peak discharge of over 30,000 cubic feet per second, killed 145 people and caused over $35 million in property damage. Clearly, the conditions causing this 500-year flood could have occurred a few miles to the south and resulted in the inundation of downtown Boulder and university housing. Yet the challenge remained to persuade the city council, and especially developers, that subdivision development some distance from any creek could nonetheless pose an unacceptable risk to future homeowners. Fortunately, with Gilbert's encouragement, the city earlier had mapped the region's 500-year floodplains, even though the NFIP only required 100-year maps.

Near the turn of the twenty-first century, Gilbert and Ken reasserted their community influence in floodplain management by participating on the city council–appointed Independent Review Panel (IRP). The panel's first review involved an assessment of floodplain management and mitigation alternatives for North Boulder's Four Mile Creek drainage basin. During the course of the IRP actions, the Boulder Housing Authority was persuaded to forgo part of a planned affordable housing development and elevate, with fill, the remainder of the project to ensure that all homes would be above Four Mile's 500-year floodplain. Gilbert was especially gratified with this decision. He and Anne were particularly fond of and knowledgeable about Four Mile Creek; its floodway included a bit of property they owned, and a primitive trail down toward Boulder became their favorite during Anne's last years. When a developer queried them about selling their property, they desisted, deciding instead to promote use and improvement of the trail for public

The Anne U. White Trail. From left to right, Mary White, Gilbert, and Boulder Friends Meeting members of "El Grupo": Mary Hey, DeAnne Butterfield, Ann and Wolfgang Thron, and John Huyler

benefit. The year before her death, the county renamed this Four Mile trail the Anne U. White Trail in recognition of Anne's commitment and work in preserving Boulder County's scenic, natural resources and developing a countywide trail system.

A similar trail system applying the earlier established CECEP floodplain policy guidelines incorporated a 5-mile recreational greenway corridor along Boulder Creek. The greenway preserves wetlands and riparian habitat, offers stormwater conveyance and retention, and maintains a highly prized scenic corridor through the middle of the city. On a typical summer day, over 5,000 people travel the corridor's jogging, bicycling, and handicapped-accessible paths, making this Boulder's most used recreational facility. Even trout fishing and whitewater boating are now possible in the heart of Boulder. The Whites' third-story condominium, after they relocated from Sunshine Canyon to the heart of Boulder, overlooks this greenway corridor, which Gilbert traversed daily as he walked to and from his office.[9]

To their credit, university, city, and county officials worked together to create this highly complex corridor that requires the coordinated maintenance of five city departments, the university, and a trail ranger program. For his part, Gilbert steered the city away from a Corps of Engineers proposal in the 1970s to straighten, line with cement and stone, and thus channelize Boulder Creek. Instead, the community adopted a "noncontainment" policy, which emphasizes purchasing land to create an undeveloped floodway comparatively free of structural controls (Birch 1989).

In another controversial floodplain matter, Gilbert's influence as chair of the IRP led to significant protections in the development of the Boulder Community Foothills Hospital in east Boulder, adjacent to Boulder Creek. Gilbert had opposed the site of the hospital, given its location in the floodplain, but community pressure convinced him to give way to the selection of this site after an extensive review process. In order to meet multiple community objectives, city staff proposed a requirement to elevate the hospital site and protect the structure to 500-year flood levels in line with Gilbert's philosophy. It was the first time the 500-year standard was applied to a critical facility and marked a growing change in the city's approach to floodplain management. Meanwhile, although unsuccessful in preventing construction of the Boulder Library expansion alongside the Boulder Creek floodway, Gilbert did manage to reverse a citizen task force's otherwise unanimous recommendation to the city council that would have added to and expanded the civic center in the downtown floodplain as well. When the task force submitted its report, Gilbert was permitted to attach his minority opinion along with their recommendation. The council noted that opinion, heard Gilbert's arguments, and accepted his recommendation over that of the task force. Ken Wright described Gilbert as "dogged against all odds when convinced he is right" (K. Wright 2000). Over time, Boulder decision makers assumed as a matter of course that any major floodplain issue would require a citizen task force, if not also an independent review panel of experts. Moreover, if the task force's recommendation was not shared by Gilbert, they also learned to expect Gilbert to submit a minority opinion. To his credit, when he chaired such a task force or independent review panel, which he often did, Gilbert invited members to exercise the same prerogative.

Gilbert's greatest challenge over his many years of involvement in Boulder floodplain issues was his own university's inflexibility and disregard for city and county initiatives to limit development in floodplains. Beginning with his 1960s involvement in shaping zoning regulations, he raised the ire of university officials by urging that construction of foreign student housing adjacent to Boulder Creek be abandoned. Despite the consequent 1969 ordinance that included this request, the university did not relent and in fact proceeded to build even more intensively in the floodplain (White 2000–2005).[10] In the face of this intransigence, Gilbert urged the university and city to institute an educational program to warn students of the hazard they faced and to advise them regarding mitigation measures to lessen the risks to their belongings and personal safety. Gilbert's persistence ultimately resulted in a city agreement to appoint an emergency management official responsible for this education process. The resultant booklet of instructions, subsidized by the university, is now published in six languages, and an ambitious program of instruction in flood preparedness is administered annually to university students. In anticipation of the next "big flood" that will test the adequacy of these measures, Gilbert funded the development of a questionnaire, now on file with the university, to be administered to flood victims following major flooding. The money for the project came from the Volvo Environment Prize, which Gilbert won in 1995. He had similarly donated the 1964 stipend he received from the city for his consultation concerning zoning ordinance to PLAN Boulder.

Starting in 1996, yet another issue in the ongoing controversy among the city, county, and university regarding floodplain use involved Gilbert and the Wrights. The city of Boulder was considering purchase of a 300-acre property of undeveloped land (the "Flatirons property") in the South Boulder Creek floodplain (the city's largest floodplain) that was formerly a gravel mine. In an unanticipated move, the university purchased the land and announced tentative plans to build a south campus in the floodplain. With the announcement the university also promised to protect some 2,500 houses downstream from the site by constructing a diversion levee. Surprisingly, these announcements came before the university had consulted with city or county officials regarding safe, environmentally sound, and comprehensive floodplain management for the South Boulder Creek watershed. Given the size of the property and its obvious potential to become open space, as well as citizen and professional concerns regarding the adequacy of proposed university structural mitigation measures, Gilbert agreed to again chair the IRP to address South Boulder Creek, as appointed by city council.

The mandate of the Flatirons IRP was to review the Phase "A" Mitigation Planning Report prepared by Taggart Engineering Associates as jointly commissioned by the Urban Drainage and Flood Control District, the city, the county, and the university. For this endeavor, Gilbert worked with other IRP members, including Natural Hazards Center codirector Mary Fran Myers and hydrologists and geologists with the Colorado Water Conservation Board and the U.S. Geological Survey. Assisting the panel was Alan Taylor, Boulder's long-term floodplain manager, who had advocated Gilbert's principles for local floodplain management.[11] As a result of the Phase "A" study, Gilbert's vision of truly integrated structural and nonstructural floodplain management was clear in the IRP report submitted to the city council, county commissioners, and the administration of the University of Colorado. In fact, the IRP reports for South Boulder Creek and Four Mile Creek may comprise as succinct a summary of the principles of integrated floodplain management as is available:

1. The benefits and costs of all floodplain functions should be considered in solutions to flood problems including flood conveyance, natural and beneficial functions such as riparian habitat, open space and aesthetics, and recreation.

2. Flood issues should be addressed from the perspective of the entire contributing watershed, and problem solving should be done on an overall basis

for various portions of one large floodplain, recognizing that different reaches may deserve different action. In particular, consideration must be given to the possible effects of upstream land use on stream flows and possible mitigation measures for downstream areas.

3. A full range of floodplain management tools should be used to address flooding problems, and assessing the effectiveness of these tools should be done on individual buildings and reaches for floods of up to 500-year frequency (White et al. 2001).

The IRP report was critical of the Phase "A" report's failure to provide advice on mitigation measures for flooding of lesser or greater severity than the estimated 100-year event, even though half the nation's flood losses by century's end resulted from floods larger than 100-year events. Moreover, the hydrologic analysis was judged lacking on eight counts, requiring in Gilbert's opinion redoing the analysis and, on the basis of the additional data, revising the flood insurance rate maps for the city and county. Finally, a host of recommended interim actions to increase protection of habitat and people in the event of flooding concluded with an admonition to city, county, and university authorities to coordinate and cooperate fully in using

a wide variety of floodplain management tools to deal with flood hazards including: floodplain regulations, zoning, subdivision regulations, building codes, housing codes, sanitary and well codes, disclosures to property buyers, design and location of utility services, land acquisition and open space, redevelopment, permanent evacuation, disaster preparedness, disaster assistance, land treatment, on site detention, tax adjustments and emergency measures (White et al. 2001).

The report closed by reminding readers of the newly elected George W. Bush administration's proposal to reduce federal support for local natural hazard studies and any resulting mitigation projects. Prompt action was prudent. As Mary Fran Myers observed, "Gilbert certainly has become more vocal and willing to push as he has become older!" (Myers 2002). In this instance, all parties that had agreed to negotiate the use of the Flatirons property (including the university) listened carefully to the IRP. The $250,000 needed to redo the hydrology study and implement the interim six-month work plan appended to the IRP report was approved and funded within two months.

Graciously, Gilbert was quick to acknowledge the sacrifices for the university caused by the consequent delay. Redoing the hydrology analysis alone would require considerable time and could result in substantial modification of university plans. As of 2005, the matter remained unresolved but under conciliatory study.

Regents of the university acknowledged Gilbert's contributions on many fronts, including his persistence on behalf of all Boulderites at risk from severe flooding of Boulder's floodplains, by conferral of an honorary degree at commencement exercises in May, 2006.

Notes

1. The planners in Tulsa (and not a few of its citizens) were aware of several major floods just that year. Rapid City, South Dakota, suffered a severe flash flood, as did Buffalo Creek, West Virginia. The latter was due to dam failure. At the same time, the American town most associated with flooding, Johnstown, Pennsylvania, where over 2,000 people lost their lives after a dam collapse in 1889, also incurred flooding, albeit minor, due to a hurricane. (Five years later, Johnstown was devastated by a 500-year flood.) In 1976 the Teton Dam in Idaho also collapsed. Indeed, within two decades of its construction, the Keystone Dam proved inadequate. In 1986 so much impounded storm water had to be released to protect the dam that major flooding occurred in Tulsa.

2. The director of this undertaking, Dr. Keith Muckleston, had resigned just one month prior to the Minnesota conference. At that meeting, Muckleston decried the foot-dragging of the WRC's membership (ten federal agencies, whose consensus was required for any recommendation). Even when sufficient consensus had produced a draft recommendation in 1973 for unified national floodplain management, the Department of Interior representative on the WRC had lobbied successfully behind the scenes with the same OMB to squelch the draft report.

3. The lobbying of Bob Miller and Carol Williams for floodplain acquisition finally bore fruit three years later. By then, the city had hired engineer Charles Hardt as the city's first hydrologist and Stan Williams as a city planner. Commissioner Norma Eagleton asked these two for an acquisition proposal, and they responded with a plan to purchase another thirty houses in the Mingo Creek floodplain that were standing in the way of a proposed detention basin. The proposal carried, bringing the number of dwellings in Tulsa's floodplains relocated or leveled during the 1970s to sixty-three.

4. Flanagan subsequently was hired by the city's engineering department to develop a pilot master drainage plan for one of Tulsa's thirty-three urban drainage basins. With Gilbert White's help, Flanagan contacted a group of national leaders in drainage planning located in Denver, Colorado, headed by Boulder resident Ken Wright—Wright-McLaughlin Water Engineers—who helped him develop a planning process that resulted in a Corps of Engineers Tulsa Urban Study, completed in 1982. The study detailed the extent of the Tulsa flood problems and recommended solutions within each of Tulsa's drainage basins. Flanagan's study was modeled on the highly regarded *Denver Metro Urban Drainage Manual* developed by Ken Wright with White's help in the late 1960s—a document still referred to across the nation.

5. Another bright spot at the national level during this era was OMB's reassignment, from the WRC to FEMA, of responsibility for the Unified Program of Floodplain Management.

6. Victims' responses to the suggestion that the most damaged homes might not be eligible for federal assistance to rebuild, as formerly had been the case, met with mixed reactions. The prospect raised hope among some, especially those who had rebuilt multiple times, but the majority of homeowners, eager to begin rebuilding as soon as possible, felt tremendous anger, mixed with comparably strong grief. Two of the five commissioners opposed any acquisition program, arguing that the proposed buyout

only rewarded people who should have known they were living in a flood zone. Moreover, these commissioners feared unfairly raising hopes if the bailout fell through. "False hopes are better than none," countered one flood victim whose home was flooded to the ceiling—his sixth flood in fourteen years. After bitter commission debate, an acquisition project was approved.

7. This compared with over 90 percent local funding of the total cost of the previous decade's acquisition of sixty-three homes. Tulsa, fortunately, had unallocated capital sales tax funds available in 1984. The city sold revenue bonds (pledging the sales tax toward their repayment) and used the resulting interest to finance the city's share of the flood buyout. FEMA's disaster coordinator was initially opposed to the buyout and blocked use of NFIP funds until Mayor Young promised to provide 50 percent city matching funds for eligible NFIP rebuilding grants. FEMA and the city thus divided the cost of acquisition 50–50 after deducting flood insurance claims. The buyout program also involved federal temporary housing assistance and Small Business Administration involuntary relocation loans.

8. Properties within the floodplain were subject to a 40 percent surcharge, and the boundaries of the 100-year floodplain were redefined to include properties where the depth of floodwater would be 2 feet or greater, water velocities 2 feet per second or greater, and the area that, when inundated, would cause at least a half-foot rise in the water level. To the city's credit, these were more ambitious, stringent requirements than those called for by the federal government when Boulder joined the NFIP in 1978.

9. Because the condominium complex, initiated and planned by the Whites and several close friends, was located in the 100-year floodplain, Gilbert endured countless jibes. He remained unapologetic, explaining that the projected 100-year flood comes up just below the foundation and that even a 500-year flood would not endanger any of the building's elevated condominiums. The building has no basement, and the first floor provides only storage and parking (Human 2002).

10. The Colorado Supreme Court had previously ruled that the university, a state institution, was not bound by local development regulation.

11. Taylor recalled Gilbert once saying that he would slow down only when he finally convinced his own community to adopt the policies he had so long recommended. Taylor remarked, "I don't know what we'll do when he's not here anymore" (Human 2002).

11 *Teaching Geography*

What is important is where we stand in relation to the tasks of society. . . . What shall it profit a profession if it fabricates a nifty discipline about the world while that world and the human spirit are degraded?

—GFW

G ILBERT WHITE BECAME AN ABLE LEADER, although he never read a book on management. He also became an outstanding teacher, although (like most faculty at the university level) he never took a course in pedagogy or studied educational psychology. Gilbert simply observed what did and did not work and then enlisted others in experimentation and testing to improve education. In virtually all aspects of his varied work, Gilbert was a pragmatist (Wescoat 1992).

From the outset of his career, Gilbert assumed that a scientist's responsibilities included dissemination of new knowledge as faithfully as possible through both teaching and publishing. His Chicago mentor did not set a very good example in the latter realm: Harlan Barrows published very little. White, however, published avidly but parsimoniously. He decried the all-too-common academic practice of accruing a long list of career publications by publishing essentially the same research findings in slightly different forms in various professional journals. Although he was not critical of scientists who popularized their research to reach the wider public, Gilbert wrote almost entirely for professional and practitioner audiences that could use his ideas for the common good.[1] Even the writing of textbooks in geography he left to others.

The Association of American Geographers and the National Geographic Society

Reflecting his reluctance to publish articles for a mass audience, Gilbert published only two of his over 400 pieces (1986 and 1988) through the National Geographic Society (NGS), the most popular source of geographic information for the general public in North America (and increasingly in Latin America and abroad) since its founding in the late nineteenth century. In fact, throughout the first half of the twentieth century, very few professional geographers sought funding or publication with the NGS. Early in the 1960s, Gilbert decided to address that lamentable situation.

In 1960 White was elected vice president of the Association of American Geographers (AAG), becoming president during 1961–1962. Prior to his presidency, leadership of the AAG was primarily an honorary position. The term was only one year, and there was no budget for a permanent office or salaried staff beyond a secretary. When he assumed office, Gilbert established four goals for the AAG: (1) to secure funding for a national office and a salaried director, (2) to update and disseminate the latest information about both the practice and substance of geography education at the college level, (3) to improve significantly the quality and relevance of high school geography teaching materials, and (4) to appraise how well and to what extent geographic research findings were being used to inform public policy and programs. The association addressed all but the fourth objective with considerable success.

Through a mutual friend Gilbert suggested a meeting with Melville Grosvenor, who several years previously had succeeded his father, Gilbert Grosvenor, as president of the NGS. Melville Grosvenor agreed to the meeting and brought several of his staff. "After introducing me," Gilbert later related, "Melville turned to me and in his usual direct, cheerful manner asked, 'What do you want?' I explained that I wanted to see the two organizations work together and that we needed assistance in establishing a national AAG office. After brief discussion with his colleagues, Melville stated that the NGS would provide free office space for the AAG in the Sixteenth Street building of the NGS in Washington, D.C., and would contribute ten thousand dollars a year toward its expenses. We were in business!" (White ss). Gilbert's first objective for the AAG was accomplished with gratifying ease.

Cooperation between the two organizations steadily increased over the next half-century, due, in part, to the interest that Martha Church, a former graduate student of Gilbert's, had in both the AAG and the NGS. One of the first women to receive a University of Chicago doctorate in geography, Church went on to become the third woman to serve on the board of directors of the National Geographic Society, where she took particular interest in White's third objective for the AAG: improving geography instruction in secondary schools. Gilbert's contributions in this regard are recounted below, but first it will be instructive to look at Gilbert's legacy as a teacher himself.

Gilbert's Educational Philosophy

Like most academic geographers, White never taught geography at the secondary level, and his first experience teaching at the postsecondary level came at Haverford, where, while president, he offered a course annually in the conservation of natural resources. Thereafter at the Universities of Chicago and Colorado, he taught forty different classes at the undergraduate and thirty-seven at the graduate level. He loved teaching.

Gilbert not only taught but also helped define the way the entire discipline was presented. Indeed, the distinctive curricular reforms instituted in the Geography Department at Chicago under White's leadership (White 1958) and similar innovations with which he was associated thereafter at the University of Colorado (Wescoat 2000) affected postsecondary education at many other institutions because of the large number of Chicago and Colorado graduates who went on to teach geography elsewhere.[2] White had nine principal geography colleagues during his Chicago tenure: William Ackermann, Brian Berry, Karl Butzer, Wesley Calef, Norton Ginsburg, Chauncey Harris, Harold Mayer, Marvin Mikesell, and William Pattison. Collectively they revised the first semester curriculum at the graduate level, introducing a student-centered program designed to acquaint faculty with the strengths and weaknesses of each student in dealing with geographic ideas and methods. Simultaneously, students became acquainted with the faculty's research interests (all faculty participated in this introductory fall semester course) and with the major concepts and skills that the faculty considered essential for professional work. Students submitted field reports and maps, appraisals of published maps, bibliographic analyses, papers, oral reports, and outlines for more intensive work. At semester's end, the entire faculty's assessment of each student's performance and needs resulted in a program individually tailored in consultation with the student. In some cases the faculty recommended that a student not proceed further or that he or she seek remedial training in skills as basic as writing. White was adamant that neither students nor faculty waste the other's time. More commonly, a student might be counseled to broaden his or her background in related departments and disciplines that would complement or strengthen the student's competence in geography.

Robert Kates, a graduate student under White from 1958 to 1962, recalled how disarming, even frightening, many fellow students (especially the few women graduate students) initially found Gilbert's no-nonsense directness. Gilbert's strong leadership as department chair, coupled with his strong loyalties as well as strong prejudices, was divisive among students as well as faculty. "Gilbert was very loyal to some students, with no particular correlation between those loyalties and the student's general popularity. Gilbert at times would jump on a student—unjustly so—and Ian Burton and I confronted him on this. I was impressed with how he took the criticism" (Kates 2001). Although empire building was not Gilbert's intent, his "White 'water boys'" among the graduate students became a highly visible and highly motivated coterie of very able aspiring geographers. Understandably, those students who were not "his" by either his or their preference coped with a fair amount of ambivalence and jealousy, feelings variously shared by his faculty colleagues as well. To varying degrees other faculty competed with White for student attention. Given his commitment to team teaching, showcased in the introductory graduate seminar, departmental politics were complex and contentious throughout Gilbert's years at Chicago (Harris 2001).

By contrast, at the University of Colorado, Gilbert was much less central to the Department of Geography by virtue of joint appointments with the Institute of Behavioral Science. Moreover, he shared the limelight with several colleagues who enjoyed high visibility in other subfields of geography, notably geomorphology and climatology (Jack Ives, Nel Caine, and Roger Barry). The departments at Chicago and Colorado were linked historically by virtue of the forty years' influence at Colorado of Geography Department founder Harold Hoffmeister, like Gilbert a student of Harlan Barrows at Chicago. But geography at Colorado strengthened slowly, with the first doctorate awarded in 1968, just two years prior to Gilbert's joining the department. He joined 13 colleagues in 1970, and in contrast to the waning future of geography thereafter at Chicago, the department at Colorado flourished. By the late 1990s, the Department of Geography had 19 professors, 185 undergraduate majors, and 85 graduate students. Some 3,500 nonmajors enrolled in geography classes annually. In a national survey of 28 geography departments granting the doctorate, conducted by Michigan State University in 1997, Colorado's department ranked first in teaching productivity, third in book authorship, third in journal publications, and fourth in doctoral graduates employed in academia (unpublished "Milestones" study, drafted by A. David Hill).

Even before moving to Chicago, while at Haverford, White advocated interdisciplinary, team-based inquiry and fieldwork-based teaching that involved student participation in faculty research. His annual course at Haverford on resource management and conservation had involved as much time in field trips and Socratic discussion as it did in lectures, reading, and the writing of papers. Karl Manwiller, a Haverfordian, credited that course for his pursuit of a master's degree in social studies (including geography) and a career in high school teaching and administration. The course involved his talking to strip miners, farmers, and a forest ranger about wildfire and traversing the Brandywine floodplain to view pollution from raw sewage.

Thereafter at the Universities of Chicago and Colorado, White treated both undergraduate and graduate students as professional colleagues, asking them to work on projects in which Gilbert had both a scientific and personal interest. His success in attracting funding supported a long line of graduate student research projects with clear public consequences. He often invited student coauthorship of publications and instituted a Chicago Series of Geography Department Research to ensure that student findings (including dissertations) would be heard. All geography graduates left Chicago with at least one major publication to launch their careers. At Colorado, White's most popular undergraduate course was on natural hazards, with the Natural Hazards Center providing support for both scholarly research and fieldwork. In the geography graduate program Gilbert regularly taught a seminar called "Comparative Environmental Systems," choosing a new issue each time the course was offered. The popularity and timeliness of the seminar's topics (e.g., water development and environmental policy, environmental effects of a "nuclear winter" following a nuclear war, or an analysis of the estimates of environmental change contained in the reports *Global 2000* and the U.N. Environment Programme's *The World Environment*) resulted in White's offering this seminar almost annually until age seventy-five, well beyond his formal retirement. Typically, the required research papers were addressed to specific audiences, such as a newspaper, a federal agency, or the chief executive officer of a local business. His final seminar topic was, "What are the probable environmental effects of a nuclear strike on the local area?" That was not an unreasonable question, since a plant that then produced plutonium triggers for nuclear weapons was located 8 miles south of Boulder. (It has since been converted to a wildlife refuge.) The students' findings were published in scholarly journals.

In selecting, organizing, and teaching the relatively few, simple, powerful geographic ideas that he assumed even high school students should master, Gilbert had a concise performance standard in mind:

> A liberally educated person should know sufficiently about the processes which shape the spatial distribution of selected landscape features so that with a minimum of memorization of basic facts and anomalous relationships he can state with a fair degree of accuracy the complex of landscape features he would expect to find on any given part of the earth's surface, expressly noting the amount of diversity present at any given scale, and the changes he would expect to result from any given shift in conditions affecting the processes (White 1965).

While convinced that geography, more than any other earth or social science, trains the user to make such predictions and understand the meaning of likenesses and differences among places, Gilbert neither felt nor claimed that that was the extent of geography's usefulness or worth.[3] Nor did he maintain that geography integrated these complementary disciplines better than any of the others did. "If our concern is with cultivating analytical power," he said, "our interest should not be in advancing geography as a subject, whatever our emotional ties to it, but rather in using geographic discipline to the fullest in advancing this educational aim" (White 1965).

Thus Gilbert saw the learning of geography as both a means to develop students' broad analytical skills and as a way to focus students' attention on the key real world issues that geography can address. As Gilbert admonished his geography colleagues in 1972:

> Let it not be said that geographers have become so habituated to talking about the world that they are reluctant to make themselves a vital instrument for changing the world. This position will no longer do for research, for teaching at the college level, or for teaching at the high school level. It can survive only at the peril of the society which permits its comfortable and encapsulated existence. If we wish to direct geography's very modest contributions to the structuring of new social process and organization, we can act now in three ways. We can commit ourselves to a continuing and persistent questioning of our own teaching and research in relation to its definition and reduction of social problems. We can advocate the adoption by our Association of measures to sharpen and support such activity by groups of us here and on the international level. We can give our thoughts to the reshaping of the university as an educational institution.... What is important is where we stand in relation to the tasks of society.... What shall it profit a

profession if it fabricates a nifty discipline about the world while that world and the human spirit are degraded? (1972)

Needless to say, such remonstration was not universally welcomed. One reaction, printed in a subsequent issue of *The Professional Geographer,* took polite but firm exception:

> One can approve of those individual geographers having a strong altruistic bent contributing their professional expertise in the cause of advancing society's well-being. But I am inclined to remonstrate with those, like Gilbert White, who seek to rally geographers in general to the cause of social engineering. To be sure, White disavows any intention of evangelizing . . . yet in fact, he does so when he insinuated himself as a model to be imitated. . . . This is the manifesto of a social and political activist. But the zealot must pay a price, for there can not help but lurk a suspicion that his research may be lacking in objectivity. . . . From its beginning, the unique purpose of the Association of American Geographers has been to advance the cause of geography and geographers; it was never intended to be a social-action organization. . . . How regrettable it would be if the editors of our geographical periodicals came to look with special favor on manuscripts which dealt with socially-oriented research (Trewartha 1973).[4]

Trewartha also challenged Gilbert's warning that the human race has "entered into an unprecedented period of crisis," countering that "grave and stubborn as many social ailments are, most of them have not yet reached crisis proportions. Indeed, a number of the felt crises are a consequence of our aspirations constantly outrunning our considerable accomplishments." But time and events were on White's side in this argument. The Association of American Geographers would in time honor Gilbert with lifetime achievement awards conferred by the Hazards Specialty Group and, in 2005, the Water Resource Specialty Group.

Awards and Reflections

Gilbert was persistently mindful of the issues, the substance, involved in the teaching of geography, but he also devoted much time and energy during the 1960s to advancing the methods, the form, of that discipline. Thirty years later another Gilbert, Gilbert Melville Grosvenor, who succeeded his father, Melville, as president of the National Geographic Society, became comparably central in rethinking geography education needs for a subsequent generation of Americans in the public schools. Well aware of White's legacy in geography education and testimonial to the cooperation that Melville Grosvenor and Gilbert White had forged in the 1960s, Gilbert M. Grosvenor was instrumental in White's selection for receipt in 1994 of the National Geographic Society's prestigious Hubbard Medal. The award was presented only thirty-three times in the twentieth century. Previous recipients included such pioneers as Robert Peary, Roald Amundsen, Ernest Shackleton, Richard Byrd, Charles Lindbergh, Anne Morrow Lindbergh, Edmund Hillary and Tenzing Norgay, Louis and Mary Leakey, John Glenn, Neil Armstrong, Richard Leakey, and Jane Goodall.

Several of White's former students were invited to the ceremony to speak on his contributions to geography and geography education. A. David Hill had obtained a master's degree in geography at the University of Colorado before receiving his doctorate from Chicago. He joined the geography faculty at Colorado two years before Gilbert joined that department. By then, some of the most ambitious and sophisticated curriculum materials in geography at the secondary level had been generated by the High School Geography Project (HSGP) of the Association of American Geographers (discussed below). White had chaired the steering committee of the HSGP while at Chicago, and a close collegial bond had evolved between White and Hill at Colorado. Hill invited White to speak at the organizing meeting of the Colorado Geographic Alliance in 1986, making it one of the first five state alliances in the nationwide network of alliances formed by the NGS to encourage the teaching of geography at the precollegiate level.

As a graduate student, Hill in 1959 had taken the aforesaid introductory seminar that White pioneered at Chicago, and in his Hubbard Medal ceremony remarks, Hill recalled that experience. When Gilbert began a class, as he did an interview or even a casual student encounter, he posed a question. The conversation seldom advanced until an answer was proposed. With Gilbert, one could not be passive. In the seminar Gilbert challenged the young scholars to think about problems, problems at the interface between human populations and the natural environment central to Gilbert's own interests and expertise. However, in the last meeting Gilbert addressed an entirely different topic, geography education. "White obviously wanted us to think of ourselves not only as budding geographic scientists," Hill recounted, "but also as prospective educators, and he urged us to begin thinking about some of the educational challenges we would face." Even at that early stage of the graduate students' training, White was asking them to consider the roles geography could and should play in a liberal education and specifically encouraging them to think about how they would organize and teach an introductory course. Characteristically, Gilbert did not give his own answers to these questions. Hill quoted White from his class notes: "It is probable that your answers to these questions will change from time to time—and probably for the better." White was advising students to pay attention to change, which is more likely than constancy, and to be optimistic about people's capacities to adapt to change (Hill's remarks at the Hubbard Medal ceremony, published in expanded form in 2001).

Robert Kates was another of the former students of Gilbert's at the Hubbard Medal ceremony. Kates had been introduced to White at Chicago by a graduate student, Martha Church, who was Kates's instructor in an extension service introductory geography course in Gary, Indiana. Although Kates, a steel mill worker, lacked an undergraduate degree, Church urged his meeting with White. Comparably impressed with Kates's potential, Gilbert enabled him to enroll in Chicago's graduate program, where Kates quickly distinguished himself. He later received one of the coveted MacArthur Foundation "genius awards" (one of the foundation's initiatives for which Gilbert provided consultation as a friend and mentor of MacArthur Foundation officer, Gerald Freund, a student leader at Haverford during Gilbert's presidency).

For his part in the Hubbard Medal ceremony, Kates provided a comprehensive yet concise summary of Gilbert White's many contributions to geography:

> Overall, Gilbert made three seminal contributions to geographic science: the concept of human adjustment, describing the broad theoretical and practical range of adjustment, and the role of perception and decision-making in resource management. The choice of human adjustment, as a range of alternative actions intended either to control nature or to adapt to nature, was initially developed for floods in the 1930s. In what must be the most influential dissertation ever in geography, *Human Adjustment to Floods,* White provided in the concept of human adjustment a practical guide to action that would be applied eventually to many other resources and hazards. And perhaps most important of all human adjustment is a profound aspiration for humane coexistence with the natural world. . . . The subjects of all this work are specifically water, more generally resources, hazard, and environment. The key actors are managers, the process is decision-making, the goal is human adjustment. His work is invariably functional: to answer a question of social interest, to identify the choices open to individuals and society, to influence the selection of a public policy. . . . Over time the scale of his research expands from the local and particular to the national and the worldwide, culminating in global analysis. . . . Underlying his pragmatic social involvement are deeply held views of the sanctity of human life, the stewardship of nature, and the liberating values of education and science. Thus the responsibilities of respecting and understanding nature, sustaining life, and learning and teaching what one knows, are united in a single moral imperative (Kates 1994).

The previous year, White had been similarly honored by his colleagues at the Cosmos Club in Washington, D.C. (where he had been a member since 1942), with their thirtieth annual award.[5] His acceptance address, entitled "Perceptions of the Earth," traced the change in such perceptions both in the United States and increasingly across the globe. Beginning with the observations of the surveyor, John Wesley Powell, founder of the Cosmos Club, White characterized late-nineteenth and early-twentieth-century perceptions of the earth as the view or belief that the planet was an assortment of natural resources still to be adequately "surveyed." Implicit in Powell's own surveys was the conviction that the earth awaited further development for human benefit. The challenge then became to provide prudent stewardship so that the earth could optimally and most efficiently be "developed."

Technology could make this task easier and even increase the earth's abundance. Wise use and protection of resources were the bases for federal agencies such as the U.S. Forest Service, the Soil Conservation Service, and the National Park Service. As thinking evolved in the twentieth century, an earth "at risk" due to human activity became an increasingly salient perception. (Indeed, this concern is the focus of the following chapter.) Characteristically, Gilbert's address to the Cosmos Club ended on a hopeful note. He suggested that an emerging perception was the earth as a "spiritual home":

> The essential point, I believe, is that people around the world in the 1990s are perceiving the earth as more than a globe to be surveyed, or developed for the public good in the short term, or to be protected from threats to its well-being, both human and natural. It is all of those in some degree, but has additional dimensions. People in many cultures accept its scientific description as a matter of belief. They recognize a commitment to care for it in perpetuity. They accept reluctantly an obligation to come to terms with problems posed by growth in humanity's numbers and appetites. This is not simply anxious analysis of economic and social consequences of political policies toward environmental matters. The roots are in a growing solemn sense of the individual as part of one human family for whom earth is its one spiritual home (White 1993b).

Earlier than most of his contemporaries in geography, White raised questions about human beings' perceptions of the world they live in, the world inside people's minds. In time these questions both broadened and became more specific. They initially focused on human perception of risk posed by hazardous environments and how such perceptions form, change, and influence attitude and behavior. But White's international work broadened his perspective so that he began to incorporate cultural differences among the variables affecting the diversity of perception of landscape and environment. Indeed, understanding similarities and variations across cultures in such perceptions became for Gilbert an important focus for several years (and a career-long commitment of his Chicago graduate student, Thomas Saarinen):[6]

> Differences in culture do not necessarily make for differences in perception but they probably do, and they may be expected to show in unlike valuations of life and environment. To attempt to shape uniform world images among all men would be absurd. To look to cultivating universal appreciation of similarities of these images among the human family and of the reasons for their chief variations would seem profoundly important. I can think of no higher goal for all of us who study the earth as occupied by man and who seek to help ourselves and our fellows to perceive it more accurately. That it would be practicable remains to be demonstrated (White 1967).

This challenge concluded his remarks in 1967 to the National Council for Geographic Education. The address was entitled, "Images of the World," and in it Gilbert posed the questions: What shapes such images? How can we describe the image that another has of a section of the environment? What significance does the image bear to the individual's life in society? How do our worldviews relate to our values, to our experiences? In asking what is known about training students to form new images, Gilbert cited C. S. Lewis's observation that we cannot see things until we know roughly what they are. "Facts there must be," Gilbert said, "and no one has a conceptual scheme which can substitute for the outlines of continents and the major variations in land elevation, but these probably have greatest value in supporting an intellectual habit of looking for process which gives order to the landscape features related to them" (White 1967). Development of this intellectual habit of expanding one's ways of looking at the world and its features inspired and guided the High School Geography Project, led by Gilbert.

The High School Geography Project

The subjects that students are introduced to in high school are often strong determinants of their interests in college. In the mid-twentieth century, geography commonly was grouped with other social and behavioral sciences in a general social studies curriculum in elementary and secondary schools. Geography already was inherently interdisciplinary, linking as it did by midcentury the four "environmental sciences" of geology, physics, astronomy, and biology with the four "human sciences" of history, anthropology, sociology, and economics. Most colleges did not offer a geography major and could not afford a department solely dedicated to the discipline. Quite often, the geography faculty, if such existed, consisted of one or two geographers, who in most instances were trained primarily in the physical (environmental) sciences rather than in the cultural (human) sciences. To White (whose mentor, Harlan Barrows, had emphasized geography as the study of human ecology), the largely physical geography curricula of most high schools and colleges accordingly was woefully inadequate. White's first encounter with public school geography curricula came with his move from Haverford College to the University of Chicago. Four years thereafter (and four years before Sergeant Shriver invited Gilbert to join him in Peace Corps leadership), Shriver as chairman of the Chicago Board of Education asked Gilbert's counsel on the kind of geography instruction appropriate in high schools. The query proved to be an important catalyst to Gilbert's participation in the AAG-sponsored, NSF-funded, High School Geography Project (White 1961).

At midcentury, for the more clearly defined sciences such as mathematics and the physical and natural sciences, the National Science Foundation funded research to improve teaching. Geography, however, was not supported, in part because the National Council for Geographic Education (NCGE) did not have tax-exempt status. But curricular reform across the disciplines was in vogue throughout the nation. The movement was led by Harvard University's Jerome

Bruner, who, in 1960, published *The Process of Education,* which emphasized curriculum innovation based on theories of cognitive development. Bruner asserted that learning was an active process in which students constructed new paradigms based on current knowledge. Further, he felt that the leaders of secondary education reform should be the professionals generating the information and knowledge to be conveyed by scholars at the college and university levels. Professional geographers at both the high school and college levels embraced Bruner's approach. In the absence of an inclusive, well-organized association of secondary school geography teachers, the NCGE and AAG formed a joint committee to assess geography instruction in the secondary schools of the United States. In 1959, soon after White's encounter with Shriver and Chicago's Board of Education, Gilbert agreed to cochair the committee just prior to his becoming president-elect of the AAG. Indeed, he welcomed the prospect of serving as AAG president in 1961 and 1962 in part because the position would provide both a foundation and legitimacy for the high school geography assessment.

Only fifty years old at the time, but already highly respected as chair of arguably the nation's leading geography department at the graduate level (serving by 1969 only a dozen undergraduate majors but six dozen graduate students, four of whom were enrolled in the department's master's in geography teaching program), Gilbert was bold in challenging his fellow geographers to dramatically reform the education of future geographers at both the secondary and postsecondary levels. In public remarks Gilbert declared that once geography was properly and widely taught in high schools, introductory college courses would also undergo sweeping revision and the textbooks currently in use would be discarded. (This was a daring pronouncement, given that seven of the eight members of the HSGP steering committee had vested interests in one or more of the texts then being used or written.) Initially the High School Geography Project received $178,000 in funding from the Ford Foundation's Fund for the Advancement of Education. The HSGP was unabashedly radical in focusing on geography as a research-based discipline. Many professional geographers regarded this focus as overly innovative and ambitious because its implementation would depend on teachers with little or no formal preparation in geography. The assumption was that experienced teachers would be able to use the teaching materials as a point of departure, while the inexperienced could gain sufficient confidence from student materials and teacher's guides to move ahead with classroom activities that inspired student thinking. The guides would not lend themselves to teaching in a plodding, pedestrian way: they would require inquiry on the part of both student and teacher. Description of parts of the physical world would be less the focus than the formation of attitudes toward one's fellow humans populating the globe and their adaptation to varying habitats and utilization of natural resources. The globe's surface would not be systematically covered region by region. Rather, methods of understanding the complexity and variety of the planet's typography and ecosystems were to be developed by referring to whatever areas were deemed appropriate to a particular teaching objective.

The above description of the HSGP objectives, summarized from White's "Assessment in Midstream" contribution to *From Geographic Discipline to Inquiring Student: Final Report of the HSGP* (Patton 1970), does not allude to the diverse philosophical theories hotly debated during the mid-1960s in determining the selection of project themes. An initial plan, drawn up largely by Gilbert, envisioned fourteen units, most of which would compose a flagship course, "Geography in an Urban Age"; the remainder would be covered in alternative courses. However, only the units composing "Geography in an Urban Age" eventually were developed, and they resulted in a flexible, multifaceted course intended for a full academic year but adaptable to shorter periods. The course was aimed at tenth graders but was suitable for students a year younger or older. Each course unit was developed by a research geographer, with the assistance of a team of research, cartographic, visual aid, and writing assistants, as well as high school instructors and an educational psychologist who provided advice on evaluation methods. None of the resulting units involved a teacher in the traditional lecturer-demonstrator role. Instead, the units consisted of learning activities that teachers could use to challenge students, pose questions regarding interpretation, and require students to draw on their personal experience and knowledge—all in order to expand their understanding of the world around them and their ability to function effectively in it. Several of the most successful activities were simulations or games, an educational approach rarely used in schools at that time (Helburn 1998).

When NSF funding was finally obtained two years into the project (over $1,000,000 through 1970), the directorship of the HSGP changed. The steering committee selected the unit directors, while the new project director, Nicholas Helburn, served as a group facilitator, educator, and motivator. He promoted a projectwide sense of enthusiasm and adventure, sharing lessons from various unit directors' experience as well as from parallel earth science, anthropology, and sociological resource committees for secondary schools.

Altogether, a diverse group of more than 600 classroom teachers, 20 psychologists, and 300 geographers from 100 colleges and universities helped create, test, and revise radically new course materials (Pattison 1970). Their work was perhaps the most ambitious rethinking of a discipline's curriculum that either the Ford Foundation or the Fund for the Advancement of Education had financed. In 1970 the project office moved to Boulder, where both Helburn and White became faculty members at the University of Colorado.

By then, *Geography in an Urban Age* had been published by the Macmillan Company. Eight years later, roughly 250,000 students in 300 schools (5 percent of high school students taking geography courses in the United States) were using the materials annually. The course was even used in a number of English-speaking countries beyond the United States, as well as in Germany and the Netherlands. By this time Gilbert was little involved in the project, but his influence was clearly evident in the material's emphases on "a concern for process; a commitment to undermine ethnocentrism; an appreciation of the limits of technology; an enunciation of general rules helping prediction—particularly of the environmental consequences of human behavior; and a devotion to learning in service to mankind" (Feldman 1986). Still, testing and refinement continued, and new materials published in 1979 heavily emphasized the environmental issues that were coming to dominate Gilbert's own career.

By that time, most NSF funding went to support summer training of high school geography teachers, with Helburn monitoring the results of the training. He found that, paradoxically, within a year of their training most of the teachers had moved out of secondary education to obtain higher degrees or to become administrators. Many who did continue teaching had difficulty obtaining funding to purchase the HSGP materials. The varied and somewhat bulky set of resources discouraged school systems that wanted a single package between two covers. By the end of the twentieth century, the materials for "Geography in an Urban Age" had gone out of print.

Forty years after the HSGP began, Helburn suggested why the materials were not widely adopted (1998). Fundamentally, and not surprisingly, the problem seemed to lie in shifting from an approach of lecturing to a focus on student inquiry. "We wanted to develop habits of thinking about the where of things," Helburn said. "Connected to what? why there? influencing what else? and how do you know? or was it just a matter of chance? and is there more than one answer? And if you could do it over again, knowing what you know now, would you do it differently?"

Such skillful, experience-based teaching, not widely practiced in the United States at the time, threatened school administrators, many teachers, and some parents who feared the materials might make their children too independent, even rebellious. "Some in education assert that most schools are more interested in training for obedience than for creativity, for acceptance of authority than skepticism, for certainty than ambiguity, for passivity than for empowerment," Helburn stated. "Such schools found that they were uncomfortable with HSGP's inquiry materials" (1998). But others argued that HSGP was ahead of its time, and the enthusiasm of teachers for the pedagogical innovations did not adequately compensate for their often insufficient preparation.

Reform at the Postsecondary Level

White's and Helburn's discouragement with the lack of the HSGP's measurable influence on high school geographic instruction was ameliorated somewhat by the numbers of young teachers who, after being exposed to the HSGP curriculum, went on to study geography at the undergraduate and graduate level. At both of these postsecondary levels, movements were afoot to strengthen training of geography teachers (another of Gilbert's four objectives when serving as AAG's president in 1961–1962). An AAG Commission on College Geography was initiated in 1963 that focused primarily on untraditional content (as opposed to the learning processes), such as spatial political organization, spatial diffusion, and locational analysis (Hill 2001). The HSGP had less influence in this content domain than it did several years thereafter, when a new AAG Commission on Geographic Education (COMGED) began focusing on process. HSGP-trained college geography reformers initially spearheaded a year of regional conferences (popularly known as "road shows"), each conference inviting three dozen instructors of introductory geography courses for participant observation in the latest experiments with teaching and learning techniques that attended as fully to student emotions and feelings in the affective domain of social psychology as to the cognitive domain of conceptual content. The National Science Foundation was disinclined to venture this far afield in its funding (the U.S. Department of Education provided one year of funding), but the NSF did fund the subsequent four-year COMGED project, "Teaching and Learning in Graduate Geography" (TLGG). Pattison, the Chicago colleague of White's responsible for advising the few Chicago students focusing on pedagogy careers, directed TLGG in addressing the question, "How might graduate training in geography incorporate training for the role of college teacher?" The Geography Department at Colorado, to which Gilbert by then had moved, was among the half dozen universities (Chicago was not one of them) that mounted experimental programs with TLGG funding (Pattison and Fink 1974).

Of the legacy of all the aforesaid endeavors flowing from White's 1960 vision to reform secondary and postsecondary geography education, only the TLGG experiments have yielded longitudinal studies of their impact on participants: the postaudit Gilbert always championed (Fink 1978, 1983, 1984, 1985). Sam Natoli, for many years in the 1960s and 1970s the AAG's education affairs director, offered his perspective on the legacy of reforms initiated in geography education in those decades (Monk 1986). Eternal vigilance, Natoli emphasized, always is the price of reform. When grant money dries up and reformers fall victim to the entropy of psychic exhaustion from "staying the course" of more student-centered instruction than is the norm in public education, the status quo returns to await the next wave of reform. A. David Hill, when presenting the keynote address at the Conference on Research in Geographic and Environmental Education, hosted by the Gilbert M. Grosvenor Center for Geographic Education at Texas State University–San Marcos in 2003, posed the question: "Are we developing enough intellectual and political capital for the next generation of geography educators?" He closed his remarks by returning to what he considers our most important question:

> Why geography education? . . . This question needs answering again and again by each new generation of geography educators. I recommend to you Gilbert

White's answer to this question, because it seems to me as cogent today as it did when he offered it over three decades ago:

> "The opportunity lying ahead is to help the young people of the world recognize in similar ways the processes that account for diversity and order on the earth's surface. From such common inquiry might come a more sensitive understanding of the images which the human family shares of its domain, as well as of its own capacity to live together in peace while modifying that habitat for the human good. The time is not far off when through some international channel social and natural scientists will work together to cultivate appreciation of the different images of the globe perceived by the human race." (White 1970, quoted in Hill 2003)

NGS "State Alliances"

If Gilbert White was the most visible pioneer in geography education reform during the 1960s and 1970s, by the 1980s this distinction had passed on to another Gilbert, Gilbert Melville Grosvenor, whose career with the National Geographic Society began when Gilbert White was ending his tenure at Haverford College. Gilbert Melville Grosvenor served first as a writer and photographer with *National Geographic* magazine and then as president of the NGS and now as chairman of the NGS Board as well as chairman of the National Geographic Education Foundation. His seventy-fifth birthday in May 2006 was celebrated with establishment of the Gilbert M. Grosvenor Fund for Geography Education. No one during the latter two decades of the twentieth century has been more visible in promoting ᴋ–12 geography education in the United States. That his legacy benefits in part from the cooperation between the NGS and academic geography flowing from the 1962 meeting between his father and Gilbert White was publicly acknowledged in his conferring upon Gilbert in 1994 the Hubbard Medal. Such acknowledgment of the deepened ties between academic geography and NGS education and research is ongoing in the NGS Education Foundation's publication, *What Works in Geography Education* (NGS 2005), wherein the U.S. AAG and International Geographical Union journals and annals are described alongside national projects of Activities and Resources for the Geography of the World (ARGWorld) and Mission Geography. These projects have roots that A. David Hill (Hill 2001) attributes to not only the Geography Alliance Network of the NGS but also to the HSGP of the Association of American Geographers and the National Council for Geographic Education.[7]

Since 1986, the NGS has worked with ᴋ–12 teachers and administrators, college and university geographers, and other educators dedicated to improving geography education across the United States. Each state alliance is based in a state education department or, more commonly, a university or college geography department, matching the funding by the state departments of education specifically for geography instruction. Academic geographers are linked with ᴋ–12 teachers through teacher professional development workshops and conferences, field trips, and provision of resources such as lesson plans and maps. The Geography Alliance Network recognizes outstanding student achievement through state and nationwide competitions. Such national examinations in geography, along with the institution of advanced placement courses, are strategies utilized in encouraging colleges and universities to add high school geography to their entrance requirements.

Geography Alliance Network members have provided training for over 100,000 teachers, and the resultant experiments in schools across the nation are described in *What Works in Geography Education* (NGS 2005). The publication's Introduction opens with a sobering reminder: "Studies conducted over the past twenty years consistently show that Americans possess a poor understanding of geography. This fact stands in stark contrast to the leadership role America plays in the rapidly globalizing and interconnected world of the 21st century." The vision of Gilbert Melville Grosvenor for today's schoolchildren and tomorrow's leaders, as summarized in the announcement of the establishment of an endowment fund for geography education in his name, is applauded by Gilbert White. It is a vision he also has shared:

> As globalization begins to homogenize the world's population and technology brings people closer, there has never been a more important time to understand the complex web of science, politics, culture, economy, history, environment, and place that make up geography. Not to gaze from afar as curious bystanders, but to dive in and truly understand and appreciate others' realities (NGS 2005).

Notes

1. Gilbert truly was not critical of those scientists who sought the limelight through writing and public speaking. His closest Quaker academic friend and University of Colorado colleague, economist Kenneth Boulding, sought public acclaim as much as Gilbert disregarded it. Boulding wrote more frequently for wider audiences, including the Society of Friends. Among his colleagues, Boulding made little effort to conceal his aspiration to receive a Nobel Prize. Such need for acclaim was not uncommon among Gilbert's academic friends; indeed, it was the norm.

2. White's changes at Chicago reflected the complaints of Haverford graduates concerning the depersonalized introduction and instruction they received in graduate school. They were given little orientation to the range of options in their field, and any diagnostic review of their interests and related needs was rare. Even more alarming to Gilbert were student reports that expectations at the graduate level were lower than those they had experienced at Haverford.

3. A contrasting view of scientific geography at the time equated geography with locational analysis, a rigorous mathematical approach producing a highly ordered scheme linking geographical facts and their spatial distribution, associations, and interactions

(discussed in Pattison 1970). William D. Pattison himself argued that geography had four traditions: earth science, human relationships to land, area studies, and spatial analysis.

4. This debate between theoretical and applied science has characterized all the social sciences, and as in the case of geography it also raged in the 1960s in the author's discipline of anthropology. It was no coincidence that, upon my enrollment in graduate study at the University of Chicago in 1961, Gilbert steered me toward Sol Tax, the one applied anthropologist in Chicago's distinguished Department of Anthropology. But departmental eminence in either geography or anthropology was remarkably difficult to attain in the 1960s if the department's reputation rested heavily on application of knowledge rather than its groundbreaking extension. This was the paradox of Gilbert White's accomplishment at Chicago: as chairman of Chicago's Geography Department, he advanced the department's reputation based on its commitment to science in the public interest ahead of knowledge for its own sake.

   Concurrently in the Department of Anthropology, Sol Tax's brand of applied science ("action anthropology": learning through helping to solve indigenous problems, with both as coequal goals of science) was variously received within the discipline. It played only a small role in the department's national reputation, however, and despite the exhilaration of being a part of that Chicago anthropology endeavor for two decades, I ultimately concluded that anthropology had lost its soul in marginalizing its members who—like Gilbert White in geography—unabashedly judged and pursued social science to address societal problems. During a sabbatical semester I wrote, for the *Annual Review of Anthropology*, a review of anthropology's contributions to public policy and administration (Hinshaw 1980). My extensive review of anthropologists' influence on public policy (including environmental issues) since midcentury was sufficiently discouraging that I forthwith left academic anthropology and moved into academic administration.

5. Theodore Schad, with whom Gilbert worked on the Senate Select Committee on National Water Resources, and Thomas Malone, a colleague on SCOPE for many years, nominated Gilbert for the Cosmos Club award.

6. During his tenure at the University of Arizona, Thomas Saarinen considerably advanced Gilbert's appreciation of cultural differences in geographic perceptions. Following extensive research of students' and others' perceptions of local and regional geography in Tucson and the southwestern United States, Saarinen extended his research abroad from 1988 to 1996, eventually with funding from the National Geographic Society. Working through public school teachers, he and a cadre of graduate students compared pupils' perceptions of their own communities and nations, indeed their world images, in schools from Scandinavia through Europe across Asia to Australia (Saarinen and MacCabe 1995).

7. Activities and Resources for the Geography of the World (ARGWorld), directed by Phil Gersmehl, are interactive curricular activities consisting of eleven global units developed by the AAG with NSF funding. Mission Geography, directed by Sarah Bednarz, focuses on how the National Aeronautics and Space Administration's missions

aid our ability to explore earth from space, through learning modules suitable for grades kindergarten through 4, 5 through 8, and 9 through 12. Other NSF funded k–12 interactive learning materials benefiting from HSGP experimentation, in A. David Hill's judgment (Hill 2001), are Geographic Inquiry into Global Issues, directed by Hill, and Activities and Readings for the Geography of the United States, directed by Phil Gersmehl.

12 *The Crisis of the Global Environment*

We can stabilize human populations, improve people's quality of life, provide more food, save tropical forests and disappearing species, and protect the environment. . . . If we remain inactive, whether through pessimism or complacency, we shall only make certain the darkness that many fear.

—**World Resources Institute (1984)**

I N 1949, THE NEWLY CREATED United Nations sponsored the first international conference to discuss use and conservation of natural resources. Developing nations, in particular, expressed concern and frustration regarding inequities in access to and use of the planet's natural resources, but no one expressed concern regarding the adequacy of those resources—if shared equitably—to meet humanity's needs.

In 1972, a second U.N. conference was convened in Stockholm. By then, environmental issues such as depletion of the ozone layer, contamination by acid rain, climate change by greenhouse gases and other atmospheric pollutants, desertification and mismanagement of water resources, depletion of forests, and pollution of oceans with resultant extinction of species had become much larger concerns than development of resources. Twenty years later, at another U.N.-sponsored environmental summit in Rio de Janeiro, the international community examined both resources and environment and confronted the issue of human exploitation of resources deleteriously influencing global ecosystems. Gilbert White attended both the Stockholm and Rio conferences; to the former he provided expertise on two critical resources: water (and lack thereof—drought) and energy as developed for and used by humankind. The previous decade he had chaired the steering committee of a project on U.S. energy strategies financed by the Ford Foundation, the Ford Energy Policy Project (FEPP, discussed below). By the 1992 Rio conference, White's perspective was even broader because he had served in the intervening years as president of the Scientific Committee on Problems of the Environment and of Resources for the Future. Environmental pollution had become a particularly salient issue for him, in part because he had chaired the Technical Review Committee of the Nuclear Waste Project of the state of Nevada in 1987 and had also been a member of the Committee on Technical Bases for Yucca Mountain Standards in 1992.

The latter group was appointed by the National Academy of Sciences to advise the Environmental Protection Agency on standards to ensure protection of public health from high-level radioactive (nuclear) wastes in an underground repository proposed for construction beneath Yucca Mountain, Nevada.

Midway between the publication of FEPP's extensive report in 1974 and the Yucca Mountain Standards recommendations in 1995, Gilbert also served on the steering committee of a World Resources Institute study, *The Global Possible: Resources, Development, and the New Century* (1984), one of the first of several global assessments of resources and environmental trends undertaken in the last quarter of the twentieth century. Thus, in the last three decades of the twentieth century, Gilbert was central to several studies that both provided scientific understanding of the global environmental crisis and outlined steps to achieve sustainable use of natural resources. Before proceeding with detailed review of these specific endeavors, their national and international contexts of environmental concern and study warrant brief summation.

The Earth at Risk

Before governments or academia became generally aware of the risks to the global environment, the perception first emerged locally and individually. In the United States some of the issues were first set forth by Rachel Carson in her landmark book *Silent Spring* (1962) and by Charles Reich in *The Greening of America,* serialized in the *New Yorker* before its publication in 1970. These works preceded a spate of federal legislation between 1969 and 1973, including the National Environmental Policy Act, the Clean Air and Water Acts, and the Endangered Species Act, as well as the establishment of the Council on Environmental Quality and the celebration of the first Earth Day. It was not until the following decade that the global scientific community, initially in the United States, Canada, and Japan, and subsequently in a host of other countries, led the campaign to increase awareness of the environmental crises facing the planet (Speth 2004; White 1993b). The International Council of Scientific Unions and the International Union for the Conservation of Nature and Natural Resources were leaders in this movement, aided by the United Nations Environment and Development Programmes (UNEP and UNDP) and by national scientific societies such as the U.S. National Academy of Sciences. The popular books that fueled the national debate were joined by comparably popular global reviews such as Richard Falk's *The Endangered Planet* (1971), Garrett Hardin's *Exploring New Ethics for Survival* (1972), Donella Meadows, Jordan Randers, and Dennis Meadows, *The Limits to Growth* (1974), Barbara Ward and Rene Dubos's *Only One Earth* (1972), Harrison Brown's *The Human Future Revisited* (1978), and Lester Brown's *The Twenty-Ninth Day* (1978).

In the mid-twentieth century, when the first U.N. conference on use and conservation of resources was convened, the world's population was less than half what it would be at the end of the century. This population growth, aggravated by increased per capita use of natural resources such as fossil fuels and water, in large part led to the shift in perception from an earth "developing" at midcentury to an earth "at risk" by the 1970s.

In the United States local issues precipitating this shift included air, water, and noise pollution, clear-cutting of forests, strip mining, construction of dams and channelization of rivers, urban sprawl and highway construction, hazardous waste disposal, nuclear power plant safety problems, toxic chemical exposure, and oil spills. Two of the galvanizing events were the Cuyahoga River fire in Cleveland and the Santa Barbara oil spill, both in 1969. Enthusiasm for development faded even more as scientists and citizens realized that many well-intended initiatives were resulting in unintended deleterious consequences. Perhaps the earliest worldwide manifestation of such concern came in reaction to evidence of strontium 90 pollution of mothers' milk from the radioactive fallout from nuclear bomb tests. By 1963 the treaty prohibiting such testing in the atmosphere, outer space, and under water had been adopted. DDT and selenium were killing birds and other wildlife. Entire species were endangered by timber cutting and river modification. Timber growth was curtailed by acid rain caused by coal burning. And human health was endangered by toxic emissions, particularly from automobiles.

By the early 1970s, a science of toxicology had taken root, addressing questions of what substances are toxic to other organisms in a united biosphere. Production of chemicals mounted from 10 million pounds annually in 1940 to over 100 billion pounds by 1980. It was estimated that as many as 500 new chemicals were being put on the market each year. During the 1970s, additional land of about 10 million hectares (25 million acres) annually was brought under cultivation in developing countries, concurrently with 15 million hectares (37 million acres) annually being degraded for agriculture through such toxification, erosion, and desertification.

By the early 1980s ozone depletion by chloroflurocarbons (CFCs) and the accumulation of greenhouse gases and consequent global warming had become accepted facts among the global scientific community. A core of ice drilled in a Siberian glacier in 1980 "demonstrated a perfect correlation between fluctuations in temperature and carbon dioxide levels and helped embolden a few researchers to make the first global warming forecasts with real confidence" (McKibben 2006). Pre–industrial revolution concentrations of carbon dioxide in the atmosphere were 275 parts per million, compared with 315 parts by the late 1950s (and nearly 380 parts per million by 2005). Then, in 1986 the world learned emphatically that environmental problems knew no borders, as radioactive fallout from the Chernobyl nuclear power accident spread far beyond Ukraine.

In the United States three principal nongovernmental agencies monitored these global conditions—the Worldwatch Institute, the World Resources Institute, and Resources for the Future, all located in Washington, D.C. The latter was funded by the Ford Foundation, as were, in part, the Environmental Defense Fund and the Natural Resources Defense Council. Abroad, the major intergovernmental programs included the Foundation for Environmental Conservation and World Meteorological Organization in Geneva, the Scientific Committee on Problems of the Environment in Paris, the International Program for Global Change Research in Japan, the International Union for the Conservation of Nature and Natural Resources, and the United Nations Environment and Development Programmes.[1]

❧

GILBERT WHITE did not devote much attention to reviewing this history for publication, with two notable exceptions. In 1980 he identified trends in an article for the centennial issue of *Science*. Then, in 1986, the Institute of Behavioral Science in Boulder mounted an impressive assessment of behavioral science from the disciplines (political science, sociology, economics, anthropology, psychology); at their boundaries (law, language, and health/medicine); and in relation to the world problems of population, environment, war, and peace. Gilbert addressed the "environment" in his most comprehensive published overview of the history and status of our consciousness of Planet Earth at risk, "Greenhouse Gases, Nile Snails, and Human Choice" (1991b). Rather than identifying trends as he had done in the *Science* article (White 1980b), he focused on the challenges of understanding the interactions of physical, biological, and social systems; and our assessments of risk and environmental choices. In closing, he observed: "We probe why the environmental movement emerged when it did in various cultures, and what continues to advance it so widely. . . . We know that behavioral scientists were not wise enough to predict it, and now, confronted with the intent of physical and biological scientists to launch a holistic attack upon understanding the changing earth, do not yet have a behavioral component to espouse" (White 1991b).

The holistic attack to which White alluded was the formation of the Intergovernmental Panel on Climate Change (IPCC), consisting of approximately 1,000 physical and biological scientists. Their international monitoring was facilitated by new modes of looking at the globe and of understanding its processes. Satellite photography recorded transformation in cloud cover, ice, temperature, soil moisture, vegetation, and urban settlement. Plate tectonic theory, first suggested in 1912 but not widely accepted until the 1960s, presented a view of the land masses of Planet Earth moving against each other. The concept of biogeochemical cycling offered a framework within which the movements of the basic nutrients (carbon, nitrogen, oxygen, phosphorus, sulfur) could be analyzed as affecting atmosphere, soil, vegetation, and water. Meteorological theory and advances in computer technology produced models of global atmospheric circulation, explaining how acid deposition, stream pollution, fertilizer policy, and climate change could interrelate. The term "human environment" was popularized by the 1972 Stockholm Conference on the Human Environment, where these environmental consequences of human management of global resources were first addressed in collective fashion. This perception of the earth at risk—at least relative to other problems—

developed unevenly around the world, with almost all nations having some form of environmental legislation and administration by the mid-1980s. In some developing countries, however, enforcement of laws has remained weak to nonexistent.

Many advocates for development, especially (but certainly not exclusively) in lesser developed countries, have taken issue with environmentalists' efforts to protect fragile habitats and reduce pollution of air and water, arguing that the eradication of poverty and all its consequences—from poor health to social unrest—justified the potential ecological risks that might accompany the development necessary to meet humanity's requirements for food, water, energy, and housing. At the least, this faction argued, if sacrifices had to be made to preserve ecosystems, they should be made by the wealthiest countries—those that were consuming the most resources and contributing the most to pollution and other environmental problems (White 1993b).

At the same time, an even more contentious debate was under way. More than population growth among the poor and voracious material consumption among the wealthy, a greater threat to the earth's environment seemed to be posed by nuclear war and consequent nuclear winter, global climate warming, and stratospheric ozone depletion. Although population growth and unbridled consumption might endanger humanity's numbers and standard of living, the latter threats involved potential destruction of the entire planet.

Gilbert White's professional interests and research bridged these debates. First, his work on natural hazards suggested that threats to humanity's welfare from extreme events could be significantly reduced by ensuring that populations examine *all* possible solutions and, foremost, stay out of harm's way. Second, as mentioned earlier, his studies regarding water quantity and quality suggested practicable approaches for sustainably managing this resource. Some of this work on water quality, especially in developing countries in Africa and the Americas, involved collaboration with his wife, Anne.[2] His appreciation of energy issues was greatly broadened by his chairing the FEPP. Similarly, his understanding of toxic threats to the environment was enhanced by his early work with SCOPE on nuclear winter (discussed in Chapter 6) and later by his work regarding disposal of radioactive waste.

As significant as are Gilbert's scientific contributions mentioned above, history may accord him even more gratitude for his efforts from 1974 to 1981, while president of SCOPE, to galvanize international and interdisciplinary attention on the earth's biogeochemical cycles. That was the informed opinion expressed by Canadian Ted Munn, former SCOPE colleague and more recently editor of the *Encyclopedia of Global Environmental Change*.

> Gilbert White representing SCOPE and Mostafa Tolba as Executive Director of UNEP in 1979 issued their joint statement, "Global Life Support Systems" (White and Tolba 1979), on behalf of a committee of about fifteen scientists. Of these it had been Gilbert who first saw the *inter-relations* among these cycles that people had been talking about for a half dozen years by then. No one had

thought about the effect in the atmosphere of all the nitrogen in our fertilizers on the ground, for example. Once you see these connections, the research agenda radically changes. After the ball got rolling, Gilbert was not inclined to expend his own energies at such a level of integration where the knowledge wasn't yet up to the tasks that most concerned him. But I consider his initial suggestion that we look at the interconnections to be his most important contribution to science. No one rivals Gilbert in perception of interrelationships. He was one of the very few scientists who could get that far outside his own discipline (Munn 2001).

Gilbert, typically, described his role more modestly:

It was hard at first to get people interested. In fact, I got a grant from the Ford Foundation to pay somebody to go around and see if they could drum up interest among scientists in working on global biogeochemical cycles. One of the results was a series of studies that began in the early 1980s and culminated in October, '85, at the Villach Conference in Austria. This was the first full-scale discussion among U.N. agencies about the potential of greenhouse gas warming to change the climate of the world. From there it was only a matter of a few years before the whole world was caught up in it (White 1991a).

This breadth of Gilbert's interests and concerns made him a central figure in a number of the early debates about the management of the earth's resources. His persistent clarion reminder was that, although time has not yet run out on our ability to reduce planetary risks, our progress toward that goal depends more on understanding human behavior than on increasing our knowledge of natural processes. In this vein, he concluded his remarks at the Institute of Behavioral Science symposium with which we began this section of the chapter:

It would be rash to conclude that, on balance, the environment of the globe as a whole is either deteriorating or improving, or that the survival of the societies we know depends upon filling a simple set of prescriptions. It is all too complex and dynamic, whether it involves managing greenhouse gases or Nile snails. . . . The future condition of the globe's interlocking natural and social systems depends more on human behavior than on the further investigation of natural processes, however desirable that may be (White 1991b).

Gilbert was seventy-five years old when he reached this conclusion, and to fault him for not making more of an effort at that point to chide Congress and federal agencies for lack of action regarding the accumulation of carbon dioxide and other greenhouse gases would be unfair. He chose to continue focusing his attention during the 1990s on his principal goal: integrating local, state, and national initiatives to achieve more efficacious floodplain management (see Chapter 9).

The scientist who did shoulder that burden was James Hansen, of the National Aeronautics and Space Administration, who in 1988 testified before the hearing of the Senate Committee on Energy and Natural Resources. He was convincing enough regarding the reality of temperature rising as a result of accumulation of greenhouse gases to produce U.S. government and international funding of the Intergovernmental Panel on Climate Change. By 1995 the IPCC had concluded that "the balance of evidence suggests that there is a discernable human influence on global climate." The resultant furor produced an effort within some offices of government and some sectors of the energy industry to cast doubt on the evidence rallied by IPCC to support its claims (Gelbspan 1997). To this exposé of calculated misinformation were added Gelbspan's sequel on global warming, *Boiling Point* (2005), and Mark Bowen's *Thin Ice: Unlocking the Secrets of Climate in the World's Highest Mountains* (2005), in which Bowen reports the findings of, among others, scientists Lonnie Thompson and Charles Keeling, who in 2005 were awarded the Tyler Prize for Environmental Achievement (the prize awarded to Gilbert White in 1987).[3]

In the closing plenary session of the 2005 July Workshop of the Boulder Natural Hazards Center, Roger Pielke of the University of Colorado and William Hooke of the American Meteorological Society assessed the difficulties we face in predicting what lies ahead in natural hazards management. Leading the list is the "gulf between the climate change community of scientists involved with the IPCC and the natural hazards community in conceptualization of mitigation." The IPCC promotes "reducing the changes in climate," whereas the natural hazards community encourages "reducing the impact of extreme events and risky conditions." As a result, the IPCC still defines the scope of its inquiries to exclude the most important contributors to vulnerability, including the dramatic increase in exposure of property and lives to hazards (Pielke 2005).

A brief summary of issues raised by the Western Hemisphere's experience with hurricanes during 2005 illustrates the difficulty of explaining disaster losses solely in terms of climate change. The year 2005 was not only the warmest year on record in North America but also produced the most force 1–5 hurricanes on record. Ocean surface temperatures averaged 1 degree warmer worldwide from 1990 to 2005, suggesting that global warming is partially responsible for the increased strength of hurricanes. Also, over the same fifteen-year period, one-third of all hurricanes annually, on average, were categories 3–5, in contrast to the fifteen years prior to 1970, when only one in five reached such magnitude. But there was a similar spike in categories 3–5 hurricanes early last century; we may be experiencing a cyclical phenomenon that global warming possibly exacerbates. Similarly, the number of tropical depressions becoming hurricanes annually (regardless of strength) cycled over periods of one to two decades during the twentieth century. It appears premature to attribute recent increases in number or strength of hurricanes primarily to global warming, even as evidence suggests that warming of ocean surface temperature is a factor in hurricane formation. Also cyclical and not yet understood are the paths of Atlantic hurricanes in the twentieth century, with most making East Coast landfall from Florida to Maine throughout the first half of the twentieth century, before shifting to a preponderance of landfalls from Honduras up the Gulf of Mexico and around to Florida's west coast toward century's end.

While the IPCC has focused on the above considerations, including their role in explaining disaster losses from hurricanes, the Natural Hazards Center community has urged more attention to the socioeconomic changes that are putting more people and property in harm's way. In 1920 the U.S. population occupying coastal areas from Texas to Maine numbered no more than the combined populations of Miami and Fort Lauderdale in 2005. Projecting ahead to 2050, if current weather conditions changed not at all, while human land use trends continued unabated, our losses from hurricanes would increase 220 percent. By contrast, if our land use remained as is through the next forty-five years, while climate trends continued unabated, our losses would increase a mere 10 percent. In terms of stemming losses in lives and properties, we are largely the master of our fate. (Most of the predictions above were given in unpublished presentations at a Natural Hazards Center Hurricane Katrina Symposium, September 21, 2005, at the University of Colorado.)

We turn now to the three specific tasks with which Gilbert was heavily involved in the 1970s (energy policies), the 1990s (toxic nuclear waste disposal), and throughout this time period (environmental degradation and mismanagement of natural resources). The reader may wish to refer to Appendix 1 to keep in mind the temporal sequence of Gilbert's other, parallel involvements, over these three decades.

The Ford Foundation's Energy Policy Project

In 1971, two years prior to the energy crisis precipitated by the Arab oil embargo, the Ford Foundation presciently selected U.S. energy policy as a priority and allocated two million dollars for a year-long study. The effort involved a project director, S. David Freeman, his staff, and a twenty-one-member advisory board chaired by Gilbert White. The study incorporated several dozen specialized research projects commissioned by the director and his staff and resulted in a preliminary report that was widely disseminated in 1973. This preliminary report was even adopted as a selection by the Book of the Month Club. The final assessment of options and policy recommendations, *A Time to Choose* (FEPP 1974), incorporated findings from the research projects as well as the advisory board's independent assessment of the report's recommendations.

Collectively, the research studies and reports of the FEPP represented an ambitious study of public policy and options for meeting the nation's projected energy needs—beyond anything previously undertaken, in or out of government. The timing was auspicious; very little energy planning was being done by government, universities, corporations, or not-for-profit research agencies. Between budgetary restraints and the pressure of more immediate problems, government agencies typically cannot mount such comprehensive studies. For their part, universities also have difficulty marshalling either the financial or breadth of intellectual resources needed for a sustained study. Corporate interests are typically narrow, and few not-for-profit agencies possess the broad base of expertise needed to address such a large, complex national issue. Indeed, few organizations could have taken on a project of this scope, involving identification and clarification of issues, analysis, technical assistance as well as exploratory research, and even advocacy. The Ford Foundation did have this capacity, however, and the agency's reputation ensured attention to its report in and out of government, despite the low level of government and public concern at the time.

Unfortunately, despite its visibility, the FEPP report seems to have had little effect on national policy, judging from the nation's failure, even thirty years later, to act decisively on the report's main recommendations. Some basic flaws in the organization and management of the project are probably to blame for this lack of influence. Although early on Gilbert identified some of these weaknesses, it was difficult for him to change the approach, given the strictly advisory role he and his board played relative to the director and his staff. This constraint was particularly exasperating since Gilbert's advisory board incorporated significant knowledge and experience from the corporate world, academia, and government. For example, the petroleum and public utilities industries were represented by chief executive officers (CEOs) of Westinghouse Electric Corporation, Eastern Gas and Fuel Associates, the Independent Petroleum Association of America, the American Public Power Association, Pacific Lighting Corporation, Mobil Oil, and Commonwealth Edison; and environmental interests were represented by executive directors of the Sierra Club and the Institute for Environmental Medicine. Not surprisingly, with such power and influence represented, Gilbert found chairing the board a daunting task, particularly because of the adversarial position assumed by the CEO of Mobil Oil, William P. Tavoulareas.[4]

Tavoulareas and several other members strongly objected to the project director's undisguised use of the FEPP "to alert the public to the profligate energy waste by American consumers, excesses of oil companies and electricity utilities, and environmental degradation due to energy production" (Deutch, Joskow, and Rowen 1975). White and his board consistently counseled the director and his staff to make identification, clarification, and analysis of issues their primary objective. However, in part because the project could commission technical assistance and specialized studies, the advisory board was unsuccessful in suppressing staff advocacy of such measures as conservation and government control over production in lieu of the free market competition favored by utilities and petroleum producers.

The Ford Foundation also financed an independent evaluation of the FEPP (Deutch, Joskow, and Rowen 1975), which suggested that the FEPP report's emphasis on conservation, a broader base of energy resources, and reduced energy consumption had caught the attention of the White House and Congress. In fact, the evaluators found that the report inadvertently encouraged some public complacency, given its basic conclusion that energy resources were adequate for the nation's projected needs, if use of existing sources was restrained and new sources were developed. However, the nation was unwilling to do either in any concerted manner, due in part to opposition to the final FEPP report by several members of the advisory board. Gilbert, while largely sympathetic to the approaches suggested in the report, remained true to his charge as chair of the board and to his beliefs as a group facilitator; he ensured that advisory board disagreements with the staff report, as well as disagreements within the advisory board, were fully noted and disclosed. Since the complete board achieved consensus regarding only a bland set of recommendations, White encouraged individuals to submit supplementary reports. Seventeen dissenting opinions accompanied the unanimous, but weak, endorsement of the principal recommendations of the final report.

At the end of his career, Gilbert judged the FEPP to be one of four major disappointments among projects with which he was heavily involved. The others were the inability of his Ford Foundation task force to shift the U.N. Mekong River Committee's member nations from conflict to cooperative development of the river's resources in time to avert the Vietnam War; the continuing high losses from flooding despite more integrated floodplain management in the United States; and the stalled negotiations among federal agencies, states, and local citizens to ensure safe disposal of radioactive waste—the battle over Yucca Mountain.

The Yucca Mountain Standards for Disposal of Radioactive Waste

Proper management of radioactive waste from nuclear weapons production and nuclear electric power production had become, by the end of the twentieth century, a national problem defying solution. High-level defense wastes were (and still are) primarily stored in steel tanks underground at three U.S. Department of Energy (DOE) locations in Washington, South Carolina, and Idaho. Spent commercial nuclear fuel is stored in water pools and above-ground dry-storage containers at more than seventy sites in the United States. By century's end, there were roughly 7,000 metric tons of defense nuclear waste and 63,000 metric tons of spent commercial nuclear fuel at these various sites.

The DOE has been charged with developing a permanent underground repository for all such waste in the United States. Doing so requires first finding an appropriate site that meets regulatory requirements and then constructing and operating the repository. The Environmental Protection Agency (EPA) and the U.S. Nuclear Regulatory Commission are responsible for regulating the disposal program to ensure adequate protection of public health and safety. The process of selecting a suitable storage site and applying to Congress for site approval has been going on since 1975, but as of 2004 the DOE still had not filed a single site application. In 1987, however, Congress directed the DOE to concentrate only on the Yucca Mountain, Nevada, site, after earlier calling for an East Coast as well as a West Coast option. The Yucca Mountain waste repository, as currently designed, would house up to 70,000 metric tons of radioactive waste deep underground. Ninety percent of this waste would be spent nuclear fuel from commercial power plants, and 10 percent would be waste from the nation's nuclear weapons program.

In the 1990s, Gilbert became involved in the site selection process when he served on a National Academy of Sciences/National Research Council (NAS/NRC) committee. The Committee on Technical Bases for Yucca Mountain Standards was charged with recommending the requisite standard of safety needed to protect public health if Yucca Mountain were selected as a nuclear waste repository by the projected deadline of 2010. If the site was not deemed appropriate, Congress required that DOE submit other recommendations for the permanent or temporary disposal of waste. The standard-setting process had actually begun in the mid-1970s and resulted, in 1985, in a standard promulgated by the EPA that was intended to apply to any disposal site deep underground. State agencies promptly challenged that standard, and it was reviewed in the courts. The standard was remanded to the EPA in 1987, and the agency was directed to reconsider the challenged provisions. However, before the EPA could respond, the 1992 Energy Policy Act was passed, mandating a separate process for setting a standard specifically for Yucca Mountain. Section 801 of the 1992 act requested an analysis by the National Academy of Sciences of the scientific bases for a Yucca Mountain standard and directed the EPA to develop health and safety guidelines for protection of the public near the Yucca Mountain site, based upon and consistent with the findings and recommendations of the NAS study.[5] The NAS assigned this analysis to its National Research Council. The NRC was given one year to present its recommendations, after which the U.S. Nuclear Regulatory Commission had one more year to issue its specific regulations, requirements, and criteria consistent with the NAS/NRC Yucca Mountain standard commissioned by the EPA.

The NAS/NRC committee was asked to respond to three questions: (1) whether releases of radioactivity to the environment could be limited to a level that constituted protection of the general public; (2) whether it was reasonable to assume that a system for oversight of the repository could be developed that would prevent an unreasonable risk of the repository's engineered barriers being breached or the public being exposed to radiation beyond allowable limits; (3) whether it was possible to make scientifically supportable predictions of the probability that a repository's engineered barriers would be breached as a result of human intrusion over a period of 10,000 years (100 centuries was the time estimated by EPA for the radioactivity of the wastes to decay to levels no greater than those emitted by natural uranium) (NRC 1995). But limiting the criteria to the decay level of uranium is arbitrary, given the much longer life of some other radionuclides scheduled for burial at Yucca Mountain (for example, iodine-129 has a half-life of seventeen million years, and neptunium-237 has a half life of over two million years).

The same year that the NRC Yucca Mountain Standard report was issued (1995), another study was published. The result of eight years of work, it was entitled *One Hundred Centuries of Solitude: Redirecting America's High-Level Nuclear Waste Policy* (Flynn et al. 1995). Its nine coauthors dedicated the report to Gilbert White, chair of the Technical Review Committee for research authorized by Nevada's Nuclear Waste Project Office (NWPO). In 1986 the NWPO selected representatives of assorted points of view from outside the state with no connections to the project to evaluate the research that had been done. Gilbert agreed to serve on the subsequent, aforesaid NAS/NRC Yucca Mountain Standards Committee by virtue of this concurrent Nevada NWPO assignment. It had familiarized him with the history and issues of the entire national program of high-level radioactive waste management.

The first meeting of the NWPO Technical Review Committee was held in 1987 at what was then Bally's Hotel in Reno, Nevada. The meeting brought together the ten committee members with about two dozen researchers who worked under the auspices of the state's impact assessment contractor, Mountain West Research, and its president, Jim Chalmers.

> Jim was a take charge guy with considerable talent for managing projects requiring a diverse and eclectic team of investigators. He also was used to having things his way. Upon arriving early to inspect the meeting room at the hotel, Jim deemed unacceptable the seating arrangements, with tables set out in a large egalitarian square. He proceeded to rearrange the room into a classroom setting, with participants facing a head table at the front. Jim was just finishing up the realignment when a distinguished, white-haired gentleman walked through the door. One look at the room and those piercing blue eyes radiated intensity and purpose. In his characteristic low-key manner, Gilbert walked around the room and quietly inquired who had arranged to have the room set up the way it was. He smiled that radiantly purposeful smile of his, thanked Jim for his efforts, and proceeded to rearrange the room back to the large square. From that moment on, through the almost ten years of his chairmanship, there never was any doubt about who was in charge, even though I don't think I ever heard Gilbert raise his voice or do more than "suggest" courses of action (Strolin 2001).

Like floodplain management, the challenges were as much political and social as scientific and technological. Success depended on engendering cooperation among multiple levels of government, ensuring transparent fairness in distributing the costs and benefits of the program, and earning the trust of a public fearful of nuclear waste and suspicious of the motives of the institutions managing them. By 1995, the Yucca Mountain project had become so mired in political, financial, legal, and public relations issues that the team that prepared *One Hundred Centuries of Solitude,* chaired by James Flynn, judged the problems to be virtually insurmountable. In their report, the group recommended a full-scale overhaul and redirection of national nuclear waste policy. They suggested that Yucca Mountain, which had originally been scheduled to open in 1998, would not be ready before 2020. The original 1982 cost estimate of sixty million dollars for site selection had soared to six billion dollars, and there were scientific questions about the safety and suitability of Yucca Mountain, the only site under consideration. DOE's dismal record for handling the temporary storage of defense wastes had further eroded support for the permanent disposal program, which was already fiercely opposed by state government and the public in Nevada.[6] Nevadans were concerned that Yucca Mountain's location just 90 miles north of Las Vegas would adversely affect tourism, gaming, and entertainment—by far the city's chief sources of revenue—as well as the community's attractiveness as a place to live. As the authors of *One Hundred Centuries of Solitude* said, "Even in a state that thrives on betting, it's a gamble Nevadans would rather not take" (Flynn et al. 1995).

Although national attention has focused on the Yucca Mountain controversy, the general public is mostly unaware of DOE's umbrella High-Level Nuclear Waste (HLNW) program that employs more than 2,000 people and has a multimillion-dollar budget. Logistical dilemmas and general public distrust have plagued this program, as have management issues (for example, the DOE had seven directors of the HLNW program during the 1990s, five of whom never got beyond the status of acting director). Some of the program's major problems include determining what kind of transportation system would be safest, most efficient, and most acceptable for moving nuclear waste and how long present interim storage facilities can be considered safe while new disposal technologies are under study and development. Still, the most troublesome issues concern scientific uncertainty surrounding high-level nuclear waste. Demonstrating that such materials can be successfully isolated for 100 centuries exceeds our current ability to predict natural and human events. The uncertainty is especially true with a first-of-its-kind facility with innovations that involve numerous unknowns. Reactions and interactions among wastes, storage casks, and the surrounding environment are difficult, if not impossible, to predict. For example, groundwater level, a critical variable, is subject to change due to seismic activity, but that activity is very difficult to predict over such a long period of time. As the authors of *One Hundred Centuries of Solitude* state, "Indeed, predictions about the future behavior of the geologic structure, the stored wastes, their containers, and the repository itself rest on many assumptions that are themselves uncertain to varying degrees and, according to a 1990 statement from the National Academy of Sciences, 'will remain uncertain no matter how much additional information is gathered'" (Flynn et al. 1995).

The leading recommendation of Flynn and his associates was to place a moratorium on the current program and to reevaluate the efficacy of, and thus the commitment to, underground geologic disposal. Interim dry-cask storage facilities exist that can be used to store waste for at least 100 years, allowing the program time to respond to the technical and socioeconomic problems that have plagued the efforts to abide by the arbitrary schedule established for the Yucca Mountain solution.

A judgment handed down on July 9, 2004, by the District of Columbia Circuit of the U.S. Court of Appeals was the latest obstacle, as of this writing, to proceeding with use of Yucca Mountain for the projected storage. It ruled on behalf of the State of Nevada, the Natural Resources Defense Council, and several other environmental groups that the EPA's decision to establish a safety compliance period extending only

10,000 years into the future "is arbitrary and capricious" and inconsistent with the findings and recommendations of the NAS/NRC committee. That committee's work, with which Gilbert had assisted (as reviewed earlier in this chapter) and that was published in *Technical Bases for Yucca Mountain Standards*, found "no scientific basis for limiting the time period of the individual-risk standard to 10,000 years or any other value" (NRC 1995). Accordingly, the EPA must either issue a revised standard that is based upon and consistent with the findings of the NAS/NRC committee's work or return to Congress and seek legislative authority to deviate from the report produced by the NAS/NRC. "It was Congress that required EPA to rely on NAS's expert scientific judgment, and given the serious risks nuclear waste disposal poses for the health and welfare of the American people, it is up to Congress—not EPA and not this court—to authorize departures from the prevailing statutory scheme" (U.S. Court of Appeals D.C. Reports 2004).

The Global Possible Conference

With Gilbert White's encouragement as chairperson of Resources for the Future, James Gustave Speth founded the World Resources Institute (WRI) in 1982. Gilbert enthusiastically offered his support despite the overlapping agendas of the two organizations (Speth, personal communication). Two years later Speth and WRI undertook an ambitious conference on "The Global Possible" involving seventy-five scientists representing twenty nations who reexamined the relationship between earth's resources and the human future. White served on the conference steering committee. The central, resounding message of the conference was that determined action, despite bleak predictions concerning economic and environmental crises, could yet result in a secure and prosperous world. Global warming, expanding deserts and retreating forests, mushrooming cities in poor countries reflecting impoverished rural populations, and wasteful domination of natural resources by wealthier nations were deemed reversible trends. "We can stabilize human populations, improve people's quality of life, provide more food, save tropical forests and disappearing species, and protect the environment," the final report said. "We must mobilize now to achieve the global possible. If we do, the future can be bright. We have sufficient knowledge, skill, and resources—if we use them. If we remain inactive, whether through pessimism or complacency, we shall only make certain the darkness that many fear" (WRI 1984).

The Global Possible conference addressed eleven problem areas: population, poverty, and development; the urban environment; fresh water; biological diversity; tropical forests; agricultural land; living marine resources; energy; nonfuel minerals; atmosphere and climate; and international assistance and the environment. It concluded with an assessment of conditions, trends, and capabilities and a discussion of business, science, and citizens. Of course, Gilbert's primary contribution was in the area of fresh water, and his tone of cautious optimism reflected the tone of the report in general:

The good news about fresh water is that, even after accounting for the larger volume of water that is unavailable to people from the hydrologic cycle, there is enough on a global scale to support current and anticipated populations on a sustainable basis. . . . Three essential goals are dependable and safe supplies for people, protection and management of the environmental systems through which water moves, and efficient water use. Meeting these goals will require that fresh water not continue to be treated as a free good or as the principal means for disposing of human and industrial wastes (WRI 1984).[7]

The environment was not highlighted, as were resources and their development, in the subtitle of the resultant publication, *The Global Possible: Resources, Development, and the New Century,* possibly reducing the influence of the conference and its report in comparison with other global assessments of that decade. In particular, the World Commission on Environment and Development, chaired by Gro Harlem Brundtland (who was among the participants in the WRI conference) issued a study that was much more widely cited and used.

The WRI and the World Commission meetings were but two of several conferences and resulting reports during the 1980s on global trends and challenges. The reports were largely produced by scientists and directed at policy makers. In his 2004 reassessment of these same challenges, *Red Sky at Morning: America and the Crisis of the Global Environment,* James Gustave Speth characterized the reports from the 1980s as having ten principal concerns:

1. Depletion of the stratospheric ozone layer by CFCs and other gases;

2. Climate change due to the increase in greenhouse gases in the atmosphere;

3. Loss of crop and grazing land due to desertification, erosion, conversion of land to nonfarm uses, and other factors;

4. Depletion of the world's tropical forests, leading to loss of forest resources, serious watershed damage (erosion, flooding, and siltation), and other adverse consequences;

5. Mass extinction of species, principally due to the global loss of wildlife habitat and the associated loss of genetic diversity and resources;

6. Rapid population growth, burgeoning Third World cities, and ecological refugees;

7. Mismanagement and shortages of freshwater resources;

8. Overfishing, habitat destruction, and pollution of the marine environment;

9. Threats to human health from mismanagement of pesticides and persistent organic pollutants; and

10. Acid rain and, more generally, the effects of a complex mix of air pollutants on fisheries, forests, and crops.

Speth's 2004 volume is notably darker than the 1984 report with which Gilbert assisted; he emphasizes the same concerns but with little of the optimism that pervaded

The Global Possible. Given his perspective (Speth had been involved in global monitoring for over thirty-five years), his 2004 reassessment is instructive—and ominous. (One of the reviews of *Red Sky at Morning,* in the *New York Times,* was titled "Be Afraid. Be Very Afraid.") Speth's citation of too little political will, too late, is particularly sobering. He opines, sadly, that United Nations summits such as Rio and Stockholm served up agendas for action more palliative than substantive. They permitted "pitifully weak" responses, especially on the part of the United States, shattering the notion that the United States has been the world's environmental leader.

With the energy policy recommendations of the Ford Foundation Energy Policy Project still under debate three decades after the project's report was issued and the Yucca Mountain nuclear waste storage debate still raging a decade after the two 1995 studies were published, Gilbert White had come to share Speth's discouragement with the lack of will among U.S. political leaders. Both of these knowledgeable scientists believed that humanity's need had become less the acquisition of additional knowledge regarding environmental trends and resources than enlightened leadership with the will to act on the knowledge that already existed (White, Kates, and Burton 2001).

The nation's experience with national, state, and local government response to Hurricane Katrina late in 2005 only deepened the conviction of scientists and practitioners associated with the Boulder Natural Hazards Center that private and local hazards mitigation and disaster response holds the most promise for the future. In November 2005, Gilbert and Stephen Leatherman of the National Hurricane Center cowrote an article for the *Hazards Observer,* "Living on the Edge: The Coastal Collision Crisis," that drew this conclusion, echoing the remarks of William Hooke in the closing plenary session of the July workshop of the Natural Hazards Center. Hooke saw little hope for top-down strategies for hazards management, given the Katrina-magnitude surprises that will accompany even the modest global warming already detectable. As extreme events become messier, the lag time between disaster and reaction will increase, the recovery resources will be diminished, and frustration will increase from addressing tomorrow's challenges with yesterday's answers. "Although all organizational levels must be involved, the private sector will be the major player" (Hooke 2003).

To the Leatherman and White article (2005), the senior policy adviser of the Mitigation Division of FEMA, H. Joseph Coughlin, Jr., responded with understandable concern, "Any change in course in how the Nation deals with coastal hazard issues must, in my view, begin at the Federal level. Why, because Federal programs and the public policy they implement have such a direct impact on the decision-making process that impacts the use of our nation's coastal areas" (Coughlin 2005).

Although Gilbert came to his conclusion slowly, following remarkable patience with and faith in federal coping capacity throughout his career, even by the early 1990s he had become more impressed by private and local than by public and national mitigation planning. In his acceptance address in Sweden, on receiving the Volvo Environment Prize in 1995, the mitigation initiatives worldwide that he reviewed were all from the private sector. Former student and colleague Ian Burton attended the ceremony and heard Gilbert's acceptance speech. "This is a theme I have heard Gilbert express many times," Burton later said.

> Innovation never comes from government, and governments never evaluate themselves. He keeps harping on this. So there is the contradiction of his devoting his life to influencing public policy, seemingly never discouraged about this, believing that government is the answer, and yet as the "rugged individualist" simultaneously urging all of us to work at the grassroots, not waiting for government to bail us out (Burton 2001).

In closing this chapter, it is fair to say that Gilbert never despaired of enlightened leadership emerging at all levels of organization to work in concert with scientists in addressing our environmental dilemmas. Ian Burton and Bob Kates encouraged his optimism and in turn, no doubt, were reassured by his. Kates suggested their adoption of the motto, "Between a bright future and a descending darkness, always a candle" (personal communication).

Notes

1. For monitoring specifically the resource of water, in the United States a National Water Commission was established in 1971, with Gilbert serving as a consultant from 1971 to 1973. In 1998 a World Water Council (WWC) was founded, with Gilbert offering his reflections on the previous half-century's quest for integrated water management in the inaugural issue of the WWC's journal (White 1998b).

2. Anne's research following *Drawers of Water* included a contract with the International Development Research Center (Ottawa, Canada) to produce a selected annotated bibliography on rural water supply and sanitation in developing countries, consultation for the World Bank on appropriate technology for water supply and waste disposal, consultation for the U.S. Agency for International Development identifying household preferences for and feasibility of alternative water supply and sanitation systems in low-income housing in Nairobi, Kenya, and household behavioral patterns regarding water and sanitation in two Egyptian villages.

3. This history of research on global warming as reported through 2005 was helpfully reviewed by Bill McKibben in 2006.

4. Lee Botts, executive director of the Lake Michigan Federation, was one of the two environmentalists appointed to the advisory committee chaired by Gilbert White. In a letter to Gilbert on his ninetieth birthday, Botts reviewed the dynamics of the committee:

> The advisory committee was set up because of the objections of the oil industry to selection of David Freeman to direct the project. William Tavoulareas led the appeal to Edsel Ford, then CEO of the Ford Motor Company, against Freeman. Ford replied that, while he could not overrule the foundation's selection, he could make certain that industry would have a role in the project through an advisory committee whose individ-

ual comments would be published in a final report. Even you were challenged by the extreme differences of opinion and strong personalities.

So much hostility developed between Tavoulareas and McCloskey (executive director of the Sierra Club) that when one spoke in the advisory committee meetings, the other would leave the room. Finally in hope that closer acquaintanceship would lead to more amiable relations, the foundation arranged for a full five day meeting in California where everyone would stay at and be wined and dined at the Santa Barbara Country Club. It did not work, but greater civility was achieved at the follow up meeting that you arranged in Estes Park (Botts 2001).

5. The 1992 Energy Policy Act made the task of Gilbert's NRC committee a bit easier (unfortunately) by weakening the health protection provisions of the Nuclear Wastes Policy Act. The 1992 legislation required the DOE to meet potentially less stringent standards for radiation exposure than the EPA had planned.

6. Since 1988 Congress and the DOE had repeatedly cut federal funding for Nevada's own state studies challenging the suitability of Yucca Mountain. Again, no alternative site was under review, and almost all provisions of the Nuclear Wastes Policy Act for ensuring a fair site selection process had been rescinded or compromised. In 1989 the Nevada state legislature passed two resolutions opposing the Yucca Mountain project and a bill that made it illegal to dispose of high-level nuclear waste in the state.

7. Eight steps for accomplishing these three goals were listed:

1.) Prepare national analyses of existing fresh water uses and supplies and likely future demands as a basis for sound future planning. Incorporate environmental and social factors and public participation into the planning of projects.

2.) Ensure that water users are charged rates that encourage efficiency and reflect the costs of providing water on a sustainable basis.

3.) Give greater attention to opportunities for underground water storage, as opposed to surface storage, for stabilizing inter-year variations in supply.

4.) Achieve sharp increases (as much as 50 percent) in the efficiency of water use in irrigation by using readily available, cost-effective means such as pricing water to cover the true cost of supply, harmonizing cropping practices and water delivery, modifying water-application techniques, and managing water supply systems more reliably.

5.) Emphasize the construction of smaller, community-based irrigation systems (which can be locally managed and designed for local needs) and the rehabilitation, better operation, and maintenance of existing systems as alternatives to new, large projects.

6.) Manage fertilizers and pesticides in a way that protects surface- and groundwaters. Nations that export agricultural chemicals and firms that manufacture them have an obligation to help educate users about prudent application rates and techniques.

7.) Give precedence to the development and demonstration of simple, low-cost, decentralized urban water supply systems and sanitation technologies that minimize water conveyance, promote nutrient recovery, and reduce human exposure to pathogens.

8.) Control potential industrial water pollutants at the source through required application of available and effective processes and technologies and through "chemically tight" management that recycles or contains hazardous industrial waste (WRI 1984).

13 Gilbert White: The Man

Go placidly amid the noise and haste,
and remember what peace there may be in silence.
As far as possible without surrender
be on good terms with all persons.
Speak your truth quietly and clearly;
and listen to others,
even the dull and the ignorant;
they too have their story.
　　　　　—Max Ehrmann, *Desiderata*

I believe that each of us finds greatest use and greatest satisfaction in a
life which respects and kindles the spark of the divine that is found in
the conscience of every other member of the human brotherhood.
　　　　　—GFW

REATNESS IN A PERSON is popularly measured by power in politics, authority in religion, or creativity in the arts, sciences, and other realms. And indeed, Gilbert White's legacy certainly stems in part from his creative thinking as a geographer. But the people who know Gilbert well invariably say that they admire his "person" as much as his accomplishments. His greatness is due in large part to a union of creative and utilitarian scientific ideas and honorific character that allowed him to effect significant social change in his lifetime. Gilbert's success is a lesson for anyone, whether his or her contributions are social or political leadership, scientific or philosophical ideas, works of art, or in any other endeavor. Those persons who are most revered live exemplary lives.

Gilbert White was blessed with such examples in several accomplished ancestors on both sides of his family, but he benefited from neither wealth nor position at birth. He was, to large degree, a "self-made" man, and he thus constitutes a fitting model for anyone who wants to live a life that makes a difference. Most of us do not enjoy great wealth or opportunity by birth. Gilbert demonstrated that a person without that birthright, but with a few personal and intellectual gifts—and perhaps more importantly, with a will to "amount to something"—can leave this planet a better place.

In his poem "Desiderata," Max Ehrmann wrote: "If you compare yourself with others, you may become vain and bitter, for always there will be greater and lesser persons than yourself." Rather than comparing himself, Gilbert tried to learn from the people he met, particularly his teachers, elders, and others in leadership roles; he rarely, if ever, "looked up" to or "looked down" on anyone (or if he did, he was loath to show it). He seemed to respect every person he encountered unless he was given a strong reason not to.

To better understand Gilbert White, one might set aside Ehrmann's caveat, compare himself or herself to the man, and ask, What were those "few personal gifts" of Gilbert's that enabled him to lead such a distinguished career and life? Certainly a strong intellect, a distinguished bearing, an engaging personality, good health, and consequent longevity all partially explain Gilbert's influence on people and history, but none of them are singular gifts. Similarly, his stable and carefree childhood as the lastborn in a loving family, followed by a good education and timely career opportunities, also account in part for Gilbert's early success, but they, too, are not extraordinary circumstances for many people in academic or public service careers. Gilbert's assets also included a talented and wise spouse, a wide and earnestly cultivated circle of friends, and a religious faith practiced with caring and committed companions. Together, all these qualities and benefits certainly set Gilbert apart from many colleagues and other professionals, and yet even these conditions do not seem sufficient to account for the remarkable stature and reputation that Gilbert White acquired in his seventy years of public life. His distinctiveness lay in his expectations of himself.

This resolve commenced, in his memory, from his uncle Gilbert's query, "Do you think you will ever amount to anything?" And it certainly was strengthened by his grandmother Julia, who annually quizzed him about the steps he had taken toward this goal of making a difference (in particular, his steps toward the goal of helping others). As a result, Gilbert entered adulthood committed to leaving the world—its people, as well as other life forms—better for his passage.

If "character" and "intellect" best summarize the prerequisites for "making a difference" over which an individual has some control, then perhaps the term that best summarizes the conditions for making a difference beyond one's control (particularly in Gilbert's case) is "serendipity." Chance plays a role in everyone's life: for example, when Gilbert narrowly missed a flight that crashed, killing all on board; or when he and Anne flew to Japan on two different airlines with similar schedules to reduce the risk of leaving their children parentless, only to experience the two airplanes nearly colliding on landing. But for Gilbert serendipity was inevitably positive—unanticipated, often unexplained, opportunity. Some people might see a mystical hand in such fortune, but Gilbert never went that far, even though he agreed with Einstein that life is through and through a miracle. Similarly, Gilbert would not object to anyone's suggesting that "God helps those who help themselves," but he would not find that quite adequate, either, as an explanation of much that he considered serendipitous in his life. At age ninety-two, when asked to explain the fortuitous events and opportunities that punctuated and at times dramatically redirected his life, Gilbert simply defined serendipity as "the factors influencing a decision that were not initially present in the decision-making process" (White 2000–2005). Gilbert's approach to decision making included creative thinking and attentive listening, but it also included alertness to the unexpected, seizing the moment, and openness to redirection.

Gilbert's "style of conduct" is the principal focus of this chapter; his career "mission" is the focus of the final chapter. Both constitute his legacy, and the distinction between ends and means is of course arbitrary. But among the characteristics or virtues that bear on his conduct (how he lived his life) are several that illuminate an unusually high level of social centeredness, as compared with self-centeredness. These are humility and self-effacement and commitment to service. Another cluster of characteristics centers on stewardship of his personal resources and the natural resources of our planet: efficacy in pursuit of that mission in terms of collaborative leadership, dedication, efficiency, and parsimony. These latter virtues are more germane to Chapter 14. Underlying all the foregoing characteristics are his basic beliefs.

White's Convictions

Gilbert never hesitated to talk about our shared responsibility to leave the planet a better place for our having been here, but he felt no similar need or responsibility to dwell upon his basic religious and philosophical beliefs about human nature or human relationship to the divine. In 1951, when he was Haverford's youthful president, he did accept, with some trepidation, an invitation to appear on Edward R. Murrow's radio program, "This, I Believe." In that broadcast interview, Gilbert focused on his convictions regarding his life's mission, while trying to put those convictions in a Christian context:

> I have studied many streams from their rushing mountain headwaters to their sluggish tidal mouths—great giants of rivers, tiny tributary brooks, streams flowing from clear springs, streams disappearing in sandy deserts. In all of them one finds the same forces of nature at work, making for the slow carving out of valleys and for the enrichment of plants and wildlife. Everywhere there is a delicate balance among water, soil, plants and animals. Man can change this moving balance of nature for the good by stabilizing it at new levels and by adding new harmonious elements, as when he stores the water of ephemeral streams to create green oases. Or he can throw it out of balance by selfish or ignorant use of resources so as to set in motion a vicious chain of destruction, as when he slashes a forest and launches a new cycle of soil erosion.
>
> Whether one explores the nearby stream or the mysteries of inter-stellar space, one finds order and a sense of divine direction in the physical universe. The biologist in his laboratory learns that there is a law of mutual aid which is dominant in the animal and plant world. Each of us learns for himself in the innermost laboratory of his conscience that there is a law of love among

mankind. I believe that this is the law which Jesus preached. This is the law which He lived supremely.

I believe that each of us finds greatest use and greatest satisfaction in a life which respects and kindles the spark of the divine that is found in the conscience of every other member of the human brotherhood, and which nourishes the harmonious growth of individual men and women. To set the welfare of any national or racial group ahead of the development of individuals, or to coerce individual expression of thought and worship is to unloose a destructive erosion of human values to gain the temporary prosperity of a state. While watching the German occupation of France I became convinced that man can no more conquer or preserve a civilization by war that he can conquer nature solely by engineering force. I found that an occupying army or a concentration camp can repress men's basic beliefs but cannot change them.

The good life, like the balance of all the complex elements of a river valley, is founded upon friendly adjustment. It changes slowly but it leads always toward a more fruitful development of individual men in service of each other. It embraces confidence in fellowship, tolerance in outlook, humility in service, and a constant search for the truth. To seek it in our own lives means imperfection and disappointment, but never defeat. It means, I believe, putting ourselves in harmony with the divine order of love, with the great stream of forces that slowly are shaping, in spite of man's ignorance and selfishness, an enrichment of the human spirit.

Following his tenure at Haverford, Gilbert became more cautious about using religious terminology, and he acknowledged two concerns that became more and more apparent during his life. First, the popular vocabulary available to discuss spirituality is too limited to adequately describe or express this domain. Second, religious terms and labels seem to be divisive rather than unifying in achieving either ecumenicalism within the United States or harmony among cultures and societies internationally. As an example, within the Boulder Friends Meeting (one of the more liberal Quaker communities in the United States), some members preferred to describe themselves as Quaker Christians rather than Protestant Christians. The distinction helped those members disassociate from orthodox Christian doctrine in order to focus simply on the historical teachings of Jesus. When he was asked if he remained comfortable describing himself as a Protestant Christian as well as a Quaker, Gilbert replied, "Yes, but I hope there aren't any follow-up questions!"

When discussing God, Gilbert clearly had harmony in nature in mind more than a supernatural creator. Indeed, he often preferred to talk about the "divine spark" rather than God. Gilbert described his father, A.E., as a confirmed agnostic, and for much of his life Gilbert appeared to some friends and family members to be the same, although he himself was uncomfortable with the label. In his later years, this ambivalence diminished, and Gilbert seemed more open to affirming a God and divine purpose in the universe and in our lives. Even though he believed that the universe, both living and nonliving, is essentially sacred, Gilbert recognized that humankind might have an uncommon, if not unique, role in the world. In a word, this role was service—to our fellow human beings and the earth we share. Indeed, for both Gilbert and Anne White, religion was service. They speculated little about any broader implications of spirituality. As their daughter, Mary, said (quoting Henry Cadbury), "If you can't see the spirit, do service, and maybe through the service you will see the spirit."

Gilbert's beliefs about spirituality and divinity probably owed more to his science than to either his Baptist upbringing or his Quakerism. The importance to both Gilbert and Anne of Quaker teachings lay in the guidance they provided for living responsibly, rather than for any explanation they might provide regarding humanity's place in the universe. For Gilbert, origins or first causes were of little concern; all was sacred and miraculous. Scientific knowledge could never fully explain the universe, but it could increase our awe and wonder of it.

Gilbert even conceptualized morality in basically scientific terms, equating the mutual aid dominant in the animal and plant world with love among humankind. He found no need for the words "evil" or "sin," preferring the terms "ignorance" and "human frailty." The lack of good intent or irresponsible action was as much of a definition of sin as Gilbert required. Similarly he viewed nature's ecosystems and biogeochemical cycles as basically harmonious (nature's way) unless degraded or forced into unnatural disequilibrium by intrusive human behavior.

Gilbert was no more inclined to study philosophy than he was to study theology. His familiarity with the pragmatism of John Dewey and Dewey's mentor, William James, seems to have provided him with all the philosophical underpinnings he needed. William James, however, was also criticized for his inattention to the problem of evil. One response of James and White (and many other Quakers) has always been that when human beings no longer depend on the "revealed truth," strict ideology, and interpretation of scriptures, but instead focus on "direct access," or enlightened intuition, in order to discern correct behavior, the possibility arises for both unusual virtue and great mistakes. For that reason, among others, Quakers feel that individual seekers must ground their search in *collective* seeking, meditation, and worship. Hence, Quakerism provides a means for understanding Gilbert's belief in the responsible channeling of free will, trusting the individual seeker to pursue truths ("leadings," in Quaker language) that can improve our human condition, and subjecting those leadings to group assessment while encouraging humility in the seeker and support of the collective.

Gilbert was slow to articulate most of these spiritual beliefs. His convictions regarding his mission in the world (shared with others), however, were often articulated both passionately and eloquently, as his words throughout this book demonstrate. His career involved the pursuit and dissemination of scientific knowledge in the public interest, and he believed strongly in sound science, keen discernment, useful collaboration, careful evaluation, clear language, and effective teaching.

We continue now with the principal topic of this chapter, Gilbert's stature in terms of his social consciousness and personal conduct.

Social Centeredness

Humility

Many friends, colleagues, and acquaintances found Gilbert unforgettable specifically because of his relative lack of ego and his unassuming grace in living his most basic beliefs. For example, in 2000 he penned this two-sentence unpublished self-description of "an ordinary teacher":

> A well-intentioned, routine teacher, who occasionally notes something in nature that others have missed, consistently tries to explain this to others with whom he feels he belongs. Those persons are his children or, more often, his students who continue to be inquiring about the world around them and share the excitement of discovery of meaning in life.

This is hardly "preaching," even as he exemplified admirably the following truths expounded by the renowned Parker Palmer, a comparably gifted Quaker teacher who was also unabashedly a preacher:

> External tools of power have occasional utility in teaching, but they are no substitute for authority, the authority that comes from the teacher's inner life. The clue is in the word itself, which has author at its core. Authority is granted to people who are perceived as authoring their own words, their own actions, their own lives, rather than playing a scripted role at great remove from their own hearts. When teachers depend on the career powers of law or technique they have no authority at all (Palmer 1998).

For reasons not altogether clear, Gilbert White consciously denied himself the charisma of the pulpit. Ironically, discouraging adulation is likely to encourage it. Gilbert's graciousness and avoidance of the limelight ensured that others looked up to him.

Gilbert's acquaintances often wondered how much of the man's humility reflected his Quaker faith and its practice. When asked about it, Gilbert would rephrase the question. He decided to join the Society of Friends, he would recall, because he already was in agreement with core Quaker tenets; he did not "convert" to Quakerism and then reorder his actions and priorities because of the dictates of the faith. To attribute his basic beliefs or behavior to being Quaker was misleading. This distinction was important to Gilbert, since he worked primarily with non-Quakers throughout his career and wanted his work (including the consensus decision-making process he constantly advocated) to be judged on its utility and responsible approach to addressing some of the key issues of our time. If some of his work and behavior reflected Quaker beliefs, that was incidental. Gilbert felt that to attribute his behavior to being a Quaker might imply to some people that a person who was not a Quaker need not take as seriously the responsibility we share to cultivate discernment (wise judgment and responsible behavior) regarding a specific issue or one's larger role on earth.

Service

To the extent that religion equated with service in Gilbert's experience, service was his fundamental commitment. His social consciousness and his corresponding selflessness in focusing on being "his brother's (and planet's) keeper" were remarkable. He might have resisted the label of servant, but for him the gift of existence deserved the return gift of helping and facilitating, collaborating with the people and world in which one finds oneself. Leader as servant; servant as leader. Because of this interpretation of service, Gilbert led very well.

As previously mentioned, Gilbert achieved his wisdom gradually through experience and observation rather than through any structured study of leadership. His models included, in graduate school, his mentor, Harlan Barrows, a comparatively unassuming man, and, a few years later, Franklin Delano Roosevelt, an effective listener.

In many ways Gilbert's long career can be seen as a series of service/leadership opportunities to which he was invited or that he filled out of necessity. His innate abilities and reputation resulted in an abundance of satisfying employment and service opportunities without his applying for a single position in his adult life. (He acknowledges that in his youth he harbored more pride and need for recognition. These needs lessened after he ran for class president his freshman year in college and won.) It was his mother's desire that after elementary school, he receive all his formal education at the University of Chicago, and on graduation he accepted Harlan Barrows's invitation to join him in Washington. He might well thereafter have returned promptly to Chicago as an instructor, had Barrows's hope materialized to secure a position for Gilbert in the Geography Department (even in advance of conferral of his Ph.D.). Instead, a career of other invitations commenced in Washington: to serve as staff secretary for a succession of planning committee chairmen in the FDR administration, followed by employment with the Bureau of the Budget; an assortment of roles with the American Friends Service Committee—from his early refugee work, to assisting Clarence Pickett in the Philadelphia international office, to his directorship of the Conferences for Diplomats, and finally his chairing the national committee of the AFSC in the 1960s; to serve as president of Haverford College; to chair the Geography Department at the University of Chicago, at Chauncey Harris's instigation; to direct the Institute of Behavioral Science in Boulder, at Kenneth Boulding's suggestion; to collaborate with Ian Burton and Robert Kates on international research on natural hazards; to assist the graduate students at the University of Colorado, who urged him to establish the Natural Hazards Center; to participate on the committee that recommended the Peace Corps, at the suggestion of Maurice Albertson; and to assist the many U.S.

agencies, foundations, and international scientific organizations that asked Gilbert to chair several dozen committees, task forces, and commissions in the latter part of the twentieth century.

It should be quickly noted that Gilbert did not do everyone's bidding. He turned down probably as many invitations to be of service as he accepted (while not yielding to the temptation to follow Kenneth Boulding's example of awarding his secretary a star for each invitation she convinced him to decline!). Gilbert learned early to be parsimonious with his time and careful in discerning what he could do well, given his knowledge and skills. Most significantly, he accepted the opportunities that advanced his scientific agenda. In a few cases, he simply occupied an obvious void, as when in 1972 he volunteered to work all night during a planning conference in Kiel,Germany, to map out the agenda for the fledgling Scientific Committee on Problems of the Environment, after bickering among the many natural, physical, and social scientists involved threatened to destroy the committee. As SCOPE colleague Ted Munn recalled,

> The original focus of SCOPE was on climate, the oceans. But there was a crowd of ecotoxicologists who wanted to run their own program but who were off in left field as far as other SCOPE participants were concerned. Then there were the health folks focusing on World Health Organization business, who weren't any more welcomed than the ecotoxicologists. And finally there were the "limits to growth" people. Without being asked, Gilbert overnight pulled together an agenda that he thought would fly with all three groups, and it did! (Munn 2001)

Personal Relationships

Gilbert's one-on-one relationships with others are marked by at least five distinct qualities: respect, kindness, generosity, loyalty, and veracity. Discussion of these is based on the observations of many friends, colleagues, and acquaintances; Gilbert's correspondence archived in the Department of History of the Corps of Engineers; testimonials and anecdotes offered by friends on Gilbert's ninetieth birthday in 2001; and the citations included with many of the national and international honors awarded Gilbert White.

Respect

Gilbert respected whomever he encountered, be it a repairman making a house call or a head of state. That was perhaps best demonstrated in his ability and desire to listen. A friend observed: "The secret to Gilbert's ability to communicate directly is his starting point: his ability to listen. He focuses on others, hearing them out, so that when he responds he really has heard what you have said. He may differ in his opinion, but there is little miscommunication due to his not having understood you" (Hooke 2000). When chairing a meeting, Gilbert usually began by asking,

"Friends, shall we begin with brief introductions and share a sentence about what each of us hopes to accomplish together here?" Gilbert recognized the importance of understanding where people were "coming from." By developing such understanding and respect in a group, Gilbert felt that a collaborative spirit and consensus could be achieved.

Similarly, in one-on-one discourse he respected not only each person's individual position but also his or her ability to discern a proper solution or path. Hence Gilbert was always reluctant to state his position or provide advice without first engaging in a dialogue. His approach was Socratic; he invariably responded to an opening question with a question of his own. He was not simply trying to be self-effacing or polite. Indeed, his insistence on listening before responding was often disquieting and sometimes seemed unkind, since it could result in an awkward silence until the question was answered. But Gilbert was simply making the point that the most useful answers result from joint insight—that the questioner had the responsibility to share his or her thoughts and position before Gilbert offered a response. This approach reflected both Gilbert's respect for the other person as well as his pragmatism. He recognized that, by sharing their thinking, his colleagues, students, and friends would clarify the issues for themselves much more than if they just listened to Gilbert.

Gilbert never was chatty; he took to heart the admonition, "Let your words be few." Unless he had something useful (or kind) to say, Gilbert said nothing. Again, his reticence could be intimidating or make him appear aloof, but as he aged, Gilbert became less reserved. In his later years he talked more easily, and conversation with him became less demanding.

Even when his views were not sought, if Gilbert had an insight or opinion he wanted to share, he would most often offer those ideas by asking a probing question rather than making a pronouncement. He very much tried not to attack the person, even if he strongly opposed the idea. For example, at age ninety Gilbert attended a talk about the funding of social science research following the tragedy of September 11, 2001. The presentation focused on opportunities to obtain support and conduct research on ways to protect the nation from terrorist acts, including the development of high-technology surveillance systems and other such technology. Gilbert sat quietly with his eyes closed (some thought he was asleep) through the entire presentation. But when the discussion had almost concluded, he raised his hand and asked simply, "Are there funds available, or has anyone actually conducted research, on why terrorism occurs?"

Gilbert's penchant for listening more than talking, even deferring to others endeavoring to expound the ideas or positions that he advocated, was not always welcomed in his leadership roles. For some Arabs (and people of other cultures, for that matter), Gilbert's degree of humility could be interpreted as weakness rather than as virtue. Ayman al-Hassan, a Jordanian who participated in the National

Academy of Sciences committee on Middle East water resource cooperation chaired by Gilbert (see Chapter 14), initially struggled with Gilbert's unusual humility, which challenged his cultural assumption regarding effective leadership. But as he came to know Gilbert, he came to admire the man. He likened the reorientation required of him each time the committee met to "changing with remote control one television channel to another" (al-Hassan 2001).

Another Arab, the Egyptian geographer Sherif el-Kassas, was one of the Whites' closest foreign friends following their collaborative research and work on Egyptian-U.S. bilateral programs, Nile basin issues, worldwide desertification problems, global ecology, and climate change. El-Kassas's tribute to Gilbert on his ninetieth birthday was especially meaningful: "I am fortunate to have known Gilbert for fifty years: a friend who fills the heart with comfort and tranquility, a companion who fills the soul with joy and pleasure, and a teacher who fills the mind with knowledge and vision. . . . As a Muslim I came to admire and deeply respect the type of Christianity that Gilbert lives and practices, beautiful and angelic" (el-Kassas 2001).

Kindness

First Gilbert and Anne and then Gilbert and Claire, were members of El Grupo (The Group), one of several associations of members of the Boulder Friends Meeting who met periodically as a sort of informal extended family. One of El Grupo's couples adopted a daughter, Jesse, who was in turn informally adopted by the group. When she was eleven years old, Jesse chose Gilbert as her adult "hero" and subsequently asked him for his advice regarding what to do with her life. Gilbert's counsel: "If you are kind to people, you will have a good life."

While a student at Haverford College, I was dating Ardith, my wife-to-be, who attended college in Ohio. Upon learning that she would be coming to Haverford for the junior prom, Gilbert offered the use of the Whites' one automobile for those two days. Imagine her surprise on being met at the station in the president's car!

Gilbert typically ended conversations by asking, "Now, is there anything that I can do for you?" He truly expected a candid answer and was eager to help if possible. Often a house guest of friends when traveling, Gilbert always insisted on helping with the chores—at least with the cleanup and washing of dishes following dinner. One admiring couple who decided to follow his example explained their behavior as simply "doing a Gil."

First with their cabin in Sunshine Canyon and subsequently with "The Meadow" near Allenspark, Colorado, the Whites always felt that "mi casa es su casa" (my home is your home). When Anne and Gilbert were not using these retreats, they were always available to acquaintances for anything from a brief overnight stay to much longer retreats, and a large number of friends from around the United States and abroad accepted the offer. All that was asked and expected in return was responsible care of the house (including recycling!).

Santa, at age eighty, the night before Christmas at "The Meadow" cabin, 1991

Generosity

A thoughtful act is also generous when some sacrifice is entailed. When Gilbert was imprisoned in Baden-Baden by the Germans, he gave his only spare pair of shoes to a young Russian prisoner whose only shoes had given out. Following their release from prison, Yaroslav Tiajoloff attempted to repay Gilbert, only to have Gilbert return the money twice, explaining that Yaroslav was not indebted to him. Finally, on Gilbert's ninetieth birthday, Yaroslav decided to try again. He calculated the interest over sixty years and sent $125 along with a drawing of a pair of shoes bearing angel's wings and floating in heavenly clouds. He also enclosed a note, imploring Gilbert to accept the payment. "Over the years, in trying to overcome your resistance, I have explored many devices," he explained. "I even telephoned shoe stores in Boulder, seeking a gift certificate. But they did not have any. *Please be as generous in accepting as you are in giving.*" After that gentle reprimand, Gilbert assented and did not return the money. Instead, he donated it (for shoes) to the homeless shelter in Boulder in Yaroslav's name. Although deeply, even stubbornly, principled, Gilbert recognized the Russian's criticism and relented. Claire Sheridan once stated that Gilbert had the ability to receive criticism and make amends—an interesting blend of pride and humility that Gilbert retained even into his nineties.

Gilbert generously supported dozens of organizations and institutions by donating any money he received in association with the many prizes he was awarded.
In the end, he gave several hundred thousand dollars to causes and institutions
that were involved in the problems that formed the center of his life's work. The
largest of such financial awards, $75,000 from the Tyler Prize for Environmental
Achievement in 1987, was divided among eight organizations in the United States,
Canada, Switzerland, and France. He retained $15,000 for his and Anne's projected
use in research abroad (which did not happen due to Anne's declining health). In
some instances, his generosity conflicted with his selflessness. For example, he directed that an honorarium from Western Illinois University be given to the National Council for Geographic Education, but with the stipulation that his name
not be associated with the contribution in any public announcement.

Loyalty

Gift giving was very important to both Gilbert and Anne. Important occasions in
the lives of his students and colleagues, especially, were marked by highly personalized gifts, often geographically significant (such as a historical map suitable for
framing, cork coasters from Portugal, or an enamel pin from Toledo, Spain). The
Whites sent out hundreds of personalized end-of-year greetings—usually cards
that Anne designed herself. At the close of the year of her passing in 1989, the card
Gilbert mailed was a sketch of the tree-lined path where her ashes had been dis-
persed (each card hand-painted). The greeting read: "Looking ahead along the
Anne White Trail. May the year ahead be a time for happy reflection on days past,
and for exploration of the days ahead with curiosity and optimism." Even in old
age, Gilbert remained steadfast not only in staying in touch with former students
and colleagues but also in helping them, when asked, with advice and contacts that
could aid them in their work and careers.

Gilbert and Anne remained enduringly committed to their friendships. For example, Gilbert's first undergraduate course in geography at Chicago was taught by
John Morrison, who himself was a graduate student, working on a dissertation based
on research in Central Anatolia (Turkey). Morrison received his Ph.D. in 1939, after
Gilbert had already left for Washington. However, because Morrison subsequently
focused on the Soviet Union and water use in the Middle East, Gilbert remained in
touch with John and his wife, Fritzi, for many years. When Gilbert was reminded late
in life that John's dissertation had never been published, he endeavored for the next
two years to get it published. He contacted universities in Turkey, U.S. universities
with programs in Turkish studies, and even the Turkish Embassy in the United States.
After John died, Gilbert persisted for Fritzi's sake, but finally both Fritzi's and
Gilbert's declining health required that he give up his efforts.

The Korean War overlapped Gilbert's tenure as president of Haverford College.
At the school a number of students objected to military service either by applying

for alternative nonmilitary service or by refusing to register for the compulsory draft altogether. The latter conscientious objectors faced possible imprisonment. However, if asked, the college would vouch for any student's integrity at a draft board hearing, and the college promised assistance to these students in pursuing their studies, should they be imprisoned. One of the students who chose to object by not registering was Paul Cates, who lived in Maine. Gilbert chose to receive an award from the American Association of Geographers in absentia so that he could speak on Paul's behalf at his draft board hearing.[1]

Veracity

Gilbert spoke honestly and directly, even when convention might have dictated that he say nothing. For example, at Haverford, the Whites usually invited the cast of a campus theater production to their home following the opening performance. On one occasion, when he was asked for his opinion of the performance, Gilbert replied honestly that he was disappointed. The faculty director, flabbergasted, said, "But you, the president of the college, can't say that!" Gilbert clarified why he was disappointed, and later told Anne that when a president could not speak his mind candidly it was probably time to move on.

His correspondence with former students and close associates was comparably frank, to the point of bluntness. A University of Chicago colleague wrote, "Dear Gil, For the past several days I have been intermittently reading *Small Is Beautiful* by E. F. Schumacher, a maverick British economist. It is an extraordinary volume, and I recommend it to you most emphatically." Gilbert replied, "The Schumacher book leaves me warm with appreciation for the rhetoric but cool as to its message. Perhaps I am uninfluenced unduly by having seen some of his intermediate technology experiments, very few of which bore any significant fruit."

Although he was certainly honest and most often candid, when the occasion dictated, Gilbert could also be tactful and, at the same time, witty. The following letter, sent to Keith Muckleston of the U.S. Water Resources Council on June 19, 1975, illustrates both Gilbert's diplomacy and his dedication to following through on his commitments:

Dear Keith:

I reviewed the draft report on "A Unified National Program for Flood Plain Management" which you forwarded on June 3 and attach a set of comments.

In looking through the document I had the feeling that my reactions might be somewhat like those of a person called upon to advise a boxer who, having completed 14 rounds of a very tough and tiring fight, is being offered advice as to how he might get through the final round. To any suggestion, he might reply that he had already tried it. And his chief concern would be with surviving that final round and still remain on his feet.

At almost every point at which I felt moved to make suggestions I had the impression that the ambiguous language was the product of long negotiations and compromise, or that a proposal to strengthen the argument would turn out to be one that had been tried and failed. In the process of drafting this type of document groups sometimes reach the stage at which they find it extremely difficult to make any further changes even though all the members may recognize that the result falls short of their initial aspirations.

With this as background, I have arranged my comments in three groups: (1) those which I would make if given a few minutes in which to comment upon the report before a national conference or congressional committee, (2) those addressed to possible ways of strengthening the main thrust of the document, and (3) detailed suggestions for improvement of wording.

Best regards, Gilbert (White 1975c)

Anne White–Gilbert's Collaborator and Support

Gilbert's social commitments were both balanced by and reflected in his two marriages. He loyally nurtured both, and his forty-five years with Anne, in particular, flourished despite heavy professional commitments. His second marriage, some years following Anne's death, was to Claire Sheridan.

Anne and Gilbert were similar in personality, gentle and very warm even as they were comparably reserved. Anne clearly was more artistic. She was a painter and potter early in life, and she wrote poetry regularly throughout adulthood, something Gilbert never attempted (one of his closest friends, Kenneth Boulding, was also a poet; that friendship is discussed later in this chapter). Indeed, Anne's poetry probably revealed her inner life even more than did interviews about her with Gilbert, their children, and friends. Unfortunately, however, Anne chose to destroy almost all her poetry from the middle decades of her life, and it was Gilbert's idea, not Anne's, to have her remaining poems published following her death. Anne's poetry, along with oral history interviews she conducted with children, reveal a reflective personality, particularly compared to Gilbert's detailed, factual approach to recounting his ancestry and upbringing.[2]

Several close friends described Anne as Gilbert's equal in intelligence, wit, and wisdom. In their marriage, it became increasingly important to both Anne and Gilbert that, given her undergraduate training in economics and data gathering techniques, Anne have opportunities to conduct academic research. It is not clear, however, whether to Anne it was more important to demonstrate this ability to herself or to Gilbert. After her death, Gilbert recalled that the only tension between himself and Anne resulted from differing priorities regarding her academic career. It was Anne, initially, who wanted to pursue academic research and work collaboratively with her husband, and she took an active interest in geographic field research when Gilbert returned to Chicago in 1956. Their cooperative research in East Africa in the 1960s, resulting in *Drawers of Water,* clearly benefited from her insights into the critical role of women in households as well as her expertise as a statistician. In Gilbert's memory, "Anne loved doing research. Her innate charm and pleasure in getting to know all sorts of people was an asset. Her own consulting projects later in her life were exciting and energizing."

Because of her interest and work on domestic water supply issues, Anne was invited to join the professional staff of the Institute of Behavioral Science at the University of Colorado when the Whites moved to Boulder. From 1974 to 1978, she wrote seven journal articles and book chapters herself, but thereafter she restricted herself to collaborative research and authorship, coauthoring four articles with Gilbert and two with other researchers thereafter. Her final work, published posthumously, occupied her as long as her declining energy permitted. But Anne also felt some pressure to continue her academic role as long as she could, perhaps from Gilbert's example in this regard. Late in life she admitted to weariness with such work and relief that her ill health was reducing such pressure. Still, *Drawers of Water*—the fieldwork as much as the scholarship and resulting publication—stood out in Gilbert's memory as the most enjoyable and productive effort that he and Anne ever undertook.

Anne's wit was very dry, and she was fun-loving. In the early years of the Natural Hazards Center, office staff (including manager Mei Mei Pan, editor Sarah Nathe, project manager Susan Tubbesing, editor Penny Waterstone, and Penny's student-husband, Marv) would periodically take off at lunch to find "the perfect piece of pie." Anne, who frequented the center, would join them, but Gilbert never did. When finished with the day's work, he would listen to office talk, obviously enjoying ("from the great twinkle in those blue eyes") the latest gossip but characteristically remaining only a listener. Getting Gilbert to laugh was considered an office accomplishment; his countenance, always composed, was customarily also steely—until he smiled.

Family humor expressed itself in gentle kidding and in practical jokes. Gilbert grew up in a family where such humor was a key part of relationships. He enjoyed recounting the time in his youth on the Wyoming ranch when he inserted Ex-Lax in gum he generously passed out to the hired hands. "This caused some consternation in an area where about the only places to make oneself inconspicuous were behind sagebrush plants." His daughter Frances recalled countless table and—in later years—telephone conversations when Gilbert would share a good joke. He had his favorites, to which the family circle was subjected intermittently. "Mummy and I were always a great audience because we usually had forgotten the punch line!"

Having initially focused on history at Vassar, Anne was more a historian and follower of politics than Gilbert (she passed both these interests and her wry wit on to her son Will, who developed a keen collector's interest in U.S. political lampoonery). Indeed, several acquaintances credited Anne with sensitizing Gilbert to women's rights and needs in the workplace. From 1973 to 1974, she was codirector of Womanpower, Inc., an early nonprofit employment service for women in Boulder. She was also a member of the Women's Forum of Colorado and the Society of Women Geographers (as well as of the Association of American Geographers).

Anne fought a losing battle keeping the cabin orderly, even as she succeeded admirably in creating a calm ambience. The White's dog for many years, Shona, learned to navigate the cabin's floors through piles of Gilbert's work without disturbing a single sheet of paper. And throughout the children's years at home, Anne arbitrated Gilbert's and the children's claims to the available desk and table space. After Gilbert retired from teaching in 1978 (he continued as director of the Natural Hazards Center), Anne allowed him one bookcase and told him to leave anything that would not fit in that bookcase at his office in the center. Fortunately, after being named the University of Colorado Gustavson Distinguished Professor Emeritus of Geography in 1980, Gilbert was given a small office in the basement of the center, which he used almost daily, when not traveling away from Boulder, until the end of the century.

Anne was the hostess of the many social gatherings the Whites held at their home for professional associates, while Gilbert typically engaged in one-on-one conversations on the periphery. In many senses, Anne was Gilbert's "manager," protecting him from many of the people who would place demands on his time— even his children—but also encouraging him to become engaged when needed. She enjoyed entertaining and having opportunities to strengthen friendships with Gilbert's associates, who were often the topics of the couple's late night talks. She also managed to become knowledgeable about, even engaged in, a wide range of Gilbert's professional interests. At Gilbert's invitation, Anne agreed to serve as interim coeditor of the *Natural Hazards Observer* from 1976 to 1978, and the largely female staff with whom she worked found her to be as decisive, efficient, and well-organized as her husband, strengthening their conviction that Anne influenced Gilbert's life more than most people realized.

Anne and Gilbert's children knew even better the assertive yet nondictatorial management style that Anne exercised. Gilbert willingly let her be his personal barometer and tell him when he needed to redirect his attention from work to family or relax and even take a nap. However, in public Anne willingly granted Gilbert center stage. Her personal reward seems to have been simply knowing how much she anchored Gilbert's life. Dick Jessor, Gilbert's colleague and a former director of the Institute of Behavioral Science, once observed, "Anne made Gilbert know who he was. He came to treasure her vitality, her intelligence and wisdom. She was probably as committed to his career as was he, and he valued her insights" (Jessor 2002).

One of Anne's poems, from 1969, wittily reminded Gilbert of their collaboration:

A scientist is a man, says C. P. Snow,
More moral than most, perhaps, and yet a man.
Yet now a man who matters more than most
Holding the heavens from falling on all our heads.
Both worlds together (including women, and others
who do not speak the tongue or comprehend it).
Our passion now that these will venture forth
Moved by our common love of home and food and children
Partial to truth, partial to knowing, and kind,
To grasp like an apple, firm, and round,
Some saving aspect of the universe.
Yet they are men, he says, and I will wonder
If any set of men can do this all alone.

Gilbert, Staff, and Students

Gilbert was described by some as a bit patronizing to men, and more so to women, early in his career as an employer. Some of his Haverford correspondence suggested that he felt the high standards of excellence there were more easily maintained with an all-male student body. The graduate programs in geography at both Chicago and Colorado were almost exclusively male domains. The 1972 first assessment of natural hazards included only one woman, Jackie Beyer, among the several dozen graduate students and faculty involved; and only three women were invited to the Natural Hazards Center's first annual July workshop. This gender gap, if not bias, rapidly changed under pressure from Anne and center female staff. There is also, however, evidence that the gap was more tolerated than welcomed, with Gilbert's attitudes reflecting the cultural norms at midcentury. The few women students who did persevere in graduate study, with Gilbert chairing their dissertation committees, received from the Whites as a couple fully as much attention as did Gilbert's male advisees. In fact, Gilbert's first doctoral student was Jackie Beyer, who, like Martha Church (see Chapter 11), saved for the remainder of her long career in geography all her correspondence from both Anne and Gilbert. Anne was as faithful a correspondent as Gilbert, and, indeed, even the Whites' children corresponded with students close to the family. Jackie was virtually adopted into the Whites' household, frequently house- or pet-sitting in their absence and on several occasions joining the family for out-of-state travel and in-state backpacking. Gilbert shepherded Jackie through employment searches, even assembling a curriculum vitae for her during her fieldwork in South Africa.

Gilbert was among the few members of the Cosmos Club in Washington, D.C., who objected to the club's policy of limiting membership to men. When he learned of this policy after being inducted into the club, Gilbert considered resigning, but he decided to remain a member and work for a change in policy. After fifty years of persistent efforts, the policy was changed in 1988. Subsequently, Gilbert sponsored several women for membership.

Many University of Colorado students in geography and related fields were employed by the Natural Hazards Center, hired as teaching assistants, or had Gilbert as their adviser. All were adopted into the Whites' extended family and treated almost as caringly as Gilbert and Anne treated their own children. One of Gilbert's students, Burrell Montz, recalls that some in that "family" even began calling each other cousins, "related through Gilbert." For almost all of Gilbert's students, that sense of belonging continued after graduation, through both the annual center workshops and the collaborative research they conducted. Many former students admitted that they return to the workshops primarily to reconnect with the center's extended family.

When the Whites entertained at home, guests encountered a different Gilbert White. In the company of his antiques and memorabilia of four generations and especially the many family pets, Gilbert truly relaxed. Above the fireplace was a pastoral photograph of grazing sheep (a reminder of Wyoming summers in his youth), which established a mood of serenity. The kitchen always had a faint aroma of curry or other exotic spices, reminiscent of the many travels abroad. And throughout their home, as in his office, could be found keepsakes from those travels, even mementos from Gilbert's work with refugees in France (a metal medallion from a fence, used as a paperweight) and internment in Germany (a metal oxen shoe found when walking in the forest near Baden-Baden).

In the living room was a deep recliner that Gilbert always offered to his guest, preferring a straight-backed chair for himself, which then left the guest looking up at Gilbert. On one occasion his students managed to get Gilbert into the recliner. He sat on the edge initially, ramrod straight as usual. But as he (uncharacteristically) accepted one and then another rum-laced eggnog, he sank slowly into the chair until he finally reclined fully, with his triumphant students gathered around mischievously looking down. The shoe was sometimes on another's foot: Gilbert enjoyed telling the story of his good friend Roy Popkin, a Red Cross official who attended the Natural Hazards Center workshops regularly for twenty-five years, falling headlong into the Whites' hot tub. Tom Heberlein, a rural sociologist who sometimes worked with the Natural Hazards Center, recalled his astonishment when, as an overnight guest of the Whites, he was invited to join them in the hot tub—without swimming suits, since he, of course, had not brought his own!

The Whites and the Bouldings

Gilbert first met Kenneth Boulding at a meeting for worship at Haverford College in 1955, and by 1958 the Whites and Bouldings had become good friends. Within a year of acquiring their Sunshine Canyon property, the Whites invited Kenneth and Elise to

Kenneth and Elise Boulding, 1980

Gilbert at the desk of his maternal grandfather W. W. Guthrie, in his home at the communal housing venture at 624 Pearl in Boulder, 2003.

vacation with them for a week, including rafting the Colorado River through the Grand Canyon. Over the years of their relationship, Kenneth became a scholar as eminent in economics as Gilbert was in geography. Elise became a prominent sociologist.

The two men, as well as the two marriages, offer striking and instructive contrasts. Each scholar was charismatic in his own way. Boulding had an attractive aura, great charm. He was magnetic and welcomed the limelight. Meteorologist William Hooke offered a somewhat different definition of Gilbert's charisma: "He embodies those special gifts of mind and character which are the source of the personal power of exceptional individuals and upon which they depend for their capacity to secure the allegiance of, and exercise decisive authority over, large masses of people" (Hooke 2000). Gilbert's charisma was perhaps slower to take hold but equally commanding.

Whereas Anne White eschewed academic prominence for herself, evidencing no competition with Gilbert, Elise Boulding did not conceal her envy of Kenneth's scholarly fame.[3] Gilbert surmised late in life that his and Anne's happy academic collaboration, absent of competition, may have benefited from observing the Bouldings' subtle struggle in this regard.

Most of their common friends and colleagues recognized that Gilbert and Kenneth shared some, but not all virtues. Gilbert admired Kenneth's imagination and enjoyed his irreverent playfulness.[4] Gilbert attributed to Boulding, more than to any other colleague, his appreciation for the limitations of disciplinary compartmentalization of knowledge. It was, after all, Boulding who, soon after joining the University of Colorado's new Institute of Behavioral Science, suggested that the university invite Gilbert to direct the institute. Kenneth learned from Gilbert's humility and respected his popularity among students; Boulding was mentor to many fewer students, despite being a more frequent public lecturer. Indeed, the wonder of the two scholars' abiding friendship was their tolerance of and preparedness to benefit from their differences.

Gilbert and Kenneth never discussed their differences in style or their marriages. Thanks to their steadfast friendship, the Bouldings and Whites were able to spearhead the planning and implementation of a communal four-story housing venture in the heart of Boulder, at 624 Pearl Street. The Whites enjoyed this home during the final years of Anne's life, and Gilbert and Claire Sheridan reside there today.

Failing Health

Anne and Gilbert shared adversities as well as joys. They helped each other through several serious illnesses and accidents, and they also were the principal caretakers in his final years of Gilbert's brother, Warren, an alcoholic.

Soon after moving from Chicago to Colorado in 1970, Gilbert and Anne each began to experience health problems with which they would contend the rest of their lives. Anne first dealt with cancer (of the skin) in 1971. A year earlier, at age fifty-nine, Gilbert suffered severe lower back pain (probably the result of his accident aboard ship returning to the United States during World War II), as well as flu and shingles during his first hectic year at the University of Colorado. Then Anne fell from her horse and seriously injured her leg, requiring a long convalescence and rehabilitation. From 1976 to 1978, Gilbert experienced intermittent urinary infections that resulted in prostate surgery in 1978. Fortunately, throughout the 1980s, Gilbert had no major health problems and was able to help Anne as she coped with declining health. For their part, the White children were impressed with Gilbert's readiness to reorder his priorities when Anne became ill, particularly because they felt that their parents had gradually grown apart over the preceding decade because of Gilbert's demanding work and travel commitments. Indeed, they felt that Gilbert could have been more sensitive to Anne's loneliness in those years and more quickly acquiesced to her desire to accompany him on foreign travel. This the couple finally did together in the 1980s, sometimes with one of the children.

Absence

It is not just the passion that hurts me,
The guts turning over beneath a melting look.
But small things I cannot share with you;
The incandescent candle of a sunlit pine.

—Anne

In the early 1980s Anne exhibited some worrisome health signs, especially a slowly declining blood count. In May 1987, a CAT scan disclosed a colon tumor, and the physician prescribed chemotherapy. Gilbert's daily notes that evening recorded "a dull, deep chill." With possibly a year to live, Anne gallantly decided to make the most of it. In August they vacationed with daughter Frances's family (including their only two grandchildren at that point—Gilbert became a grandfather at age seventy), and Gilbert and Anne continued on to Sydney for the International Geography Congress and a tour of Australia's outback. En route home, they vacationed in Hong Kong and Tokyo. Later in the autumn, they visited Hyde Park and then Vassar in conjunction with Gilbert's schedule of commitments across the country.

That winter Anne managed to join the family for Christmas dinner, but she welcomed in the New Year in the hospital. She insisted on a final visit to "The Meadow" cabin in March when she realized the end was near. Then she took to heart the counsel of her hospice nurse: "Dying provides your opportunity to teach one of the most important lessons in life: how to die well." Anne met with each child and close friend and offered advice in her usual straightforward, unapologetic way. For example, she told Gilbert's secretary of many years, Mei Mei Pan, to lose weight and to let go of her children. (Anne had given the latter advice to several other married friends over the years, counsel that Anne herself had followed with her own children.) Mary, after listening to the parting counsel that her mother had reserved for her, offered to return for a final farewell, but Anne matter-of-factly said that would not be necessary, that she had said what she had to say. Anne's final verse, penned a few days before her death, reflected her gratitude for what she had been given, her satisfaction with her stewardship of those gifts, and her readiness to move on:

Well, That's That

Well, that's that now, and it's over.
And I remember tender,
Think of sweetness.
Shed no tear.
For in this hand
Is peacefulness.
And in this clasp
Pure joy.

Anne died on April 10, 1989, less than a month shy of their forty-fifth wedding anniversary. Just off the Anne U. White Trail below Four Mile Canyon in the foothills of Boulder, Anne's ashes are at rest, inconspicuous to passersby.

Gilbert, who always had assumed that Anne would outlive him, was inconsolable. He considered taking his life and so confided to one of his closest former students. If Gilbert's life was lived in response to requests for assistance and guidance from the persons he respected, the death of Anne, the person he most respected and cherished, left him profoundly alone for the first time in his life. Understandably, he remained depressed for months.

His left leg suddenly collapsed in 1992 because of what would later be diagnosed as spinal stenosis, and in 1993 he suffered the first of several strokes. Physical therapy helped bring down his blood pressure, and after insertion of a pacemaker in 2005, coronary problems ceased to be a major concern. But the spinal stenosis worsened, producing back discomfort and unsteadiness when walking for the remainder of his life. It was difficult for Gilbert to accept that he needed aid in walking, particularly because his sight, hearing, and mental abilities remained so acute. Fortunately, he survived several serious falls, and by mid-2006 he remained, with the help of a cane and finally a walker, remarkably ambulatory. His mind and his will seemingly would not let his body give up as long as any work, any commitment, remained undone.

☙

IN THE LATE 1990S, Gilbert declined an invitation from the Boulder Friends Meeting to share his spiritual journey, something that members occasionally are asked to do following Sunday worship. Instead, he offered to review his history of

Claire Sheridan and Gilbert, 1990

The Sheridan-White wedding at Wild Basin Lodge near "The Meadow" cabin, 2003

Quaker service and discuss his long-standing concern regarding the comparative lack of voluntary service opportunities available to young Friends in recent years (White 1998a, 2000). Nevertheless, one suspects that Gilbert's spiritual journey, particularly his deepening social consciousness, was unusually intertwined with Anne's. Perhaps Gilbert could not share that journey, even with Quakers who were among the Whites' closest friends, lest that betray a confidence shared only with Anne of how deeply indebted to her he was for the gift of his career.[5] After all, Gilbert and Anne came to Quakerism concurrently, albeit independently, and Anne participated in his budding career almost from the start, even sacrificing a traditional courtship for the frantic completion of a doctoral dissertation on the eve of their separation when Gilbert left for France and Germany. Gilbert's mission became Anne's, although she also wisely pursued her own life with her own gifts. Because she was Gilbert's pilot and his anchor, Anne's passing left him despairingly adrift for many months.

Moving On—Claire Sheridan

His closest friends, and especially his children, readily agreed that Claire Sheridan, a mutual friend of Gilbert and Anne, was perhaps the most serendipitous, unforeseen good fortune to come Gilbert's way in later life. Several days before her death, Anne suggested to Gilbert that after she was gone, he take Claire for a walk on the foothills trail that he and Anne so often frequented. She thought that Claire and Gilbert had much in common and that they should become better acquainted. Some weeks after Anne's death, Gilbert did invite Claire to take that walk. Afterwards they had tea. They took many walks in the months that followed, usually talking about Anne and the life that she and Gilbert had led, the work that they had done together, and his deep sense of loss. Finally Claire suggested that Gilbert consult a grief counselor in Fort Collins who had made a career of helping people deal with loss. Gilbert did so, and in a few weeks he again called Claire. His counselor had advised him to continue to read Anne's diaries in the morning, and then afterward, if he wanted, he could call Claire and go for a walk. This was a comforting transition for Gilbert and became a prelude to what turned into a long and happy relationship. In 2003 they were married under the care of the Boulder Friends Meeting near their Allenspark cabin alongside the North St. Vrain River.

Notes

1. Were it not for Haverford's and Gilbert's commitment to supporting conscientious objectors, it is unlikely that this biography would have been written. Anticipating not registering for the draft upon turning eighteen and considering a number of colleges, I chose to enroll at Haverford because of an encouraging letter from Gilbert himself, who

promised ongoing aid and instruction if imprisoned. The imprisonment never occurred, but the letter became the foundation of my long association with Gilbert White.

2. Yet Gilbert was even more committed than Anne to preserving family records and keepsakes, giving and receiving gifts, and remaining in touch with old acquaintances. Gilbert was also a collector. He had the half-dozen academic hoods he received when given honorary degrees woven into a quilt, and he retained over 500 playbills from theatrical performances that he had attended. Perhaps his most prized collection includes several dozen first editions of the works of Bret Harte and Mark Twain.

3. Gilbert felt that the Bouldings' competition subsided when Beloit College in Wisconsin named a library after both of them in appreciation for their donating their respective book collections.

4. In the 1960s both men served on a State of California Commission for water planning. In frustration, Kenneth indiscreetly circulated summaries in humorous verse of the commission's lackluster progress. Subsequently (and consequently, Gilbert believes), the commission was suspended and its funding retracted.

5. When he was interviewed about the meaning of Anne in his life, Gilbert was generally reluctant to share much in depth. His reticence seemed to reflect not only love and respect for Anne, but a comparable respect for and loyalty to Claire. Nor did Gilbert supply the author any letters to or from Anne or their children. They apparently corresponded by mail very little, and perhaps Anne and Gilbert considered their correspondence too intimate for retention.

14 *Gilbert White, His Legacy*

It is striking that in a century of evolving public policy the prevailing aim has been to minimize losses from floods and not to optimize the net social benefits from using floodplain resources, including the preservation of the basic associations of soil, vegetation, biota, and water. In simplest terms, it is the contrast between "loss reduction" and "wise use."

—GFW

Stewardship of Floodplains

A central struggle of Gilbert White's career was to convince others to accept extreme events of nature as natural hazards and to recognize that their potentially disastrous consequences could be mitigated by a broader range of human adjustments than were recognized by policy makers and federal agencies prior to the mid-twentieth century. Gilbert's distinct contribution was to educate those officials and others regarding the full range of nonstructural adjustments available to manage floodplains and mitigate losses from flooding. By the 1970s, his mission had broadened substantially to include the promotion of understanding, respect, and protection of the global natural order, which includes inevitable extremes. In a word, Gilbert championed stewardship—preserving nature and promoting sustainable use and husbandry of the natural resources employed by human beings. Recognition of the need to pursue these goals, these ways of living, led to the emergence of a science of sustainability in the late twentieth century.

The term "sustainability science" was first used in Sweden, home of the Volvo Corporation, which awarded its Environment Prize in 1995 to Gilbert White for the breadth of his vision and his efforts in advancing environmental stewardship.

Gilbert's counsel in this arena was, characteristically, measured. He cautioned against overreaching expectations in undertaking such formidable challenges. In 1992, at the National Forum on Water Management Policy sponsored by the American Water Resources Association, he served as discussant for the section on "Sustainable Development." Other career-long associates provided retrospective and prospective assessments of the primarily national issues that had dominated Gilbert's career: U.S. floodplain management and water infrastructure needs, risks, and uncertainties, as well as perspectives on water resources policy from economics, geography, political science, and engineering. It was a nostalgic moment for Gilbert; the forum was dedicated to the memory of his early Washington mentor, Abel Wolman, "who understood better than some of his contemporaries the obligations of the engineer as an agent of social change. Indeed, for Wolman the distinction between social and technical engineering loses meaning" (Reuss 1993b). Others in attendance whom Wolman and/or White had mentored (and who are mentioned in this biography) included Allen Kneese of Resources for the Future, Rutherford Platt, a University of Chicago graduate student in the 1960s, Theodore Schad of the Senate Select Committee on National Water Resources, James Wright of the Tennessee Valley Authority, Martin Reuss with the Corps of Engineers (who, as historian and chairman of the forum, edited its proceedings), and Leonard Shabman, an academician who had served government (including the army) in advisory roles.

Gilbert's comments at the close of the session on sustainable development were succinct:

> We are all aware that the goal of sustainable development has a wide spectrum of connotations in the current scene. While several of the definitions are tantalizing in their ambiguity, and others are mutually opposing, I suspect that there is something close to consensus on a few elements. The time horizon is the indefinite future, rather than an investment period. The capacity of the environment is seen as providing opportunity for cultural as well as economic satisfaction, without any impairment of natural systems. . . .
>
> Obviously, the challenges posed by the sustainable development concept in water management are enormous and unprecedented. Two of the possible steps to meet them are to focus on simple demonstrations of what is envisaged in practice, and to join in specifying an agenda for needed research. The agencies and scientific groups involved should lose no time in demonstrating exactly what they mean by a plan for sustainable water development of an area. To only describe appropriate technologies and standards and regulations will not be enough (White 1993c).

White considered the design concepts outlined in the forum by the Corps of Engineers challenging and highly ambitious, noted that public officials' expressed views are not necessarily a guide to future behavior ("What people say often contrasts with what they do"), and reminded attendees of the paradoxes revealed by the media discussion of that year's U.N. Conference on Environment and Development in Rio de Janeiro:

> The controversy over setting emission limits on greenhouse gases, and over strategies to reduce further loss of species, obscured consideration on the world scene of the forces driving continued deterioration of air, water, soil, and biota. . . .
> Limiting carbon dioxide emissions is important, but far more important is action on problems of population and consumer demand (White 1993c).

Perhaps most satisfying for Gilbert in those four June days of fellowship with old "comrades in arms" was the remarkable unity of vision (embodied in Abel Wolman) among the participating scientists, civil and Corps engineers, and practitioners. The rivalries of the past century, discussed in this book's Preface, had been largely overcome and replaced by the common cause of "implementation of the institutional changes that will be needed to put our scientific and technical knowledge to use in the service of mankind" (Schad 1989).

The year 1992 provided yet another nostalgic moment for White. In October, Gilbert became the first recipient of the Sustained Achievement Award of the Renewable Natural Resources Foundation (RNRF). This award was instituted on the twentieth anniversary of the founding of this consortium of seventeen professional, scientific, and educational organizations, with many of which Gilbert had had long-standing involvement over the course of his career, most notably the American Water Resources Association, the Association of American Geographers, and Resources for the Future. "Renewable resources" lies at the heart of sustainable development and sustainability science, and accordingly Gilbert was moved by this award's acknowledgment of a pioneering role he regarded as modest.

When Gilbert was presented the Volvo Corporation's Environment Prize two years later, it was fitting that Ian Burton, of the White-Burton-Kates triumvirate, was able to attend. Moreover, by then Robert Kates was in the forefront of this new discipline of sustainability science.[1] Gilbert already had passed the baton.

༄

BESIDES HIS STUDENTS, many other people who knew and worked with Gilbert helped further his goals. One example, William Hooke, deputy chief scientist with the National Oceanic and Atmospheric Administration in 2000 and an astute participant-observer of both the scientific and bureaucratic worlds of natural hazards research and mitigation, said of Gilbert:

> He is both the Thomas Jefferson, the conceptualizer, and the George Washington, the implementer, of the field of natural hazards. He has influenced a generation of hazards experts by being their community's image of what the ideal member of that field should be. The popular wisdom is that the founding fathers had a great vision of a strong presidency leading the new nation. But they weren't such visionaries. They knew that Washington would be the first president. If they had foreseen that the second president would be John Adams we perhaps would have a parliamentary form of government. It was Washington's strength of character that carried the day in establishing the form of government we now revere. Gilbert has had the same influence in establishing the character of the Hazards Center. He is a weighty figure, and weighty leaders do two things: they have a great dream; and they wisely give it away. Gilbert had the dream of sustainability in our adjustments to natural hazards, and he mobilized hundreds of people marching to the same drummer. He entrusted the dream to a Hazards Center and with it drew others into that dream. Thereafter his role was the rudder, revitalizing and annually renewing commitment of the hazards community to the

fundamental truths he elaborated. In particular, he saw more clearly than most that the earth as a natural system relies on extreme events to do its business and that catastrophe is less a natural event than a consequence of social decisions. Thanks to Gilbert White, the public needs now less to be convinced of these ideas than simply reminded and kept on track (Hooke 2000).

The idea of living with nature's extremes was Gilbert's Jeffersonian conception. The Natural Hazards Center (as well as many of Gilbert's other efforts) represented his Washingtonian implementation. Through the Natural Hazards Center, "a large number of federal agency employees, local emergency managers, ecologists, geographers, and other social scientists, were brought together and helped to see how they were members of the same community" (Hooke 2000).

During his thirty-year career, Hooke saw both houses of Congress establish natural hazards caucuses. Senator John Edwards's office created a website for the twenty-five institutions supporting the Senate caucus, and Hooke used the site to promote the knowledge and resources available through the Natural Hazards Center.

Another Natural Hazards Center workshop participant and Gilbert observer over several decades was Brigadier General Gerald Galloway of the U.S. Army Corps of Engineers and the U.S. Military Academy. Galloway noted that attitudes toward property rights at the commencement of Gilbert's career were little different from those of centuries earlier: property owners had not only the right but the responsibility to defend their land and homes in floodplains from flooding through whatever means available. Clearly, White's suggestion that government should decide whether or under what conditions victims of flooding could rebuild on their own property directly challenged this widely held belief that a man's home is his castle and he can do what he will with his property. To change such fundamental ideas in a few decades, to persuade even the Corps of Engineers that they had been unwise in emphasizing the control of rivers while disregarding the stewardship of floodplains, was an enormous accomplishment. Galloway recognized that here again, Gilbert was a master at enlisting help.

> Gilbert recruited, trained, and fostered disciples of his radical philosophy for half a century, and he never ceased beating us up the side of our head (in his gentle way) if we didn't continue doing our part. I gave a speech in a conference in Chicago in the 1990s, and Gilbert said to me afterwards that it should be published in the IWR journal [*International Water Review*]. The next time I saw him, he asked me if I had gotten that done yet! (Galloway 2001)

Gilbert was untiring in his commitment to the cause of stewardship and expected no less from others. His success in this area was due to at least four of his approaches to work: sharing the ownership of ideas, communicating effectively, acting efficiently (employing serenity and a sense of proportion, parsimony, and focus), and increasing the efficacy of institutions sharing his mission.

Sharing the Ownership of Ideas

If Gilbert was determined in seeking out disciples, he was also more than willing to share the ownership of ideas and publications while downplaying his own role. He was sole author of relatively few books and of only one-third of the three dozen other publications (among his 400) that he considered the most significant. The four books that he regarded as his most seminal were *Human Adjustment to Floods* (1945), *Drawers of Water* (1972), *Environmental Effects of Complex River Development* (1977), and *The Environment as Hazard* (1978). Only the first of these (his doctoral dissertation) was solely his own. Virtually all his graduate students shared authorship of one or more of his publications, and a few of those who most benefited from this collaboration believed that, in so doing, Gilbert may have hindered his own scholarly reputation early in his career among his professional colleagues.

Gilbert's commitment to parsimonious writing (as well as to parsimonious speech) and hence to keeping his books as short as possible, also ran contrary to usual academic practice. But in the 1980s he did begin planning a monumental work that would weave together international water resource management and environmental policies. For example, in a law school course on water law, the focus would be on ownership and supply, whereas a completely separate course on environmental law would deal with the issues of water quality and environmental effects. Gilbert believed that the marriage of these two fields warranted a book. Cambridge University Press concurred, and for well over a decade Gilbert worked on the endeavor. But advancing age with no concurrent reduction in the claims on his time again led him to seek assistance, in the person of James Wescoat, then a colleague in the Geography Department at the University of Colorado. Wescoat's own interests (Wescoat 2003) made him an ideal partner to provide the historical perspective for *Water for Life*. With his usual generosity, Gilbert insisted that Wescoat's name precede his own on the title page (Wescoat and White 2003).

Gilbert rejected many (perhaps most) invitations to speak, write, or chair committees, in part to promote associates whom he felt were capable of or even better suited for the task. For example, when he was approached to take the job, Gilbert suggested that Gerald Galloway chair President Bill Clinton's commission on the massive Mississippi Valley floods of 1993 (see Chapter 9). Similarly, Barbara Richman, managing editor of the journal *Environment* in the 1980s, when Gilbert was one of four scientists on the publication's executive editorial board, found Gilbert reluctant to write articles for the peer-reviewed scholarly magazine. He agreed to write only three articles during their joint tenure with *Environment* (overlapping the last half of Gilbert's term as executive editor from 1983 until 1992) because he believed that the opportunity to use this platform should be left open to others. He was particularly reluctant to write on the Middle Eastern water deliberations that he had chaired for the National Research Council (discussed below), because such an article represented a career advancement opportunity for one of the Middle Eastern representatives on the committee (Richman 2001).

Communicating Effectively

Gilbert's approach to chairing a National Research Council committee, a federal task force, or a city council advisory committee on Boulder's vulnerability to flooding was essentially the same as his approach to chairing a Quaker business meeting (or Haverford faculty meetings—see Chapter 5). Gilbert acknowledged that, at times, he declined chairmanships if constraints of group size or participant allegiance (i.e., if a participant was exected to represent the views of an organization or constituency to the exclusion of his own) precluded this approach. This reluctance partly answers the question posed by some of his associates: What kept Gilbert White from competing for more visible political leadership?

As his career advanced, however, Gilbert did accept some appointments that were very challenging, as detailed in Chapter 12. In his final National Research Council assignment, in the late 1990s, he chaired a committee of Jordanian, Palestinian, and Israeli water experts that examined cooperative use of Jordan River and Dead Sea resources, "among the first analyses of international river basins to recognize the provision of ecosystem services as an essential water need along with domestic use" (White et al. 1999). Even among these Arab Muslim and Jewish scholars, he was able to orchestrate considerable agreement, something the participants thought impossible before they began working together under White's leadership (al-Hassan 2001). After receiving the committee's report (White et al. 1999), NAS president Bruce Alberts commended Gilbert and acknowledged that possibly only a Quaker could have created the mutual trust needed for this group to collaborate under such trying circumstances.[2]

In potentially adversarial situations, where the willingness to pursue Gilbert's approach or position was weak or lacking altogether, Gilbert could use friendly persuasion. He was usually an uncensorious but canny lobbyist. These skills were particularly evident in his efforts to protect Boulderites from unnecessary flood losses along Boulder Creek (see Chapter 10). They proved less effective, however, when he served on the FEMA committee established to oversee the postaudit of the National Flood Insurance Program (see Chapter 9). In that case he responded to some members' lack of commitment to the work by threatening to report to the relevant congressional committee his disappointment with the committee's efforts.

Similarly, when he was told that the city of Boulder was considering allowing the use of a basement floor of new construction in the 100-year floodplain for housing the Boulder Historical Museum, he told the museum director that he would withdraw from all involvement in Boulder community affairs if the plans went forward (Butterfield 2001). Those who knew Gilbert knew this was not an idle threat, and the location was changed.

One of Gilbert's commitments was to encourage the expression of minority opinions. After they were presented, he typically acted as mediator and tried to promote viable reconciliation and consensus. He had the ability to deal with opposing views without personalizing the disagreement, further increasing the likelihood that any group of which he was a part could forge a minimal consensus. At times, Gilbert's willingness to accept less than full realization of a committee's assignments in the short run (because he was optimistic about building upon that success in the long run) could frustrate his allies. They feared that in his eagerness to build ownership and consensus he would sacrifice a potentially stronger outcome from a less than unanimous majority. But Gilbert's patience often resulted in more progress than skeptical participants would have deemed possible.

Acting Efficiently (Serenity, Proportion, Parsimony, Focus)

Former Chicago graduate student Ken Mitchell recalled Gilbert's reaction to the student protests at the University of Chicago in the late 1960s. A group of faculty and students from the Geography Department examined the administration building following a student sit-in. After noting some typewriters into which ink had been poured and hearing one of the faculty complain about the damage, Mitchell observed that really determined protestors could have done much more harm. Gilbert, silent until then, agreed, and suggested that the whole affair was a "tempest in a teacup." Peter Jutro, senior policy adviser for Environment and Security with the U.S. EPA and for many years an ally of Gilbert's regarding environmental policy, said, "It is easy to be indignant in the environmental area and to lose the balance between academic discourse and political advocacy. Gilbert was never guilty of this" (Jutro 2001). On the occasion of Gilbert's ninetieth birthday, Tom Mayer, an Institute of Behavioral Science colleague at the University of Colorado, summarized in verse a number of Gilbert's virtues. He wrote: "He keeps an even keel in the crisis strewn landscape of modern life. A gyroscopic sameness pervades his daily manner. Gilbert bestows a cool ounce of serenity on all those who languish near."

Gilbert's students valued the manner in which Gilbert taught precision and brevity. He often assigned position papers limited to 500 words, recognizing that it is harder to write less than to write more. "[This practice] proved especially helpful in testifying before Congressional committees," Ken Mitchell said. "Twenty minutes was the recommended length, and I would get it down to less than that. If I had pursued a more theoretically guided career, I would not have mastered the difference between 'blue-sky' theorizing and Gilbert's practical, defensible theorizing" (Mitchell 2001). As Barbara Richman noted, "Gilbert's style, in his quiet way, was to assess needs in their most quintessential form, boiling each issue down to its most simple solution" (Richman 2001).

When collaborating with other scientists in consulting (when services are costly and time limited), Gilbert was sensitive to gathering only the information required to address the task at hand. Conversely, when he judged the available knowledge insufficient to support a policy decision, he would not overreach. For example, in the 1970s, when the American Friends Service Committee was considering taking a public stand against increased reliance on nuclear energy in the United States, Gilbert joined with Kenneth Boulding in arguing (without success) that the AFSC should not act until the risks were better understood. Similarly, in the interest of efficiency, Gilbert supported any "sunset provision"—any rule that mandated that a committee, even an institution, be terminated before outliving its usefulness.

Focus was central to Gilbert's efficiency, as well as a principal lesson he endeavored to teach others. He paced himself for the task at hand, even as he made seemingly superhuman demands on himself in staying on task until completion. Despite his considerable patience with others, his example often was formidable. He would routinely ask of himself more sacrifice and single-mindedness than his associates were accustomed to asking of themselves. Many of his students recall that on field trips, Gilbert would require them to show up earlier in the morning and persevere later than they, half Gilbert's age, usually expected of themselves.

Ruben Mendez, as a novice economic adviser for the 1997 U.N. Conference on Desertification with which Gilbert was involved, telephoned Gilbert for advice on estimating rates of land degradation worldwide. Gilbert had a particularly hectic schedule and suggested that they confer during an upcoming flight from Denver. Mendez flew from the East Coast to rendezvous at the Denver airport as suggested.

> In about ten minutes, Gilbert wrote out a simplified classification of land types and the kind and degree of their degradation, and outlined a conceptual scheme. By the time we landed in Washington I was fortified with ideas, leads, a systematic approach and, most important for me at the time, a sense of confidence about how to handle the project.... Gilbert never claimed credit for it, but he was one of the main architects of the World Plan of Action adopted by the Conference and later by the United Nations General Assembly (Mendez 2001).

Gilbert assumed that imagination and experimentation could also increase the focus of groups. Reds Wolman, professor of geography at Johns Hopkins University (and son of Abel Wolman, Gilbert's Washington mentor in the 1930s) recalled meetings of a Committee on Water that were proceeding rather unproductively in Washington, D.C. Members were constantly excusing themselves to make or receive telephone calls. Gilbert, as chair, finally suggested holding a meeting away from Washington, at the Four Way Lodge on the Great Egg Harbor River, where a single telephone (outside the lodge) and a minimum of other distractions might enable the committee to complete its assignment in one weekend. "The committee rose and retired quickly in the cold bunk-house, drew chairs around the fireplace to meet, talked over dishwashing and the stove, canoed in fog at breaks, and designed and assigned the writing of the Alternatives in Water Management report (about the Colorado River)." Few, if any, calls were made, and no subsequent meetings were needed (Wolman 2001).

Shepherding Institutions

Many of the causes that Gilbert espoused were contentious, even unpopular, given their long-term (and usually expensive) goals that advanced environmental welfare ahead of human short-term interests. Achieving these goals usually required cooperation among allied organizations as well as funding from assorted sources. In 1976, Kenneth Thompson, of the Miller Center for Public Affairs, wrote to Gilbert asking about the most efficacious way for the center to assist groups dealing with problems related to population pressure on the environment. In his response Gilbert first reviewed the strategies other funding agencies had taken. The Population Council was providing small grants to investigators needing a little encouragement to push on with promising ideas. By contrast, the Ford and Rockefeller Foundations, Resources for the Future, and the U.S. Agency for International Development favored large grants to a few agencies for more comprehensive programs. He then advised:

> If I were to explore possibilities for a series of small grants in the field I think I would begin by talking to whomever was the responsible officer for the joint Ford-Rockefeller awards on population problems with a view to identifying people or institutions which did not qualify for that program but which seemed to display competence, enthusiasm, and imaginative definition of problem. My hunch would be that those individual applications might be more likely to unearth some highly promising proposals than would the type of project that now is espoused by Planned Parenthood at the Population Reference Bureau. The Ford-Rockefeller appeal is likely to have generated inquiries from a number of applicants who would not fit into their program as outlined (White 1976b).

Gilbert's postscript to his letter to Thompson was typical: "Incidentally, I have been in touch with a most unconventional but bright young investigator who drives a taxi in Toronto while preparing to do some field work in the Galapagos on a population-environmental issue. If you think your group might be interested in an application from him let me know to whom he should apply."

Again, on Gilbert's ninetieth birthday, former Ford Foundation vice president Marshall Robinson wrote the following:

> In 1973, when the Ford Foundation discovered that "care of the environment" was a worthy goal to pursue, we turned to Gilbert White to show us how that goal could be best served with money. Gil rose to the task, beginning with a suggestion that we enlist Resources for the Future. Essentially a research institute, RFF had long been a Ford client, which he said could be helpful—if Ford

would help RFF to broaden their mission to pursue this new objective. It was a brilliant idea which, given his reputation for solid and balanced research, was a comfort for those nervous Ford trustees who saw "environment" as a form of creeping socialism. From then on, we checked controversial proposals with Gil (who turned some down and suggested how to fix up others). He was our research quality screener and professional ethics mentor (Robinson 2001).

Gilbert went out of his way to assist institutions and scientists in countries such as the Soviet Union and China, where institutional frameworks were lacking and funding was difficult to obtain. For example, for more than two decades the Whites annually contributed modest financial support to a dozen Russian geographers to supplement their inadequate public salaries. Gilbert first became involved with the Russian scientific community through the American Friends Service Committee Conferences for Diplomats. Because he spoke Russian (which he had learned while interned in Baden-Baden), Gilbert made several good friends, one of whom, Vasily Smirnyagin, was elected president of SCOPE in the 1970s. Other friendships evolved from his associations with the Institute of Geography, the Russian Academy of Science, and the Department of Geography at Moscow State University (where Genady Golubev hosted Gilbert as a Fulbright visiting scholar early in the 1970s). The friendships deepened with Gilbert's efforts through SCOPE and the AFSC Conferences for Diplomats to de-escalate East-West tensions and reduce the threat of nuclear war and nuclear winter (see Chapter 6).

In addition to SCOPE meetings held in Russia, Gilbert chaired two major conferences in the Soviet Union, a Volga River cruise symposium on Man and Environment in conjunction with the twenty-third International Geographical Union (IGU) Congress in Moscow in 1976, and a UNEP Commission investigating the declining size and health of the Aral Sea in the early 1990s. At the IGU Congress, attendees who were unaccustomed to Soviet life were surprised by the bureaucratic red tape, formality, and ponderous decision-making procedures. To reduce this culture shock for non-Russians and facilitate socializing on board the cruise ship, Gilbert insisted on eliminating all academic and public titles during the symposium (a practice that Gilbert frequently used even in the United States because of the Quaker preference for using only first and last names to promote an egalitarian spirit). Tatiana Zvonkova, one of the two Soviet scientists supervising the symposium, responded happily to Gilbert's suggestion and exclaimed, "What a democrat!"

Similarly, in Central Asia, Moscow, and Switzerland, where the contentious Aral Sea deliberations were held,

> Gilbert's was the calming voice of the American geographer that everyone knew and respected, which was instrumental in reaching compromise and in the end turning out a credible Diagnostic Study, acceptable to all sides.... He not only clearly understood the key aspects of the problem, but also was so insightful about the "political" maneuvering that was going on between the

Moscow people, particularly the Institute of Geography, and the Central Asian scientists (Micklin 2001).

In the mid-1970s Gilbert advised the Treasury of Australia regarding the establishment of a viable national insurance program as part of a comprehensive disaster mitigation plan analogous to the U.S. flood insurance program. Rodney Smith of the Australian Treasury had been referred to White by a staff member of the U.S. Senate Committee on Banking, Housing, and Urban Affairs. White in turn enlisted the assistance of Howard Kunreuther of the University of Pennsylvania's Wharton School and Robert Simpson, counselor for Economic and Commercial Affairs in the U.S. Embassy in Canberra. But Gilbert's pleasure helping another nation avoid some of the pitfalls of the U.S. experience ensured his personal involvement for the next fifteen months.

Gilbert's personal papers abound with requests to provide advice to institutions and agencies and requests to serve on boards. He was cautious in the invitations he accepted to serve on boards, declining if he suspected that the organization was seeking his name rather than substantive assistance.[3] But when declining, Gilbert sometimes offered instead to provide specific advice or consultation, particularly if he thought he could contribute to the solution of a concern that he shared with the organization. His judiciousness in making commitments and his trustworthiness once a commitment was made only encouraged yet more such requests. As Tom Mayer said in his tribute:

> *Trust morning not to abscond*
> *Trust water to slake thirst.*
> *Trust the pathway to reach home.*
> *Promises GW gives not easily and not often.*
> *When given, a GW promise resembles*
> *Pathways, water, and morning.*

Invitations to accept honorary degrees were especially problematic for Gilbert. He accepted only eight over the course of his long career, turning down as many more. Unless he could enhance the status of the geography profession or discipline, he was reluctant to accept. Moreover, when he did accept, he urged that the bestowing institution ask him and other recipients to visit and participate in campus life for several days, a practice he had instituted at Haverford when he was president.[4]

White accepted positions with very large philanthropic foundations, as well as some small family foundations, if the institutional goals and his personal commitments overlapped. At one time or another, he worked with the Rockefeller, Carnegie Corporation, Ford, General Services, Andrew Mellon, and MacArthur Foundations. The Compton Foundation, one of the smaller family foundations with which he worked, helped fund a number of research and/or publication efforts important to Gilbert (including this biography). Gilbert was exceptionally persuasive in raising money, and from him many associates and students (as well as his children) learned the importance of identifying the most likely funding sources and knowing how to obtain their assistance.

In addition to securing funding, effective stewardship involves steadfast maintenance of institutions. Although, as mentioned above, Gilbert was ready to turn over an idea, project, or institution to others (both his colleagues and employees have cited this readiness to "empower" others as one of his more admirable—and sometimes disconcerting—characteristics), he was reluctant to allocate work to others without shouldering his share of the effort. His filling in a second time, with no compensation, as interim director of the Natural Hazards Center is one notable example.[5]

Gilbert's various secretaries at the University of Colorado all attested to his organizational skills, keen memory, and attention to detail in managing the many projects and services he provided to a multitude of organizations, agencies, institutions, and individuals. He modeled, rather than instructed staff on time-saving techniques. The Natural Hazards Center's secretary for twenty years, Fay Tracy, recalls how rapidly the staff adopted Gilbert's practice of abbreviating the names of everyone in his family, the office, and circle of closest associates, using the three initials of each person's name in all memos, even in conversation. It became an honor to be so referenced by Gilbert; you had become a member of his extended family. In his office there was an assigned place for everything, and everything was in its place. Gilbert wasted no time finding what he needed, be it a publication or simply a name and address.

Enhancing efficiency was Gilbert's reason for advocating postaudits (retrospective assessments) of programs. Although officials could rarely, if ever, justify their failure to fund and conduct such postaudits (how could they defend not taking available steps to increase efficiency?), Gilbert was continually frustrated in his efforts to promote such analysis. For example, his efforts to have a thorough postaudit conducted of the National Flood Insurance Program were consistently thwarted for several decades. Gerald Galloway was sympathetic to Gilbert's efforts in this regard but felt that Gilbert was unrealistic in his expectations:

> Gilbert on the issue of post-audits is much like the voice of John the Baptist crying in the wilderness. Without being disrespectful, until the Messiah comes along and shakes the roots of the Congress and the government, it is unreasonable to expect officialdom to pay money for a critique of something that may prove embarrassing. It isn't going to happen on the Hill, it isn't going to happen in state legislatures, and it isn't going to happen in the federal agencies. On small scales my and others' efforts have met with some success, but when I mention this within the Corps as a possible agenda on any sizeable scale, people say "You've got to be kidding!" So, has White's effort in this regard been a failure? Not with people with a conscience, who continue to be bothered by the challenge he regularly puts forth. But there are always excuses, such as no funding to do it or it being a diversion from our primary function (Galloway 2001).

The inefficiencies that resulted from not assessing the consequences of policy actions tried even the patience of Gilbert White.

Gilbert turned down as many opportunities as he accepted to assist others and advance his own career objectives. Reaching even the many career goals that he did set for himself—especially the publication of *Water for Life* (2003)—required both longevity and the postponement of retirement until age ninety-three. Even at ninety-two he managed to attend the inaugural Gilbert F. White National Flood Policy Forum in Washington, D.C. Established under the auspices of the Association of State Floodplain Managers Foundation, the forum assessed the efficacy of the 1 percent chance (100-year) flood standard used by the U.S. Army Corps of Engineers for much of the twentieth century and adopted by the National Flood Insurance Program early in the 1970s. In a sense the forum was a postaudit, and it could not have been more fitting or welcomed by Gilbert (ASFPM Foundation 2004).

Paradoxes

In every person there are paradoxes, tensions among beliefs and commitments. Despite Gilbert's remarkable consistency and integrity, several paradoxes persisted throughout his life. Perhaps the most noteworthy was his enduring fascination with the workings of government (especially the presidency and federal agencies of the executive branch) in contrast with his reluctance to encourage his students to pursue careers in government. Indeed, Gilbert recalled only one graduate student who chose a career in government (with the Corps of Engineers), and only one Haverford College alumnus contacted for this biography acknowledged Gilbert's influence regarding his choice of a government career.[6] One colleague suggested that Gilbert was so charismatic and so influenced his students that many learned to speak with his voice and let him use them to pursue his agendas. Moreover, his students rarely would make a job change without consulting Gilbert, and he would not initially think of government when passing along news of job openings.

Of course, Gilbert himself, following his eight years in the FDR administration from 1933 to 1942, turned down all subsequent invitations to return to government. Many associates expressed puzzlement over why Gilbert eschewed political office with such determination. Certainly, part of the answer lies in the challenge to personal integrity inevitably posed by political wheeling and dealing. In Gilbert's case, however, the answer probably also reflected his comparative lack of ambition and ego. Political ambition and success are often associated with a strong ego and the need for attention and fame, traits that are not very pronounced in Gilbert. But the question still persists: did Gilbert's convictions, reinforced by his Quakerism, prevent him from having a greater impact on the policies he sought to influence? Probably his reply would have been that knowing and being true to oneself is the first prerequisite to service and stewardship.[7] His path was as a citizen-scientist, offering the insights and truths of geography and related fields to government leaders when and wherever needed.

Another paradox in Gilbert was a consequence of his strong belief in the potential of each individual human being. He rarely gave up on anyone. To the contrary, he remained optimistic—some would say naïvely so—about every person's ability to rise to challenges. However, at the same time, perhaps without being entirely conscious of forming a judgment, Gilbert would scrutinize a person's behavior relative to their word. He extended every benefit of the doubt before forming a judgment, but then, if disappointed, he would reduce his contact and his investment in the relationship.

He rarely reprimanded anyone, and therefore, when he did criticize, it could be devastating. On occasion, his closest and most successful students, understanding from their own painful experience how devastating such criticism could be, cautioned Gilbert when they sensed that he was pushing a student too hard. Nevertheless, a few students found Gilbert so intimidating and feared his censure so much that they gave up pursuing degrees in geography. Hence, Gilbert's great respect for human potential and expectation of best efforts (although coupled with patience and kindness) paradoxically resulted in only the more gifted and self-assured surviving his guidance and supervision. However, once within Gilbert's circle of respected colleagues, a person received almost boundless loyalty, and Gilbert subsequently forgave occasional mistakes.

As an adult, Gilbert observed twelve U.S. presidents (often consulting for their administrations). He also watched closely a number of other leaders in public and private life, some of whose careers were transformed by the weight of the responsibility they assumed (and by other personal adversity in a few instances). He also witnessed several instances in which power corrupted. The personal improprieties of three presidents (FDR, JFK, and Bill Clinton), whose optimistic and idealistic political leadership Gilbert nonetheless admired, bemused Gilbert. He was surprisingly tolerant of such frailty, given the high standards he set for himself, but he was completely blindsided by the misuse of university and federal funds, coupled with philandering, of Gilbert's colleague Gene Haas during the first assessment of natural hazards conducted by the Institute of Behavioral Science in the early 1970s. He had never before experienced anything comparable, and he simply could not fathom or deal with such betrayal.[8]

In a few cases, Natural Hazards Center staff questioned Gilbert's judgment when, over the years, he hired new employees who they thought were unqualified. When their concerns were confirmed by the poor performance of a new employee, the staff found Gilbert oddly reluctant to take action. He would promise to counsel or even dismiss the new employee but would then drag his feet, trying to salvage the situation or at least avoid embarrassment to the employee. Clearly, the conflict between his optimism regarding individual human beings and the reality of some of those human beings' failure to live up to expectations was difficult for Gilbert to reconcile, and he therefore did not enjoy the role of employer.

Still, Gilbert thoroughly enjoyed people, and because of the deep respect he generated, his associates were always on their best behavior around him. Accordingly, Gilbert was most often heartened by his personal experiences with others.

Gilbert White and the Problem of Evil

The foregoing stories reflect Gilbert's ambivalence about acknowledging willful undermining of the natural or moral order. In the previous chapter this issue was explored vis-à-vis Gilbert's liberal Quaker worldview, assumptions that helped him reconcile, if not sidestep, the issue. But the problem deserves to be examined in greater depth and within the broader context of the twentieth century's many devastating and incomprehensibly large acts of suffering inflicted by one person or people on others, as well as modern philosophy's responses to those events. Indeed, those events, along with the erosion of confidence in government and science to deliver us from the depredations that threaten humankind, raises the key question that prompted this biography: What does Gilbert White's example teach us about living a life that makes a difference in an increasingly perilous and morally ambiguous world? What does his life mean in light of the events of our time?

When the Corps of Engineers honored the careers of Arthur Maass and Gilbert White in 2001, Leonard Shabman of the Department of Agricultural and Applied Economics at Virginia Tech University and director of the Virginia Water Research Center was invited to review their influence on the Corps' and the nation's attitudes toward resource management. In his talk Shabman pointed out a significant change in the preceding forty years:

> There has been a loss of public faith in government bureaus and bureaucrats (it used to be a compliment to be a bureaucrat). From the political right and political left government bureaus are accused of being a problem for natural resources and not a solution. A new faith in mini-democracy, stakeholder participation, collaborative decision-making, or whatever term you care to use, has replaced the progressive era faith in the expert with skepticism about expertise. Today we are past the time of progressive era and "new deal" top down, hierarchical model of bureaucratic responsiveness and responsibility. This new decision model does not have a place for the Corps to do a study of what it deems to be best for the nation and announce its findings to all interested publics. There is the need to involve BOTH the cost-sharing partners AND the agencies and other interests that have the power to delay and block projects. How one incorporates planning and evaluation into this new decision-making environment has not been well addressed—or even understood—by the Corps (Shabman 2001).

Gilbert White was a child of that Progressive era that produced New Deal idealism, and he has acknowledged its salutary influence on him. However, in the early 1940s Gilbert went from that optimistic world of charismatic, top-down leadership into the

European cauldron of fascist totalitarianism, from which he emerged with the previously mentioned perspective that balanced responsible leadership and grassroots activism. He never relinquished a determined commitment to achieving both, despite the subsequent sixty years during which confidence in government generally faded, as Shabman suggested.

When Gilbert encountered the Gestapo in 1942–1943, he had been a member of the Society of Friends less than one year and a participant in Quaker worship for less than ten. Certainly, the philosophical foundation underlying his interactions with Nazism derived from his study of Quaker faith and practice (in particular, the writings of Rufus Jones), but it probably was as much based on the secular pragmatism of William James, the neo-Enlightenment optimism and rationalism of philosopher and pacifist Bertrand Russell (whose career overlapped that of the older James at the turn of the century), and the emerging secularism in liberal Christianity of the twentieth century. One such theologian, Reinhold Niebuhr (who wrote the foreword to one of the reprints of James's *The Varieties of Religious Experience*) said of evil, "It is always the assertion of some self-interest without regard to the whole, whether the whole be conceived as the immediate community or the total community of humanity, or the total order of the world. The good is, on the other hand, always the harmony of the whole on various levels" (Niebuhr, quoted in Ross 2002). That clearly was Gilbert's assessment as well. And his response to critics pressing him on the matter was to redouble his efforts to better understand why political leadership was not attending to the findings of science that could help illuminate the causes of resource depletion, unjust distribution of those resources, and the resultant suffering, violence, and war (White, Kates, and Burton 2001).

At the start of this millennium, Jonathan Glover wrote *Humanity: A Moral History of the Twentieth Century* (2000), which examined the psychology underlying the philosophy of Friedrich Nietzsche and the political leaders of the twentieth century who followed in Nietzsche's intellectual footsteps (including, but not limited to, Adolf Hitler and Joseph Stalin). Nietzsche's idol was Johann Wolfgang von Goethe, and of him Glover wrote, "What he aspired to was totality; he strove against the separation of reason, sensuality, feeling, will; he disciplined himself to a whole, he created himself." Glover adds that "self-creation requires self-discipline. Cultivating some characteristics and curbing others requires 'hardness,' as Nietzsche called it, towards oneself. As advocated by the Stoic philosophers, desires and impulses have to be strictly under control. The reward of hardness towards yourself is to become what you have the potential to be: the artist and creator of your own life" (Glover 2000).

William James described the religious quest in similar terms, and upon reading James's *The Varieties of Religious Experience* in his late teens, Gilbert began to try to live his life with just such discipline. Glover essentially describes attempts at such self-creation in the twentieth century that went wrong, just as James a century earlier described various attempts—the varieties of religious experience—

that had gone right. Hitler will be long remembered as the twentieth-century archetype of such efforts gone wrong. Gilbert White is worthy of examination as an example of an effort gone right.

In his analysis Glover "de-demonizes" the men responsible for inhuman acts by showing that their actions were the result of poor discernment of a proper path, rather than the result of any essential, inherent "evil." Gilbert, reflecting the liberal Quakerism of his experience, similarly refused to demonize the Gestapo in his encounters during 1942 and 1943. Glover attributed to the rationalist scientist Bertrand Russell a pre–World War I optimism that scientific progress would diminish (if not eliminate) war and the worst forms of human cruelty. (It is one of the saddest ironies of our time that that science actually resulted in previously unimaginable tools of destruction.) Speaking of that nineteenth-century optimism, Glover says dryly, "In the light of these expectations, the century of Hitler, Stalin, Pol Pot and Saddam Hussein was likely to be a surprise." A century later, the late nineteenth and early twentieth century hope of progress and humanitarianism fed by scientific knowledge was revealed as tragically naïve, or "brittle," as John Maynard Keynes described Bertrand Russell's philosophy of human nature and diagnosis of human affairs. However, the optimism of Russell and James regarding the triumph of reason and goodness is certainly understandable, given the relatively peaceful time in which their outlook was formed. Gilbert inherited that optimism, which was reinforced by the confident Quaker view that human beings and their institutions could be perfected through spiritual insight, collective discernment, and imitation of the example of Jesus. The brittleness that Keynes attributed to Bertrand Russell and William James is probably similar to the problem that fellow Quaker commentators found in Gilbert's address, "Stewardship of the Earth" (White 1975a), presented at the Friends' 1978 Right Sharing of World Resources conference. They suggested that Gilbert underestimated the structural violence (corporate evil) unleashed during the twentieth century (FWCC 1978). It was the same criticism that Paul Rasor, director of the Religion and Social Issues Forum at Pendle Hill (a Quaker retreat center in Philadelphia), addressed to religious liberals more generally following the horrific attacks of September 11, 2001: "Religious liberals have historically failed to acknowledge that there is also an inherent potential for evil in human beings. Having no theology of evil has weakened our prophetic voice in trying to resist it" (Rasor, quoted in Ross 2002).

Challenges to Gilbert's Optimism

Susan Tubbesing, the first project manager at the Natural Hazards Center, recounted that when she was hired in the early 1970s, Gilbert warned her that the center would last only two—at the most three—years. "By that time all hazards researchers would know, and readily exchange information and research findings with, all practitioners and would be carrying out new research to solve all the challenges faced in the 'real world.' So there would no longer be a need for a Hazards Clearinghouse and I would again be out of a job. . . . One of the times that Gilbert's optimism got the best of his seasoned judgment" (Tubbesing 2001).

Similarly, Gilbert and his student Robert Kates were once granted an audience with an administrator of the United Nations Development Programme to present their concerns about the failure of the UNDP to address the extreme events of nature that frequently undermine development objectives, especially in poorer countries. Because UNDP did not include the evaluation or funding of measures to mitigate hazards in their projects, both vulnerability and losses were increasing. The UNDP administrator asked for a follow-up memorandum summarizing their concerns, which Gilbert promptly and thoroughly provided. He received no response. Thereafter, Gilbert would sometimes complain, "But we told UNDP what to do!" "This illustrates a charming naiveté in Gilbert," Ian Burton once said, "thinking that a scientist can influence policy at that level with a memo. I have come to see how crowded the national and international policy arena is and how ineffectual social scientists usually are in trying to intervene" (Burton 2001).

Again, the paradox was that, despite his (and other's) extensive knowledge regarding the deteriorating prospects for sustainable management of the earth's natural resources, Gilbert maintained his enduring (and endearing) confidence and never despaired that the worrisome trends could be reversed, if only the requisite leadership could be married with the knowledge and solutions offered by science. He was as unshakeable in this faith as was Bertrand Russell. How did he maintain this optimism? In part, no doubt, through the "charming naiveté." But Gilbert also maintained a serenity that manifested itself, from time to time, in a curious distancing from the cares of the world, perhaps so that he could then become passionately re-involved. Gilbert succeeded in being very much in the world, but peculiarly not of it.

Paradoxically this tranquility enjoyed by Gilbert did not derive from or nurture a fascination with the past or speculation and prophecy about the future. He focused on—was preoccupied with—human betterment here and now and was almost constantly in the company of others similarly committed. Although he probably would object to the label, philosophically Gilbert could perhaps best be described as an existential pragmatist—an existentialist for his living in the moment, a pragmatist for experimenting to determine what approach would yield the most efficacious results. Herein may lie a key to appreciating the role that live theater played in Gilbert's life. His preoccupation with getting needed things done in the here and now may have reflected priorities rather than lack of interest in diversions to other times and places. By allowing himself the luxury of frequent theater outings, he perhaps removed himself from the doubtless wearying preoccupation with pressing societal needs more effectively than he could with other, less absorbing forms of entertainment, such as reading and television. That said, he did do a lot of reading.

Because of his ability to curtain-off the outside world in pursuit of periodic tranquility and peace of mind, one of his closest students and colleagues ventured that probably no one other than perhaps Anne or Claire ever really knew Gilbert White. If Anne had been alive and available for interviewing for the writing of this book, we perhaps would have an answer to this question: what happened in Gilbert's life and their marriage in the 1970s that produced, on the one hand, serious consideration of Gilbert's actually retiring when the University of Colorado rules called for an end to his faculty tenure and, on the other hand, the period of several years when Gilbert seemed unresponsive to Anne's need to spend more time with him on his travels abroad? His daily notes in the mid-1970s revealed at least a momentary period of discernment with Anne about a traditional kind of career ending and settling into a postretirement life style. But when queried about those notes twenty-five years thereafter, Gilbert had no memory of ever having seriously considered retiring. One can only assume that it was at Anne's urging that the idea arose and that possibly Gilbert's need to continue his professional lifestyle contributed to any distancing thereafter.

However, Gilbert's daily notes during the late 1970s and early 1980s also mentioned periodic bouts of depression, which he and Anne suspected were caused by allergies or medications (although the suspicions were never confirmed).[9] Anne probably is the only person who could have perceived and understood the effects on Gilbert of the series of discouraging, perhaps even unsettling, developments of the 1970s that would have tried the optimism of even a Gilbert White. They included the transition from Chicago to Boulder in 1970 (with Gilbert's associated disappointment with the University of Chicago and sadness over the Geography Department's rapid decline soon thereafter); disappointment also with the American Friends Service Committee's organizational dilemmas and priorities that only deepened with the AFSC's disinterest in White's and Kenneth Boulding's proposal of joint Institute of Behavioral Science and AFSC collaboration on a more environmentally oriented AFSC agenda for the 1970s; the turmoil within SCOPE that led to Gilbert's willingness to undertake its presidency; the escalation of the Cold War that deepened the threat of a nuclear war (and nuclear winter) and helped persuade Gilbert to become heavily involved with the journal *Environment*; and finally the crisis for the fledgling Natural Hazards Center precipitated by the adjudication over center director Gene Haas's improprieties, which virtually demanded that Gilbert step into the breach as director to avoid the center's demise.

Gilbert had but dim memories by 2000 of recurring periods of depression two decades previously, and indeed they may have been produced by medications for the assorted ailments (described earlier) with which he struggled. But perusal of Appendix 1's enumeration of Gilbert's many commitments in those years will suggest reasons aplenty for weariness, if not depression. The wonder is that he mustered the physical strength and mental resolve to persevere. Anne's role in that renewed commitment to "making a difference" with their lives in all likelihood was pivotal and may help explain the plunge into depression her unanticipated death precipitated.

By the time that Claire Sheridan entered Gilbert's life following Anne's death in the late 1980s, Gilbert exhibited (according to Claire) brief periods of discouragement but never depression. And even when temporarily ill, he was loath to complain. Claire was impressed with his ability to avoid talking about or even acknowledging "trouble." He was averse to viewing television or film violence and avoided discussions about worrisome political trends and environmental conditions. "I think there is a conscious naiveté, a protective naiveté, about Gilbert. The only way that you can think lofty thoughts is if you don't get mired in the muck. My reaction after 9/11 was to be vengeful. I wanted to kill them! But Gilbert wouldn't venture an opinion on what should be done and was unwilling even to engage in the conversation" (Sheridan 2002). Given his career dealing with natural disasters and their aftermath of suffering, Gilbert's avoidance of the painful details of human-caused disasters and violence is unsurprising.

Ultimately, his protective naiveté, even if it was a conscious naiveté in the interest of serenity, permitted Gilbert White to adopt and maintain the only approach that does offer a solution to the environmental perils resulting from increasing population and careless use and management of resources. In the end, the alternatives are simply either resignation, if not despair, or the belief that people are capable of choosing a better path and the world can be improved. Gilbert, throughout his long life, was not interested in examining the psychological and spiritual impediments to fulfilling human potential. Such an approach was pointless to him; it was not pragmatic. Instead, he defied popular assumptions about inherent selfishness. He expected unusual selflessness of himself, and his approach was sufficiently successful in making a difference in the world and the people with whom he dealt that he persisted and many others followed. The example he offered was, in the end, profoundly simple. Developing a pure spirit and wise judgment is not only a human possibility, a gift, but a weighty responsibility. Gilbert remained unconcerned about where this gift comes from, whether from the grace of God or a process of natural evolution. But he remained deeply concerned with the implications of this gift for the future of the Earth. If more of us understood the responsibility implied by this gift, if more of us then made as much of a difference as Gilbert White did, the planet just might still be inhabitable for our grandchildren's grandchildren. Gilbert recognized the need to pass on recognition of this gift and responsibility. He taught wildfire mitigation to his grandchildren, enlisting the help of even the youngest in periodically removing the lower dead branches on trees surrounding their mountain cabin. And, of course, each one also learned the importance of recycling and conserving water from the cabin well; "Save Water" stickers were placed by all the faucets . . . even the toilet.

In his characteristically efficient manner, Gilbert put his own personal affairs in order soon after attending to Anne's after her death. He even wrote his own obituary. But, as the adage goes, "The Lord was not yet through with Gilbert White." It is now fifteen years later, fifteen years of another enduring partnership later. The consequences of White's refusal to retire, encouraged no doubt by Claire's comparatively youthful exuberance, are apparent in all that he accomplished since the Institute of Behavioral Science sponsored an eightieth birthday celebration for him in 1991 (see Chapters 9 through 12). Moreover, untold numbers of his former students and colleagues and associates closer to his own age may remain uncommonly productive as well, judging from the several volunteered testimonials of those consciously electing not to retire because of Gilbert's example and wishing not to disappoint him. "I can't retire until Gilbert is gone!" was the admission of several when interviewed. Such a poignant tribute to his influence.[10]

As this writing comes to a close, Gilbert is in New Mexico helping Claire ready a newly purchased retirement residence in Taos for her use in conjunction with their residence in Boulder. On that trip, I suspect he will gather a few pebbles from his beloved Ghost Ranch in New Mexico (a retreat center where Quakers in the central and southwestern mountain states hold their annual meetings) to add to the circle where his ashes will eventually commingle with Anne's off the trail down Four Mile Canyon. In 2002 Gilbert pondered the history and future of such pebbles, and that short essay is a fitting geography lesson with which to end this story of his life.

> These pebbles are a product of the sandstone in one of the great walls overlooking Ghost Ranch. Reddish brown, granular, smooth surface, uneven form from deposition in what were probably desert conditions some 200–300 million years ago, chunks of the sandstone fell into the eroded valley and were divided into smaller forms by rain, freezing and thawing water, and plant roots. Some of the original solid rock still hangs in the cliffs, some is in great boulders, some is in water-washed pebbles, and some is mixed in the soils of the gentle slopes and valley bottoms. The processes that formed them over tens of thousands of years were diverse, and they promise to be even more so in the future. Depending upon a diversity of natural and human factors, the pebbles like these in my hand will be found in widely different locations and forms.
>
> In a variety of shapes and products the pebbles will be essential parts of the future Ghost Ranch and Rio Chama basin. Just what natural and social forces will affect them—and how—is far from certain. The interaction of physical and biological forces is complex. The future role of human activity—road building, new houses, irrigated fields—cannot be predicted with confidence. There is even less ability to predict the future of the Upper Rio Chama human landscape than there is to predict its physical configuration. The forces that shape the number, occupations, and spiritual and economic state of the basin's people are more

Gilbert at Ghost Ranch, New Mexico, for the yearly business meetings of the Intermountain Region of the Society of Friends

complex and more variable than those shaping the soils, water, and vegetation. And speculation has begun on possible effects of climate change.

The shape of these pebbles resulted from the interaction of changing natural and human forces. The shape of the people of the Upper Rio Chama in the years ahead will result from more rapid and diverse human forces. They evolved slowly in Anasazi, Spanish, and Anglo periods. Now, they are changing rapidly from season to season and from year to year with new technologies and community systems, and we can only speculate as to what shape they will have a century hence.

Notes

1. Kates served as vice chair of the National Research Council's Board on Sustainable Development, which published *Our Common Journey: A Transition Toward Sustainability* (NRC 1999). A succinct summary of that emerging research program and articles by Kates and Thomas Parris on "Long-Term Trends and a Sustainability Transition" and "Characterizing a Sustainability Transition: Goals, Targets, Trends, and Driving Forces" were published in *Mapping Economic and Environmental Vulnerabilities: Proceedings of the National Academy of Sciences* (Kates and Parris 2003a, 2003b).

2. Gilbert was one of four scientists who were particularly effective in chairing study committees of the National Research Council who were interviewed on videotape by Bruce Alberts for a pamphlet, *Roles of the Committee Chair* (Alberts et al. 2000).

3. Late in his career, when he was trying to reduce his commitments, he first declined but then two years later accepted an invitation to serve as a public member of the American Board of Industrial Hygiene. He concluded that the board needed a "voice of conscience"; he felt that the organization had a good code of ethics in occupational and environmental health but lacked an adequate policing system.

4. The following letter from May 31, 1977, to Norman Moline in the Geography Department of Augustana College in Rock Island, Illinois, followed Gilbert's acceptance of an honorary degree at Augustana. Typically, he used the occasion to help his former student.

> We arrived back in Boulder last night and were happy in our recollections of the Commencement stay at Augustana. Upon returning to my office this morning I inquired about the status of the Fulbright appointment for Australia, and learned that they are going ahead with consideration of appointments for this coming academic year. In the circumstances, there would be no prospect for your applying this year. It is possible that something new might come along next year, but for the present you should not give any consideration to it.
>
> As for people in Washington, I would suggest that after you arrive you should get in touch with Salvatore (Sam) Natoli at the Association of American Geographers on 16th Street. In addition, I think you would find it useful to make yourself known to Jeffrey Zinn at the Conservation Foundation, 1717 Massachusetts Avenue, N.W., telephone 797-4342. Jeff has been particularly interested in problems of natural hazards for the coastal zone. Next door to you on the Council on Environmental Quality the senior scientist is Lee Talbot who has an early geography background and a very broad view of environmental problems. I think you would enjoy calling up and making an appointment to see him and letting him know of your interest in environmental matters.
>
> Sincerely, Gilbert

5. Two examples from Gilbert's work with the National Academy of Sciences also demonstrate this point. In 1976 the World Conservation Union sought his assistance, as a former NAS representative member of the union's Executive Board, in obtaining dues three years in arrears from the NAS. He freely acquiesced. Then, in 1994 at age eighty-two, he agreed to serve as an unpaid private individual (not as an organizational representative) on the Review Panel of the National Research Council's Young Investigator Program on Management of Water Resources with Turkmenistan and Uzbekistan.

6. At Gilbert's suggestion, Robert Wickham applied for and received an appointment with the Department of the Interior in his senior year at Haverford. Gilbert also advised him "to come and see him before resigning, if ever I became frustrated with government service" (Wickham 2000). A year later Wickham dutifully returned, having just resigned! (He subsequently served twenty-four years with the Ford Foundation, following an interview also arranged by White.)

7. In Gilbert's case, self-knowledge included knowledge of the physical frailty and difficulties that resulted from two years in a German prison camp. Although Gilbert appeared robust and lived a long life, he may have felt that the stress of leadership would have been hard on his body.

8. Gilbert was very slow to recognize this problem and was so removed from office personnel and daily conversation in the Institute of Behavioral Science that the staff were unable to share their concerns in a timely fashion. Consequently, Gilbert was initially reluctant to accept the evidence of malfeasance and then to confront Haas. But when the evidence was irrefutable and Haas still did not admit his guilt, even to legal authorities, Gilbert became outraged. He subsequently had no contact with Haas following his dismissal from the university, and Gilbert also reduced his contacts with Haas's previous institutional colleagues who had recommended Haas, despite awareness of his prior history of improprieties.

9. When Gilbert needed cheering up, Anne would seek excuses to get him together with his closest former students, Ian Burton and Bob Kates (described as Gilbert's acolytes by fellow student Tim O'Riordin and teased for their "sibling rivalry" by Claire).

10. Although, without exception, Gilbert's former students acknowledged their debt to and respect for Gilbert, many also volunteered that they were unwilling to make the sacrifices that Gilbert (and Anne) had made to pursue such a productive career. Many students and colleagues saw the balance between work, outdoor recreation, and relaxation that Gilbert and Anne did succeed in achieving as nonetheless too ascetic, particularly with respect to the couple's relationship with and time commitment to their children.

Epilogue

Why is the sea the prince of a hundred streams?
Because it lies below them.

If the sage would guide the people, he must serve with humility.
If he would lead them, he must follow behind.
In this way when the sage rules, the people will not feel oppressed;
When he stands before them, they will not be harmed.
The whole world will support him and will not tire of him.
Because he does not compete, he does not invite competition.
> **—Lao Tsu, *Tao Te Ching***

THERE IS GREAT NEED for more effective leadership in managing conflicts over natural resources, exacerbated by nature's extremes, than the United States and the world have experienced of late. In the Introduction I posed two questions that, in part, prompted this biography. The first was, "Thinking globally, in today's complex world, what constitutes effective leadership in decision making that will leave our planet a better place for our presence?" In this Epilogue I move beyond the story of White's life to share what I have learned from my study of the man and to ponder the potential of his legacy to address our leadership dilemma. I hope, and suspect, that because of the widening influence of his students and colleagues, together with his own writings and those about him, White's influence will grow for many years to come. Blessed with his opportunities and longevity, I suspect that Gilbert hopes so, too, as the following anecdote suggests.

Gilbert is proud of his name, in part because another Gilbert White (1720–1793), whom British schoolchildren still come to know as England's first ecologist, combined pastoral care of his parish of Selbourne with meticulous observation and documentation of every life form he encountered in that small parish. In August 2000, our American Gilbert White penned his reflections on the 200-year legacy of his British namesake, about whom scores of books have been written. Gilbert suggested, in fact, that the author of *The Natural History of Selbourne* "was the first person in human history to observe and write down what was the state and activity of each plant, bird, and rodent that lived in the woods, fields, and streams around him." In closing, Gilbert wrote, "I wouldn't choose another name, and I continue to hope that I might in my own efforts reflect a bit of the original discernment of *the* Gilbert White." It will come as no surprise to those already acquainted with America's Gilbert White if his influence comparably broadens long after the man himself has left this earth.

This first attempt to interpret Gilbert's meaning through biography comes early, while he is available to contribute to it—because he did not maintain a personal journal or compile many reflections (such as the aforesaid on his name) on his life, work, and basic beliefs. Hence, this book is only an initial account of Gilbert's life, and I look forward to future assessments of this virtuous "prince of a hundred streams."

As suggested throughout this book, Gilbert's virtues, born of his beliefs and values, involved pragmatic wisdom in fashioning a way of living that is profoundly moral while also profoundly ecumenical. His marriage of faith in science with the practice of Friends (and of others similarly committed to collective discernment of truths and consensus building to ensure effective action) resulted in a life that some have described as saintly. Gilbert's example does indeed reflect his Christian upbringing and culture, even as he laid aside the more exclusionary and divisive aspects of Christian doctrine that can disguise the fundamental moral accord of all major religions and our common humanity.

"Saintly" is perhaps not the best descriptor for Gilbert White. Clearly, he never fancied himself a preacher, and he never would have wanted to be thought of as an anointed representative of the divine. However, he certainly did feel that a spark of the divine resided in all human beings, and on occasion he voiced the opinion that part of any person's reason for being was to help others discover that spark. Perhaps "princely" is a more apt description. The good prince is a consummate statesman, with wisdom wed to grace, authority wed to humility, and conviction wed to courage. Hence, I have substituted "prince" for "king" in the quotation from the *Tao Te Ching* above.

ॐ

GILBERT ALWAYS URGED great caution in predicting what lies ahead for North America or the planet regarding climate change, extremes of nature, and their consequences for the ever-increasing population at risk. Obviously, our planet comprises highly variable and complex systems, and Gilbert was always quick to point out the importance of local conditions and local variability. Deleterious climate changes in some regions could be matched by more agreeable effects in others. Gilbert was similarly hesitant to forecast the societal consequences of the increasing inequities in the use of our natural resources, even as he decried the growing disparities in wealth and power. He was concerned that our civilization, indeed our species, might perish, but he was not an alarmist or himself given to despair. Some considered Gilbert unduly optimistic; he considered himself a realist.

From left to right: William Hooke, Gilbert, and William Anderson at the Natural Hazards Research Center workshop, July 2005

I respect Gilbert's caution about not extrapolating beyond what our knowledge supports and the obvious truth that there is far more not fully grasped about the workings of our natural environment than is understood. I also accept that we know not what evolving capacity resides with humankind to rise to any challenge, moral as well as technological.

Still, although Gilbert's perspective was continually broadened through interdisciplinary work, his career interests did not include archaeology. And archaeology shows us that civilizations do perish; it even teaches lessons about how and why any number have done so. Another scholar and contemporary of White, Jared Diamond, expanded his initial training in geography to include anthropology. The result was pioneering (and highly popular) work in the study of comparative civilizations (*Guns, Germs, and Steel: The Fates of Human Societies,* published in 1997, and *Collapse: How Societies Choose to Fail or Survive,* published in 2005), in which Diamond traces the rise and fall of numerous cultures around the world and down through history.

Their fall, or unraveling, in most instances resulted from pressure upon and competition for natural resources, often exacerbated by a natural hazard (such as drought) that became an unmanageable disaster. All such experiments with civilization, in both the old and new worlds, benefited from approximately the last 10,000 years of abnormally constant and hence dependable climate across the temperate latitudes of our planet. That comparative predictability led gradually to more sedentary—even urban—settlement patterns and the domestication of plants and animals that supplemented and in some contexts supplanted the nomadic hunting and gathering of food upon which humans had relied for tens of thousands of years. All civilizations reviewed by Diamond experienced expanding population based on agriculture and on social stratification based upon unequal access to the benefits of the more efficient exploitation of natural resources such labor specialization permitted.

In short, civilizations evolved during and because of a period of remarkable calm in the evolution of a very turbulent planet. Although climate changes were usually a factor in the demise of those civilizations, the available data suggest that recent climatic volatility is greater than such civilizations confronted. If so, our current environmental challenge is compounded by our concurrent experience with the increasing volatility of globalization's deepening interdependencies. Unprecedented levels of wealth and power stratification, based on escalating resource utilization and depletion, pose the great risk that interlocking social and natural hazards may become disastrous beyond our coping capacities.

That is the theme of J. F. Rischard's book, *High Noon: Twenty Global Problems, Twenty Years to Solve Them* (2002). Rischard, a German economist and vice president of the World Bank, provides a comprehensive assessment of these natural and societal interlocking hazards, all of whose consequent risks must be reduced, in his opinion, to avert collapse on a scale utterly unprecedented in human history. At the closing plenary session of the July 2005 Natural Hazards Workshop, climatologist William Hooke ended a sobering litany of natural hazards trends (see Chapter 12) by asking how many of the roughly 300 in the audience had read Rischard's book. Only a half-dozen hands were raised, suggesting that even within the natural hazards professional community, collective denial may already have set in.

We entered the new millennium with, already, a sprinkling of "failed states" around the world. Four decades of research and monitoring trends in Guatemala have convinced me that this small country bordering Mexico is one of these states. The July–August 2005 issue of *Foreign Policy* listed Guatemala thirty-first among sixty "weak or failed states" on the basis of a dozen social, economic, political, and military indicators. To these indicators should be added population pressure: Guatemala is the size of Ohio but has 13 million people—two-fifths the population of Canada. One million Guatemalans are temporary workers in the United States and Canada for lack of adequate employment in Guatemala. Guatemala's vulnerability is the greater for the natural hazards its residents face from hurricanes, earthquakes, and volcanic eruptions, all of which typically produce massive landslides. In the twentieth century, Guatemala experienced five major landslide disasters, most recently Hurricane Stan in October 2005.

The Natural Hazards Center funded a month of reconnaissance research by me in December 2005, focusing on the environmental and economic impacts of Stan's heavy precipitation (Hinshaw 2006).[1] Stan teaches us that even a comparatively low-intensity storm (a category 1 hurricane with winds no stronger than 80 miles per hour) can push a failing nation over the edge. If we continue on our present trajectory, we will witness such national collapses until the tipping point is reached when a natural disaster triggers the collapse of a region, if not a meltdown of the world's globalized economic interdependencies and political checks and balances.

From the research undertaken for this biography, I conclude that one telling indicator of such a tipping point is the declining willingness of the "haves" to step into the breach of natural disasters to assist their more vulnerable brethren to rebuild, especially when those victimized are forced to relocate and become competitors for scarce resources of soil, water, and energy. Migration always has been a human coping adjustment, but relocations due to severe natural and human-caused disasters already are posing challenges that defy solution, particularly in Africa (the continental region on which, primarily, Robert Kaplan based his 2000 book, *The Coming Anarchy*). Even North Americans have begun to realize, with back-to-back hurricanes Katrina and Rita, how contentious the issues of forced and voluntary relocation (within the broader array of adjustments to disaster) can be following disaster.[2]

It is not simply a matter of supposedly responsible individuals and institutions failing to address the critical environmental and social issues challenging humanity. The "haves" are becoming less willing to help the have-nots. In his 2005 book, *The Moral Consequences of Economic Growth*, Benjamin Friedman correlated first the steady improvements in U.S. economic performance from the 1940s through the 1960s, and then the decline of gross national product (GNP) commencing in the 1970s, with national commitment to social equity and public investment during those decades. When the economy was strengthening, social welfare legislation, tolerance, and philanthropy benefited. When the economy slowed, so did the nation's egalitarian openness and altruism. As Jeffrey Madrick (2006) says, "Friedman urgently and convincingly describes a society that is failing in many respects but is strangely unable to understand why." Indeed, the federal government's discouraging response following Hurricane Katrina in 2005 and even into 2006 may reflect the will of the broader electorate more accurately than we wish to believe. As discussed in Chapter 12, most leaders in the natural hazards community, if not also in government, feel that top-down approaches to disaster preparedness, response, and recovery are less efficacious than grassroots, local initiatives and leadership. However, given Friedman's findings regarding decreasing altruism and the implied erosion of a sense of community, this conclusion is not encouraging in our age of decreasing resources. It appears that our collective welfare will depend on improved strategies and, perhaps most importantly, on leadership that rebuilds that sense of community.

THIS BOOK PROVIDES a model for such leadership. Increasing competition for natural resources in conjunction with massive dislocations of populations (particularly impoverished populations) are already challenging the abilities of nations large and small to manage the resulting conflicts. Gilbert White's long career in shepherding natural resources has involved not only the study of resource issues but also a distinctive ability to establish and strengthen communication and cooperation across contentious boundaries. Admittedly, many of the issues he engaged proved too intractable and the assignments he undertook too ambitious for the degree of progress he optimistically sought. But his efforts abundantly demonstrated that trust in due process and able leadership can result in open dialogue, secure incremental agreements, and, ultimately, change for the common good.

Since White's special expertise involved water, the epigraph from the *Tao Te Ching* that begins this Epilogue seems particularly apt. The interdependence of rivers and oceans in maintaining life on earth through continuous cycling of moisture (in the process, providing much of the energy that supports Western civilization's remarkable comforts) is, indeed, a miracle, just as is every other natural process we seek to comprehend. It is hardly a peaceful cycle, given the tumultuous "nature" of both the oceans and the rivers that feed them. But it is reliable—the essence of cooperation and trust. It is perhaps a metaphor for an ideal human condition. The sea accepts the discharge from its rivers without fail, and the rain upon the land provided by evaporation from the sea falls on the just and the unjust, the rich and the poor, without prejudice. The sea leads the process from below, encouraging its tributary streams to relinquish their discharge from reenergized soils.

In human affairs, trust among cultures and societies sharing earth's bounty depends upon unprejudiced listening and acknowledgment of disagreement until the most humane and sustainable course of action has been collectively discerned and agreed upon. A host of leaders embodying the virtues that Gilbert has demonstrated—people who can lead from below—are needed at all levels and in all domains. These virtues have been exhibited by wise persons in many times and places; in this respect they are nothing new. However, White is exceptional because of the diligence and persistence with which he committed to the practice of these beliefs.

The second question posed in the Introduction was, "Thinking locally, how important for humanity's and the Earth's future is it that *our* lives 'matter'—that we each make a difference, if only in our immediate environs?" In this Epilogue's review of assorted perspectives from geography, anthropology, political science, and economics (and with the illustrative example of Guatemala, one of North America's closest neighbors), I have endeavored to make the case that we have no choice but to do whatever we can to "make a difference." Otherwise, our grandchildren and great-grandchildren, to whom the book is dedicated, may well live amid the rubble of our own collapsed civilization.

The globalization on which we have come to depend is, of course, a mixed blessing. With its increasing efficiencies in communication, it greatly amplifies the "power of one" for good or for ill. We possess the ability to learn, and then to teach, more rapidly and efficiently than ever before. Given the opportunities posed by this contemporary human condition, what can one do to acquaint others with the message of Gilbert's life? Sharing this book is an obvious first step. But more to the point of Gilbert's message, what can each of us do to embody and model his example, that spirit?

Notes

1. The Guatemala Human Rights Commission/USA reported that 2005 was the worst year for human rights abuses in Guatemala since the signing of the Peace Accords in 1996, ending forty-five years of civil war. Amnesty International issued more urgent action alerts for Guatemala in 2005 than for any other country in the Americas, with the exception of Colombia (GHRC/USA 2005). The same December issue of the *Bulletin of GHRC* reported Guatemala's human development index, measured in terms of life expectancy, GNP per capita, adult literacy, and school enrollment, to be the hemisphere's second lowest, behind only Haiti. Also summarized in this useful publication are findings by Guatemala's Human Rights Procurator's Office regarding thirty-seven issues causing social tension that may well ignite "social explosion in Guatemala" if not addressed. Sadly, among the regions of the nation described as most prone to conflict are the very areas hardest hit by Hurricane Stan.

2. Dislocations and attempts at relocation will increase, not only for the reasons apparent to date in some areas of Africa, but also due to reduction in habitat suitable for human occupancy due to rising sea levels and changes in temperature and precipitation. Some regions may be facing warmer climates, but some areas of the temperate and polar latitudes, especially in the Northern Hemisphere, are at risk of colder temperatures from possible rapid alteration of ocean currents. More inevitable, but probably less dramatic (unless large ice sheets, lubricated by ice melt, slip rapidly into the oceans), will be gradual shrinkage of landmass globally due to melting icecaps at both poles. Unfortunately, much of the world's population lives in coastal regions at or near sea level, where only a few inches rise in sea level will trigger massive relocations.

Appendixes

Appendix 1: Vitae of Gilbert F. White

1934	1940	1945	1950	1955	1960	1965	1970	1975	1980	1985	1990	1995	2000	2005 →

POSITIONS HELD:

Staff Member, Mississippi Valley Committee, National Resources Committee (NRC), National Resources Planning Board, 1934–40

Staff Member, Bureau of the Budget, Executive Office of the President, 1940–42

Volunteer and Assistant to the Executive Director, American Friends Service Committee: France, Germany, and U.S., 1942–46

President, Haverford College, 1946–1955

Chair, Dept. of Geography, University of Chicago, 1956–69

Visiting Professor, Oxford University, 1962–63

Professor, Dept. of Geography, and **Director**, Institute of Behavioral Science, CU, 1970–78

Director, Natural Hazards Research, Applications Information Center, 1976–84, 1992–94

Gustavson Distinguished Professor Emeritus of Geography, 1980–present

OTHER PROFESSIONAL ACTIVITIES:

Member, Hoover Commission Task Force on Natural Resources, 1948

Vice Chair, President's Water Resources Policy Commission, 1950

Chair, various Quaker Conferences for Diplomats, 1952–97

Member, UNESCO Advisory Committee on Arid Zone Research, 1953–56

Member, NRC Committee on Renewable Natural Resources, 1957–62

Consultant, Senate Select Committee on National Water Resources, 1961–62

Consultant, Lower Mekong Coordinating Committee, Cambodia, Laos, Thailand, and Vietnam, 1961–62, 1970

Chair, American Friends Service Committee, 1963–69

Member, Special NSF Commission on Weather Modification, 1964–65

Chair, NRC Committee on Water, 1964–68

Chair, Steering Committee on High School Geography Project, AAG, 1964–70

Chair, Bureau of Budget Task Force on Federal Flood Policy, 1965–66

Member, Resources for the Future Forum on Formation and Role of Public Attitudes, 1966

Adviser on Man-made Lakes to Administrator of U.N. Development Programme, 1966–71

Member, UNESCO Advisory Committee on Natural Resource Research, 1967–71

Trustee, Resources for the Future, 1967–79 (Chair, 1974–79)

Member, Advisory Committee on Environmental Science, NSF, 1968–71

Chair, Commission on Man and Environment, International Geographical Union, 1969–76

Member, Economic Commission for Africa, Working Group on Water Planning, 1970

Member, Scientific Comm. on Problems of the Environment, ICSU, 1970–82 (Pres., 1976–82)

Member, Universities Council on Water Resources Task Force, 1971

Member, U.N. Interregional Seminar on Flood Damage Prevention, Soviet Union, 1971

Member, Advisory Committee of the Office of Interdisciplinary Research, NSF, 1971–72

Consultant, National Water Commission, 1971–73

Member, SCOPE, Working Group on Man-made Lakes, 1972

1970 1975 1980 1985 1990 1995 2000 2005

Consultant, UNESCO Committee of Experts on the Statistical Study of Natural Hazards, 1972

Senior Consultant, U.N. Development Programme, 1972

Member, AFSC Delegation to China, 1972

Chair, Advisory Board, Ford Energy Policy Project, 1972–74

Chair, NRC International Environmental Programs Committee, 1972–76

Member, Technology Assessment Advisory Council, U.S. Congress, 1973–76

Member, Earthquake Studies Advisory Panel, U.S. Dept. of the Interior, 1973–76

Member, Advisory Panel on Environmental Quality, U.S. Geological Survey, 1975–77

Chair, NRC Environmental Studies Board, 1975–77

Adviser, Ford Foundation Program on Resources and the Environment in the Middle East, 1975–77

Consultant, Water Quality Studies on the Nile River and Lake Nasser, 1975–79

Member, National Oceanic and Atmospheric Administration Committee on Natural Hazard Management in Coastal Areas, 1976

Member, Advisory Board of the Energy Laboratory, MIT, 1976–77

Member, Advisory Committee on Natural Resources, United Nations University, Tokyo, 1977–79

Chair, NRC Commission on Natural Resources, 1977–80

Chair, Joint Committee, Egyptian Academy of Scientific Research and Technology, and U.S. NAS, 1978–86

Member, NRC Governing Board on Security and Disarmament, 1980

Member, SCOPE, Steering Committee on Interaction of Biogeochemical Cycles, 1980

Chair, Advisory Committee for the Ecosystems Center of the Woods Hole Marine Biological Lab, 1981–82

Chair, U.N. Environment Programme Committee report on the "State of the Environment," 1982

Member, SCOPE, Steering Committee on the Environmental Consequences of Nuclear War, 1983–88

Executive Editor, *Environment*, 1983–92

Member, American Association for the Advancement of Science Committee on Arid Lands, 1985–86

Member, Working Group on Drought and Desertification, National Center for Atmospheric Research, 1986

Member, Advisory Group on Greenhouse Gases—WMO, UNEP, and ICSU, 1986–90

Chair, Nevada State Technical Review Committee on Socio-Economic Effects of Nuclear Waste Disposal, 1986–93

Member, Advisory Group on Water, UNEP, 1987–93; Chair, Aral Sea Basin Diagnostic Panel, 1990–93

Member, U.S. National Committee for Man and Biosphere, 1989–92; ad hoc special commission, 1993–95

Member, Advisory Committee on Environment, International Council of Scientific Unions, 1989–96

Member, Carnegie Corp. Task Force on the Organization of Federal Environmental R&D Programs, 1990

Member, International Conference on Global Warming and Climatic Change: African Perspectives, 1990

Member, Steering Committee of Intl. Geo. Union/UN Conf. Global Critical Zone Mapping Project, 1991

Member, NRC Committee on Technical Bases for Yucca Mountain Standards, 1993–95

Member, Nat. Forum on Nonpoint Source Pollution, NGS and Conservation Fund, 1993–95

Chair, Advisory Panel on Reducing Earthquake Losses, Off. of Tech. Assessment, 1994

Vice Chair, Steering Committee, Human Dimensions Program, ISSC, 1994–1995

Member, Steering Committee for Heinz Center on Coastal Erosion, 1997–2000

Member, FEMA Steering Committee for Evaluation of National Flood Insurance Program, 2001–present

Appendix 2: Honors and Awards Received by Gilbert F. White

American Water Resources Association
    Eben Award, 1972
    Caulfield Award, 1989
Association of American Geographers
    Distinguished Service Award, 1955, 1974
    Anderson Medal for Applied Geography, 1986
    Lifetime Achievement, 2002
    Water Resource Specialty Group Lifetime Achievement Award, 2005
National Academy of Sciences
    Environmental Award, 1980
    Public Welfare Medal, 2000
University of Chicago, Quantrell Award for Excellence in Undergraduate Teaching, 1967
American Geographical Society, Daly Medal, 1971
University of Colorado, Thomas Jefferson Award, 1973
Royal Geographical Society of London, Honorary Corresponding Member
Russian Geographical Society, Honorary Member, 1976
National Academy of Sciences, Member, 1973–present
American Academy of Arts and Sciences, Member
American Philosophical Society, Member, 1973–present
Soviet Academy of Sciences (replaced by Russian Academy of Sciences), Foreign Member
University of Colorado Medal
University of Chicago Alumni Medal
Plan Boulder County, Achievement, 1984 and 1994
National Council for Geographic Education, Master Teacher Award, 1985
United Nations Sasakawa International Environment Prize, 1985
National Wildlife Federation Conservation Award, 1986
United Nations Environment Programme Global 500 Roll of Honour, Laureate, 1985
Tyler Prize for Environmental Achievement, 1987
Society for Risk Analysis, Distinguished Contribution Award, 1987
International Geographical Union, Laureat d'Honneur, 1988
Bonfils-Stanton Foundation Award for Science and Medicine, 1988

Vautrin Lud International Prize in Geography, 1992

Renewable Natural Resources Foundation, Sustained Achievement Award, 1992

Cosmos Club Award, 1993

American Rivers, Lifetime Achievement, 1994

Federal Emergency Management Agency, Outstanding Public Service Award, 1994

National Geographic Society, Hubbard Medal, 1994

Volvo Environment Prize, 1995

Universities Council on Water Resources, Hall Medal, 1995

National Academy of Sciences, Public Welfare Medal, 2000

National Medal of Science, 2000

International Water Resources Association, Millennium Award, 2000

City Council of Boulder, Commendation, 2001

American Academy of Water Resources Engineers, Honorary Diplomate, 2005

Water Resources Engineer, 2005

Honorary Degrees Conferred on Gilbert F. White

Augustana College

Earlham College

Hamilton College

Haverford College

Michigan State University

Swarthmore College

University of Arizona

University of Colorado

Awards and Institutions Established in Honor of Gilbert F. White

The Goddard-White Award

The Goddard-White Award honors the contributions made to floodplain management by Gilbert White and Jim Goddard (1906–1994). This award is given by the Association of State Floodplain Managers (ASFPM) to individuals who have been instrumental in carrying forward the goals and objectives of floodplain management throughout the United States. It is an indication of the level of esteem the association holds for the two namesakes as well as the recipients and is the association's highest honor.

Gilbert F. White National Flood Policy Forum

To promote discussion on national floodplain management policy and issues, the Association of State Floodplain Managers (ASFPM) Foundation has established a forum that brings together leading experts in the field. The forum seeks to develop policy recommendations and establish an ongoing record of flood policy issues and directions for the future. The forum has been named in honor of Gilbert F. White, whom the association describes as "the most influential floodplain management policy expert of the twentieth century." The forum is not only a tribute to his work but also a recognition of the success of his deliberative, consensus-building approach to policy analysis and research.

Periodically, the forum explores one pressing flood policy issue by hosting a dialogue among approximately fifty experts, including government, industry, and academic stakeholders. Again, the goal of each forum will be to provide recommendations for policies that will reduce the human casualties and economic losses associated with flooding, as well as policies that will protect and enhance the natural and beneficial functions of floodplains. The discussions and recommendations of each forum are summarized and distributed as a report by the ASFPM Foundation.

ASFPM Flood Hazard Fellowship

The Association of State Floodplain Managers Flood Hazard Fellowship Fund, established by the ASFPM Board of Directors in 1988, supports a fellowship to recognize and encourage individual achievement in the profession of flood hazard management. The fund was established in the spirit of advancement of the field of floodplain management as practiced by Gilbert White, the initial contributor to the fund. In establishing this fund and award, the association cited White as devoting "a lifetime ... to promoting floodplain management concepts and reducing the human and material impacts of floods and other hazards. ... [He] embodies the spirit of advancement and achievement to which the Association subscribes." The fellowship is not necessarily awarded every year.

Resources for the Future Gilbert F. White Postdoctoral Fellowship Program

Resources for the Future (RFF) offers resident fellowships for each academic year in honor of Gilbert F. White, "retired chairman of the RFF board of directors, distinguished geographer, and statesman of science." The fellowships are intended for researchers who have a doctoral degree and wish to devote a year to scholarly work in areas related to natural resources, energy, or the environment. Social scientists, as well as natural scientists interested in policy-relevant interdisciplinary research, are encouraged to apply.

Arthur Maass–Gilbert F. White Reference Room, U.S. Army Corps of Engineers, Institute for Water Resources

In 2001 Gilbert White and Harvard scholar Arthur Maass donated their extensive personal research libraries to the Corps of Engineers' Water Resources Institute in Alexandria, Virginia. The collection is considered one of the most extensive in the world on water resources planning. This room was established to hold these collections and is dedicated to the contributions made by White and Maass to the profession of water management. The institute has said that "no other scholars in the twentieth century had more influence on the Corps of Engineers. Their ideas have not been overcome by time; if anything, the world is still catching up to the concepts they articulated fifty years ago."

Gilbert F. White Award, Association of American Geographers Hazards Specialty Group

The Association of American Geographers Hazards Specialty Group encourages students writing Ph.D. dissertations and master's theses to consider applying for the Gilbert F. White Award, which is presented to the author of an outstanding thesis or dissertation completed within the previous two years about natural or man made hazards. Recipients of the White Award receive $500, a plaque, and an autographed copy of Robert W. Kates and Ian Burton's two-volume work, *Geography, Resources, and Environment: Selected Writings of* and *Themes from the Work of Gilbert F. White.*

Gilbert F. White Doctoral Fellowship, Department of Geography, University of Colorado

This award was established to provide fellowship funding for one or two outstanding Ph.D. students in geography at the University of Colorado who are in their final semester of dissertation preparation. The award is based on both financial need and scholarly merit.

References

Alberts, Bruce, et al., eds. 2000. *Roles of the Committee Chair*. Washington, DC: National Academy of Sciences.

Albertson, Maurice. 2003. Interview with Robert Hinshaw.

Anderson, William. 2001. Interview with Robert Hinshaw.

Arnold, Joseph L. 1988. "The Flood Control Act of 1936: A Study in Politics, Planning, and Ideology." In *The Flood Control Challenge: Past, Present, and Future*, edited by Howard Rosen and Martin Reuss. Chicago: Public Works Historical Society.

ASFPM. 1996. *Floodplain Management in a Multifaceted World*. Proceedings of the 21st Annual Conference of the Association of State Floodplain Managers in Little Rock, AK. Madison, WI: ASFPM.

———. 2002. *Mitigation Success Stories in the United States*. 4th ed. Madison, WI: Association of State Floodplain Managers.

ASFPM Foundation. 2004. *Reducing Flood Losses: Is the 1% Chance Flood Standard Sufficient?* Report of the 2004 Assembly of the Gilbert F. White National Flood Policy Forum. Washington, DC: National Academies Keck Center.

Baker, Jeanette. 2004. "Gilbert White: Using Science to Help People." In *Lives That Speak: Stories of Twentieth-Century Quakers,* edited by Marnie Clark. Philadelphia: Quaker Press of Friends General Conference.

Barrows, Harlan H. 1940. Letter of 2/9 to GFW, Alexandria, VA: Office of History, U.S. Army Corps of Engineers, GFW Archives, Box 4, Folder 1A 45.

Barry, John M. 1997. *Rising Tide: The Great Mississippi Flood of 1927 and How It Changed America*. New York: Touchstone, Simon and Schuster.

Beyer, Jackie. 2005. Personal communication.

Binson, Boonrod. 1965. "Southeast Asia's Old Man River." SR, Oct. 30.

Birch, Daniel R. 1989. "Partnerships Toward Multi-objective Projects in Boulder, CO." In *Partnerships: Effective Flood Hazard Management*. Proceedings of the 13th Annual Conference of the Association of State Floodplain Managers in Scottsdale, AZ. Madison, WI: ASFPM.

Birch, Daniel R., and Robert L. Wheeler. 1987. "The Changing Focus and Continuing Development of Boulder, Colorado's Floodplain Management Program." In *Realistic Approaches to Better Floodplain Management*. Proceedings of the 11th Annual Conference of the Association of State Floodplain Managers in Seattle, WA. Madison, WI: ASFPM.

Birky-Kreutzer, Pauline. 2003. *Peace Corps Pioneer*. Self-published.

Block, Jean F. 1978. *Hyde Park Houses: An Informal History*. Self-published.

Boggs, D. Lee, III. 1986. *Determining the Effectiveness of Efforts to Reduce Flood Losses: The TVA Experience.* Knoxville: Tennessee Valley Authority.

Botts, Lee. 2001. Letter to GFW. GFW home files.

Bowen, Mark. 2005. *Thin Ice: Unlocking the Secrets of Climate in the World's Highest Mountains.* New York: Henry Holt.

Boyer, John W. 1999. "Annual Report to the Faculty of the College," *University of Chicago Record* 34, no. 1.

Bronner, Edwin. 1993. "Oral History Interview with Gilbert White." Haverford College Library.

Brown, Harrison. 1978. *The Human Future Revisited.* New York: W. W. Norton.

Brown, Lester. 1978. *The Twenty-Ninth Day.* New York: W. W. Norton.

Burton, Ian. 2001. Interview with Robert Hinshaw.

Burton, Ian, Robert W. Kates, and Gilbert F. White. 1978. *The Environment as Hazard.* New York: Oxford University Press.

———. 1981. "The Future of Hazard Research: A Reply to William I. Torry." *Canadian Geographer* 25, no. 3.

Butterfield, DeAnne. 2001. Interview with Robert Hinshaw.

Carson, Rachel. 1962. *Silent Spring.* Boston: Houghton Mifflin.

Cary, Stephen. 1999, 2001. Interview with Robert Hinshaw.

Clark, Bronson. 1997. *Not by Might: A Viet Nam Memoir.* Clastonbury, VT: Chapel Hill Publishers.

Clawson, Marion. 1966. *With the Task Force on Federal Flood Control Policy.* Insurance and Other Programs for Financial Assistance to Flood Victims, Committee Print no. 43, 89th Congress, 2nd session.

———. 1981. *New Deal Planning: The National Resources Planning Board.* Baltimore: Published for Resources for the Future by the Johns Hopkins University Press.

Collett, Stephen. 2002. "History of the American Friends Service Committee and Quaker United Nations Office: Washington Seminars and Conferences for Diplomats." Mimeographed manuscript. American Friends Service Committee, Philadelphia.

Coughlin, Joseph. 2005. Letter of 12/01 to Leatherman and White.

Cutter, Susan. 2001. "Celebrating Geographers." *AAG Newsletter,* January.

De Buys, William. 1999. "St. Francis in the Low Post." In *Human Nature,* edited by John P. Herron and Andrew G. Kirk. Albuquerque: University of New Mexico Press.

Deutch, John, Paul Joskow, and Henry Rowen. 1975. "Evaluation of the Ford Energy Policy Project." Unpublished manuscript. Alexandria, VA: Office of History, U.S. Army Corps of Engineers, GFW Archives, Box 135, Folder 54A.

Diamond, Jared. 1997. *Guns, Germs, and Steel: The Fates of Human Societies.* New York: W. W. Norton.

———. 2005. *Collapse: How Societies Choose to Fail or Survive.* New York: Viking.

Emlen, Betty. 2001. Interview with Robert Hinshaw.

Falk, Richard. 1971. *The Endangered Planet.* New York: Random House.

Feldman, Elliot J. 1986. "The Citizen Scholar: Education and Public Affairs." In *Geography, Resources, and Environment.* Vol. 2: Themes from the Work of Gilbert F. White, edited by Robert W. Kates and Ian Burton. Chicago: University of Chicago Press.

FEMA. 1995. *National Mitigation Strategy: Partnerships for Building Safer Communities.* Washington, DC: Federal Emergency Management Agency.

FEMA and the Interagency Task Force on Floodplain Management. 1986. *A Unified National Program for Floodplain Management.* Washington, DC: Federal Emergency Management Agency.

FEPP (Ford Energy Policy Project). 1974. *A Time to Choose: America's Energy Future,* edited by David S. Freeman et al. Final Report by the Energy Policy Project of the Ford Foundation. Cambridge, MA: Ballinger Publishing.

Fink, L. D. 1978. "A Discipline's Experiment in Higher Education: A Report on the TLGG Project." *Journal of Geography in Higher Education 2.*

———. 1983. "First Year on the Faculty: Getting There." *Journal of Geography in Higher Education 7.*

———. 1984. "First Year on the Faculty: Being There." *Journal of Geography in Higher Education 8.*

———. 1985. "First Year on the Faculty: The Quality of Their Teaching." *Journal of Higher Education 9.*

Flynn, James, et al. 1995. *One Hundred Centuries of Solitude: Redirecting America's High-Level Nuclear Waste Policy.* Boulder, CO: Westview Press.

Frawley, Margaret. 1942. Letter of 12/23 to Anne Underwood. Philadelphia: American Friends Service Committee Archives, Foreign Service, Relief and Refugees, Personnel.

Friedman, Benjamin. 2005. *The Moral Consequences of Economic Growth.* New York: Alfred A. Knopf.

Friedman, John, and Clyde Weaver. 1979. *Territory and Function: The Evolution of Regional Planning.* Berkeley: University of California Press.

Fromkin, David. 1995. *In the Time of the Americans.* New York: Alfred A. Knopf.

FWCC. 1978. "Right Sharing of World Resources Conference." Friends World Committee for Consultation. Unpublished manuscript, Alexandria, VA: Office of History, U.S. Army Corps of Engineers, GFW Archives, Box 241, Folder 102.

Galloway, Gerald E. 1994. *Sharing the Challenge: Floodplain Management into the 21st Century—A Blueprint for Change* (Galloway Report). Washington, DC: U.S. Government Printing Office, G16.

———. 1998. "What's Happened in Floodplain Management Since the '93 Mississippi Flood?" *Natural Hazards Observer 22* (March).

———. 2001. Interview with Robert Hinshaw.

Gelbspan, Ross. 1997. *The Heat Is On.* New York: Basic Books.

———. 2004. *Boiling Point.* New York: Basic Books.

GHRC/USA. 2005. *The Bulletin of the Guatemala Human Rights Commission/USA 1,* no. 1.

Glover, Jonathan. 2000. *Humanity: A Moral History of the Twentieth Century.* New Haven, CT: Yale University Press.

Gotaas, H. B., and Gilbert F. White. 1966. *The Water Resource in Northeastern Illinois: Planning Its Use.* Chicago: Northeastern Illinois Metropolitan Area Planning Commission.

Greenwood, John Ormerod. 1975. *Quaker Encounters: Friends and Relief.* York, England: William Sessions.

Hallie, Philip. 1979. *Lest Innocent Blood Be Shed.* New York: Harper and Row.

Hardin, Garrett. 1972. *Exploring New Ethics for Survival.* New York: Viking Press.

Harris, Chauncey. 2001. Interview with Robert Hinshaw.

al-Hassan, Ayman A. 2001. Interview with Robert Hinshaw.

Heath, Douglas H. 1968. *Growing Up in College: Liberal Education and Maturity.* San Francisco: Jossey-Bass.

———. 1976. "What the Enduring Effects of Higher Education Tell Us About a Liberal Education." *Journal of Higher Education 47.*

———. 1999. *Schools of Hope: Developing Mind and Character in Today's Youth.* Bryn Mawr, PA: Conrow Publishing.

———. 2001. Interview with Robert Hinshaw.

Helburn, Nicholas. 1998. "The High School Geography Project: A Retrospective View." *Social Studies* (September–October).

Hewitt, Kenneth. 1983. "The Idea of Calamity in a Technocratic Age." In *Interpretations of Calamity,* edited by K. Hewitt. Winchester, MA: Allen and Unwin.

Hiatt, Burritt. 1942–1944a–d. "Journal of France and Germany." In the possession of Muriel Hiatt, Wilmington, Ohio.

Hill, A. David. 2001. "Geography Education: Episodes in Building its Intellectual Capital." *Research in Geographic Education 3,* no. 2.

Hinshaw, David. 1951. *Rufus Jones: Master Quaker.* Toronto: G. P. Putnam.

Hinshaw, Robert E. 1980. "Public Policy, Administration, and Anthropology." *Annual Review of Anthropology 9.*

———. 2006. "Quick Response Report on Hurricane Stan." Natural Hazards Center, http://www.colorado.edu/hazards/qr/qrrepts.html.

Hooke, William. 2000. Interview with Robert Hinshaw.

———. 2005. "Climate Change and Unpredictability in Hazards Management." Unpublished Abstract SO5-2 of presentation in Plenary II session. Natural Hazards Center workshop, Boulder, CO.

Hori, Hiroshi. 2000. *The Mekong: Environment and Development.* Tokyo: United Nations University Press.

Hoyt, William G., and Walter B. Langbein. 1955. *Floods.* Princeton: Princeton University Press.

Human, Katy. 2002. "White: A Pioneer of Flood Control Planning." *Boulder Daily Camera,* April 7.

Jessor, Richard. 2002. Interview with Robert Hinshaw.

Jutro, Peter. 2001. Interview with Robert Hinshaw.

Kaplan, Robert D. 2000. *The Coming Anarchy*. New York: Random House.

el-Kassas, Sherif. 2001. Letter to GFW. GFW home files.

Kates, Robert W. 1962. *Hazard and Choice Perception in Flood Plain Management*. Research Paper No. 78. Chicago: University of Chicago, Department of Geography.

———. 1994. Unpublished remarks at the NGS Hubbard Medal Award.

———. 2001. Interview with Robert Hinshaw.

Kates, Robert W., and Ian Burton, eds. 1986. *Geography, Resources, and Environment*. Vol. 1: Selected Writings of Gilbert F. White; Vol. 2: Themes from the Work of Gilbert F. White. Chicago: University of Chicago Press.

Kates, Robert W., and Thomas M. Parris. 2003a. "Long-Term Trends and a Sustainability Transition." In *Mapping Economic and Environmental Vulnerabilities: Proceedings of the National Academy of Sciences*. Washington, DC: National Academy of Sciences.

———. 2003b. "Characterizing a Sustainability Transition: Goals, Targets, Trends, and Driving Forces." In *Mapping Economic and Environmental Vulnerabilities: Proceedings of the National Academy of Sciences*. Washington, DC: National Academy of Sciences.

Kennedy, David M. 1999. *Freedom from Fear: The American People in Depression and War, 1929–1945*. The Oxford History of the United States, Vol. 9. Oxford: Oxford University Press.

Krimm, Richard. 2001. Interview with Robert Hinshaw.

Kunreuther, Howard, Paul Slovic, and Gilbert F. White. 1974. "Decision Processes, Rationality, and Adjustment to Natural Hazards." In *Natural Hazards: Local, National, Global*, edited by Gilbert F. White. New York: Oxford University Press.

Kunreuther, Howard, and Paul Slovic. 1986. "Decision Making in Hazard and Resource Management." in *Geography, Resources, and Environment*, Vol. 2. Themes from the work of Gilbert White, edited by Robert W. Kates and Ian Burton. Chicago: University of Chicago Press.

Kunreuther, Howard, and Gilbert F. White. 1994. "The Role of the National Flood Insurance Program in Reducing Losses and Promoting Wise Use of Flood Plains." *Water Resources Update 95* (Spring). Special issue on "Coping with the Flood: The Next Phase."

Kusler, Jon, and Larry Larson. 1993. "Beyond the Ark." *Environment 35*, no. 5: 6–11, 31–34.

Lacey, Paul A. 2003. Letter to GFW. GFW office files.

Lao Tsu. 1972. *Tao Te Ching*. Translated by Gia-fu and Jane English. New York: Random House.

Larson, Larry. 2005. Letter of 7/23 to Robert Hinshaw.

Leatherman, Stephen, and Gilbert F. White. 2005. "Living on the Edge: The Coastal Collision Course." *Natural Hazards Observer 30*, no. 2.

Leopold, L., and T. Maddock. 1954. *Big Dams, Little Dams, and Land Management*. New York: Ronald Press.

Leslie, Jacques. 2005. *Deep Water: The Epic Struggle over Dams, Displaced People, and the Environment*. New York: Farrar, Straus, and Giroux.

L. R. Johnston Associates. 1992. *Assessment Report of Floodplain Management in the United States*. Washington, DC: Federal Emergency Management Agency.

Maass, Arthur. 1951. *Muddy Waters: The Army Engineers and the Nation's Rivers.* Cambridge, MA: Harvard University Press.

Madrick, Jeffrey. 2006. "The Way to a Fair Deal." *The New York Review of Books 53*, no. 1.

Marston, Sallie. 1983a. "Natural Hazards Research: Towards a Political Economy Perspective." *Political Geography Quarterly 2*, no. 4.

———. 1983b. *The Political Economy Approach to Hazards in California.* NHRWP no. 49. Boulder, CO: Natural Hazards Center of the University of Colorado.

Mayer, Thomas. 2001. Letter (in verse) to GFW. GFW home files.

McKibben, Bill. 2006. "The Coming Meltdown." *The New York Review of Books 53*, no. 1.

McReynolds, Elaine. 1994. Letter to GFW. GFW office files.

Meadows, Donella H., Jorgen Randers, and Dennis L. Meadows. 1974. *The Limits to Growth.* New York: Universe Books.

Mendez, Ruben. 2001. Letter to GFW. GFW home files.

Meyer, William B., and Charles H. W. Foster. 2000. *New Deal Regionalism: A Critical Review.* Cambridge, MA: Harvard University Press.

Micklin, Philip. 2001. Letter to GFW. GFW home files.

Mileti, Dennis S. 1996. "Managing Natural Hazards into the Next Century." In *Floodplain Management in a Multifaceted World. Proceedings of the 21st Annual Conference of the Association of State Floodplain Managers in Little Rock, AK.* Madison, WI: ASFPM.

———. 1999. *Disasters by Design: A Reassessment of Natural Hazards in the United States.* Washington, DC: Joseph Henry Press.

Mitchell, James K. 1988. "Confronting Natural Disasters: An International Decade for Natural Hazard Reduction." *Environment 30*, no. 2.

———. 2001, 2005. Interviews with Robert Hinshaw.

Moline, Norman. 2001. Interview with Robert Hinshaw.

Monday, Jacqueline. 2001. Interview with Robert Hinshaw.

Monk, Jan. 1986. "The Association of American Geographers' Role in Educational Leadership: An Interview with Sam Natoli." *Journal of Geography in Higher Education 10*.

Moore, Jamie W., and Dorothy P. Moore. 1989. *The Army Corps of Engineers and the Evolution of Federal Flood Plain Management Policy.* Program on Environment and Behavior Special Pub. No. 20. Boulder, CO: Institute of Behavioral Science.

Munn, Theodore. 2001. Interview with Robert Hinshaw.

Murphy, Francis G. 1958. Regulating Flood Plain Development. Research Paper No. 56. Chicago: University of Chicago, Department of Geography.

———. 1959. "Auxiliary Report on Regulating Flood-Plain Development." Folder: Flood Plain Use, File: 1501–07, PD-OCE.

Myers, Mary Fran. 2002. Interview with Robert Hinshaw.

Myers, Mary Fran, and Gilbert F. White. 1993a. "Floods—and Floods of Studies." *Natural Hazards Observer 18*, no. 2.

———. 1993b. "The Challenge of the Mississippi Flood." *Environment 35*, no. 10.

NAPA. 1993. *Coping with Catastrophe.* Washington, DC: National Academy of Public Administration, National Performance Review.

Nathe, Sarah, 2002. Letter to Robert Hinshaw.

NGS. 2005. *What Works in Geography Education.* Washington, DC: National Geographic Society Education Foundation.

NRC (National Research Council). 1995. *Technical Bases for Yucca Mountain Standards.* Washington, DC: National Academy Press.

———. 1999. *Our Common Journey: A Transition Toward Sustainability.* Washington, DC: National Academy Press.

O'Riordan, Tim. 1997. "Commentary 2, on *Human Adjustment to Floods.*" In *Progress in Human Geography 21,* no. 2.

Paley, William. 1972. *Resources for Freedom* (Paley Report, issued in 1952). President's Materials Policy Commission. 5 vols. New York: Arno Press.

Palmer, Parker J. 1998. *The Courage to Teach.* San Francisco: Jossey-Bass.

Pattison, William D. 1970. "The Producers: A Social History." In *From Geographic Discipline to Inquiring Student,* edited by Donald J. Patton. Washington, DC: Association of American Geographers.

Pattison, William D., and L. D. Fink. 1974. *Preparing Others to Profess: A Trial Year. Directors Report, Phase I* (July 1973–June 1974). NSF grant to AAG, GZ1816.

Patton, Ann. 1975. "Report on the National Forum on the Future of the Flood Plain." Draft of an article for the *Tulsa World.*

———. 1993. *From Harm's Way: Flood-Hazard Mitigation in Tulsa, Oklahoma.* Tulsa, OK: Public Works Department.

———, ed. 1994. *From Rooftop to River: Tulsa's Approach to Floodplain and Stormwater Management.* Tulsa, OK: Stormwater Drainage Advisory Board and Public Works Dept.

Patton, Donald J., ed. 1970. *From Geographic Discipline to Inquiring Student: Final Report of the HSGP.* Washington, DC: Association of American Geographers.

Philipson, Morris. 1970. "The Difference Between a Ruin and a Relic." Foreword for republished 1899 William Rainey Harper University of Chicago address, "University and Democracy." Chicago: University of Chicago Press.

Pielke, Roger. 2005. "Climate Change and Unpredictability in Hazards Management." Unpublished Abstract SO5-2 of presentation in Plenary II session. Natural Hazards Center workshop, Boulder, CO.

Platt, Rutherford H. 1986. "Floods and Man: A Geographer's Agenda." In *Geography, Resources, and Environment.* Vol. 2: Themes from the Work of Gilbert F. White, edited by Robert W. Kates and Ian Burton. Chicago: University of Chicago Press.

———. 1996. "Hazard Mitigation: Cornerstone or Grains of Sand?" *Natural Hazards Observer 20* (September).

———. 1997. "Commentary 1 on *Human Adjustment to Floods.*" In *Progress in Human Geography 21,* no. 2.

————. 1999. *Disasters and Democracy: The Politics of Extreme Natural Events.* Washington, DC: Island Press.

Poertner, Herbert G. 1988. *Stormwater Management in the United States.* Bolingbrook, IL: Stormwater Consultants.

Quinn, James R. 2000. *Thirty Years in Deep Water: The NFIP and Its Struggle for Significance.* Belleville, Ontario: Epic Press.

Raskin, Marcus G., and Bernard B. Fall. 1965. *The Viet-Nam Reader.* New York: Vintage Books.

R. D. Flanagan, and Associates. 1994. *Tulsa's Flood Management Program.* Tulsa, OK.

Reich, Charles. 1970. *The Greening of America.* New York: Random House.

Reilly, Frank. 1994. Letter dated 8/23 to GFW. GFW office files.

Renner, George T. 1935. "A Preliminary Exploration of Regions." In *Regional Factors in National Planning and Development* by George T. Renner. Washington, DC: National Resources Committee.

Resch Synnestvedt, Alice. 2005. *Over the Highest Mountains: A Memoir of Unexpected Heroism in France During World War II.* Pasadena: International Productions.

Reuss, Martin. 1985. "Andrew A. Humphreys and the Development of Hydraulic Engineering: Politics and Technology in the Army Corps of Engineers, 1850–1950." *Technology and Culture 26*, no. 1.

————. 1989. *Water Resources People and Issues: Interview with Arthur Maass.* Alexandria, VA: Office of History, U.S. Army Corps of Engineers.

————. 1993a. *Water Resources People and Issues: Interview with Gilbert F. White.* Alexandria, VA: Office of History, U.S. Army Corps of Engineers.

————. 1993b. "Introduction." In *Water Resources Administration in the United States,* edited by Martin Reuss. American Water Resources Association. East Lansing: Michigan State University Press.

Richman, Barbara. 2001. Interview with Robert Hinshaw.

Riecken, Henry W. 1952. *The Volunteer Work Camp: A Psychological Evaluation.* Cambridge: Addison-Wesley Press.

Rischard, J. F. 2002. *High Noon: Twenty Global Problems, Twenty Years to Solve Them.* New York: Basic Books.

Roberts, Janet. 2001. Letter to GFW. GFW home files.

Robinson, Marshall. 2001. Letter to GFW. GFW home files.

Ross, Warren. 2002. "Confronting Evil." *UUWorld 16*, no. 1.

Saarinen, Thomas, and Charles MacCabe. 1995. "World Patterns of Geographic Literacy Based on Sketch Map Quality." *Professional Geographer 47*, no. 2.

Scawthorn, Charles. 2005. Letter to Robert Hinshaw.

Schad, Theodore M. 1989. "Past, Present, and Future of Water Resources Management in the United States." In *Water Management in the 21st Century.* Bethesda, MD: American Water Resources Association.

Schmitt, Hans A. 1997. *Quakers and Nazis: Inner Light in Outer Darkness.* Columbia: University of Missouri Press.

Shabman, Leonard. 2001. "The Principles of White and Maass and the Future of the Corps." Address delivered at the inauguration of the Maass and White Collection, Alexandria, VA: Office of History, U.S. Army Corps of Engineers.

Sheaffer, J. R. 1960. *Flood Proofing: An Element in a Flood Damage Reduction Program.* Department of Geography Research Paper No. 65. Chicago: University of Chicago.

———. 2005. Correspondence with Robert Hinshaw.

Sheridan, Claire. 2002. Interview with Robert Hinshaw.

Speth, James Gustave. 2004. *Red Sky at Morning: America and the Crisis of the Global Environment.* New Haven, CT: Yale University Press.

Stakhiv, Eugene, Richard Cole, Paul Scodari, and Lynn Martin. 2001. *White Paper on Improving Environmental Benefits Analysis.* Alexandria, VA: Institute for Water Resources, U.S. Army Corps of Engineers.

Stein, Lloyd E. 1971. *Hutchins of Chicago: Philosopher-Administrator.* Chicago: University of Chicago Press.

Stevens, Robert. 1983. "The Case of Haverford College." Speech on the 150th anniversary of the founding of Haverford College. Philadelphia: Newcomen Society.

Stinnett, Robert B. 2001. *Day of Deceit: The Truth About FDR and Pearl Harbor.* New York: Simon and Schuster.

Strolin, Joseph. 2001. Letter to GFW. GFW home files.

Thompson, John. 2001. Letter to GFW. GFW home files.

Thompson, John, et al. 2001. *Drawers of Water II.* London: International Institute for Environment and Development.

Thorndike, Rosanna. n.d. Interview with John Baskin.

Tjossem, Wilmer. 2001. Interview with Robert Hinshaw.

Torry, William I. 1979. "Hazards, Hazes, and Holes: A Critique of *The Environment as Hazard* and General Reflections on Disaster Research." *Canadian Geographer 23.*

Trewartha, Glenn T. 1973. "Comments on Gilbert White's Article, 'Geography and Public Policy.'" *Professional Geographer 24,* no. 2.

Tubbesing, Sarah K. 2001. Letter to GFW. GFW home files.

U.S. Court of Appeals, DC Reports. 2004. Petitions for Review of Orders of the Environmental Protection Agency, Dept. of Energy and the Nuclear Regulatory Commission. Washington, DC.

Ward, Barbara, and Rene Dubos. 1972. *Only One Earth.* New York: W. W. Norton.

Wescoat, James L. 1992. "Common Themes in the Work of Gilbert White and John Dewey: A Pragmatic Appraisal." *Annals of the Association of American Geographers 82,* no. 4.

———. 2000. "History, Theory, and Graduate Education: A Vitruvian Challenge." *Progress in Human Geography 24,* no. 1.

———. 2003. "Water Resources." In *Geography in America at the Dawn of the 21st Century,* edited by Gary L. Gaile and Cort J. Willmott. Oxford: Oxford University Press.

Wescoat, James L., and S. J. Halvorson. 2000. *Ex-Post Evaluation of Dams and Related Water Systems.* Report to the World Commission on Dams. Capetown: WCD.

Wescoat, James L., and Gilbert F. White. 2003. *Water for Life: Water Management and Environmental Policy.* Cambridge: Cambridge University Press.

White, Anne U. 1991. *Poetry of Anne U. White.* Boulder, CO: Privately printed.

White, Gilbert F. 1934. Letter of 1/25 to Harlan Barrows, Alexandria, VA: Office of History, U.S. Army Corps of Engineers, GFW Archives, Box 4, Folder 1A 45.

———. 1935. "Shortage of Public Water Supplies in the United States During 1934," *Journal of the American Water Works Association 27,* no. 7.

———. 1940a. Letter of 8/8 to Harlan Barrows. Alexandria, VA: Office of History, U.S. Army Corps of Engineers, GFW Archives, Box 4, Folder 1A 45.

———. 1940b. Letter of 2/14 to Harlan Barrows. Alexandria, VA: Office of History, U.S. Army Corps of Engineers, GFW Archives, Box 4, Folder 1A 45.

———. 1941. Letter of 1/27 to Harlan Barrows. Alexandria, VA: Office of History, U.S. Army Corps of Engineers, GFW Archives, Box 4, Folder 1A 45.

———. 1942a. Letter of 3/20 to Harlan Barrows. Alexandria, VA: Office of History, U.S. Army of Engineers, GFW Archives, Box 3, Folder 1A 40.

———. 1942b. Letter of July 30 to Lindsley Noble. Philadelphia: American Friends Service Committee Archives, Foreign Service, Relief, and Refugees.

———. 1942c–f. Letters to Philadelphia AFSC Office. Philadelphia: American Friends Service Committee Archives, Foreign Service, Relief, and Refugees.

———. 1942g. Personal Notes re "Miracles." GFW home file on France/Germany.

———. 1943a–d. Letters to GFW's family, excerpted by AFSC office in "Life of the Nord-Amerikanische Diplomatengruppe at Bremmer Kur Park Hotel, Baden-Baden, February to October, 1943." Philadelphia: American Friends Service Committee Archives, Foreign Service, Relief, and Refugees.

———. 1945. *Human Adjustment to Floods: A Geographical Approach to the Flood Problem in the United States.* Ph.D. diss., submitted June 1942. Research Paper No. 29, Chicago: University of Chicago, Department of Geography.

———. 1952. "America's Dual Responsibility." In *Building Leadership for Peace: Report of the 21st Annual Forum.* New York: New York Herald Tribune.

———. 1953. "A New Stage in Resource History." *Journal of Soil and Water Conservation 8,* no. 5.

———. 1958. "Introductory Graduate Work for Geographers." *Professional Geographer 10,* no. 2.

———. 1960. "The Changing Role of Water in Arid Lands." *Arizona Bulletin Series 32,* no. 2.

———. 1961. "A Joint Effort to Improve High School Geography." *Journal of Geography 60.*

———. 1964a. "Vietnam: The Fourth Course." *Bulletin of the Atomic Scientists 20,* no. 10.

———. 1964b. *Choice of Adjustment to Floods.* Department of Geography Research Paper No. 93. Chicago: University of Chicago.

———. 1965. "Geography in Liberal Education." *Geography in Undergraduate Education: A Report of the Geography in Liberal Education Project.* Washington, DC: Association of American Geographers.

———. 1966a. With the Task Force on Federal Flood Control Policy. *A Unified National Program for Managing Flood Losses: Report by the Task Force on Federal Flood Control Policy.* House Doc. 465, Washington, DC: U.S. Government Printing Office.

———. 1966b. "The World's Arid Areas." In *Arid Lands: A Geographical Appraisal,* edited by E. S. Hills. London: Methuen; Paris: UNESCO.

———. 1966c. "Deserts as Producing Regions Today." In *Arid Lands: A Geographical Appraisal,* edited by E. S. Hills. London: Methuen; Paris: UNESCO.

———. 1966d. "Arid Lands." In *Future Environments of North America,* edited by F. Fraser Darling and John P. Milton. Garden City, NY: Natural History Press.

———. 1967. "Images of the World." Unpublished address to the National Council for Geographic Education.

———. 1969. *Strategies of American Water Management.* Ann Arbor: University of Michigan Press.

———. 1970. "Assessment in Midstream." In *From Geographic Discipline to Inquiring Student,* edited by Donald J. Patton. Washington, DC: Association of American Geographers.

———. 1972. "Geography and Public Policy." *The Professional Geographer 24.*

———. 1973. "Natural Hazards Research." In *Directions in Geography,* edited by Richard J. Chorley. London: Methuen.

———. 1975a. "Stewardship of the Earth." In *Geography, Resources, and Environment.* Vol. 1: Selected Writings of Gilbert F. White, edited by Robert W. Kates and Ian Burton. Chicago: University of Chicago Press.

———. 1975b. "National Perspective." In *The Water's Edge: The National Forum on the Future of the Flood Plain.* Minneapolis: Department of the Interior.

———. 1975c. Letter of 6/19 to Keith Muckleston. Alexandria, VA: Office of History, U.S. Army Corps of Engineers, GFW Archives, Box 202, Folder 86–11.

———. 1976a. Letter of 6/26 to Wesley Calef. Alexandria, VA: Office of History, U.S. Army Corps of Engineers, GFW Archives, Box 223, Folder 95–11.

———. 1976b. Letter of 11/19 to Kenneth Thompson. Alexandria VA: Office of History, U.S. Army Corps of Engineers, GFW Archives, Box 223, Folder 95–11.

———. 1977. Letter of 5/31 to Norman Moline. GFW office files.

———. 1980a. "Overview of the Flood Insurance Program." Statement to the Senate Committee on Banking, Housing, and Urban Affairs, February 28.

———. 1980b. "Environment." *Science Centennial Review 209,* no. 4452.

———. 1985. "Foreword." In *Environmental Consequences of Nuclear War,* edited by B. Pittock et al. 2 vols. Chichester: John Wiley and Sons.

———. 1988. "When May a Post-audit Teach Lessons?" In *The Flood Control Challenge: Past Present, and Future,* edited by Howard Rosen and Martin Reuss. Chicago: Public Works Historical Society.

———. 1991a. "Profile: Gilbert White, Part I." *IBS Newsletter,* December.

———. 1991b. "Greenhouse Gases, Nile Snails, and Human Choice." *Perspectives on Behavioral Science: The Colorado Lectures,* edited by Richard Jessor. Boulder, CO: Westview Press.

———. 1992a. For the Task Force. "Retrospect and Prospect." In *Floodplain Management in the United States: An Assessment Report.* Boulder, CO: Federal Interagency Floodplain Management Task Force, Vol. 1, 67–69. Vol. 2, V1-1-VI-4.

————. 1992b. With ten others. *Action Agenda for Managing the Nation's Floodplains: An Assessment Report.* Boulder, CO: Natural Hazards Research and Applications Center, Special Publication No. 25.

————. 1993a. "25 Years of Flood Insurance in Perspective." Unpublished address at the WYO Conference of NFIP.

————. 1993b. "Perceptions of the Earth." Thirtieth Cosmos Club Award. Washington, DC: Cosmos Club.

————. 1993c. "Comments," in *Water Resources Administration in the United States,* edited by Martin Reuss. American Water Resources Association. East Lansing, MI: Michigan University Press.

————. 1994a. "Anecdotes: 1914–1998." Boulder, CO: Unpublished recollections at GFW residence.

————. 1994b. "Reflections on Changing Perceptions of the Earth." *Annual Review of Energy and Environment 19.*

————. 1994c. Letter of 8/4 to Lieutenant General Gerald Galloway. GFW office files.

————. 1994d. Letter of 11/4 to Elaine McReynolds. GFW office files.

————. 1994e. "The Midwest Floods of 1993: Flood Control and Floodplain Policy and Proposals." Statement to the House Committee on Public Works and Transportation, October 27, 1993.

————. 1995. "Decision or Procrastination in Floodplain Management." *Water Resources Update 97.*

————. n.d.a–c. Interview with John Baskin in Boulder in the mid-1990s. Wilmington, OH.

————. 1996. "Looking Toward the Horizon: Prospects for Floodplain Managers." In *Floodplain Management in a Multifaceted World. Proceedings of the 21st Annual Conference of the Association of State Floodplain Managers in Little Rock, AK.* Madison, WI: ASFPM.

————. 1998a. "Quaker Volunteer Service for the Future." *Friends Journal,* January.

————. 1998b. "Reflections on the 50-Year International Search for Integrated Water Management." *Water Policy 1.*

————. 1999a. "A Decade of Missed Opportunities?" In *Natural Disaster Management,* edited by Jon Ingleton. Leicester, England: Tudor Rose.

————. 1999b. "Water Science and Technology: Some Lessons from the 20th Century." National Research Council Wolman Lecture. Washington, DC: National Academy of Sciences.

————. 2000. "Quaker Volunteer Service: A 70-Year Perspective." *Friends Bulletin,* March.

————. 2000–2005. Interviews with Robert Hinshaw.

————. 2001. Letter of April 27 to Larry Larson and Donald Vogt. GFW office files.

————. 2002. "Autobiographical Essay." In *Geographical Voices,* edited by Peter Gould and Forrest R. Pitts. Syracuse, NY: Syracuse University Press.

————, ed. 1974. *Natural Hazards: Local, National, Global.* New York: Oxford University Press.

————, ed. 1977. *Environmental Effects of Complex River Development.* Boulder, CO: Westview Press.

White, Gilbert F., David Bradley, and Anne U. White. 1972. *Drawers of Water: Domestic Water Use in East Africa*. Chicago: University of Chicago Press.

White, Gilbert F., and Charles C. Colby. 1961. "Harlan H. Barrows, 1877–1960." *Annals: Association of American Geographers 51*, no. 4.

White, Gilbert F., and J. Eugene Haas. 1975. *Assessment of Research on Natural Hazards*. Cambridge, MA: MIT Press.

White, Gilbert F., Robert W. Kates, and Ian Burton. 2001. "Knowing Better and Losing Even More: The Use of Knowledge in Hazards Management." *Environmental Hazards 3*.

White, Gilbert F., and Daniel A. Okun. 1992. "Abel Wolman." Memorial Tributes, National Academy of Engineering. Washington, DC: National Academy Press.

White, Gilbert F., et al. 1943. "Activities in France." Final Report. Philadelphia: American Friends Service Committee Archives, Foreign Service, Relief, and Refugees.

White, Gilbert F., et al. 1958. *Changes in Urban Occupance of Flood Plains in the U.S.* Research Paper. Chicago: University of Chicago, Department of Geography.

White, Gilbert F., et al. 1975. *Flood Hazard in the United States: A Research Assessment*. Boulder, CO: University of Colorado, Institute of Behavioral Science.

White, Gilbert F., et al. 1999. With the Committee on Sustainable Water Supplies in the Middle East. *Water for the Future: The West Bank and Gaza Strip, Israel, and Jordan*. Washington, DC: National Academy Press/National Research Council.

White, Gilbert F., et al. 2001. "South Boulder Creek, Boulder, CO—Independent Review Panel Report." Boulder, CO: City of Boulder.

Wickham, Robert. 2000. Letter to Robert Hinshaw.

Witt, James Lee. 1993. "Remarks." Prepared for the 1993 Natural Hazards Workshop of the Natural Hazards Research and Applications Information Center. Boulder, CO: University of Colorado.

Wolman, Abel. 1942. Letter of 2/13 to the American Friends Service Committee. Alexandria, VA: Office of History, U.S. Army Corps of Engineers, Archives of Gilbert F. White, Box 3, Folder 1A 40.

Wolman, Reds. 2001. Letter to GFW. GFW home files.

WRI. 1984. *The Global Possible: Resources, Development, and the New Century*. Washington, DC: World Resources Institute.

Wriggins, Howard. 2004. *Picking Up the Pieces from Portugal to Palestine: Quaker Refugee Relief in World War II*. Lanham, MD: University Press of America.

Wright, Barbara. 2003. *Plain Language*. New York: Simon and Schuster.

Wright, James. 2000. *The Nation's Response to Flood Disasters: A Historical Account*. Madison, WI: Association of State Floodplain Managers.

Wright, Kenneth. 2000. Interview with Robert Hinshaw.

Index

ROBERT HINSHAW's acquaintance with Gilbert White began in 1951 when enrolled at Haverford College, outside Philadelphia, during White's tenure as president of Haverford. Following graduation in 1955, Hinshaw served as teacher and then director of Olney Friends School (Ohio) until earning an M.A. and Ph.D. at the University of Chicago. Doctoral research in predominately Maya communities bordering Lake Atitlan in Guatemala led to publication in 1975 of *Panajachel: A Guatemalan Town in Thirty-Year Perspective*, among other Guatemala and Mesoamerica-related publications. He taught anthropology at the University of Kansas and the National University of San Carlos (Guatemala) before serving as president of Wilmington College (Ohio). Thereafter, teaching appointments at Beloit College (Wisconsin) and the University of Colorado alternated with administrative posts: academic dean at Bethel College (Kansas), director of the Associated College of Central Kansas, and director of the Kansas Institute for Peace and Conflict Resolution (Bethel College). He resides in Allenspark, Colorado, and Kansas City, Missouri.